Tennessee

Tennessee

Sally Walker Davies

with photographs by the author

The Countryman Press ✳ Woodstock, Vermont

Explorer's Guide Tennesee
ISBN 978-0-88150-898-7

Interior photographs by the author unless otherwise specified
Maps by Erin Greb Cartography, © The Countryman Press
Book design by Bodenweber Design

Published by The Countryman Press, P.O. Box 748, Woodstock, VT 05091

Distributed by W. W. Norton & Company, Inc., 500 Fifth Avenue, New
York, NY 10110

Printed in the United States of America

10 9 8 7 6 5 4 3 2 1

To James and Maddie, the loves of my life.
The last year has been a journey in so many ways,
and the road not always smooth.
You both continue to amaze me,
and to quote one of our favorite books:
I love you all the way to the moon, and back (times infinity!).

To my parents, Lou and Moe Walker, for a childhood filled with books
and a lifetime filled with love.

To Susie, for being my rock. Love you more.

Finally, to Peggy Reisser Winburne,
my editor at *The Commercial Appeal*.
You changed the course of my life
the day you published my first travel article,
and I will never be able to fully express
my gratitude for your guidance,
your support, and your friendship.

EXPLORE WITH US!

In the beginning of the book, you will find an alphabetical listing of special highlights, with important information and advice on everything from antiques to zoos.

LODGING

Tennessee offers an exquisite array of lodging possibilities, from rustic yet lush mountain lodges to historic inns and ultraplush historic hotels. That's why you will find few references to chain hotels throughout the lodging sections in each chapter. Where there's no local alternative, or if a local version of a chain hotel is the most convenient or particularly good option—or the only game in town—you will find a listing. But as with the restaurant listings, the goal in the hotel listings is to provide information on hotels, inns, bed & breakfasts, and rentals that are unique to Tennessee and offer the best atmosphere and experience.

Rates: Prices are per night and range from low, off-season rates to higher summer and holiday weekend rates. Please note that prices (and price ranges) were accurate at press time in 2010, and don't hold it against us or the innkeepers if those prices have fluctuated.

Inexpensive	Less than $100 (for hotels, inns, and B&Bs)
	Less than $50 (for campgrounds, state park facilities)
Moderate	$100–200
Expensive	$201–300
Very expensive	More than $300

RESTAURANTS

A few things to note about the restaurant listings in this book: First, there's a difference between *Dining Out* and *Eating Out.* The establishments listed under *Dining Out* are fine-dining establishments, some more casual than others but still with the air (and price tag) of fine dining. *Eating Out* listings showcase less-expensive dining options.

Secondly, you will find very few references to any kind of chain restaurant here, whether fast-food or casual dining. Why? Because you can find those restaurants anywhere, and they don't add anything unique or local to a Tennessee experience. So our recommendations focus on local eateries (with a few local chains thrown in), owned by local restaurateurs, whether a white-tablecloth restaurant or a lunch counter in a local pharmacy.

Rates: Average prices refer to a per-person price for dinner consisting of an entrée, appetizer or dessert, and a glass of beer or wine (taxes and gratuities not included).

Inexpensive	Less than $16
Moderate	$16–30
Expensive	$31–50
Very expensive	More than $50

KEY TO SYMBOLS

🖉 The kid-friendly symbol appears next to establishments that appeal directly to kids, if not already obvious.

🏵 The special value symbol appears next to those establishments that offer an extra value, over-the-top service, or are considered a worth-the-splurge experience.

🐾 The pet-friendly symbol appears next to hotels, campgrounds, and parks that allow pets. Remember, most lodgings will charge a surcharge for pets, and if pets are accepted, they are expected to be leashed and as well behaved as their owners.

☙ The ecofriendly symbol appears next to accommodations, restaurants, and bars that are especially environmentally friendly and/or use local and natural products.

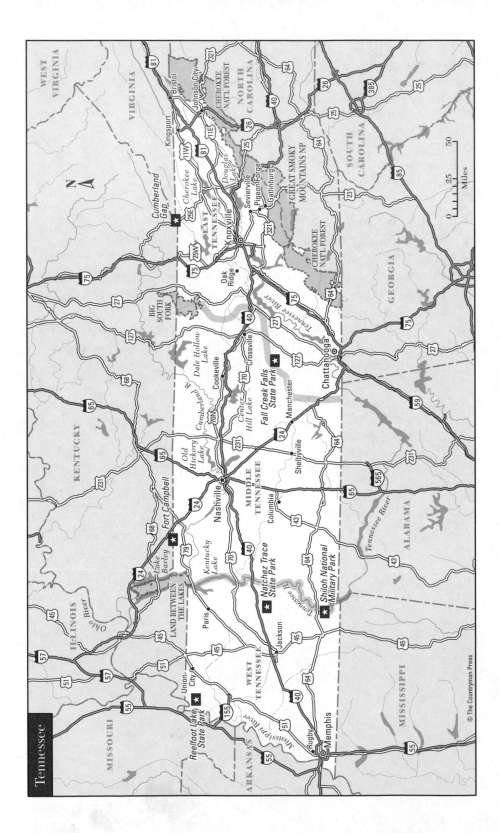

Tennessee

© The Countryman Press

CONTENTS

1 Eastern Tennessee: The First Frontier / 25

2 Middle Tennessee: The Heart of Tennessee / 141

3 Western Tennessee: Music and the Mighty Mississippi / 249

List of Maps

ACKNOWLEDGMENTS

So many people across Tennessee—and beyond—played a part in helping me with this book.

Tons of thanks to the Countryman Press team, especially Kim Grant and Justine Rathbun, for excellent guidance and amazing patience.

Stephanie Jones has gone from dear friend to partner in crime in the last year, and her photographs and research assistance have been invaluable.

Tom Adkinson, Heather Middleton, and the Geiger team went out of their respective ways to get me where I needed to go.

Marlene Shaw, Leanne Kleinmann, Susan Mahoney, Gigi Gould, Leanne Owens, Anca Marr, Shelby Terry, and Angie Gardner at St. Mary's Episcopal School in Memphis were more supportive and encouraging than I ever thought possible—thank you all.

Finally, Sheryl, Linda, Julia, Kim, Stephanie, and Kristi—what can I say? I couldn't have made it through without you all.

INTRODUCTION

This book is based on multiple trips I have taken since 2002, as I have had the good fortune to roam Tennessee in search of its delights for a variety of media outlets since becoming a resident that year.

From lodging to dining to exploring, everything in this guide was chosen for its worthiness and written for an audience that appreciates the unique characteristics of local business while experiencing some of the country's best attractions, both natural and man-made.

In this book, you will find very little mention of chain anything, whether hotel or restaurant. I am a huge believer in experiencing the unique flavors of every city or town, so the usual suspects get little coverage here. Rest assured, the inclusion of any hotel, restaurant, or attraction in this guide was not paid for with assurances of coverage.

Think of these suggestions as a jumping-off point for your own exploration, but not as a checklist. These are *my* favorite spots around Tennessee, but so many more are worth experiencing as well. Would that I could include them all—and believe me, I've already started my list of those spots I must revisit or must learn about for future editions of this guide.

The guide is organized by the geographic sections that the state of Tennessee divides itself into: East Tennessee, Middle Tennessee, and West Tennessee; from there, again, the guide follows the state's regional dividers.

Each chapter begins with a brief overview of the city or town(s) covered, with historic highlights as well as current information about the destination. Complete contact information, including addresses, phone numbers, and Web sites, is included with each listing.

Guidance gives information for the local convention and visitors bureau or tourism agency.

Getting There and **Getting Around** give you the closest major airport, basic highway and driving routes, plus information on public transportation and taxi service, where available.

Medical Emergency provides contact information for the closest local hospital or clinic. Of course, in case of emergency, dial 911, being sure to note your exact location, including the closest major intersection, if possible.

To See and **To Do** offer my picks for the best the destination has to offer, including enough information to pique your interest but not so much that you'll find no reason to visit. From museums and historic sites to boating and cavern tours, there's a variety of options for exploration.

Green Space highlights parks, botanic gardens, and other natural wonders, all of which are prevalent in Tennessee.

Lodging is where you'll find hotels, bed & breakfasts, inns, camp-grounds, and cabin rentals—again, very little in the way of franchise or chain establishments.

Where to Eat offers a mix of fine dining (*Dining Out*) and casual dining (*Eating Out*), focusing on local flavors and favorites.

Entertainment features live-music venues, performing arts centers, and outdoor concert venues and events. There's something for every taste.

Selective Shopping features a mix of local boutiques, art and antiques galleries, and in the case of larger cities, shopping neighbor-hoods or retail centers.

Special Events highlights the top annual events and festivals in each town.

Every effort has been made to ensure the information contained in this guide is accurate at the time of writing—summer and fall 2010—and is intended to be a guide for trip planning. Change, however, is inevitable, and it is only to be expected that prices will always be on the increase, and establishments will come and go, so be sure to take this into consideration during your planning process.

WHAT'S WHERE IN TENNESSEE

AGRICULTURE There's a rich agricultural heritage in Tennessee, from the abundant cotton crops in the delta along the Mississippi River to broad acres filled with fruit trees and vegetable patches in Middle and East Tennessee. During the spring, summer, and fall, there's always the opportunity to visit pick-your-own farms, wander through pumpkin patches, and enjoy the variety of fresh produce from the state's farmers. The Tennessee Department of Agriculture (picktnproducts.org) offers a listing of those farms that welcome visitors, as well as farmer's markets and breweries, distilleries, and wineries across the state.

AIRPORTS There are five major airports offering commercial airline service in Tennessee, with all of the major airlines offering service into the state. **Knoxville (TYS)** serves as the major hub for those wishing to explore the Smoky Mountain region; **Chattanooga (CHA)** also serves some Smokies visitors but generally provides service to regional gateways like Atlanta and Charlotte, and has the added cachet of being a two-hour drive from Atlanta's Buckhead neighborhood. The Tri-Cities area (Johnson City, Kingsport, and Bristol) is served by **Tri-Cities (TRI),** with a surprising amount of direct flights into Atlanta, Detroit, and Charlotte. **Nashville (BNA)** is the only game in Middle Tennessee, as **Memphis (MEM)** is for West Tennessee; both these airports serve international passengers as well, so those arriving from overseas may connect in one of these cities before traveling on to other regions of the state.

AMTRAK There's limited AMTRAK (amtrak.com) service in Tennessee, and it surprises most folks to know that there's no choo-choo running into Chattanooga these days—at least not of the passenger train variety. The City of New Orleans runs daily between Chicago and New Orleans with stops in Newbern/Dyersburg and Memphis, but there are no services offered in Newbern.

ANTIQUING Tennessee is a treasure trove for antiques lovers; those looking for fine furnishings will do well to shop in **Nashville's Belle Meade** and **Green Hills** neighborhoods, along **Central Avenue** in **Memphis,** and on **Chattanooga's Southside.** And be sure to browse through shops in **Columbia** and **Franklin** as well; these charming towns outside of Nashville have been and still are home to some of Middle Tennessee's most fabulous antebellum homes, so the finds tend to be excellent around these parts. If you're looking for primitives, farm implements, and bits of Americana, the small towns are where to find the best collections.

AREA CODES Tennessee has six area codes spread across the state. In East Tennessee, **423** covers the Chattanooga area, while **865** is used in Knoxville, Oak Ridge, the Smoky Mountain region, and the northeast. In Middle Tennessee, **615** is for Nashville and the immediate metropolitan area, while most destinations in the Upper Cumberland use **931.** Memphis and its surrounding area use **901;** while northwest Tennessee, including Reelfoot Lake, Union City, and Martin, use **731;** as does the southwest area outside of Memphis, including Jackson, Pickwick, and Paris Landing.

BARBECUE If Tennessee had a state meat, it might well be pork—barbecued pork, that is. **Memphis** is ground zero when it comes to barbecue and serves up slew of 'cue at dozens of eateries. (See "Memphis and Surrounding Area.") Yes, you can find fine barbecue across the state—**Calhoun's** in Knoxville, **Jack's** in Nashville, and **Bennett's** in Gatlinburg are a few of the prime choices.

B&BS There's a heavy concentration of bed & breakfast lodgings in the Smoky Mountain region, in the surrounding communities of **Sevierville, Pigeon Forge,** and **Gatlinburg,** with fewer of these lodgings as one heads west. **The Bed and Breakfast Association of Tennessee** (931-924-3869; tennessee-inns.com) offers a comprehensive listing of member properties with complete contact information and descriptions.

BICYCLING There are plenty of bike routes for those who want to hit the road on two wheels—and pedal, that is. The **Tennessee Department of Transportation** (tdot.state.tn.us/bikeped) offers downloadable bike route maps, split into sections, for riders of all abilities. While all the routes offered are regular roads of the state, county, or local government, few have designated bike lanes. Bicycle helmets are required for all riders under the age of 16.

BIRDING Bird-watching is more than a casual thing in Tennessee; a large slice of **West Tennessee** is part of the **Mississippi Flyway** (mississippi.flyways.us) and home to hundreds of thousands of migratory birds in the winter. **East Tennessee**'s forests and mountains are also full of wonderful bird-sighting opportunities year-round; there are more than 240 species of birds found in **the Great Smoky Mountains National Park** (nps.gov/grsm), and the park's Web site offers excellent information about the topography and habitat of its native birds. The **Tennessee Ornithological Society** (tnbirds .org) offers birding sites by region, with checklists to download and print for use in the field.

BOATING Whether you're captain of your own ship or simply want to try out a pontoon for a day, marinas across the state provide full services and very often rentals for those wishing to explore Tennessee's waterways and lakes. The state's **Wildlife Resource Agency** (615-781-6500; state.tn.us /twra/boatmain.html) offers comprehensive boating information, including licensing, location of public launches, and links to a list of marinas across the state.

BREWERIES From Ghost River in Memphis to Jonesborough's Depot Street, the handcrafted-beer industry is brewing in Tennessee, if you'll forgive the pun. While there's no one resource for a list of the state's breweries, the **Tennessee Department of Agriculture** (picktnproducts.org) offers a small listing.

BUS SERVICE The major cities in Tennessee—**Memphis, Nashville, Knoxville,** and **Chattanooga**—all offer public bus service, and **Greyhound** serves a number of towns throughout the state. **Gatlinburg** has its own trolley, and **Pigeon Forge** and **Sevierville** cooperatively operate a trolley service to main attractions, as does **Chattanooga,** in addition to its regular public tran-

sit system. Information on specific service is available at the start of each chapter if bus service is indeed available.

CABIN RENTALS In East Tennessee, there's a cabin or chalet for every taste, from cozy, one-bedroom rustic retreats to grand, sprawling lodges filled with luxurious amenities and enough room to sleep 18. The cabin companies listed in the various chapters are meant to open the door for your exploration of cabins in any of the regions; the best source for reliable services is the local convention and visitors bureau or companies that also partner with the state **Department of Tourism** (tnvacation.com). Many **Tennessee state parks** (state.tn .us/environment/parks) offer cabin rentals in addition to campgrounds; most are priced under $50/night and come fully outfitted with linens, kitchens, and even

grills. State park cabins tend to book quickly given their quality and inexpensive price.

CAMPING There are more than 50 state parks in Tennessee (state .tn.us/environment/parks), so finding a campsite is easy, paying for it is affordable, and the amenities usually include trailheads, waterways, scenic views, and wildlife. Not bad for around $20/night, in most cases. Campsites at most state parks include primitive sites and combo RV/tent sites with hookups; check the individual park Web site for information on rates, reservations (not always necessary), and more details.

CANOEING/KAYAKING From the **Wolf River** in Memphis to the **Tennessee River** in Knoxville and even the **Mighty Mississippi,** there are a vast number of waterways to paddle through. Once again, state parks offer plenty of opportunity for paddlers, and some spots—including the **Pellissippi Blueway** (cs.utk.edu /~dunigan/blueway)—provide detailed route maps.

CIVIL WAR SITES The battles fought in Tennessee were among some of the most important of the Civil War, and the state **Tourism Department** (tnvacation.com /civil-war) offers an excellent overview of these battles and Civil War history in Tennessee. As the state celebrates the **Civil War Sesquicentennial** in 2011, at the time of the publication of this book, a variety of events marking the 150th anniversary will be under way. Check the Web site for

Stephanie Jones

more information. See the appendix for more information on the Civil War in Tennessee.

CIVIL WAR TRAILS As Tennessee marks the 150th anniversary of the Civil War, history buffs can follow a variety of Civil War trails throughout the state to gain a better understanding of the importance of Tennessee during the war. Go online to tnvacation .com/civil-war/trails for downloadable maps and trail information.

COLLEGE SPORTS Blue or Orange? Tiger or Vol? These are important questions across the state, as sports fans and alumni line up in favor of their teams. The **University of Memphis Tigers,** with whiz-kid coach Josh Pastner, is continuing the excellent basketball tradition in the state; the **University of Tennessee** is known not just for its top-ranked men's basketball, but also for coach Pat Summitt and her **Lady Vols,** who dominate women's college basketball, with eight national championships to date. Summitt, by the way, is the all-time winning-est college basketball coach, male or female.

EVENTS With rich musical, cultural, and natural heritage, the state always has an event going on, whether it's May's Beale Street Music Festival in Memphis or the sparkling, months-long Winterfest in the Smokies. The state's tourism Web site (tnvacation.com) has a searchable feature for events and is an excellent resource. In addition, each chapter in this book highlights the annual events and festivals for the featured town.

FALL FOLIAGE One of the most spectacular times in Tennessee is October and November, when the lush greenery that blankets the state bursts into spectacular, fiery colors. The Smokies and points in East Tennessee are particularly brilliant, with a cascading hue throughout the mountains. All things fall in the state, from color reports to pumpkin picking and other fall events, can be found online at fall.tnvacation.com.

FISHING Anglers love Tennessee, from casting lines in the **Little Pigeon** or **Green River** in the **Smokies** to johnboating in **Reelfoot Lake** and casting for catfish in **Pickwick.** The state requires fishermen of all ages have a license, available at all state parks and plenty of bait shops and marinas throughout the state. For a complete rundown on fishing in Tennessee, including regulations, seasons, species, and the best fishing holes, visit the Tennessee Wildlife Resource Web site at state.tn.us/twra/fish/fishmain.html.

FLAG The Tennessee state flag features an emblem of three white stars in a blue circle on a red background; each star represents one of the three main geographic regions of the state—East, North, and West. As you travel through

Tennessee, you may spot the three stars in commercial uses—on the helmets of the Tennessee Titans, for example, or in the logo of First Tennessee Bank.

GEOCACHING Using a GPS (Global Positioning System) for outdoorsy scavenger hunts has become a popular sport in Tennessee; **geocaching clubs** throughout the state are popping up, some with excellent resources, like the **Middle Tennessee Geocachers Club** (mtgc.org) and the **Greater East Tennessee Geocaching Club** (getgc.org).

GOLF From the celebrity-owned **Mirimichi** in **Millington** to a collection of **Jack Nicklaus–** designed **Bear Trace courses,** Tennessee is a robust destination for following that tiny white ball over manicured greens. The **Tennessee Golf Trail** (tngolftrail.net) lists the public golf courses at state parks, and special courses are highlighted throughout this book.

HIKING Few would argue that Tennessee is a premier destination for hikers of abilities and endurance; from the ultrachallenging ascent up **Mount LeConte** in the **Great Smoky Mountains National Park** to an easy stroll along the **Burgess Falls route in Middle Tennessee,** our state is a hiking paradise.

HUNTING Whether it's wings or antlers that interest hunters, the moderate weather and wide open spaces of Tennessee combine for excellent hunting throughout the year. Licenses are required for all types of hunting, and complete information on regulations, hunting on public and private land, and more is available from the **Tennessee Wildlife Resource Agency** (615-781-6500; state.tn.us /twra). The **Tennessee Hunting Guide Society** (huntingsociety .org) also offers information, including lists of guides throughout the state.

INNS As with bed & breakfast lodgings, the highest number of traditional inns is found in the Smoky Mountain region, in the surrounding communities of Sevierville, Pigeon Forge, and Gatlinburg, with fewer of these lodgings as one heads west. The **Bed and Breakfast Association of Tennessee** (931-924-3869; tennessee-inns.com) offers a comprehensive listing of member properties with complete contact information and descriptions.

LIVE MUSIC Where can you find live music in Tennessee? Everywhere, from street corners in **Nashville** and **Memphis** to tiny **country bars** in Gatlinburg. Nashville highlights its more than two hundred live-music venues with special guitar-pick-shaped signs; Memphis's best source for live-music happenings is the local newspaper and weekly alternative paper, the Go Memphis section of the *Memphis Commercial Appeal* (commercialappeal.com), and the *Memphis Flyer* (memphisflyer .com).

MAIN STREET COMMUNITIES
The charming downtown areas of a number of the state's smaller towns—Collierville, Franklin, Columbia, and others—combine to give visitors a real taste of small-town Tennessee. A number of these communities are recognized as part of the Tennessee Main Street program for their redevelopment and infusion of reinvestment money from both local and state governments. Learn more about these charming communities throughout this book, or by going online to www.tennessee mainstreet.org.

MEAT-AND-THREE Restaurants across the state offer meat-and-three plates—a curious thing to those who have not traveled previously in the southern United States. A meat-and-three is a meat (usually a daily special like meat loaf or a pork chop) and the diner's

choice of three vegetables or side dishes from a long list of options. From lima beans to green beans to macaroni and cheese or creamed corn, the combinations are endless.

NEWSPAPERS Newspaper publishing is still alive, although perhaps not as well as it used to be, in Tennessee, with all the major cities continuing their daily print editions as of this writing. The *Memphis Commercial Appeal* (commercial appeal.com) is the Memphis daily, with *The Tennessean* (tennessean .com) Nashville's daily; the *Knoxville News-Sentinel* (knoxnews .com) and Chattanooga's *Times-Free Press* (timesfreepress.com) round out the top papers in the state.

MUSIC AND HERITAGE TRAILS To better market the big and small attractions along the highways and byways of Tennessee, the state developed a number of **themed trails,** including music and heritage trails. Downloadable maps and descriptions are available online, and in the annual state visitors guide available at welcome centers. For information call 615-741-2159 or log onto tnvacation.com.

NASCAR RACING NASCAR hits the tracks in both Bristol and Nashville; the **Nashville Superspeedway** (nashvillesuperspeed way.com) and **Bristol Motor Speedway** (bristolmotorspeedway .com) both host events throughout the year, as well as other car racing events.

POPULATION Just over 6 million people call the Volunteer State home; Memphis and Nashville are the largest cities, with more than 600,000 people living in Memphis proper and more than a million in the metropolitan area, and more than 500,000 living within Nashville/Davidson County and more than 1.1 million in the greater metro area.

PROFESSIONAL SPORTS With just over a million people in each of the Nashville and Memphis metro areas, it might come as a surprise these cities each host a professional sports team, and in Nashville's case, two teams. The NFL's **Tennessee Titans** and the NHL's **Nashville Predators** call Nashville home, while the home court of the NBA's **Grizzlies** is in Memphis.

SMOKING Tennessee enacted a comprehensive statewide ban on smoking in the workplace in 2007. Restaurants and bars are smoke free unless they choose to limit access to people 21 and older at all times. This includes restaurants with bars, as well as chain and hotel restaurants. Restaurants can allow smoking on outdoor patios. For hotels, smoking rooms are allowed, provided that no more than 25 percent of the rooms in a hotel or motel can be designated as smoking rooms. Many bars, restaurants, and hotels have gone completely smoke free, and usually those establishments note their status on doors and entranceways.

STATE FLOWERS Tennessee actually has two state flowers. The state wildflower, the purple passionflower, was chosen by school children of Tennessee in 1919. The state cultivated flower is the iris. Each spring, the Tennessee Iris Festival (tennesseeirisfestival .com) in Dresden celebrates this state flower.

STATE PARKS There are more than 50 state parks in Tennessee; all are free, most are pet friendly, and many offer cabins and campsites for visitors.

TIME ZONES Tennessee is a **dual time zone state,** with a general dividing line being Eastern Tennessee in the Eastern time zone, and Middle and West Tennessee in the Central time zone.

TRAFFIC UPDATES Before setting out on a car trip through Tennessee, check with the state Department of Transportation (www.tdot.state.tn.us/tdotsmart way) for the most up-to-date road closings, traffic construction, and maintenance information.

TRAILS & BYWAYS 16 self-guided trails throughout the state originate in the big cities, but take travelers on the scenic back roads for a journey into the hidden gems of Tennessee. Whimsically named and/or themed, each trail offers scenic drives which encompass a variety of sights. With imaginative names like the Walking Tall trail or Ring of Fire trail, each trail offers the chance to hit the road for a memorable trip through Tennessee history (tntrailsandbyways.com).

WALKING HORSES They're graceful, easy gaited, and excellent for riders of all levels. Tennessee Walking Horses can be found around the world, and many are bred right in Middle Tennessee's **Shelbyville.** The **National Tennessee Walking Horse Celebration** (twhnc.com) is held annually in Shelbyville, drawing thousands of equestrian fans to the state to honor these beautiful creatures.

WEATHER Generally, Tennessee enjoys moderate weather year-round, with the big variations coming in the **mountains of East Tennessee,** where snow and cold —although rarely extreme cold— take hold for about two months. **Nashville** certainly gets its share of snow and cold during the winter, with **Memphis** staying more moderate in the winter and usually warmer and more humid than the rest of the state in the summer. It's always a good plan to check weather forecasts before heading to any destination, but particularly in **East Tennessee,** where roads will close around town and in the **Great Smoky Mountains National Park** due to snow.

WELCOME CENTERS At 14 entrance points to the state, Tennessee Welcome Centers provide a chance to take a break, stretch your legs, and pick up maps and guides to Tennessee. Find locations and more information online at www.tn vacation.com/welcome-centers.

WHISKEY Middle Tennessee is home to the originator of Tennessee whiskey, Jack Daniel, and his Lynchburg distillery—but Gentleman Jack wasn't alone in trying to perfect a fine sipping whiskey. George Dickel opened a distillery just 20 miles from Lynchburg to perfect his craft, hoping to make it as fine as Scotch whisky (with no *e*, you'll note). So what makes a Tennessee whiskey different from bourbon? It's nearly identical in every way, with the exception that Tennessee whiskey is filtered through sugar maple charcoal to give it a mellower, smoother feel.

WINERIES Tennessee wineries are taking root across the state, with more than 30 wineries and vineyards now producing grapes and wines. A full list of wineries is online at the **Tennessee Wine Growers Association** Web site (tennesseewines.com).

ZOOS Some of the country's best zoos just happen to be in Tennessee. In 2010, the **Memphis Zoo** was rated the number one zoo in America by users of the online rating site TripAdvisor; **Nashville, Chattanooga,** and **Knoxville** each has its own excellent zoo.

Eastern Tennessee: The First Frontier

1

KNOXVILLE AND THE MIDDLE EAST

NORTHEAST

GREAT SMOKY MOUNTAIN REGION

KNOXVILLE AND
THE MIDDLE EAST

KNOXVILLE

In some ways, Knoxville has been the Rodney Dangerfield of Tennessee
—it rarely gets any respect. Sure, it's home to the University of Tennessee
and considered the gateway to the Smokies, but it can't claim to be the
home of country music and the birthplace of the blues and rock 'n' roll,
and it doesn't get as many raves as Chattanooga for a spectacular,
Phoenix-like rise from the ashes. But don't underestimate Tennessee's
third-largest city. Quietly, Knoxville is always evolving and improving, and
its amazing collection of cultural and historic sites certainly rival that of
Nashville and probably outstrip Memphis.

Set in a beautiful valley at the headwaters of the Tennessee River,
Knoxville was a prime settlement and hunting ground for the Cherokee
prior to European settlement. The first settler was Gen. James White,
who built a fort and group of cabins above the river in 1786 thanks to a
Revolutionary War land grant. White was able to make friends with the
Cherokee and helped other white settlers move into the area, including
William Blount, who was named governor of the territory in 1790 and
built his home, the historic Blount Mansion, in 1792. During these few
years, white settlers were illegally moving into the Cherokee lands in the
nearby French and Broad valleys; the Cherokee had not ceded these
lands, and the government ordered the settlers out, to no avail. Blount,
however, was able to negotiate with the Cherokee for the capital of the
territory—White's fort. Blount named the new capital after the first U.S.
Secretary of War, Henry Knox.

Being at the confluence of three rivers, Knoxville developed from frontier outpost to trading and shipping mecca, with riverboats and steamboats bringing cotton from farther south to trade for local products
including tobacco and corn.

The residents of Knoxville and its surrounds were deeply divided as

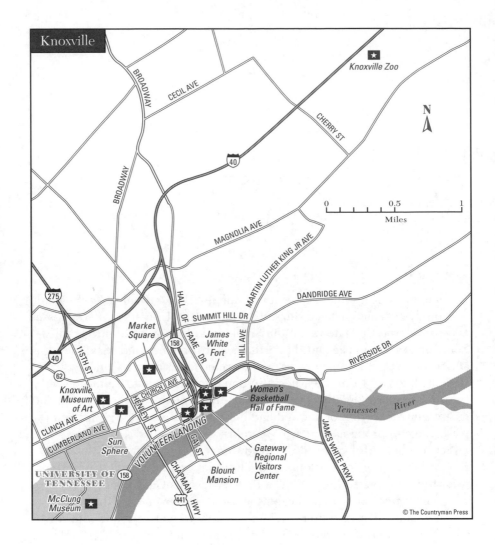

talk of secession and the abolition of slavery escalated prior to the Civil War. Blount County, directly south of Knoxville, was strongly abolitionist, while many businessmen were pro-secessionist. While the region around Knoxville and the larger portion of Knox County voted against secession in 1861, the city itself overwhelmingly voted to secede. Not long after Tennessee had joined the Confederacy, Union guerillas destroyed a hand-ful of the city's bridges, and martial law was instituted. And while efforts were made to fortify the city, Confederate troops evacuated when Union troops began a march toward the city under Ambrose Burnside in the summer of 1863. The Union moved in and stayed through the end of the war, fending off an attempt by Confederate forces to attack.

Following the war, Knoxville went on a bit of a business boom, adding almost one hundred factories by the late 1880s, including knitting mills and those producing furniture, food, and iron products. A huge quarry outside town was mined for beautiful pink Tennessee marble. Life was great in Knoxville, which was bursting at the seams with new immigrant residents and prosperity. However, between the economic crash in 1929 and the constant flooding of the Tennessee Valley, Knoxville and the surrounding area took a real hit in the early decades of the 20th century. True, many Knoxvillians were essential in the creation of the Great Smoky Mountains National Park in 1933, but industrial blight was the view from Knoxville. The economic pendulum slowly began swinging back the other way for the city in 1933 when the Tennessee Valley Authority began its ambitious dam-building program with Norris Dam. The TVA projects brought other jobs to the region, including the construction of the airport and other Works Project Administration projects.

Knoxville's roller-coaster economic ride continued as those textile mills that survived the Great Depression found themselves no match for foreign competitors in the 1950s and 1960s. As suburban housing developments began to lure residents out of downtown Knoxville, business followed. Soon, this pretty city with its distinct mix of architecture felt a bit deserted. Folks came into the city to work and escaped after five to their suburban oases. The resulting flight to suburbia meant a huge loss of tax revenue for the city; annexation attempts were combative and unsuccessful, and a variety of almost desperate attempts to redevelop the downtown area were tried.

The city's selection as the site of the 1982 World's Fair was the catalyst for the renaissance of downtown and its neighborhoods. More than 11 million people visited Knoxville during the World's Fair, and the boost to the economy—and the morale of residents—turned into a winning combination for the city. The Sunsphere—that golden-domed landmark that was the icon of the 1982 World's Fair—stands as a reminder to the world that one event can indeed change the course of a city's future.

While the revitalization has been slow, progress in creating a revitalized downtown has been steady. Market Square, once the epicenter of commerce in Knoxville, has returned to glory as a modern adaptation of the town market, with restaurants and shops, while residents have also come back to this area, enjoying the city's vibrant new energy and offerings. Theaters have been refurbished, retailers large and small have moved in, and the downtown dining scene has become one of the best in the state, not just for the cuisine itself but for the focus on sustainable dining and the use of local vendors and producers.

Knoxville boasts a number of historic districts and neighborhoods worthy of exploration. **The Old City,** also known as the **Jackson Avenue Warehouse District,** is in the northeast corner of downtown and offers a collection of restaurants and clubs, with some residential housing and boutique shopping. A young and hip crowd tends to populate the clubs here, and the area is still in transition (read: empty storefronts below, expensive flats above).

The **Fourth and Gill** neighborhood in North Knoxville is primarily a residential neighborhood and a must-visit for those interested in architecture and urban design. Originally a "streetcar suburb" of separate subdivisions, the area is a mishmash of architectural styles from the 1880s through the 1940s, and the wide, tree-lined streets often meet at funky angles, meaning getting lost is all too easy. **Volunteer Landing** is less a neighborhood and more a destination on the river, dotted with historic homes and featuring a 1-mile walking path, full-service marina, waterfalls and fountains, and a regional visitors center.

Fort Sanders—or the Fort, as locals call it—is north of downtown, on the edge of the University of Tennessee campus and on the National Register of Historic Places. The neighborhood is full of Victorian-era houses and structures, and it was named for the Civil War Battle of Knoxville, which happened smack in the center of this neighborhood. Fort Sanders

JAMES WHITE FORT, THE FIRST HOME IN KNOXVILLE

still retains its Victorian elegance, but in an interesting juxtaposition to that refined era, its residents are primarily college students. The Fort's Cumberland Avenue—known as "the strip"—is a hot spot for college students, with multiple bars, restaurants, and shops.

There's a lot of understated elegance and charm in today's Knoxville, from the very cool visitors center, where an indie local radio station hosts a daily live music show—genius!—to the vibrant performing arts scene: Knoxville has its own opera, symphony, and ballet companies. It boasts a number of excellent art museums, a delightful zoo, and of course, the blazing orange of University of Tennessee sports.

GUIDANCE Knoxville Tourism & Sports Corporation (800-727-8045; knoxville.org), 301 S. Gay Street. This could be the coolest visitors center in the state, as it includes a bookstore/retail area for picking up Tennessee maps, books, and souvenirs; there's also a café/deli/coffee shop on-site. And this is the home of the *WDVX Blue Plate Special*, the weekday radio show on independent radio dedicated to local and regional talent (see *Entertainment*).

GETTING THERE *By air:* **McGhee-Tyson Airport** (TYS; 865-342-3000; tys.org), 2055 Alcoa Highway, Knoxville. A mix of regional and national carriers serves McGhee-Tyson, including AirTran, Allegiant, American Eagle, Delta, and United.

By bus: **Greyhound** (865-534-0369; greyhound.com), 100 E. Magnolia Avenue. Greyhound offers service to Knoxville, and the bus terminal and ticket office are open 24 hours daily.

By car: Knoxville is located in East Tennessee, easily accessible from I-75 and I-40, both of which intersect the city.

BLOUNT MANSION

3000; katbus.com), 301 Church Avenue. Fares start at $1.50, with one-,
four-, and seven-day passes available. Bus service is offered seven days a
week, with schedules varying by route; most routes run 7 AM–11:30 PM,
with some offering late-night service. Download route maps and detailed
schedule information from the Web site.

By car: Knoxville's attractions are well spread out, so a car is an excellent
choice for touring Knoxville. I-640 loops around the city; I-40 is the main
east–west route into town, and I-75 is the main north–south route into
town. Once in the city, downtown Knoxville is bordered by the Tennessee
River to the south and is laid out on a grid system.

By taxi: There are about two dozen taxi services operating in Knoxville,
including **Big Orange Taxi** (865-523-3400) and **Yellow Cab** (865-523-
5151). A trip from the Knoxville airport to downtown hotels is approximately $30.

MEDICAL EMERGENCY Baptist Hospital (865-632-5210; mercy.com),
137 E. Blount Avenue. Offers 24-hour emergency care and comprehensive medical services.

✳ To See

HISTORIC SITES Blount Mansion (888-654-0016; blountmansion.org),
200 W. Hill Avenue. Open Tues.–Sat. 9:30–5. Closed on Sat. when the
University of Tennessee football team plays at home. Tours begin at the
top of the hour; last tour starts at 4. Nestled between towering buildings
of glass and steel, the stately home built in 1792 is a reminder of the
frontier days in East Tennessee. William Blount served in Congress under
the Articles of Confederation and was appointed by President Washington
to be governor of the territory south of the Ohio River; his family home
also served as the capitol of the territory. The simple sawed-wood home
was a rarity among the log cabins; the nails holding the house together
were from Blount's family business in North Carolina. Tours start in the
visitors center with a multimedia presentation about Blount and the history of the house. Many of the antiques are from the family, with others
being true to the period. The pretty garden is in the Colonial Revival
style and is included on the tour of the home. Adults $7, seniors $6, children $5.

James White Fort (865-525-6514; discoveret.org/jwf), 205 E. Hill
Avenue. Open Mon.–Sat. 9–5, Apr.–Nov.; Mon.–Sat. 10–4, Dec.–Mar.
Note: The fort is closed during UT home football games because of parking and traffic congestion. Revolutionary War veteran James White
founded Knoxville with a portion of the 1,000-acre land grant he received

for his service in the war. A friend to the Cherokee, White would negotiate between the Native Americans and incoming white settlers; his two-story log cabin briefly served as the territorial capitol and is the city's most-visited historic site. Located directly across from the Women's Basketball Hall of Fame, the fort is an authentic slice of pioneer life and an especially great spot for kids, as the stories of pioneers and Indians sparks the imagination. Adults $5, children $2.

World's Fair Sunsphere (865-951-1307; worldsfairpark.com/worlds-fair-sunsphere.html). Open daily 9 AM–10 PM, Apr.–Oct.; daily 11–6, Nov.–Mar. The gleaming Sunsphere was built as the symbol of the 1982 World's Fair in Knoxville, and today its observation deck is open to the public for a 360-degree view of the city, the UT campus, and the mountains. The Sunsphere and Tennessee Amphitheater are the only two remaining structures from the fair. Enter at the base of the Sunsphere or inside the convention center. Free.

MUSEUMS Farragut Folklife Museum (865-966-7057; townoffarragut .org/parks-athletics-leisure/museum.html), 11408 Municipal Center Drive, Farragut. Open Mon.–Fri. 10–4:30. The famed naval commander Farragut—he who said "damn the torpedoes, full speed ahead" at the Battle of Mobile Bay—was from East Tennessee; the museum in the town named for him features a broad collection of the admiral's personal items, as well as historical items from the local area and a variety of Civil War artifacts. The museum, located within the town hall, celebrates the holiday season with displays of antique toys, dollhouses, and decorations; the donation of a collection of Elvis memorabilia from a local collector in 2009 brings a twist of West Tennessee to the museum. Free.

Knoxville Museum of Art (865-525-6501; knoxart.org), 1050 World's Fair Park. Open Tues.–Sat. 10–5 (with extended hours until 8 on Fri.), Sun. 1–5. Although the Knoxville Museum of Art didn't come into being until the 1960s, it has amassed an excellent permanent collection featuring artists of regional and national prominence. Perhaps the highlight of the KMA's collection is the Thorne Rooms, nine miniature dioramas created with the collection that Mrs. James Ward Thorne of Chicago assembled with tiny furnishings and accessories she collected from across the globe. The museum's Exploratory Gallery invites children and their parents to interact with art, with hands-on experiences designed and installed by artists themselves, while traveling exhibitions regularly bring international masterpieces to East Tennessee. Free.

McClung Museum (865-974-2144; mcclungmuseum.utk.edu), 1327 Circle Park Drive. Open Mon.–Sat. 9–5, Sun. 1–5. The McClung is both an exhibiting and research museum; housed at the University of Tennessee, the permanent collection ranges from priceless artifacts from ancient cul-

WOMEN'S BASKETBALL HALL OF FAME

tures to decorative arts and a deep examination of the Battle of Fort Sanders, Knoxville's major Civil War battle. Free.

✍ **Women's Basketball Hall of Fame** (865-633-9000; wbhof.com), 700 Hall of Fame Drive. Open Tues.–Fri. 11–5 and Sat. 10–5, Labor Day–Apr. 30; Mon.–Sat. 1–5, May–Labor Day. Is it coincidence that the Women's Basketball Hall of Fame is located in the town where the all-time winning-est college basketball coach in history makes her home? I think not. Pat Summitt's astonishing record (more than nine hundred wins) aside, she's got some excellent company in the building, dedicated to all levels of women's basketball and its history—more than one hundred years' worth. Any girl who's got game needs to see this shout out to women's basketball, and guys will impressed as well. The best part of the whole museum is the lower level, where multiple courts with backboards and nets of varying height are set up, basketballs at the ready. Some serious one-on-one games get going here, and the action can be viewed from the upper level. Adults $7.95, children 6–15 $5.95, children five and under free.

✳ To Do

AQUARIUMS AND ZOOS ✎ **Knoxville Zoo** (865-637-5331; knoxville -zoo.org), 3500 Knoxville Zoo Drive. Open Mon.–Fri. 9:30–4:30, Sat.–Sun. 9:30–6. The small but excellent zoo is easy to navigate and allows kids (and adults!) some serious face time with the animals, as the habitats are designed for maximum viewing. The cute red pandas are a huge hit with the kids, as is the Kids Cove play area, home to the animals found in the Smokies. The Wee Zoo, specially designed for the toddler and preschool set, brings critters to a toddler's eye level and includes plenty of play space. Behind-the-scenes tours are available for an additional fee but allow incredible access to the animals. Note, however, those

WOMEN'S BASKETBALL HALL OF FAME

KNOXVILLE ZOO

tours are best for older children, probably seven and up. Adults $16.95, children 2–12 $12.95, children under two free. Parking is an additional $5.

FAMILY FUN ✎ **Fort Kid** (865-215-4311; knoxville.org/visitors/parks -nature/fort-kid), 1050 World's Fair Park. Open daily dawn–dusk. The all-volunteer force that built the sprawling playground couldn't have imag-ined how popular the playground would become; the mazes, tunnels, swings, and slides have kids begging their parents to stay for hours, if not longer. I suggest a picnic lunch and a shady spot for maximum enjoyment, and just let the kids run wild. Free.

SPECTATOR SPORTS **University of Tennessee Sports** (865-974-1000; utk.edu/athletics), University of Tennessee, various locations. With a women's basketball team led by Pat Summitt, the winning-est college bas-ketball coach of all time; a men's basketball team that advanced to the NCAA's Sweet 16 in 2007; and a football team that has celebrated multi-ple SEC championships and postseason bowl appearances in the last two decades, Knoxville is the heart of the college sports scene in the state. Single tickets are available on most home game days, football included. According to a 2010 Web poll by the school, when asked how they became a Vols fan, 68 percent of the respondents answered that they were "born into it." And there's no arguing with those kinds of numbers.

✳ Green Space

GARDENS AND NATURE CENTERS ✎ **Ijams Nature Center** (865-577-4717; ijams.org), 2915 Island Home Avenue. Open Tues.–Sat. 9–5, Sun. (Mar. 30–Nov. 1) 1–5. A long boardwalk connects all manner of habitats along the Tennessee River, from meadows and forests to caves and creeks. A raptor center allows the chance to glimpse predatory birds, while 5 miles of hiking trails lure runners and walkers alike. A museum features the story of the Ijams family and its dedication to conservation, a variety of exhibits on the flora and fauna of the region, as well as interactive children's exhibits that showcase wildlife and conservation. Free.

🐾 **Knoxville Botanical Gardens** (865-862-8717; knoxgarden.org), 2743 Wimpole Avenue. Open daily dawn–dusk. Atop a ridge and tucked away within a neighborhood, the gardens were opened in 2001, meaning the process of planting, identifying, and tagging all the greenery and flowers is an ongoing process. The gardens have a history of both Native American and Civil War occupation, although further research is still being conducted to confirm the property's history. Leashed pets are welcome with their owners, and a walking tour map is available online. Free.

✳ Lodging

BED & BREAKFASTS/INNS
Maplehurst Inn (865-523-7773; maplehurstinn.com), 800 W. Hill Avenue. Eleven bedrooms are scattered on four floors of this 1918 mansion in the historic district downtown; all the bedrooms include private baths and a choice of accommodations, from double beds to kings. The famous Maplehurst casserole is a breakfast staple, as is a wide array of fruits and pastries. Moderate.

HOTELS The Cumberland House Hotel (865-971-4663; starwoodhotels.com/fourpoints), 1109 White Avenue. Long the largest independent hotel in downtown Knoxville, the Cumberland House joined forces with Sheraton and now is a Four Points property. But

PRICE CATEGORIES:	
Inexpensive	Less than $100 (for hotels, inns, and B&Bs); less than $50 (for campgrounds, state park facilities)
Moderate	$100–200
Expensive	$201–300
Very expensive	More than $300

the hotel's intimate, upscale atmosphere hasn't changed despite the chain-hotel label, although some of the originality seems to have been flattened out a bit. But the bar is still a hip and sleek hangout, and rooms are spacious and luxurious—a perfectly lush spot for those seeking a bit of upscale comfort among the usual chain hotel suspects. Moderate.

☙ **Hotel St. Oliver** (865-521-0050; stoliverhotel.com), 407 Union Street. This Market Square hotel is most unexpected; each of the 24 rooms features different decor, and there's a general air of upscale dishabille about the whole place that's too fetching to ignore. The location is fantastic for exploring Market Square, downtown, and the Old Town area, with easy freeway access for those looking to explore beyond the downtown area. Breakfast is included in the room rate. Note that on UT football weekends, a two-night minimum is required. Moderate.

✳ Where to Eat

DINING OUT Chesapeake's (865-673-3433),500 Henley Street. Open Mon.–Thurs. 11:30–2:30 and 4:30–10, Fri. 11:30–2:30 and 4:30–11, Sat. 4:30–11, and Sun. 4:30–9:30. The nautical theme is a bit kitschy and overdone at this downtown eatery, but the fresh seafood—shrimp, oysters, lobster, and about everything in between —is prepared almost any way one could request. The atmosphere is quiet and the service excellent, and the price tag at the end of the night is worth it. Expensive.

The Grill at Highlands Row (865-851-7722; thegrillathighlands row.com), 4705 Old Kingston Pike. Open Mon.–Sat. 5–10. New life has come to this once-renowned spot on Old Kingston Pike; the Highlands was one of *the* fine-dining experiences in town from the 1930s through the 1960s.

The restaurant has been resurrected by a local developer who may not be old enough to remember the original's heyday but cared enough to try and capture the atmosphere of a fine-dining establishment with a more casual atmosphere. The result is a hit. The wide open dining room that's cozy at night leads to an intimate lounge space; the main dining area has wood plank walls and gas lanterns, giving it a warm and old-fashioned feel. The food is rich, both in its calorie count and its depth; traditional chops, steaks, and seafood are served up with unusual sides, including Gouda grits and okra fries, adding a bit of Southern spice to a predominantly American menu. Homemade desserts, including a selection of handmade ice cream, change on a nightly basis. Expensive.

EATING OUT Calhoun's on the River (865-673-3400; calhouns.com/CalhOnTnRiver.shtml), 400 Neyland Drive. Open Sun.–Thurs. 11–10, Fri.–Sat. 11–11. Calhoun's is a barbecue chain with locations all over the South, but one of the original Calhoun's was right on the Tennessee River, and it's still as packed as it was when it first opened. The decor is nothing spe-

PRICE CATEGORIES:	
Inexpensive	Less than $16
Moderate	$16–30
Expensive	$31–50
Very expensive	More than $50

cial, as the river view is the main backdrop, and almost every table has a river view. This Memphis girl was a bit skeptical about barbecue outside home base, but the ribs are truly some of the best I've ever tasted, with a mild yet flavorful sauce and succulent meat. Boats can pull right up and dock at the restaurant, and there's outside seating that's open almost year-round. Moderate.

Cities Cupcakes (865-588-4558; citiescupcake.com), 5201 Kingston Pike SW. Open Tues.–Fri. 10–6, Sat. 10–4. These cupcakes are large and as rich as your uncle, but they won't cost you an inheritance to indulge in city-inspired flavors like the Knoxville, made of UT-orange chiffon cake and topped with whipped vanilla frosting, or the Santa Fe, a jalapeño corn bread cupcake with spicy cream cheese frosting. Inexpensive.

❧ **La Costa** (865-566-0275; lacostaonmarketsquare.com), 31 Market Square. Open for lunch Mon.–Sat. 11–3; dinner Sun.–Thurs. 4–10, Fri.–Sat. 4–11, and Sun. 11–3. One of the state's first green certified restaurants, La Costa features loads of organic and locally grown foods, and probably isn't for those who have limited or unadventurous palates. (As in yours truly; it was hard for me to find something I liked. However, the foodies I was traveling with loved La Costa, as would most people with anything more than a meat-and-potatoes mentality. But I digress.) The Latin-inspired

menu pairs nicely with the talent at the bar, where fresh mojitos and other yummy cocktails and a lovely wine list certainly held my attention. The signature Ceviche of the Moment is a fresh fish delight, while the rubbed pork rib eye was a spicy and surprisingly juicy piece of pork. Its restaurants like La Costa that make one wish one had experimented more—with food—as a child. Moderate.

Pete's Coffee Shop (865-523-2860; petescoffeeshop.com), 540 Union Ave. Open for breakfast

Tennessee Department of Tourist Development

WDVX BLUE PLATE SPECIAL

and lunch Mon.–Fri. 6:30–2:30, Sat. 7–2. There's a surprisingly huge menu at this basic little coffee shop that offers coffee-shop-style food, from huge egg platters and stack of fluffy pancakes at breakfast to club, chicken salad, and BLT sandwiches during the lunch hour. Daily plate specials offer a meat and two sides or a veggie plate with a choice of three for less than $6. The crowd is an eclectic mix of college students, top business execs, and colorful locals. Inexpensive.

✱ Entertainment

BARS AND NIGHTCLUBS
Crown & Goose (865-524-2100; thecrownandgoose.com), 123 S. Central Street. Open Mon.–Thurs. 11–11, Fri. 11 AM–2 AM, Sat. noon–2 AM, and Sun. 11 AM–4 PM. A London gastropub in the heart of the historic district, the Crown & Goose serves up pub grub, loads of ales and lagers in pints, and darts, of course. Live music on most weekend evenings, and a beer garden in the back during the warmer months, add up to a real slice of British life.

LIVE-MUSIC VENUES *WDVX Blue Plate Special* (865-544-1029; wdvx.com/programs/Blue Plate.html), Knoxville Visitors Center, corner of Gay Street and Summit Hill Drive, downtown. The live weekday radio program is must-do in Knoxville; starting at noon on weekdays, regional and national artists from all genres,

AT THE MAST GENERAL STORE, YOU CAN GET A FAVORITE LOCAL COMBINATION: MOON PIES AND RC COLA.

but primarily bluegrass, folk, and country, perform on the small stage in the visitors center. Get there early to grab a table—and a sandwich or cup of coffee from the small deli—and settle in for a real treat. Free.

✳ Selective Shopping

BOUTIQUE SHOPPING

Bliss/Bliss Home (865-329-8868; shopinbliss.com), 24 and 29 Market Square. Open Mon.–Sat. 10–6. One Bliss is a home store with thoroughly modern classics, some outrageous and some totally affordable, while the other Bliss is full of unusual yet must-have clothing and accessories, as well as a number of funky gifts and random decor.

Mast General Store (865-546-1336; mastgeneralstore.com /knoxville.cfm), 402 S. Gay Street. Open Mon.–Wed. 10–6, Thurs.–Sat. 10–9, and Sun. noon–6. An almost overwhelming collection of outdoor gear for men, women, children, and dogs, plus a variety of giftware and quite a few gift sets of Moon Pies and RC Cola (it's a Southern thing—see the *Over the Moon* sidebar). Ski wear and outdoor clothing are the specialties, as are a vast shoe offering of outdoorsy brands.

Yee Haw (865-522-1812; yeehaw industries.com), 413 S. Gay Street. Open Tues.–Fri. 10–6, Sat. 10–5, and Sun. noon–5. Artful letterpress posters and products are simply fun to look through, and the groovy staff ranges from super-friendly to surly, but the store is absolutely worth making time for. Prints range from a few dollars to a few hundred, and as the company's artists are being featured all over the place these days, from decor magazines to hip New York galleries, best to buy at the local prices while you can.

SHOPPING DISTRICTS Market Square (865-224-6732; knoxville marketsquare.com/district/shop), bordered by Gay, Walnut, Union, and Wall streets. The eclectic collection of stores and restaurants in Market Square, plus weekends and random days filled with fairs, concerts, and events like the Wed. farmer's market, give Market Square an edgy and hip feel. Stores range from home decor to gift stores and nontraditional clothing; most stores are open Mon.–Sat.10–6.

✱ Special Events

Early April: **Rossini Festival** (865-524-0795; knoxvilleopera.com /rossini), Gay Street and Market Square. A one-day Italian street fair with opera performances (in Italian, of course), an artisan's market, and loads of Italian food. Free.

April: **Dogwood Arts Festival** (865-637-4561; dogwoodarts.com), 602 S. Gay Street, and locations around town. A huge celebration of the arts and nature, Dogwood combines fun events like sidewalk chalk art competitions and juried exhibitions; the month-long event

also incorporates performing arts with the visual arts for an overarching experience. Many events are free, although some require tickets. Check the Web site for details.

April–June: **Sundown in the City** (sundowninthecity.com), Market Square. Live concerts held throughout the summer in Market Square bring out a nice mix of families, couples, and singles to mingle and enjoy a summer evening as the sun goes down. Free.

SOME OF WHAT'S ON OFFER AT THE FARMER'S MARKET AT MARKET SQUARE

OAK RIDGE

It's one of the youngest towns in the state of Tennessee—less than 60 years old. But Oak Ridge has perhaps the most comprehensively fascinating history of any town in the entire state, and perhaps the nation.

A long, narrow valley in the hills northwest of Knoxville, Oak Ridge saw significant occupation as far back as the year AD 1000; once natives of the Woodland and Mississippian periods moved on, the rural valley was relatively deserted by the time European settlers discovered it. The long, flat valley was perfect for farming, and small farm communities were established.

In October 1942, the federal government rapidly bought up the family farms on 60,000 acres in the communities in the hills outside of Knoxville. Eviction notices were posted, giving the farmers little time to clear out. Heavy equipment came in, and a fence around the huge land mass went up. This area, which wouldn't be identified on maps, which then–vice president Harry S Truman wasn't made aware of for six months, did have a purpose: it was the site of what the government called the Manhattan Project.

Construction—on sewers and roads, houses, office buildings, and manufacturing plants—carried on 24 hours a day for more than a year, through unusually heavy rains for 10 months of that time. Mud was everywhere, and boardwalks had to be constructed so people could make their way between buildings.

Soon, people came by the busload. In the end, 75,000 people in all—scientists and engineers from all over the world and their families moved wholesale into this community behind the fence—and very few would leave the compound over the next two years. Secrecy was paramount, they were told. Neighbors in this community never talked about what work they were doing; husbands and wives, who often worked in different parts of the compound, would never reveal to each other what their exact jobs entailed.

As locals watched, truck after truck of equipment and supplies would go into what they called the Secret City, and only people occasionally came out, usually men in business suits carrying briefcases, heading off to the train or airport. Turns out those men were heading to Los Alamos in New Mexico, carrying lead-lined briefcases with small amounts of the material needed to make an atom bomb.

It was only when the news of a new weapon used against the Japanese was announced that those behind the fence knew what the secrecy was all about. The gates to the city were opened, and a parade was held to welcome the curious.

The Secret City was also supposed to be a temporary city; all the homes and most of the buildings were meant to be dismantled after the war. But the peacetime applications of all the research that had brought about the atomic bomb were obvious to the scientists at Oak Ridge, and the decision was made to keep the facility running. Research continues today on energy, supercomputing, biological systems, and neutron systems.

GUIDANCE Oak Ridge Convention & Visitors Bureau (865-482-3439; oakridgevisitor.com), 102 Robertsville Road. The Oak Ridge CVB Web site contains detailed information on city and regional attractions, and offers loads of history about the Secret City.

GETTING THERE *By air:* **McGhee-Tyson Airport** (TYS; 865-342-3000; tys.org), 2055 Alcoa Highway, Knoxville. About 30 miles from Oak Ridge, via I-140 and TN 62.

By car: Oak Ridge is about 35 miles northwest of downtown Knoxville, easily accessible from I-75 and I-40.

GETTING AROUND *By bus:* There is no public bus service in Oak Ridge; **Greyhound** (865-534-0369; greyhound.com) offers service to Knoxville.

By car: Oak Ridge was laid out by the federal government, and as you might imagine, the layout is pretty basic: grid system in the downtown area, with alphabetized streets throughout town—which makes finding a street quite a snap. Illinois Avenue and Oak Ridge Parkway are the major thoroughfares in town; the CVB offers an excellent map on its Web site that can be ordered through the mail and picked up at the visitors center.

MEDICAL EMERGENCY Because Oak Ridge is located in two counties— Anderson and Roane—be sure to note your exact location if you dial 911, as your call may routed to either county's emergency services department. The Oak Ridge Police Department number is 865-425-4399.

Methodist Medical Center of Oak Ridge (865-835-1000; mmcoak ridge.com), 990 Oak Ridge Turnpike, is the main hospital in Oak Ridge, with a large emergency room and comprehensive medical and diagnostic services available 24 hours daily.

✳ To See

HISTORIC SITES International Friendship Bell, Badger Avenue, near Oak Ridge Civic Center, 1043 Oak Ridge Turnpike. To mark the 50th anniversary of the revelation of the Manhattan Project and its purpose, a traditional Japanese bell was created to serve as a hope for everlasting peace between all nations, with a nod to the permanent bond created between this city and Japan. Free.

Oak Ridge National Laboratory (865-574-7199; ornl.gov). Tours, which depart from the American Museum of Science and Energy (see *Museums*), are offered June 1–Labor Day weekend and must be arranged in advance. Tours are open only to American citizens 10 years old and older, and proof of citizenship is required. The Oak Ridge National Laboratory was never meant to be a permanent facility, as its purpose was simply and solely to support the Manhattan Project. The first building of the project, known as 10-X, or the graphite reactor, was built here. It's almost disappointing that such an important building in the history of America is so bland from the outside, but inside, disappointment is quelled by the fascinating story the guides tell about exactly what occurred here. The three-hour tour makes stops at New Hope Center at the Y-12 Plant and the Spallation Neutron Source, and includes a drive around the old K-25 Plant, offering insightful information both into the history of ORNL and the discoveries that continue to emerge from the place that put the *secret* in Secret City. Free.

Wheat Community African Burial Ground, TN 58, Oak Ridge, adjacent to East Tennessee Technology Park Overlook. The 1850s slave ceme-

THE GRAPHITE REACTOR AT THE OAK RIDGE NATIONAL LABORATORY

A FLAT-TOP HOUSE AT THE AMERICAN MUSEUM OF SCIENCE AND ENERGY

tery has more than 90 unmarked graves; those buried here are thought to have been slaves at the Gallaher-Stone Plantation. Free.

MUSEUMS ✍ **American Museum of Science and Energy** (865-576-3200; amse.org), 300 S. Tulane Avenue. Open Mon.–Sat. 9–5 and Sun. 1–5. AMSE chronicles the amazing story of Secret City, and most of the friendly folks who work here formerly worked at the Oak Ridge National Laboratory or grew up during the time that the Secret City was still a secret—so their insider knowledge and pride of place is evident when you chat with them. Adults will particularly marvel at the story of Secret City and how so many people could keep their work secret. The historical exhibits are text and photo heavy, and quite fascinating; a flat-top house exhibit shows just how utilitarian the accommodations for workers were, with prefab houses being constructed as fast as possible. The rest of the museum is a wonderland for curious kids, as science and energy are explained and explored in understandable terms and interactive ways. Adults $5, children 6–17 $3, children under six free.

CHILDREN'S MUSEUM OF OAK RIDGE

⚓ **Children's Museum of Oak Ridge** (865-482-1074; childrens museum ofoakridge.org), 461 W. Outer Drive. Open Tues.–Fri. 9–5, Sat. 10–5, and Sun. 1–4; also open Mon. 9–5 in June, July, and Aug. What started as a single exhibit by the local Girl Scouts turned into one of the most creative spaces for children in the entire state. Opened in 1973, the museum is housed in a sprawling schoolhouse built for the children of the researchers and scientists working on the Manhattan Project. From the short history of the city to exhibits on Appalachia and the rain forest, the old classroom space is cleverly used to entice children in almost every kind of way. Adults $7, children three and up $5.

Southern Appalachian Railroad Museum/Secret City Excursion Train (865-241-2140; techscribes.com/sarm), TN 58, East Tennessee Technology Park. Trains depart from the Heritage Center (formerly K-25) and wind through the hills and valleys surrounding what was once off-limits to the public. (Construction on a new station and railroad museum at the Heritage Center site is expected to begin in 2011.) The scenic tours are on the 1940s-era rail cars; themed rides, including mystery dinner trains and fall foliage excursions, are offered seasonally. The train trips frequently sell out, so advance reservations are recommended. Non–U.S. citizens must provide passport and visa information prior to boarding. Adults $15, children 12 and under $10. Lap children two and under are free.

✳ To Do

BIKING Haw Ridge Park (865-425-3450; cs.utk.edu/~dunigan/mtnbike
/haw.html), 821 Edgemore Road. Open daily sunrise–sunset; closed some
weekends in the fall for hunting. The former off-road space for motorized
vehicles—jeeps and motorcycles—is now prime mountain biking space,
with 780 acres and dozens of routes to explore. The terrain alternates
between hilly, rocky, and rutted; steep descents are the hallmark, with
gradients in excess of 70 percent in spots. For bikers who want less of a
thrill, there are single-track trails along the lakeshore. Free.

✳ Green Space

**GARDENS AND NATURE CENTERS University of Tennessee
Arboretum** (865-483-3571; discoveret.org/utarboretum), 901 S. Illinois
Avenue. Open daily 8–sunset. The arboretum features more than 250
acres planted with native trees, shrubs, and flowering plants; four walking
trails, all moderately paced, offer the chance to wander through a landscape that's always changing. Each trail is outlined in detail on maps,
available on the Web site or at the visitors center. Free.

✳ Lodging

**HOTELS Doubletree Hotel Oak
Ridge** (865-481-2648; doubletree
.com), 215 S. Illinois Avenue, Oak
Ridge. Within an easy drive to
AMSE and just a few miles to
Clinton, the Doubletree is well
located for exploring Anderson
County, with plenty of conveniences located within a few blocks,
including a variety of chain restaurants and a shopping mall. Small
suites give families extra space to
stretch out, including a sofa bed,
and an executive level offers standard rooms with the added amenities of an exclusive continental
breakfast and evening appetizers
and drinks. A fitness center,
indoor pool, and on-site restaurant
and lounge round out the amenities, and complimentary wireless
is available throughout the hotel.
Moderate.

PRICE CATEGORIES:	
Inexpensive	Less than $100 (for hotels, inns, and B&Bs); less than $50 (for camp-grounds, state park facilities)
Moderate	$100–200
Expensive	$201–300
Very expensive	More than $300

✳ Where to Eat

DINING OUT Flatwater Grill
(865-862-8646; theflatwatergrill
.com), 100 Melton Lake Peninsula. Open Mon.–Sat. 11–2 and 4–9,
Sun. 11–3. Floor-to-ceiling glass
windows offer a view of the Clinch
River, and quite often a rowing
regatta—giving a more casual air
to the restaurant, which features a
broad range of American and

JEFFERSON SODA FOUNTAIN

international favorites, from steaks and fresh Gulf seafood to pasta choices and a huge offering of salads. The dessert menu, too, is ample—and everything is made from scratch. Moderate–expensive.

EATING OUT ✎ Jefferson Soda Fountain (865-482-1141), 22 Jefferson Circle. Open Mon.–Fri. 7–3, Sat. 6:30–2. It's no secret that the Jefferson is the spot to hit for a Fat Boy (a fully loaded hamburger named after the A-bomb), a thick and creamy milk shake, or a huge breakfast platter. The Jefferson opened in 1944 and has had just two owners in that time; the adjacent pharmacy used to be part of the business, and there's still a walk-through from the restaurant to the pharmacy side.

The Soup Kitchen (865-482-3525), 47 E. Tennessee Avenue. Open Mon.–Fri. 11–7:30, Sat. 11–2. If it comes in a bowl and has the word *soup* or *chili* in the title, then it's at the Soup Kitchen—and there's no soup Nazi to be found here. All the soups served up here are homemade and change daily, with seasonal favorites including Kansas City Beef Stew and a

PRICE CATEGORIES:	
Inexpensive	Less than $16
Moderate	$16–30
Expensive	$31–50
Very expensive	More than $50

handful of chili variations; sandwich selections and the breads they come on also change daily. Inexpensive.

✳ Special Events

Mid-June: **Secret City Festival** (865-425-3610; secretcityfestival .com), Oak Ridge Civic Center. The annual festival celebrates the city's storied history through World War II reenactments, historical displays, and tours of the Oak Ridge National Laboratory; children's activities, a crafts fair, and concerts are all part of the fun. Festival is free; tickets to the concerts are $15.

Year-round: **Rowing Regattas** (865-482-6538; orra.org/regattas .htm), Melton Hill, 697 Melton Lake Drive. Known as one of the best rowing courses in the country, Melton Hill draws thousands of rowers for spring training, college competitions, and other top-level races. Check the Web site for schedule. Free.

CLINTON, NORRIS, AND LAKE CITY

Anderson County isn't particularly large or overly populated, so it may be surprising that it is home to some of Tennessee's most important historical events.

Anderson is home to Oak Ridge, the so-called Secret City of the Manhattan Project. It is home to the first damn built by the Tennessee Valley Authority, which helped power the secret project farther down the Clinch River. It is home to deep roots of the Appalachian people, who honor their history at a variety of museums, sites, and festivals.

Coal mining has a long and ugly history in Anderson County, from the Coal Creek War through two horrendous mining disasters that resulted in the deaths of more than three hundred miners. The Coal Creek War started in 1891 when the owners of the mines in the Coal Creek watershed tried to replace their miners with convicts leased from the state. The war saw the miners-turned-vigilantes attacking prisons, freeing the prisoners, and burning the buildings; armed skirmishes and battles ensued for more than a year during the labor dispute. The conflict ended with the arrests of hundreds of miners in 1892, and the aftereffects of the fighting led to the downfall of then-governor Buchanan, as well as prompting the end of the practice of convict leasing.

AN ILLUSTRATION OF THE COAL CREEK WAR FROM *HARPER'S WEEKLY*
Tennessee Department of Tourist Development

It was just after the turn of the 20th century that Anderson County suffered not a war but a tragedy: many of the miners who fought during the Coal Creek days were employed at the Fraterville mine when it exploded in 1902, killing more than 215 men and leaving no survivors. A few years later, another mine explosion took the lives of another 80-plus miners.

Anderson is also home to one of the nation's most important moments in recent history—the desegregation of the first state-supported school in Tennessee, which saw the first African American to graduate from an integrated school in the South.

All of Anderson County's attractions are an easy drive from Knoxville, and Lake City and Clinton can easily be visited in a single day. Norris Lake, however, while also an easy drive from Knoxville, may lure you for at least an overnight with its outdoorsy activities.

Anderson's history is well told at historical attractions throughout the county, and the small towns that dot this rural landscape are pleasant spots to visit any time of year. The incredible history that took place in this part of northeast Tennessee is overlooked by many but should, without a doubt, be a part of the itinerary if visiting the region.

GUIDANCE Anderson County Tourism Council (865-457-4542; yall come.org), 115 Welcome Lane, Clinton. The county tourism council offers information and maps for Oak Ridge, Clinton, Norris, and Lake City.

GETTING THERE *By air:* **McGhee-Tyson Airport** (TYS; 865-342-3000; tys.org), 2055 Alcoa Highway, Knoxville, is about 30 miles from Clinton via I-75 north.

By car: Anderson County is northwest of Knox County and is easily accessible by I-75.

GETTING AROUND *By bus:* There is no public bus service in the area; **Greyhound** (865-534-0369; greyhound.com) offers service to Knoxville.

By car: A car is essential in Anderson County, as there is no public transportation or taxi service.

MEDICAL EMERGENCY Methodist Medical Center of Oak Ridge (865-835-1000; mmcoakridge.com), 990 Oak Ridge Turnpike, Oak Ridge, is the closest hospital, with a large emergency room and comprehensive medical and diagnostic services available 24 hours daily.

✳ To See

HISTORIC SITES Coal Creek Motor Discovery Trail (865-426-7914; coalcreekaml.com), 216 N. Main Street, Lake City. Open Mon.–Fri.

noon–5. The stories of the Coal Creek War and the area's mining disasters still loom large in Anderson County. Those disasters include the Fraterville mine explosion, in which more than 200 miners perished, and the Cross Mountain mine explosion, in which more than 80 miners were killed. In the meantime, a driving trail/tour of the significant points of interest offer insight to the events that shaped this area. Free; maps are available at the Anderson County Tourism Council (see *Guidance*) or at coalcreekaml.com.

MUSEUMS Green McAdoo Cultural Center (865-463-6500; green mcadoo.org), 101 School Street, Clinton. Open Tues.–Sat. 10–5. In the tiny schoolhouse, the story of 12 high school students is told. Known as the Clinton 12, the students were the first African Americans to desegregate a state-supported high school in the South; Bobby Cain, the oldest of the group, was the first African American to graduate from an integrated public high school in the South, according to the museum. Visitors take a seat in a 1950s-style classroom to learn the background of the Jim Crow era and the local lawsuit that led to the desegregation of Clinton High; the tour then moves through a text-heavy but fascinating pictorial display that tells every aspect of the Clinton 12 story. Included is a piece of broadcast history as well—a CBS News *See it Now* piece produced and narrated by legendary newsman Edward R. Murrow. Outside, a statue of the 12—based on photos of their first day of school—brings to life the fear and anxiety they surely felt the morning of August 27, 1956, the day they made national history. Free.

Lenoir Museum Cultural Complex (865-426-7461; state.tn.us/environ ment/parks/NorrisDam/index.shtml), 125 Village Green Circle, Norris. Open daily 8 AM–10 PM in summer, daily 8 AM–sundown in winter. A collection of pioneer and Appalachian buildings, including an 18th-century rice gristmill and thrashing barn, join a museum in this small historical part of Norris Lake State Park. At the museum, a photographic history of the construction of the TVA's first dam and its importance to the area— particularly as part of the Manhattan Project—is offered, and hundreds of historic artifacts from rural life are displayed. Free.

⚓ **Museum of Appalachia** (865-494-7680; museumofappalachia.org), 28199 Andersonville Highway, Clinton. Open daily 10–4 in Jan. and Feb., weekdays 10–5 and weekends 10–6 in Mar., weekdays 9–5 and weekends 9–6 in Apr., daily 9–6 May–Oct., and daily 9–5 in Nov. and Dec. Dedicated to preserving the stories of Appalachia, the sprawling museum showcases more than 30 southern Appalachian log buildings and countless artifacts collected by John Rice Irwin, who grew up in the region. The museum hosts a variety of concerts and heritage events, including the Tennessee Fall Homecoming, when dozens of bluegrass performers are

Tennessee Department of Tourist Development

MUSEUM OF APPALACHIA

featured and costumed interpreters offer demonstrations of Appalachian crafts. Adults $14.95, children 13–18 $10, children 6–12 $5. Family passes are available for $34.

✳ To Do

FISHING Many anglers consider the **Clinch River** to be some of the finest trout fly-fishing in the country; the Clinch is clear, slow, and shallow, which is a challenging combination for anglers and a haven for rainbow and brown trout. More than 75 yards wide in many places, the Clinch is a dream for those with patience, a steady casting rhythm, and—did I mention?—patience.

For gear, head to **CR Outfitters** (865-494-2305; croutfitters.com), 2830 Andersonville Highway, Norris. A full-service fly shop, CR Outfitters also offers classes and guide service, with full- and half-day trips available. Detailed maps are also available here, as is plenty of great advice about access points and hot spots. Guided trips start at $100/person, including gear. They're open Monday 8–noon and Tuesday–Saturday 8–5.

HORSEBACK RIDING ✒ **River Ridge Farm** (865-457-6774; riverridge farmtn.com), 220 Mike Miller Lane, Clinton. Open seasonally for tours and horseback riding; call or check the Web site for exact dates. The working farm on the banks of the Clinch River below Norris Dam offers seasonal fun as part of their farming philosophy; see draft horses in action as they plow and work, take a wagon ride through fields of spring wildflowers or on a moonlight night, or saddle up for a trail ride along the river and through the farm. Reservations are required for most activities. Prices vary depending on activity; call for rates.

✳ Green Space

PARKS **Norris Dam State Park** (865-426-7461; state.tn.us/environment /parks/NorrisDam/index.shtml), 125 Village Green Circle, Norris. Open daily 8 AM–10 PM, with the visitors center open daily 8–4:30. You could say Norris Dam powered the atom bomb; the Tennessee Valley Authority's first dam provided a significant chunk of the energy for the Manhattan Project. The scenic dam and reservoir offers almost 800 miles of shoreline for exploration, including boating, fishing, and hiking; the Lenoir Museum Cultural Complex is within the state park grounds. Seventy-five campsites are offered in two locations, with a mix of primitive and full-service (with hookups for electricity and water) sites available. There's no admission fee for the park.

✳ Lodging

CABINS **The Cabin on Cedar Ridge** (865-494-3248; oncedar ridge.com), 169 Scruggs Cemetery Lane, Norris. A 1860s log cabin was moved from its original location to the ridge and refurbished in such a way that the rustic ambience isn't overpowered by modern amenities. A small kitchen and bath were added to the cabin, which offers a sleeping loft and fireplace, antique quilts, and wide-plank wood floors with scatter rugs. Breakfast is a continental affair, with fruit, breads, and juices left in the cabin for guests to enjoy on their own time frame. Moderate.

Windrock Lodge (865-244-7045; windrocklodge.com), 315 Windrock Road, Oliver Springs. A cabin complex catering to ATVers, Windrock offers two units in a single cabin that can accommodate up to 13 people. The units

PRICE CATEGORIES:	
Inexpensive	Less than $100 (for hotels, inns, and B&Bs); less than $50 (for campgrounds, state park facilities)
Moderate	$100–200
Expensive	$201–300
Very expensive	More than $300

feature full kitchens, laundry facilities, LCD televisions with cable and DVD players, and (most importantly) access to hundreds of miles of trails throughout the region. Land use permits are required for those planning on hitting the motorized trails; information about where to purchase the permits and find ATV accessories and supplies is on the Windrock Web site. Moderate–expensive, depending on choice of unit.

HOTELS Holiday Inn & Suites Clinton (865-457-2233; hiexpress .com), 111 Hillvale Road, Clinton. Those looking for a hotel experience in Anderson County can't go wrong with the Holiday Inn Express, one of the more recent additions to the chain hotel scene. A short drive from Norris Dam State Park, the hotel offers a variety of room choices, from family-sized suites to executive-level rooms with a few extra perks, including a morning newspaper and continental breakfast served in the private space. (But there's also a complimentary hot breakfast served downstairs, too.) The hotel has not just one pool, but two—one indoors, one outdoors—plus a Jacuzzi inside. Complimentary wireless is offered throughout the hotel. Moderate.

✳ Where to Eat

Restaurants in Clinton are typically of the fast-food variety, most located on Seviers Boulevard. For dining options with more local flavor, see "Oak Ridge" or "Knoxville."

✳ Special Events

Early October: **Tennessee Fall Homecoming** (865-494-7680; museumofappalachia.org), Museum of Appalachia, Clinton. A gathering of pioneer and Appalachian craftspeople and more than three hundred musicians, with three full days of continual musical performances and craft demonstrations. Tickets range from $20 for a single day to $55 for a three-day pass— early birds get that pricing, which goes up after mid-Sept. and then again at the gate.

CHATTANOOGA

Pardon me, sir—is *that* the Chattanooga you knew?

The city made famous by the choo-choo and known for the iconic attractions of Rock City and Ruby Falls has grown into so much more than a once-vital rail connection between north and south; Chattanooga is a runaway train of fine arts offerings, excellent dining, and family-friendly attractions.

Chattanooga is a Creek Indian word that means "rock coming to a point"—namely, Lookout Mountain, which rises in Chattanooga and continues almost 90 miles into Georgia and Alabama.

Hernando DeSoto traveled along the Tennessee River, stopping in Chattanooga on his quest; the river was also an important French trade route in the late 1600s and early 1700s, when trading posts were established throughout the region. War came early to Chattanooga and particularly Lookout Mountain, as first English and French battled here over control of the Indians in 1760, while conflicts with the Native American tribes continued through the late 1700s.

Soon, the Western & Atlantic Railroad was under construction, with

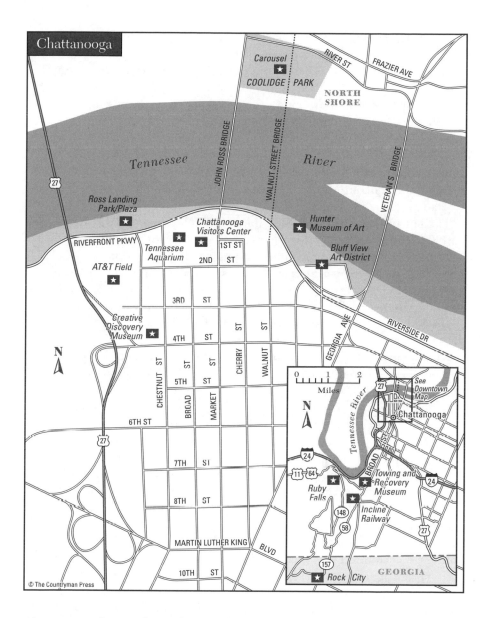

Chattanooga being the end stop; the city was soon laid out on a grid like other growing Southern towns of the era.

In 1830, the region's Indian tribes were forced out of the area, and the infamous Trail of Tears lead them west toward Oklahoma. Not long after, the city played an important role in the Civil War, with skirmishes throughout the area and the battles of Chickamauga and Chattanooga; Chickamauga saw the second-most battle casualties of the war following Gettysburg, and the battle and its stories are told in the nation's first national military park.

Reconstruction brought industry to Chattanooga, especially in iron-works, and the city began to prosper again, with a new rail station being built, a clever mechanic creating the tow truck, and the railroad industry continuing to grow.

It was one night in more modern history, however, that created the new path Chattanooga finds itself on—revitalization. In a 1969 *CBS Evening News* show, anchor Walter Cronkite declared Chattanooga to be "America's dirtiest city," a designation bestowed by the EPA for the city's industrial blight and pollution. It was a time when hardly one state was visible from Lookout Mountain, much less seven, as the vintage advertising had proclaimed.

The horror of being disgraced on national television was a wake-up call for city leaders, who came together to forge a plan for revitalization. Soon, the waterfront was developed into a prime destination for locals and visitors, with the world-class Tennessee Aquarium opening; more of the area's natural offerings were boosted with companies offering rafting and other outdoor adventures, and a pedestrian-friendly environment was created to connect the Hunter Museum and bluff-top art galleries with the main downtown attractions and the riverfront.

Chattanooga's downtown is compact enough that it is easy to get around, but big enough to have a number of distinct neighborhoods. On the **Southside,** artist studios, galleries, and boutiques now fill the previously ghostly, cavernous buildings—the baggage and storage depots that served the dozens of trains that used to cross through this city. Fine antiques stores, a smattering of casual and upscale restaurants, and an old warehouse filled with local boutique-style stores are found on the South-side, which can truthfully be a bit hit-or-miss sometimes in terms of the consistency of its offerings. Stores tend to come and go a bit too quickly for my taste, but this is the neighborhood I return to first for shopping and dining. The Southside is home to the convention center, a huge sports field, and the pavilion that houses the Chattanooga Market and Sundays on the Southside, and condos and flats are starting to pop up with more frequency in the cool old buildings in this part of town. Note that the walkability factor in this part of town is not as easy as in other parts of town—sidewalks are sometimes nonexistent from block to block as the area revitalizes.

Along the river, the **Bluff View District** is primarily residential, but it's also home to the fine arts scene, including the Hunter Museum of Art, a variety of small galleries and eateries, and the best views of the city, whether gazing across the river to the North Shore or looking down upon the aquarium and Ross's Landing area. The Bluff View area offers an inn and a nice variety of restaurants, and is a great place to leave your car (street parking can be nightmarish here; if possible, opt for a lot) and explore on foot. The Walnut Street Pedestrian Bridge, which connects

downtown to the North Shore, is accessible here, as is the gradually slop-
ing walkway from the top of the bluff down to the visitor plaza in front of
the aquarium.

Across the river from downtown lies the **North Shore**—a fun neighborhood filled with a bit of funk, a bit of kitsch, and plenty of characters.
Random festivals seem to pop up here practically every weekend. The
beautiful Coolidge Park and its much-loved carousel are the first stop
after crossing the Walnut Street bridge; the backside of the shops lining
the main business district overlook the park, creating a pedestrian-friendly
area. Coffee shops, boutiques, antiques stores, and galleries are primarily
found along Frazier, Market, and Manufacturer streets, with residential
streets flowing off those main thoroughfares.

Say **Lookout Mountain,** and most folks don't picture a gorgeous and
historic residential neighborhood; instead, they think of all those iconic
attractions—Rock City, Ruby Falls, and the Incline Railway. Along with
those signature attractions, this pretty neighborhood and a scenic drive
are in store.

While the momentum is still going strong for Chattanooga's revitalization, the new attractions and spit-polished city haven't overshadowed the
vintage attractions. If anything, the two complement each other; just as

WALNUT STREET PEDESTRIAN BRIDGE

A STATUE MARKS THE PASSAGE OF NATIVE AMERICANS ON THE TRAIL OF TEARS

one might admire a shiny new bullet train, one can still appreciate a vintage locomotive.

GUIDANCE Chattanooga Area Convention and Visitors Bureau
(423-756-8687; chattanoogafun.com), 2 Broad Street. Open daily
8:30–5:30. Conveniently located along the riverfront in downtown Chattanooga, the visitors center should be the first stop for maps, information, and discount coupons for the area's attractions.

GETTING THERE *By air:* The **Chattanooga Metropolitan Airport** (CHA; 423-855-2200; chattairport.com), 1001 Airport Road, #14, Chattanooga. Flights from 10 major airports are offered, including Memphis, Atlanta, Chicago, Orlando, and Washington, D.C., on Delta, American Eagle, U.S. Airways Express, and Allegiant Air.

By car: Chattanooga is located in the southeastern corner of Tennessee, accessible from I-75 and I-24, within two hours' drive of Nashville and Atlanta, as well as a short drive from most points in North Carolina, Alabama, Tennessee, and Georgia.

By train: Despite its long and colorful past as a major railway transportation center, Chattanooga has no passenger train service.

GETTING AROUND *By shuttle:* **CARTA Shuttle** (423-629-1473; gocarta .org). Runs Mon.–Fri. 6:30 AM–11 PM, Sat. 9:30 AM–11 PM, and Sun. 9:30–8:30. The electric shuttle buses run a loop between the Chattanooga Choo Choo and the Tennessee Aquarium, with stops every block along the way. Free.

By taxi: A handful of taxi services operate in the city, including **Mercury Cab** (423-320-4549). Taxis are readily available at the airport and near the downtown attractions; a trip from the airport to downtown hotels costs about $30.

By water taxi: **Chattanooga Water Taxi** (423-756-5060; chattanooga watertaxi.com) provides seasonal rides from the City Pier near the aquarium to the North Shore, disembarking passengers at Coolidge Park. An all-day pass is $6 for adults and $4 for kids. The schedule changes frequently, so best to check days and times prior to making plans.

MEDICAL EMERGENCY Erlanger Medical Center (423-778-7000; erlanger.org), 975 E. Third Street, offers a full-service, level-one trauma center at its main campus and a walk-in urgent care clinic (423-778-8500; erlanger.org) at 910 Blackford Street.

✳ To See

HISTORIC SITES Chickamauga & Chattanooga National Military Park (706-866-9241; nps.gov/chch). Each of the battlefields has its own visitors center; refer to the Web site for detailed directions and a map. Visitors center open daily 8:30–5; park itself open dawn–dusk. The bloodiest two-day battle of the Civil War happened at Chickamauga, when more than 35,000 soldiers were killed or injured. Despite its heavy losses, the Confederates were victorious at Chickamauga, but they lost control of the Chattanooga area to Union forces a few months later. The battles for Chickamauga and Chattanooga are recalled at the two battlefields, which

HOUSTON MUSEUM OF DECORATIVE ARTS

together make up the nation's first National Military Park. Interactive exhibits, monuments, and chilling tales of the battles are recounted by park rangers at both sites. No entrance fee for either site, although a $3 fee for adults is charged for entrance to Craven's House on Lookout Mountain.

MUSEUMS Chattanooga African American Museum (423-266-8658; caamhistory.com), 200 E. Martin Luther King Boulevard. Open Mon.–Fri. 10–5, Sat. noon–4. Closed Sun. Tracing the route—and the roots—of the Africans captured and brought to Chattanooga, the museum highlights their history, from early days of slave life to modern achievements through multimedia presentations, artifacts, and exhibits. Since there were few plantations in the Chattanooga area, African Americans were more likely to have worked in homes or businesses, as well as own their own businesses, and throughout the museum are tableaus depicting various stages of their history and impact on the city. Special attention is paid to Chattanooga native Bessie Smith, the blues singer who started her career at an early age, singing with her brother on downtown street corners. Adults $7, children 6–12 $3, children under six free.

Chattanooga Regional History Museum (423-265-3247; chattanooga history.com), 400 Chestnut Street. Open Mon.–Fri. 9–5. The history of Chattanooga, from the influence of the railroad to the infamy of the Trail of Tears and the importance of the Battle of Chattanooga in the Civil War, is told through interactive displays and hands-on exhibits. Throughout the year, traveling exhibitions bring regional and national history to life; special, topic-specific bus and walking tours delve deeper into a specific slice of the city's history. Adults $4, seniors $3.50, and children 3–18 $3. Bus and walking tours are an additional fee, and reservations are recommended.

Ø **Creative Discovery Museum** (423-756-2738; cdmfun.org), 321 Chestnut Street. Hours vary by season, but generally run 10–5 with extended hours in the summer. Closed Wed. from the Wed. after Labor Day–Feb. The ship-shaped building in downtown Chattanooga calls to kids of all ages, with its tree-house-like lookout tower a landmark for little eyes. Inside, the museum promises hands-on fun for all ages, with a river play area, a rooftop fun factory, and plenty of places to dig, create, and discover. Ages two and up $10.95, children under two free.

Houston Museum of Decorative Arts (423-267-7176; thehouston museum.com), 201 High Street. Open Mon.–Fri. 9–4 and by appointment on weekends. A small museum with a specific focus—the antique glass and ceramics collection of Anna Safley Houston—the Houston is a funky spot, and not the best for touring with little kids. But those who can keep their hands to themselves will be amazed at the extensive collection of pitchers, said to be the world's largest. Adults $9, children 4–17 $3.50, children three and under free.

Hunter Museum of Art (423-267-0968; huntermuseum.org), 10 Bluff View. Open daily at 10, with exception of Wed. and Sun., when the museum opens at noon. Closing time is 5, with the exception of Thurs., when the museum stays open until 8. Perched high atop a bluff overlooking the Tennessee River, the Hunter is a fascinating combination of old and new, both in terms of its art collection and architecture. American masterpieces from every era are housed in three buildings, from a turn-of-the-19th-century Edwardian mansion to a 1970s hunk of concrete and a shiny metal and glass building. Adults $9.95, children 3–17 $4.95, children under three free. Free the first Sun. of each month.

Ø **International Towing & Recovery Museum and Hall of Fame** (423-267-3132; internationaltowingmuseum.org), 3315 Broad Street. Open Mon.–Sat. 9–5, Mar.–Oct.; Mon.–Sat. 10–4:30, Nov.–Feb.; Sun. 11–5 year-round. Filled with antique and modern wreckers, the Towing Museum's collection will delight car buffs. The museum chose Chattanooga as its home because the first wrecker ever built was made right in the city. Members of the recovery industry are honored at the hall of fame, and there's a "wall of the fallen" to honor those wrecker operators killed while on the job. Adults $8, children 6–18 $4, children under six free.

✳ To Do

AQUARIUMS AND ZOOS ✎ **Chattanooga Zoo at Warner Park** (423-697-1322; chattzoo.org), 301 N. Holtzclaw Avenue. Open daily 9–5. This small zoo is a bit different from most in terms of the ways animals are categorized—sometimes by geography, sometimes simply by shared characteristics like being misunderstood. Rarely crowded and easy to navigate with a stroller or just little legs, the zoo feels more like a large nature park than an institution. Gorillas (especially the popular Hank) are the main attraction, and a multiyear expansion plan promises more to come. Adults $8, children 3–15 $5, children under three free. Behind-the-scenes tours are adults $15, children $8 (in addition to entrance fee).

✎ **Tennessee Aquarium** (423-265-0698; tnaqua.com), 1 Broad Street. Open daily 10–8. Twin buildings on the banks of the Tennessee River promise hours of fun for every age; one building explores river ecosystems, the other, the ocean. Journeys begin at the top of each building—

HUNTER MUSEUM OF ART

the surface of each watery wonderland—and a gently twisting walkway brings visitors deeper into the ecosystem. But this is no simple stroll through the depths of each ecosystem; rather, behind each section of river or ocean, visitors find detailed exhibits about the creatures they've just viewed, with the chance to study many species more closely. Penguins, sea horses, snakes, and giant catfish are the crowd favorites, while the expansive open-air butterfly garden atop the ocean building promises an unexpectedly serene experience. Adults $21.50, children 3–12 $14.95.

BOAT AND TRAIN RIDES Chattanooga Choo-Choo (800-872-2529; choochoo.com), 1400 Market Street. Model railroad open daily 10–6. Once home to the train route that served as the major link between the North and the South, the former Chattanooga railroad station is now a historic hotel, and antique rail cars serve as restaurants and sleeping quarters, although they do show their age. Of course, the original Chattanooga Choo-Choo no longer runs—the last left the station in 1970—but there's a model railroad with 3,000 feet of track and a variety of gift stores on the property. Train enthusiasts will most enjoy this attraction, but truthfully it's not been well maintained over the years. Adults $3, children $1.50.

River Gorge Explorer (423-265-0698; tnaqua.org), 1 Broad Street (for tickets) to the Chattanooga Pier (boat dock). The cruise schedule varies during the year; check the Web site for departure times. This is no leisurely sight-seeing trip; rather, the *Gorge Explorer*—a catamaran—whisks passengers through a winding journey along the Tennessee River gorge at high speeds. A naturalist from the Tennessee Aquarium goes along for the ride, pointing out flora, fauna, and historic sites along the way. Worry not—the boat does slow down so passengers can enjoy the natural beauty of the canyonlike gorge. Adults $29, children 3–12 $21.50, and children under three $18. (Due to Coast Guard regulations, children of all ages are considered passengers and are therefore charged.)

Southern Belle (800-766-2784; chattanoogariverboat.com), 201 Riverfront Parkway, Pier 2. A leisurely cruise along the Tennessee River, with seasonal lunch cruises and daily dinner and sight-seeing cruises offered. During the peak fall foliage months, cruises book up quickly. Prices start at $13.50 for adults, $6.50 for children for the sight-seeing cruise, with meal and special-event cruise pricing starting at $19.50 and $9.50, respectively.

Tennessee Valley Railroad (423-894-8028, tvrail.com), 4119 Cromwell Road. Seasonal service and routes; check Web site for most up-to-date schedule information. There's a trip for every taste on the historic rails in Chattanooga, from the Missionary Ridge local, an hour-long ride aboard either a vintage diesel or steam powered train; a six-hour round-trip journey to Chickamauga, Georgia, called the Turn, which includes a layover in the quaint town for shopping or a bite of lunch at a local café; and a variety of adventures along the Hiwassee River route, which runs along the scenic river gorge. Prices range $14–36 for adults and $8–26 for children, depending on route and season.

FISHING The Tennessee River and its waterways are an angler's delight, whether the rod of choice is a fancy fly rod or a simple pole and string. For fishermen with their own gear, the Tennessee Riverpark is an excellent starting point; fishing charters are also available. Check out the Outdoor Chattanooga Web site (outdoorchattanooga.com) for a full list of fishing spots and outfitters.

Feather and Fly (featherandfly.com) offers full day, guided float and wade trips on the Elk and Hiawassee rivers with experienced local guides; waders and gear are available to rent. Full-day guided wade trips are $225/person; full-day guided float trips are $375/person.

HANG GLIDING Lookout Mountain Flight Park (800-688-5637; hangglide.com), 7201 Scenic Highway, Rising Fawn, GA. Open year-round, with seasonal flight times adjusted for weather and daylight hours. The flight park is the country's largest hang gliding school; day students who want to glide in tandem with a certified instructor or fly solo have short flight or daylong training/flight options. Ages 12 and up can experience the daylong flight school, while tandem glides are available for ages four and up. Prices start at $199 and go up from there.

RAFTING A variety of white-water outfitters shoot the rapids along the Ocoee River, home of the 1996 Olympic kayak events and one of the most rafted rivers in the United States. Five miles of Class III and IV rapids make the Ocoee a challenging ride for all skill levels. Most rafting companies are located about an hour outside Chattanooga. A full list of outfitters is available online at chattanoogafun.com/outdoors.

Outdoor Adventures Rafting (O.A.R.) (423-338-5746; raft.com), 629 Welcome Valley Road, Ocoee. Hours vary by season and day; rafting trips take place throughout the summer and in May and Sept. Call ahead or check the Web site for the most up-to-date trip schedule. Advance reservations are required via Web site or phone. One of the earliest outfitters on the Ocoee, O.A.R. is now more of an adventure center than a simple rafting company, although rafting is its primary business, with trips on the Middle Ocoee or full river trips on the upper and middle sections.

Depending on the length of the rafting trip, the season, and the day of the week, pricing ranges from $35 to $95; children pay the same rate as adults. Rope courses, climbing wall, tubing, and other activities range in price from $10 to $31, with some combination packages available.

Tennessee Department of Tourist Development

INTERNATIONAL TOWING & RECOVERY MUSEUM

SPECTATOR SPORTS Chattanooga Lookouts Baseball (423-267-2208; lookouts.com), 201 Power Alley. Baseball's been played in Chattanooga since 1885, and today the Lookouts—a double-A affiliate of the Los Angeles Dodgers—spends plenty of time in the top of the standings of the Southern League. Home base is AT&T Field, built in 2000 on a bluff overlooking the Tennessee River. Single ticket prices range $2–8, and kids under six are free.

ICONIC ATTRACTIONS

In the early days of car travel, the most basic of advertising—writing on the side of a barn—implored folks to SEE ROCK CITY; that simple message brought travelers to Chattanooga's most famous attractions, which are some of America's most iconic. Tickets to Rock City, Ruby Falls, and the Incline Railway can be purchased individually or in a discounted combo pack and are sold both ways on each attraction's Web site and at their ticket offices.

Rock City (800-825-8366; seerockcity.com), 1400 Patton Road, Lookout Mountain, GA. Open daily from 8:30 AM, except during Christmas; closing times vary by season and are as early as 4 PM the first two weeks of Nov. Yes, you *really* can see seven states from Rock City, as well as navigate a suspension bridge, explore spectacular gardens, and marvel at stunning natural rock formations. During the Halloween and Christmas holidays, Rock City becomes a frightful visit or holiday wonderland. Adults $16.95, children 3–12 $8.95.

Ruby Falls (423-821-2544; rubyfalls.com), 1720 S. Scenic Highway. Open daily 8–8. The journey through the inside of Lookout Mountain is dark, damp, and dazzling, with the finale being the famed falls. One can only imagine the original journeys into the dark cave made by Native Americans, Civil War soldiers, and finally by Leo Lambert, who was determined to allow the public access to the cave after it had been shut off due to railroad construction. Lambert and his crew worked to create an elevator shaft to allow access to the cave and stumbled upon a new path that ended at the falls, which they discovered more than eight hours after they entered the cave through the opening they drilled. Lambert named the falls for his wife, Ruby. Be warned that Ruby Falls is not for anyone who's a bit claustrophobic or might have an issue squeezing through small spaces. Ruby Falls also

✳ Green Space

GARDENS AND NATURE CENTERS ✍ **Chattanooga Nature Center** (423-821-1160; chattanooganaturecenter.org), 400 Garden Road. Open Mon.–Sat. 9–5; Sun. 1–5 (Apr.–Oct.). A perfect blend of activity and serenity, the nature center offers those of any age and ability things to do, whether it be exploring a tree house; enjoying a long, quiet hike; canoeing in the Lookout Creek; or taking the kids for a stroll along the boardwalk. Best of all, there are loads of chances to see nature at its best, from offers an aerial adventure course, which includes 30 high-wire chal-lenges such as zip lines, climbing ladders, and more. Adults $16.95, chil-dren $8.95 for the falls tour; zip course pricing is $30.95 for adults and $16.95 for children 10 and up.

Incline Railway (423-821-4224; ridetheincline.com), 3917 St. Elmo Avenue. Open daily 8:30 AM–9:30 PM, Memorial Day weekend–Labor Day weekend; daily 9–6, Apr., May, Sept., and Oct.; daily 10–6, Nov.–Mar. Closed major holidays. Why drive to the top of Lookout Mountain when you can ride inside an antique railcar at a 72-degree angle? The Incline Railway opened in 1895 and offers a scenic ride up the side of Loookout, with glass windows and ceiling panels affording a sweeping view of Tennes-see and Georgia. Adults $14, children 3–12 $7, children under three free.

BIRDHOUSES RECALL THE ICONIC SEE ROCK CITY PAINTED BARNS.

the foliage to the native flower gardens and the wildlife. Adults $8, chil-dren 4–11 and seniors $5, children under four free.

PARKS ✎ **Coolidge Park/Walnut Street Bridge** (423-757-5167; chattanooga.gov/PRAC/30_CoolidgePark.htm), 150 River Street. The kids will be inclined to run, not walk, once they step onto the restored pedes-trian bridge, and you just might feel like joining them. The sturdy wood-en structure takes you from the touristy side of the city to the more sedate and funky North Shore, with its collection of boutique stores and coffee shops. The first stop once across the river, however, is the beautifully restored, hand-carved carousel at Coolidge Park. The carousel and a water play area await, and the hardest decision of the day will be which to try first.

Tennessee River Park/Walk (423-842-0177; hamiltontn.gov/TNRiver park), 4301 Amnicola Highway. Open daily 8–4, with extended seasonal hours; portion behind Tennessee Aquarium/Ross's Landing open longer. This 10-mile pathway stretching along the Tennessee River is wide and paved, welcoming both cyclists and walkers year-round. Along the route, find boat ramps, fishing piers, and public art; the park and path continues over the Walnut Street Pedestrian Bridge to the North Shore and its delights, including Coolidge and Renaissance parks. Free.

✳ Lodging

BED & BREAKFASTS/INNS

Bluff View Inn (800-725-8338; bluffviewinn.com), 411 E. Second Street. Three very different turn-of-the-20th-century homes make up this inn, including the Maclellan House, which affords bluff-top views of the Tennessee River, as well as a shady bocce court with the same view. All rooms offer a feel of Southern gentility, with a mix of antiques and antique reproductions, plenty of floral and plaid bedding paired with crisp white linens, fireplaces, and private bathrooms, some with jetted tubs. Most rooms include comfy chairs for reading and relaxing, and the public spaces are also quiet and furnished with overstuffed furniture. A gourmet breakfast on the weekends and a more moderate continental breakfast at the adjacent Rembrandt's Coffee House are included in the nightly rate, as are nonalcoholic beverages and early morning coffee service.

PRICE CATEGORIES:	
Inexpensive	Less than $100 (for hotels, inns, and B&Bs); less than $50 (for campgrounds, state park facilities)
Moderate	$100–200
Expensive	$201–300
Very expensive	More than $300

Packages offering accommodations and tickets or dining vouchers are offered throughout the year. Moderate.

The Stone Fort Inn (423-267-7866; stonefortinn.com), 120 E. 10th Street. The decidedly elegant Stone Fort Inn has 20 guest rooms decked out with lush bedding and amenities, and offers the added bonus of being smack in the middle of downtown and in easy walking distance of the Tennessee Aquarium, the river, and other

THE BLUFF VIEW INN

attractions. Many of the rooms feature fireplaces or balconies—sometimes both—and charming decor. The inn's staff always garners rave reviews for their helpfulness—especially when it comes to getting last-minute dinner reservations or accommodating an unusual request. Parking is just off-site but complimentary; wine and cheese—and warm cookies—are available in the evenings. Expensive.

HOTELS The Chattanoogan (423-756-3400; chattanooganhotel .com), 1201 S. Broad Street. A retreat on the city's bourgeoning Southside, the Chattanoogan is an unexpected surprise in this city of nice but predictable chain offerings: a boutique hotel with a snazzy, upscale feel, the Chattanoogan is the main convention center hotel but also caters to those who don't want a mainstream hotel experience, preferring more quiet and refinement than most of the downtown hotels offer. A rooftop pool, small spa, restaurant, and lounge round out the amenities, and the location affords a quick drive to just about any attraction in town. Expensive.

***Delta Queen* Hotel** (423-468-4500; deltaqueenhotel.com), 100 River Street. A bit of nostalgia can be found on the *Delta Queen*, the last of the fully operational overnight passenger steamboats in the country. The riverboat is now docked, after 2 million miles, at Coolidge Park. The boat's 88 staterooms range from master cabins with multiple windows and amenities to the more basic bunk rooms with single beds stacked bunk-bed style. Don't get the impression, however, that the *Delta Queen* offers anything in the way of roomy accommodations; sleeping quarters are tight even in the largest rooms, and the rooms could certainly benefit from new everything. But those looking for nostalgia and history will likely be happy with the riverboat hotel. The Texas lounge offers entertainment and dinner on Fri. and Sat. nights, and a buffet breakfast is included in the room rates, as is valet parking. Moderate.

Residence Inn by Marriott Downtown (423-266-0600; marriott.com), 215 Chestnut Street. The Residence Inn by Marriott Downtown is just a block from the aquarium, the riverfront, and other attractions, and offers larger rooms to accommodate a crowd, perfect for larger families. I really like the small stature of the hotel—just three stories—and its prime park-the-car, walk-every-where location. Rooms are stylish with contemporary furniture and fixtures, including large flat-screen televisions, and suites offer a full kitchen (with stainless appliances, granite countertops, and cherry cabinets no less) and separate bedroom. With all the attrac-

tions within walking distance of the hotel, the indoor pool will be a welcome refresher for kids and adults alike. Moderate.

✳ Where to Eat

DINING OUT St. John's Restaurant (423-266-4400; stjohns restaurant.com), 1278 Market Street. A white-tablecloth wonder that serves up a bit of tradition with a dash of funk, St. John's seasonal menu of locally focused food includes buffalo tenderloin, hand-made ravioli, and a Vidalia onion soup with lobster, plus unusual desserts like blood orange and buttermilk *panna cotta.* Expensive.

Table 2 (423-756-8253; table2 restaurant.com), 232 E. 11th Street. Open Tues.–Fri. for lunch, Tues.–Sat. for dinner. With a focus on seasonal food and supporting local farmers who raise hormone-free meats and organic produce, Table 2 is a relaxed yet upscale restaurant with sleek decor accented with sumptuous fabrics, and food combinations that are a winner no matter what the taste buds are asking for. Lunch runs to sandwiches, salads, and pizzas, while the dinner menu offers up some of the usual suspects with a

PRICE CATEGORIES:

Inexpensive	Less than $16
Moderate	$16–30
Expensive	$31–50
Very expensive	More than $50

twist; for instance, the traditional Southern meat-and-three gets a makeover with a choice of grilled chicken, pork, shrimp, or fish, with three farm-fresh sides. Moderate–expensive.

EATING OUT Back Inn Café (423-265-5033; backinncafe.com), 412 E. Second Street. Open Tues.–Sat. for dinner. Scenic and elegant yet casual, this restored Colonial Revival mansion is a cozy, romantic dinner-only spot featuring steak and seafood. Wine enthusiasts will enjoy the discounted prices on more than 40 selections on Wed. 5–9. Expensive.

Boathouse Rotisserie & Raw Bar (423-622-0122; boathouse chattanooga.com), 1011 Riverside Drive. Open daily for lunch and dinner. The covered deck overlooking the Tennessee River competes for attention with house-made guacamole and a giant menu of oysters served up just about any way. The deck is comfortable almost year-round thanks to cooling fans or patio heaters. Inexpensive.

⚓ Clumpies Ice Cream (423-267-5425; clumpies.com), 26 Frazier Avenue. What's not to love about an ice cream parlor opened by the son of a third-generation candy maker? Sugar and creativity run deep at Clumpies, where small batches of creamy concoctions are whipped up 10 gallons at a time. Basic vanilla and chocolate give way to more exotically flavored sorbets, and a big wooden deck overlooking the Chattanooga

THE *DELTA QUEEN*

skyline is the icing on the, well, ice cream. Inexpensive.

Hiroshi's on the Southside
(423-267-9003; hiroshisouthside
.com), 114 W. Main Street. Open
Mon.–Fri. for lunch, Mon.–Sat.
for dinner. A huge menu offers
everything from tempura to teriya-
ki, plus salads any seafood lover
would crave, including squid,
conch, octopus, and seaweed. And
then there's the sushi; with a
selection from the basics (a California roll) to the sublime (a Cali-

OVER THE MOON

It was 1917 when bakery salesman Earl Mitchell Sr., chatting with some coal miners at a company store, was told they needed something solid and filling to get them through their shifts, as they often didn't have the chance to stop for a meal. When Mitchell asked just how big this filling snack should be, one of the miners, holding his hands up to circle the moon in the night sky, replied, "about that big." When Mitchell returned to the Chattanooga Bakery and saw workers dipping graham crackers into marshmallow, he thought—why not add another graham cracker on top, and dip the whole darn thing in chocolate?

And so the Moon Pie was born—a scrumptious, hard-to-resist delight that's been produced in Chattanooga for almost one hundred years now. In the South, a Moon Pie and an RC Cola were just the ticket when something sweet and sugary was called for; a hit 1950s country song was even written about the pairing. Along the Gulf Coast of Mississippi and Alabama, the soft Moon Pies are now thrown from Mardi Gras floats in Mobile and other cities—certainly a lot easier on the body than the boxes of Cracker Jacks or other, harder treats that were once thrown from floats.

Moon Pies now come in more than the original three flavors, chocolate, banana, and vanilla; double-decker pies are also flavored in orange, strawberry, and lemon, while crunchy Moon Pies are offered in peanut butter and mint flavors.

Sadly, the Chattanooga Bakery doesn't offer a Moon Pie tour, but the Moon Pie General Store (inside Clumpies Ice Cream, 26 Frazier Avenue) does offer every size and flavor of Moon Pies and Moon Pie–branded accessories. And cold RC Cola, of course. You can also order them from home, by calling 423-877-0592 or logging onto moon pie.com.

fornia roll wrapped in eel and topped with eel sauce), even those who indulge in sushi regularly will find something to tempt. Moderate.

212 Market (423-265-1212; 212market.com), 212 Market Street. Open daily for lunch and dinner. 212 Market is a family affair and is an unusual combination of a fine dining restaurant with a family atmosphere. The state's first green certified restaurant, 212 Market focuses on local growers and producers, with the availability of crops and meats often dictating what's on the menu. The very full dessert menu always includes a selection of pies, cakes, and scrumptious crème brûlée. Moderate–expensive.

✱ Selective Shopping

FURNISHINGS Revival (423-265-2656; revivaluncommongoods .com), 12 W. 13th Street. A lush boutique of truly uncommon goods, from antique and vintage furnishings to exotic home fragrances, funky lighting, luxurious bedding, and must-haves for the home, Revival is one of those stores that makes you want to throw out all your furniture and start over. The big pieces and accessories are expensive, for sure—but there are also some fantastic finds, including Juliska stoneware, that are affordable and make great gifts. (And the way they gift wrap is simple and divine.) A huge selection of coffee table books is available, mostly on design and gardening.

SHOPPING DISTRICTS Bluff View Art District (800-725-8338; bluffviewartdistrict.com), 411 E. Second Street. Perched high above the Tennessee River, the Bluff View Arts District is more than a collection of galleries and restaurants; it is a haven within the city dedicated to the arts, from culinary creativity like pasta and bread making to the hands that sculpt, draw, and create. Peeking in the windows of businesses is perfectly acceptable here, and lucky peeping Toms will see chocolates being handcrafted or masterpieces being painted. An easy walk from the Tennessee Aquarium and other downtown attractions.

Southside District (roughly defined as between W. Main and W. 20th streets, from Broad Street to Carter Street). The city's Southside is quickly becoming a favorite with creative types, thanks to excellent galleries, antiques stores, and boutique shopping mixed with a burgeoning residential community, a few top-notch restaurants, and the weekly Sundays on the Southside at the Chattanooga Market. Most of the stores and restaurants are in historic buildings, many in former railroad sidings, baggage claim buildings, or the like. The reclaimed space of a warehouse now serves as the covered yet open-air **Chattanooga Market** (423-266-4041; chatta noogamarket.com; 1826 Carter Street), where every Sun. from Apr. through early Dec. local artists, musicians, and farmers offer their wares, provide art projects for children, and cook up some enticing food. A hip boutique hotel, the Chattanoogan (see *Lodging*), is within walking distance of the area's stores and restaurants, and is on the shuttle line for easy access to downtown's attractions.

✳ Special Events

April: **4Bridges Arts Festival** (423-265-4282; 4bridgesarts festival.org), 1826 Carter Street/ First Tennessee Pavilion. Live music from regional musicians provides the soundtrack for two days of an open-air, juried arts festival featuring local and national artists. Only 150 artists are asked to exhibit, and the festival is considered one of the top one hundred arts festivals in the nation. Adults $5, children free.

May–September: **Nightfall** (423-265-0771), Miller Plaza, 850 Market Street. The music, the crowd, and the food are hardly ever the same twice—from zydeco to rock, there's something for every musical taste. The summer concert series takes place on Fri. nights from late May through the end of Sept., with a local act opening for a headliner. Free admission.

Early June: **Riverbend Festival** (423-756-2212; riverbendfestival .com). Musical acts of every kind take center stage all around the riverfront in this nine-day music festival. $24 and up.

October: **Wine over Water** (423-265-2825; wineoverwater.org), Walnut Street Pedestrian Bridge. This heady combination—a wine tasting set on a pedestrian bridge that spans the Tennessee River— is a one-day event to benefit local historic preservation efforts and brings out the best wineries, paired with tastings from local chefs. $60; must be 21 to attend.

November: **Head of the Hooch Rowing Regatta** (404-881-9810; headofthehooch.org). The second-largest rowing regatta in America launches from the Chattanooga Riverfront, with almost nine thousand rowers taking to the river. Free.

Mid-November–January 1: ✍ **Enchanted Garden of Lights** (706-820-2531; seerockcity.com). A million-plus twinkling lights and lighted displays turn Rock City into a holiday wonderland. Adults $17.95 and up, children 3–12 $9.95 and up.

NORTHEAST

The very northeast corner of Tennessee is more commonly known as the Tri-Cities area, home to Kingsport, Johnson City, and Bristol—the tri of the Tri-Cities, plus another few dozen small communities that dot the landscape here.

Each of the three big towns has its own feel and flair, attractions and festivals, and it's easy to navigate from one to the next. History is rich here, as this area was the country's first frontier, settled by hearty, determined people who made their way across the Appalachians to discover a wild, wide-open landscape full of promise and peril.

KINGSPORT

In the mid-1700s, the push westward from the original colonies began in earnest. The desire to own land in the wilderness, rather than the "crowded" colonies of Virginia and North Carolina, led people like Daniel Boone to settle in northeast Tennessee. Boone and his followers marked a trail through the Cumberland Gap for pioneers and settlers to follow.

Kingsport straddles Sullivan and Hawkins counties, with most of the city in Sullivan County. The Holston River running through Kingsport made the location a prime area for the original Cherokee tribes that inhabited the area, and for settlers taking the Wilderness Road to Kentucky through the Cumberland Gap.

Looking forward, the city was redesigned as a "garden city" separating the town into business, housing, and industrial areas, and was the first city in the nation to use traffic circles.

Kingsport was the scene of a significant battle during the Civil War when three hundred Confederate soldiers under Col. Richard Morgan held off a large Union army commanded by Maj. Gen. Cullem Gillem for two days.

Kingsport is perhaps most notorious for the execution—by hanging—of an elephant. In 1916, the Sparks World Famous Shows Circus came to

town for its annual visit. As was the custom, local help was hired for the day to act as assistants to the circus performers and crews, including Walter "Red" Eldridge, a local hired as an assistant trainer for Mary the elephant. Eldridge was asked to take the Asian elephant to a pond for watering; although there are no actual accounts of the tragedy that followed, it's believed that Eldridge was using some kind of hook behind the elephant's ear to encourage it to move—but Mary was eating. Mary grabbed Eldridge with her trunk and hurled him against a drink stand, then crushed his head by stepping on it. The town and nearby communities were outraged, and the sheriff impounded Mary. The owner of the circus, Charlie Sparks, agreed to a public execution, and Mary was taken to Erwin, Tennessee, where a railroad crane was used to hang Mary in front of a crowd of more than 2,500.

GUIDANCE Kingsport Chamber of Commerce (423-392-8820; kcvb .org), 151 E. Main Street.

GETTING THERE *By air:* **Tri-Cities Airport** (TRI; 423-325-6000; tri flight.com), 1674 Standing Stone Parkway, Hilham. Service from major cities, including Detroit, Atlanta, and Charlotte, via Delta, American Eagle, U.S. Air, and Allegiant.

By car: Kingsport is located off I-26 between 11 W./E. Stone Drive to the north and I-81 to the south.

GETTING AROUND *By bus:* The **Kingsport Area Transit Service** (423-224-2613; kingsporttransit.org) offers shuttle service throughout Kingsport Mon.–Fri. 8–5:30. Fares are $1 each way, with free transfers. Visit the Web site for detailed route information.

By car: The major thoroughfares include E. Stone Drive and John Dennis Highway around the perimeter and Center Street into downtown.

By taxi: There are a number of taxi firms in Kingsport, including **Tri-City Cab Co.** (423-246-9037) and **Courtesy Cab** (423-230-0285).

MEDICAL EMERGENCY Holston Valley Medical Center (423-224-4000; wellmont.org), 130 W. Ravine Road, offers a level-one trauma center with comprehensive medical and diagnostic services.

✳ To See

HISTORIC SITES ✍ **Exchange Place** (423-288-6071; exchangeplace .info), 4812 Orebank Road. Open Sat.–Sun. 2–4:30 and for special heritage and event days. Check the Web site for seasonal events. The small living-history farm was a little bit of everything back in the frontier days: a relay station on the Old Stage Road; a working plantation with pigs, cows, and sheep; plus a farm with the crops to support the livestock. Nine of the 10 original buildings remain standing, earning the former relay station a place on the National Register of Historic Places. Admission varies depending on event/day; generally there is no admission or a small fee— $1 for adults.

Kingsport Downtown Heritage Trail (423-246-6550), 140 W. Main Street. The trail is a pleasant stroll through the historic area of downtown

Kingsport, with plaques and signs explaining the history or significance of various sites, including the Ohio Railroad building, the library, churches, the city mural, and the Gem Theatre. Free.

✱ To Do

WINERIES Countryside Vineyards and Winery (423-323-1660; cvwineryandsupply.com), 658 Harry Harr Road, Blountville. Open Mon.–Sat. 10–6, Sun. 1–6. This small independent family-owned winery is known for its medal-winning wines; Countryside also stocks a large selection of wine- and beer-making supplies. Tastings are free.

✱ Green Space

PARKS ⚘ **Bays Mountain Park and Planetarium** (423-229-9447; baysmountain.com), 853 Bays Mountain Park Road. The park opens Mon.–Sat. at 8:30, Sun. at noon, with seasonal closing times, generally 5 PM in the winter and 8 PM in the summer. The Nature Center at Bay Mountain

THE HISTORIC NETHERLAND INN

Tennessee Department of Tourist Development

operates on a slightly different schedule, generally closing an hour earlier than the park grounds. The 3,500-acre nature preserve, perfect for mountain biking and orienteering, also includes 25 miles of hiking trails and a 44-acre lake. Mountain biking is permitted on certain trails (register at the nature center and pay the $2 fee). In Mar., Apr., Oct., and Nov., the Bays Mountain Observatory holds free programs each Sat. night, while daily star shows are held in the state-of-the-art planetarium theater. Naturalists offer guided barge rides through the park to showcase its aquatic inhabitants, and excellent habitat programs allows close encounters with wolves, raptors and other creatures. Park entrance fee is $3/car; planetarium shows are $4 for adults and children.

🗡 **Warrior's Path State Park** (423-239-8531; tennessee.gov/environment /parks/WarriorsPath), 490 Hemlock Road. Named for the ancient trading and war path used by the Cherokee, the park includes a TVA reservoir for fishing, swimming, and boating; hiking and biking trails; as well as horseback riding. A huge, accessible-by-all, tree-house-themed playground opened in 2009, and there's an 18-hole, par 72 course for golfers. There's no entrance fee, but some activities—including horseback riding and golfing—require a fee.

✳ Lodging

BED & BREAKFASTS/INNS

Fox Manor Historic Bed and Breakfast Inn (888-200-5879; foxmanor.com), 1612 Watauga Street. Six luxurious guest rooms have been renovated and restored, melding modern conveniences with exquisite period furnishings to create the perfect ambience for travelers or vacationers. The restored late-1800s home offers private baths, king- or queen-sized beds, and all the modern comforts. Moderate.

The Netherland Inn (423-335-5552), 2144 Netherland Inn Road. Settlers traveled to the site on the Holston River to build boats for the western migration, as well as create a mini salt-shipping industry in the region. The inn was added out of necessity—a place for boat builders to eat and sleep, and house a few guests as well. Richard Netherland bought the structure at a sheriff's sale in 1818, converting the three-story building into an inn and tavern. Three presidents—Andrew Jackson, Andrew Johnson, and James Polk—have stayed at the inn. Moderate.

PRICE CATEGORIES:

Inexpensive	Less than $100 (for hotels, inns, and B&Bs); less than $50 (for campgrounds, state park facilities)
Moderate	$100–200
Expensive	$201–300
Very expensive	More than $300

HOTELS Meadowview Marriott Resort & Conference Center (423-578-6600; marriott.com), 1901 Meadowview Parkway. The rolling landscape of the foothills of the Blue Ridge Mountains and an 18-hole championship golf course combine to serve as the backdrop for this lush hotel. The renovated property was expanded and updated in early 2010 to create a more contemporary environment in a gorgeous setting, and the improvements include an indoor pool and fitness center, and guest rooms with high-tech jack pack technology and sleek bathrooms. A casual restaurant serves breakfast, lunch, and dinner, and the adjacent lounge can be quiet or quite festive, depending on the guest list at the hotel. Rock features throughout pay homage to the Appalachian setting and blend with the hotel's more contemporary than country atmosphere. Moderate.

✳ Where to Eat

EATING OUT Bone Fire Smokehouse (423-239-7225; bonefire smokehouse.com), 242 E. Main Street. Open Tues.–Sat. 11–9. Enjoy some Tennessee barbecue —baby back ribs, pulled pork, pulled and smoked chicken,

PRICE CATEGORIES:	
Inexpensive	Less than $16
Moderate	$16–30
Expensive	$31–50
Very expensive	More than $50

turkey, and brisket, some of which is brown-sugar rubbed, and all of which is smoked over oak. A choice of tangy mango or Memphis-style sauces/rubs is also available, and there are a few salad choices, but for the most part, it's all barbecue, all the time. Moderate.

✳ Selective Shopping

ANTIQUES Nooks & Crannies Antiques (423-246-8002; nooks andcranniesantiques.com), 146 Broad Street. Open Mon.–Sat. 10–5, Sun. 1–5:30. There are plenty of nooks and crannies at this huge, three-story antiques mall, so much so that the place can be a bit overwhelming. But despite its size, the mall is clean and easy to navigate, and the folks who work here are not only friendly, they can almost always point you to exactly what it is you are seeking.

FOOD PURVEYORS Ya Ya's Candy Corner (423-245-9292; yayascandycorner.com), 201 W. Sullivan Street. Open Mon.–Fri. 10–5, Sat. 10–2. A delightful find of the candy kind, Ya Ya's is filled with light and sweets, from unusual truffles to gigantic cupcakes and almost any confection one could desire.

✳ Special Events

Late April: **Spring Garden Fair** (423-288-6071; exchangeplace .info). Held at Exchange Place, the Garden Fair focuses on springtime activities at the 1850s farm, with thousands of plants, especially native plants and herbs.

The fair also features garden walks and talks, children's activities, traditional music, and baked goods.

Mid-July: **Fun Fest** (423-392-8806; visitkingsport.com/funfest), downtown Kingsport. A hot-air-balloon festival featuring balloon glows, country music concerts, and games. Concerts cost $10–15; other events are free.

Late September: **Fall Folk Arts Festival** (423-288-6071; exchange place.info), Exchange Place. Festival focuses on harvest time activities on the 1850s farm, with an emphasis on pioneer arts and crafts, traditional foods, and children's activities. Artisans offer quality crafts for sale, and the Harvest Market features autumn plants and produce. Adults $1, children 50 cents.

ANTIQUING IN DOWNTOWN KINGSPORT

Tennessee Department of Tourist Development

JOHNSON CITY

With three railroad companies crossing the town, Johnson City became a rail center for the Southeast, shuttling goods through the area and passengers on excursion trips to the Blue Ridge Mountains. As a supporter of the South, the town changed its name during the Civil War to Haynesville to honor Confederate senator Landon Carter Haynes. After the war, the town name reverted to Johnson City. With Bristol, Tennessee, Johnson City was known for its down-home old-time music and for the recording sessions conducted by Columbia Records as early as 1928.

The city was also known by a less-desirable name—"Little Chicago"—for its location as a distribution center for bootlegging activities, presumably part of the network that gangster Al Capone developed during the 1920s Prohibition era. East Tennessee State University and its 12,000 students call Johnson City home, and the town enjoys a wide breadth of cultural activities common for a college town.

GUIDANCE Johnson City Convention and Visitors Bureau (423-461-8000; johnsoncitytnchamber.com), 603 E. Market Street.

GETTING THERE *By air:* **Tri-Cities Airport** (TRI; 423-325-6000; tri flight.com), 1674 Standing Stone Parkway, Hilham. Service from major cities including Detroit, Atlanta and Charlotte, via Delta, American Eagle, U.S. Air, and Allegiant.

By car: I-81 intersects I-26 a few miles north of Johnson City.

GETTING AROUND *By bus:* **Johnson City Transit** (423-434-6260; johnsoncitytransit.org) operates Mon.–Fri. 6:15–6:15 and Sat. 8:15–5:15, and does not operate on major holidays.

By car: The city is looped by State of Franklin Road/E. Oakland Avenue, which changes names where TN 181 bisects the roadway. John Exum Parkway is a major north–south thoroughfare, with W. Market and E. Main being the major west and east roadways.

By taxi: Johnson City is served by a number of taxi companies, mostly regional; local cabbies are **Mom's Taxi** (423-975-0698) and **WW Cab** (423-929-8316).

MEDICAL EMERGENCY Johnson City Medical Center (423-431-6111; msha.com), 400 N. State of Franklin Road, is a level-one trauma center offering comprehensive medical and diagnostic services.

✳ To See

HISTORIC SITES Jake Legg's Lost State Tours (423-557-4248; lost statetours.com), 604 E. Unaka Avenue. Tours offered Sat.–Sun. at 2 and 4

PM. Mix some local history with a lot of fun during a 90-minute ride in a railcar/bus, learning about the Lost State of Franklin—an 18th-century secessionist area that North Carolina ceded to the U.S. government and eventually became a part of Tennessee. Pub crawls also available. Adults $20, seniors $16, children 5–12 $12.

Tipton-Haynes State Historic Site (423-926-3631; tipton-haynes.org), 2620 S. Roan Street. Open Tues.–Sat. 9–3. The history of Johnson City would not be complete without exploring the Tipton-Haynes Site. Tour historic buildings, including a barn and corncrib, smokehouse, spring-

ROCKY MOUNT

Tennessee Department of Tourist Development

house, and the original house, all dating from the Revolutionary War through the Civil War. This was a true frontier settlement; Daniel Boone was said to have lived here, and it's believed Native Americans lived in the cave on the site before white settlers came to the area. Artifacts from the cave include a Dire wolf tooth from the Pleistocene age. The home of a slave of the Haynes family is also present on the site. Tipton-Haynes offers a variety of holiday-themed programs, including ghostly tours and pumpkin patch gatherings during the fall, and a Civil War Christmas presentation. Adults $6, children $3.

MUSEUMS ✎ **Hands On! Museum** (423-434-4263; handsonmuseum .org), 315 E. Main Street. Open daily 9–5, June–Aug.; Tues.–Fri. 9–5, Sat. 10–5, and Sun. 1–5, Sept.–May. This fully interactive museum features play and discover areas for children from tots through teens; visitors can engage in scientific experiments, create Silly Putty, play in the Wild West, and examine the inner workings of a car from gears to motors. General admission $8, children two and under free.

✎ **Rocky Mount Museum** (423-538-7396; rockymountmuseum.com), 200 Hyder Hill Road, Piney Flats. Open Tues.–Sat. 11–5. The U.S. Territorial capital from 1790 to 1792, Rocky Mount was home to the Cobb

THE MUSEUM AT THE GRAY FOSSIL SITE

Tennessee Department of Tourist Development

family and became the capital of the territory when territorial governor William Blount came to live with the family. The story of that era is told by costumed interpreters and through games, crafts, and activities. Programs change frequently, so check the Web site for daily offerings. Adults $6, seniors $5, children 5–17 $4, children under five free.

✳ To Do

ARCHAEOLOGICAL SITES ✍ **Gray Fossil** (866-202-6223; grayfossil museum.com), 1212 Suncrest Drive, Gray. Open daily 8:30–5; closed major holidays. When highway construction workers began a road-widening project in 2000, they discovered a rare Miocene-period site filled with fossilized remains. East Tennessee State University, just down the road from the Gray Fossil site, spearheads the paleontological research, which is open to the public. All-access passes to the exhibits and research site are adults $10, children 5–12 $7; self-guided tours of the Miocene exhibit are free.

✳ Green Space

PARKS Roan Mountain State Park (423-772-0190; state.tn.us /environment/parks/RoanMtn), 1015 County Route 143, Roan Mountain. Open year-round, sunrise–sunset. At the base of Roan Mountain, the park is full of rich hardwood forests and wildflower fields; the pastoral scenery can be explored on 12 miles of hiking trails or the 2.5-mile mountain bike trail. Anglers delight in the year-round run of three kinds of trout, some native to the area, some stocked by the state game and wildlife department. Both RV and tent campsites are available, although reservations are not; both types are let out on a first-come, first-served basis. Reservations are accepted for the park's 30 cabins, which have full kitchens and wood-burning stoves. There's no entrance fee for the park.

✳ Lodging

HOTELS Carnegie Hotel (423-979-6400; carnegiehotel.com), 1216 W. State of Franklin Road. The historic hotel first opened in the 1890s, and while vintage touches remain, there's nothing old-fashioned at the Carnegie except the atmosphere. Lush rooms at the AAA Four Diamond–rated hotel feature antique-style sleigh beds with plush

PRICE CATEGORIES:	
Inexpensive	Less than $100 (for hotels, inns, and B&Bs); less than $50 (for camp-grounds, state park facilities)
Moderate	$100–200
Expensive	$201–300
Very expensive	More than $300

bedding; bathrooms are decked out in granite and have separate soaking tubs and showers. An on-site, full-service spa and fitness center bring a very big-city feel to this charming small-town hotel. Expensive.

✳ Where to Eat

DINING OUT Gourmet & Company (423-929-9007; gourmetandcompany.com), 214 E. Mountcastle Drive. Open Mon.–Thurs. 10–9, Fri.–Sat. 10–10. With a rising star in the culinary world—Chef Jackson Kramer—and an emphasis on locally grown ingredients, this well-appointed restaurant offers traditional American food with a seasonal menu that emphasizes local meat and produce. The adjacent retail shop offers gourmet foods and fine housewares. Moderate.

EATING OUT The Firehouse (423-929-7377; thefirehouse.com), 627 W. Walnut Street. Open Mon.–Thurs. 11–9:30, Fri.–Sat. 11–10. The old Walnut Street firehouse

PRICE CATEGORIES:

Inexpensive	Less than $16
Moderate	$16–30
Expensive	$31–50
Very expensive	More than $50

smokes—barbecue, that is—and offers up traditional sides like slaw and beans, as well as a variety of nonbarbecue choices, including steaks and fish. Moderate.

Heavenly Ham (423-434-4266; heavenlyhamjc.com), 701 N. State of Franklin Road. Open Mon.–Fri. 10–6, Sat. 10–3. Great club, chicken salad, and roast beef sandwiches, and a special pot roast sandwich, are the main lunch items for this casual, deli-style eatery. Inexpensive.

✳ Special Events

Early June: **Blue Plum Festival** (blueplum.org), downtown Johnson City. A two-day outdoor festival featuring live bluegrass and folk music, street vendors, and family activities. Free.

BRISTOL

It's a town split in two—with a dividing line that's not a line in the sand, but rather a full-blown light show. Bristol is half in Tennessee, half in Virginia, but it's all in when it comes to offering a slice of Americana.

Once home to Cherokee Indians, the land that would eventually become present-day Bristol was part of a huge plantation that spread over both states; it was in the 1850s that the son of the plantation owner decided a certain parcel would make the perfect site for a new town.

Before the 1800s, Bristol was busy spot for pioneers making their way to the West, starting not long after the Revolutionary War, when Fort Shelby—part trading post, part homestead—was established; Daniel

Boone came to the fort to restock and rest on his journey. The King family, who owned that original plantation upon which the town was officially established, built the first home in town; the King Department Store eventually became the first complete store in the city.

But it was during the late 1920s and early 1930s that Bristol rose to American fame, when an RCA record producer and talent scout named Ralph Peer came to town, looking for musical talent to record. Peer put out the call, and hundreds came from around the region to audition. Country music legends like the Carter family and Jimmie Rodgers were part of the famous Bristol Sessions—76 songs recorded by fewer than 20 musical acts in what perhaps remains the most famous recording sessions in American music. In 1998, Congress recognized Bristol as the Birthplace of Country Music. A new interactive museum is being built to chronicle the history of music in Bristol.

It's not the strum of a guitar, but the gunning of engines is sweet music to many in Bristol, which is also home to one of NASCAR's most acclaimed racetracks. More than a million race fans converge on Bristol each year to watch some of the stock car circuit's most famous races on what's known as the world's fastest half mile.

GUIDANCE Bristol Convention and Visitors Bureau (423-989-4850; visitbristoltnva.org), 20 Volunteer Parkway.

GETTING THERE *By air:* **Tri-Cities Airport** (TRI; 423-325-6000; triflight.com), 1674 Standing Stone Parkway, Hilham. Service from major

COUNTRY-MUSIC MURAL, DOWNTOWN BRISTOL

Tennessee Department of Tourist Development

cities including Detroit, Atlanta, and Charlotte, via Delta, American Eagle, U.S. Air, and Allegiant.

By car: Bristol is east of I-81, running from exit 74 on the Tennessee side (the last Tennessee exit on the highway) to about 8 miles up the highway into Virginia.

GETTING AROUND *By bus:* The **Bristol Transit System** (423-989-5586; bristoltntransit.org) offers bus service Mon.–Fri. 6–6, with no weekend or holiday service. Fares are 60 cents, with children under six free.

By car: Major routes into Bristol include State Street, Volunteer Parkway, and Pennsylvania Avenue.

By taxi: **Ace Cab Company** (423-764-0241) and **Elite Taxi** (423-340-2802) offer taxi service throughout the city.

MEDICAL EMERGENCY Bristol Regional Medical Center (423-844-1121; wellmont.org), 1 Medical Park Boulevard. The level-two trauma center offers comprehensive medical and diagnostic services 24 hours daily.

✳ To See

HISTORIC SITES Historic Bristol Walking Tour (423-989-4850; visit bristoltnva.org/heritage-museums/historic-downtown-walking-tours), downtown Bristol. Walking tours are self-guided, at your leisure, and downloadable maps and audio are available online. In 1901 the center of Main Street—now State Street—was designated as the state line separating Tennessee and Virginia. To commemorate the division, the Bristol Gas and Electric Company donated and erected a huge sign on the top of a hardware store with the slogan PUSH—THAT'S BRISTOL in 1910. But in 1915, the sign was moved to the actual state line on State Street, and in 1921 the slogan A GOOD PLACE TO LIVE was added. The sign is now on the National Register of Historic Places and just one stop on the walking tour, which also includes country music and NASCAR murals and historic buildings. Free.

✳ To Do

CAVERN TOURS ✂ **Bristol Caverns** (423-878-2011; bristolcaverns .com), 1157 Bristol Caverns Highway. Open Mon.–Sat. 9–5 and Sun. 12:30–5, mid-Mar.–Oct.; Mon.–Sat. 10–4 and Sun. 12:30–4:30, Nov.–Mar. 15. Travel back in time in one of the largest caverns in the Smoky Mountain region. The beautiful caverns lie far below the surface of the earth, carved out more than 200 million years ago by an ancient river; Native Indians used the huge caverns as a tool in their raids on unsuspecting settlers, as they'd emerge from the underground, attack, and then disappear. Not suitable for very young children. Adults $14, children $8.

FAMILY FUN ✎ **Caterpillar Crawl** (jlbristol.org/caterpillar), downtown Bristol. What started as a children's book—*A Very Hungry Caterpillar* by Eric Carle—became a cause for reading and literacy. A caterpillar scavenger hunt takes the curious on a journey to find 10 caterpillar sculptures designed by local artist Val Lyle hidden along State Street. Download the map at the Junior League Web site. Free.

RAFTING The Ocoee Whitewater Center (423-496-1011; fs.fed.us/r8 /ocoee), 4400 US 64, Copperhill. Open daily 9–5. The host of the 1996 Olympic canoe and kayak slalom events, the center is a one-stop shop for those looking for more information on the outfitters who provide rafting adventures, mountain biking, and fishing. The center itself hosts national and international white-water rafting competitions. Free.

SPECTATOR SPORTS Bristol Motor Speedway (423-989-6901; bristol motorspeedway.com), 151 Speedway Boulevard. Races are run seasonally; check the Web site for schedules. Tours are offered daily on the hour

BRISTOL MOTOR SPEEDWAY

Tennessee Department of Tourist Development

Mon.–Fri. 9–4 and Sun. noon–4, except during major race events. A 0.5-mile concrete track with steep banking and amphitheater seating, BMS hosts NASCAR racing, with more than a million people visiting every year. When no rubber is meeting the road, tours of the drag way, speedway, and the backstage areas of the track are offered. The holiday season brings some bling to Bristol as the speedway comes to life at night with millions of twinkling lights. Tours: adults $5, children 6–12 $3, and children under six free.

Bristol Sox (276-669-6859; bristol.sox.milb.com), 1501 Euclid Avenue, Bristol, VA. The Bristol Sox, a minor-league farm team of the Chicago variety, play in the Appalachian League. Tickets start at $4 for adults and $3 for children.

✱ Green Space

PARKS Cherokee National Forest (423-476-1212; fs.fed.us/r8 /cherokee), 2800 N. Ocoee, Cleveland. Open daily sunrise–sunset. At 640,000 acres, the Cherokee National Forest is the largest piece of public land in the state, stretching from Bristol to Chattanooga. This long, slender slice of verdant acreage offers every outdoorsy activity imaginable, from high-octane white-water rafting to sedate hikes, fly-fishing, and a dozen more adventures. Trails in the Cherokee aren't just for hikers, although there are 600 miles of hiking trails to explore; motorized vehicles have a few dozen miles of trails to ride. For those anxious to see animals in their natural habitats, the Cherokee offers ample opportunity, as more than two hundred species call the forest home, from rare salamanders to black bear and wild deer. There's no fee to enter the park, although day-use areas—boat launches, shooting ranges, and river launches—require a fee.

✱ Lodging

HOTELS Hampton Inn Bristol (423-764-3600; hamptoninn.com), 3299 W. State Street. A consistent winner in the cleanliness/friendliness stakes, the Hampton Inn Bristol, just off the interstate, is superbly located for exploring the area, whether you're off to the races at the speedway or going on a musical road trip. Every attraction is an easy drive from this location, and the hotel's friendly

PRICE CATEGORIES:	
Inexpensive	Less than $100 (for hotels, inns, and B&Bs); less than $50 (for campgrounds, state park facilities)
Moderate	$100–200
Expensive	$201–300
Very expensive	More than $300

staff is always full of good ideas for creating an itinerary. Rooms at the Hampton are nicely, if not plainly, furnished; free Internet service is available in rooms, and suites are available. Unlike many hotels, this Hampton is not smoke free; smoking and nonsmoking floors are available. There's a small fitness room, outdoor pool, and complimentary breakfast and parking. Moderate.

✳ Where to Eat

DINING OUT Troutdale Dining Room (423-969-9099; thetroutdale .com), 412 Sixth Street. Open Tues.–Sat. at 5 PM. An elegant Victorian house is home to one of the finest restaurants in the state, with a regular lineup of awards from James Beard, DiRoNA, and others. Generous pours at the clubby bar start an evening off in the right direction, and the menu never fails to surprise while still offering a traditional selection of specialties; the chef's tasting menu is a delight for the more adventurous palate. Expensive.

EATING OUT KP Duty Gourmet Shoppe & Café (423-764-3889; kpduty.net), 520 State Street. Open Mon.–Sat. 9–9. Don't be fooled by the name—there's absolutely nothing military-ish about this kind of KP duty; rather, it's as if discovering your favorite little sandwich shop had turned up the gourmet volume since your last visit. Brunch is available daily; soups and salads at lunch run from

the ordinary to exotic (a seared ahi tuna with pears and honey soy sauce, for example), and dinner fare is a bit more traditional but no less distinctive, with a rock-star lineup of culinary staples including pasta primavera and a trio of beef tenderloin. Moderate–expensive.

Macado's Overstuffed Sandwiches (423-764-1100; macados .net), 714 State Street. Open Mon.–Sat. 8 AM–12:30 AM, Sun. 10 AM–12:30 AM. The name may say *sandwiches,* but the menu promises so much more at this lone Tennessee location of a popular Virginia restaurant chain. Quesadillas and salads share the menu with $5 Reubens (on Sat.), and yes, the full menu is available starting at 8 AM—you'll find no eggs and bacon on this menu. Inexpensive.

Red Rooster Market and Deli (423-764-0716; redroostermarket .com), 1258 County Route 126. Open Mon.–Fri. 10:30–5. A sandwich shop that takes sandwiches to the next level, Red Rooster's take on classic deli food is something to crow about. A combination of pulled chicken with celery and herb-infused sauce regularly has folks begging for the recipe (don't expect them to share), and a tangy,

PRICE CATEGORIES:	
Inexpensive	Less than $16
Moderate	$16–30
Expensive	$31–50
Very expensive	More than $50

BRISTOL RHYTHM AND ROOTS REUNION

Tennessee Department of Tourist Development

chilled strawberry soup topped with caramelized onions makes one forget one is drinking fruit. Inexpensive.

✳ Special Events

Mid-September: **Bristol Rhythm and Roots Reunion** (423-573-4898; bristolrhythm.com), State Street, downtown. Bristol celebrates its musical heritage with dozens of live music performances focusing on Southern rock, country, and bluegrass. Two-day tickets $35, single-day tickets $25, children under 12 free.

JONESBOROUGH

A trip to Jonesborough, the oldest town in Tennessee, is a treat—whether you're a history buff or not. Many of this country's frontiersmen and early historic figures—including Davy Crockett, Daniel Boone, and Andrew Jackson—lived and worked here; some of the buildings can lay claim to those gentlemen as guests or residents. Founded in 1779, Jonesborough was once part of the proposed state of Franklin, the first attempt at statehood after the original 13 colonies; Jonesborough was the first capital of

Franklin, and future Tennessee governor John Sevier its first governor.
Franklin, despite its attempt at statehood, was actually part of North Carolina, whose governor didn't take kindly to the attempt to break off; the
state of Franklin was never to be. Andrew Jackson was first licensed to
practice law in Jonesborough, living here five months before moving on
to Nashville. Jackson's escapades, followed by engaging stories from the
Civil War, including those of abolitionist Elihu Embree, are recounted
here, and it's little wonder that a tiny town with such big history and lore
became the storytelling capital of the world.

Historic Jonesborough is a delight, with its wide brick sidewalks and
gorgeous and carefully tended 18th- and 19th-century buildings. Depending on one's interest in history and storytelling, a visit here can last a few
hours or a whole day. Either way, this historic town enchants from the
first moment.

GUIDANCE Historic Jonesborough Visitor Center (423-753-1010;
historicjonesborough.com), 117 Boone Street. Open Mon.–Fri. 8 5,
Sat.–Sun. 10–5.

GETTING THERE *By air:* **Tri-Cities Airport** (TRI; 423-325-6000; tri
flight.com), 1674 Standing Stone Parkway, Hilham. Service from major
cities including Detroit, Atlanta, and Charlotte, via Delta, American
Eagle, U.S. Air, and Allegiant.
By car: TN 411/11 E. and Boone Street are the major routes into town.

GETTING AROUND *By car:* Once in town, High and Boone streets are
the major thoroughfares.

MEDICAL EMERGENCY Holston Valley Medical Center (423-224-
4000; wellmont.org), 130 W. Ravine Road, Kingsport. This the closest
major medical facility, with a level-one trauma center with comprehensive
medical and diagnostic services.

✳ To See

HISTORIC SITES Strolling tour, Historic Jonesborough Visitor Center
(423-753-1010; historicjonesborough.com), 117 Boone Street. Open
Mon.–Fri. 8–5, Sat.–Sun. 10–5. A strolling tour of town is a great way to
experience its history and charm; the self-guided route includes stops at
the Chester Inn, where presidents Jackson, Polk, and Johnson all slept, as
well as the old cemetery, where graves date back to Revolutionary times.
A map, available at the visitors center for $1, is a great tool whether or
not a structured walk through town is planned; the historic anecdotes and
factoids are well worth the price.

✳ Lodging

BED & BREAKFASTS/INNS

Blair-Moore House (423-753-0044; blairmoorehouse.com), 201 W. Main Street. The 1832 house, located smack in downtown Jonesborough, features three guest rooms with canopied beds, private porches, and a beautiful garden. The suite room—the largest of the three accommodations—offers a private sitting room in addition to the private porch; the bedroom features a high bed with toile linens, reminiscent of an English country home. Breakfast is served on fine china and antique linens, and is made of locally grown and organic products whenever possible. Moderate.

Eureka Inn (423-913-6100; eurekajonesborough.com), 127 W. Main Street. Jonesborough's only historic hotel, the Eureka Inn had been a private home, a boardinghouse, and finally, a lush hotel for early-20th-century travelers. The inn underwent a $3 million refurbishment in 2000, creating 14 individually decorated rooms with private baths, antiques from the late 1800s, historic art, and photos of Jonesborough. Accommodations range from doubles with twin beds to single full-sized beds for cozy canoodling to queen-bedded rooms with a smidge of additional space—all with ironed sheets on the bed. There's advanced soundproofing, which means you get all the charm of a storied sleeping space without the usual creaking floors and overheard conversa-

PRICE CATEGORIES:	
Inexpensive	Less than $100 (for hotels, inns, and B&Bs); less than $50 (for campgrounds, state park facilities)
Moderate	$100–200
Expensive	$201–300
Very expensive	More than $300

tions. Breakfast is included in the room rate. Moderate.

Hawley House Bed and Breakfast (423-753-8870; megtrott.com/hawleyhouse), 114 E. Woodrow Avenue. The oldest house in the oldest town in Tennessee was built in 1793 and is now a bed & breakfast. Built of dovetailed chestnut logs on a limestone foundation, the house includes a huge wraparound porch, and rooms feature antique furniture, vintage quilts, and exquisite charm. Rocking chairs on the two porches are meant for whiling away the time with a book or the morning paper, or one's own thoughts—and a quick walk brings guests into town. The hearty full breakfast is served by candlelight. Moderate.

✳ Where to Eat

DINING OUT Bistro 105 (423-788-0244), 105 E. Main Street. Open Mon.–Sat. 11–4 and 5–until, Sun. 11–2. The atmosphere is historic building meets upscale dining, and the food can't really be pigeonholed in any way, except its

INTERNATIONAL STORYTELLING CENTER

quality, which is high. Steaks, lamb, seafood, and chops dominate the dinner menu; salads and sandwiches are offered at lunch; and homemade soups are offered all day. Moderate–expensive.

EATING OUT The Cranberry Thistle (423-753-0090; thecran berrythistle.com), 107 E. Main Street. Opens for breakfast at 8 on weekdays and 8:30 on weekends; closing hours vary, but dinner is

PRICE CATEGORIES:

Inexpensive   Less than $16
Moderate $16–30
Expensive $31–50
Very expensive   More than $50

served until 7 nightly, and drinks and desserts are offered into the wee hours. This café/coffeehouse offers breakfast, lunch, and dinner, as well as dessert, drinks, and coffee late into the evening. Live music is also on the menu, making for a lively spot in the historic district. Inexpensive.

Earth & Sky Confections (423-788-0202; earthandskyconfections.com), 137 E. Main Street. Open Mon.–Sat. 10–6. Luxuriously handcrafted chocolates tempt—both from the smell wafting from the shop and the intricate designs of the confections themselves. Inexpensive, unless you've got a serious sweet tooth—then the sky's the limit.

✳ Entertainment

PERFORMING ARTS Interna-tional Storytelling Center (storytellingcenter.net), 100 W. Main

A PERFORMER SPINS A TALE AT THE NATIONAL STORYTELLING FESTIVAL

Street. Open Mon.–Sat. 10–5. The history of storytelling in Jonesborough in particular and the art form in general is told through stories (of course!) and exhibits. Live storytelling sessions are held 26 weeks of the year; each week, a different storyteller takes up residence in Jonesborough and spins tales in lively performances Tues.–Sun. at 2 PM. Performance tickets are $10 for adults and $9 for students, children, and seniors; there's no admission fee to visit the center.

Jonesborough Repertory Theatre (423-753-1010; jonesborough theatre.com), 125½ W. Main Street. The regional theater group stages productions throughout the year, from classic dramas to children's plays and musicals. The annual rendition of *A Christmas Carol* is delightful, a classic example of all that's good with community theater. Adults $12, students and seniors $10.

✳ Selective Shopping

ANTIQUES Antiques district. Downtown Jonesborough is loaded with antiques stores; most feature multiple vendors. There's no need for a map or directions; simply stroll down Main Street and while away the hours browsing the stores.

ARTS AND CRAFTS Fellowship Quilters (423-753-4629), 105 Fox Street. Open Mon.–Sat. 10–5. For those who love quilts but don't actually sew, this is the place to find vintage, antique, and new quilts, ready to throw on the bed. Prices are fair, and the selection, both in terms of variety and quality, is among the best in the state.

Jonesborough Art Glass Gallery (423-753-5401), 101 E. Main Street. Open Mon.–Sat. 10–5. Chock-full of the work of regional and national glass artisans, the gallery offers pieces to hang, wear, or use from the charming (and large) renovated phone company building. Prices are incredibly reasonable, so much so that one feels as if one is almost scamming the owners sometimes. But this is one of those galleries where there's truly a chance to pick up a piece of art from a future star of the medium.

Tennessee Quilts (423-753-6644; tennesseequilts.com), 114 Boone Street. Open Mon.–Sat. 9:30–5:30. With thousands of bolts of fabric, patterns, supplies, and truly knowledgeable quilters on staff, the huge quilt shop is a treat for experienced and novice quilters alike. While the breadth of the offerings might intimidate, the friendliness—and patience—of the staff offset any feeling of stitching inadequacy.

✳ Special Events

May–October: **Music on the Square** (musiconthesquare.com), Fri. evenings, Courthouse Square, downtown. The beautiful courthouse serves as the backdrop for the weekly live music, storytelling, and dramatic performances by local and regional artists. Free.

October: ♫ **National Storytelling Festival** (storytellingfestival.net), locations around downtown. It's fitting that the oldest town in Tennessee plays host to the oldest form of entertainment. Single-day tickets start at $95, with full weekend tickets as high as $165; ticket pricing is determined by how early tickets are purchased—the early bird gets the best deal.

GREAT SMOKY MOUNTAIN REGION

SEVIERVILLE

Where the foothills of the Great Smoky Mountains meets the Tennessee Valley, an area once called Forks of the Pigeon, the land where the east, middle, and west forks of the Little Pigeon River meet is present-day Sevierville. The town's name, pronounced "Severe-ville," comes from John Sevier, a Revolutionary War colonel who routed the Cherokee out of the area.

Its believed the first inhabitants of the area lived here as early as AD 200, but it was about a thousand years later that the first large settlement of Native Americans established a village centered on a temple mound near the confluence of the West Fork and Little Pigeon. By the 1700s, present-day Sevierville was controlled by the Cherokee, but it was late in that century when Colonel Sevier would lead a battle against the Cherokee, who had aligned with the British in the Revolutionary War and remained hostile to settlers in the valley.

As more settlers moved into the area and established plantations and farms, Sevierville was named the county seat. As the country moved toward civil war, abolitionists found a friendly atmosphere in Sevierville; while some plantation owners held slaves, many African Americans were free, and the county resoundingly voted down secession from the Union.

Following the war, African American builders lead the rebuilding effort, and the town soon prospered; the next century saw its share of troubles, however, with the uprising of a Ku Klux Klan–style vigilante group and a 1900 fire that destroyed the downtown area.

It was the opening of the Great Smoky Mountains National Park that gave Sevierville prominence as a gateway to the Smokies; today, more than half the local businesses are related to tourism.

Sevierville's most famous resident is the incomparable Dolly Parton. In addition to staying true to her country girl roots, Dolly has brought her

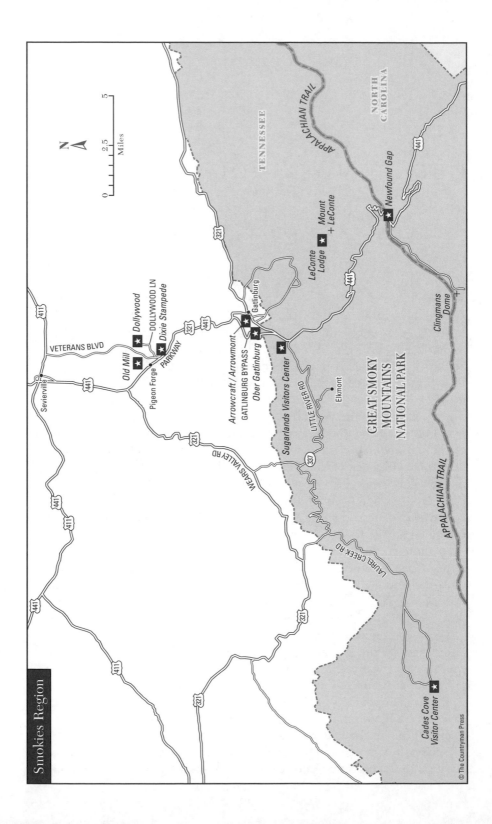

Smokies Region

N

0   2.5   5
Miles

VETERANS BLVD

Sevierville

Pigeon Forge

Old Mill

Dollywood

DOLLYWOOD LN

Dixie Stampede

PARKWAY

Arrowcraft / Arrowmont

GATLINBURG BYPASS

Ober Gatlinburg

Gatlinburg

Sugarlands Visitors Center

WEARS VALLEY RD

LITTLE RIVER RD

Elkmont

LeConte Lodge

Mount + LeConte

Newfound Gap

TENNESSEE

APPALACHIAN TRAIL

NORTH CAROLINA

GREAT SMOKY MOUNTAINS NATIONAL PARK

Clingmans Dome

LAUREL CREEK RD

APPALACHIAN TRAIL

Cades Cove Visitor Center

© The Countryman Press

own brand of tourism growth to the area, establishing Dollywood amusement park in nearby Pigeon Forge, as well as the *Dixie Stampede* dinner show featuring a retelling of the Civil War, complete with horses and heroes. She is a generous native daughter and is honored with a statue in the town square.

GUIDANCE Sevierville Convention & Visitors Bureau (865-453-6411; visitsevierville.com), 125 Court Avenue. There is no shortage of unofficial visitors centers around the area, but some are disguised as time-share companies—be warned. The Sevierville CVB, easy to get to in the downtown area, is the best source of cabin rental information for the area. (A few rental companies are listed in *Lodging*, and all cover the entire Smoky Mountain region.)

GETTING THERE *By air:* **McGhee-Tyson Airport** (TYS; 865-342-3000; tys.org), 2055 Alcoa Highway, Knoxville.

By car: Sevierville is about an hour east of the Knoxville airport via I-40.

GETTING AROUND *By car:* Traffic in and around the Sevierville/Pigeon Forge/Gatlinburg area is often congested; Gatlinburg's trolley bus system and Sevierville and Pigeon Forge's trolley are excellent for those who have the time and patience. Otherwise, driving yourself is the way to go.

Each town has its own set of numbered traffic lights along the Parkway, which is commonly referred to simply as "the Parkway" in all three towns but officially is designated as US 441 or US 321, depending on where you are. Attractions generally advertise themselves as being near a certain traffic light on the Parkway—again, numbered for each town.

By trolley: Pigeon Forge and Sevierville share the **Fun Time Trolley** (865-453-6444; pigeonforgetrolley.org), which runs two routes covering one hundred stops year-round on a seasonal schedule. Fares start at 50 cents.

MEDICAL EMERGENCY If you need to dial 911, and you're on or near the Parkway, note your exact location by specifying the stoplight number. Sevierville, Pigeon Forge, and Gatlinburg all have their own set of numbered stoplights, so be sure to specify which town, as well.

LeConte Medical Center (865-453-9355; lecontemedicalcenter.com), 742 Middle Creek Road, Sevierville, is the area's major hospital.

AMPM ER Urgent Care Center (865-908-6402), 2538 McGill Street, Pigeon Forge. Available for more routine ailments.

✳ To See

MUSEUMS Floyd Garrett's Muscle Car Museum (865-908-0882; musclecarmuseum.com), 320 Winfield Dunn Parkway. Open daily 9–5,

SEVIERVILLE'S HOMETOWN GIRL, DOLLY PARTON, IS HONORED WITH A STATUE.

Jan.–Mar.; daily 9–6, Apr.–Dec. Ninety muscle cars flex their power in the museum, which boasts one of the largest muscle car collections in the country. Adults $9.75, children 8–12 $4, children under eight free.

Tennessee Museum of Aviation (866-286-8738; tnairmuseum.com), 135 Air Museum Way. Open Mon.–Sat. 10–6, Sun. 1–6; during Jan. and Feb., the museum closes at 5. A huge aircraft hanger holds everything from vintage planes to war birds, artifacts from the early days of flight and the Tennessee Aviation Hall of Fame, whose inductees include FedEx's Fred Smith and astronaut Dr. Margaret Rhea Seddon. On good flying days, look to the skies for flybys—visiting vintage aircraft and some of the museum's collection may be buzzing by. Adults $12.75, seniors (60+) $9.75, children 6–12 $6.75, children under six free.

✳ To Do

BOATING Lighthouse Pointe Marina (865-397-7997; lighthousepointe marina.net), 1209 TN 139, Dandridge. On the huge, man-made Douglas Lake, the marina offers a variety of rentals, from pontoons to houseboats. There are 500-plus miles of shoreline on the 30,000-acre reservoir created by the Tennessee Valley Authority, so there's plenty of space for boaters of every experience level.

CAVERN TOURS ✔ **Forbidden Caverns** (865-453-5972; forbidden cavern.com), 455 Blowing Cave Road. Open daily 10–6, Apr.–Nov. One of Tennessee's claims to fame is being home to the most caves in the country—more than eight thousand recorded so far. Forbidden Caverns isn't as spectacular as many of the big names in the country, but it offers up plenty of cave lore, including a missing Indian princess, the use of the cave as a still during Prohibition and beyond, and imaginative grotto names like the Grotto of the Dead and the Grotto of Evil Souls. $14.

FISHING **Smokies Angling Adventures** (865-933-3140; smokiesangling .com), location varies depending on trip scheduled. Douglas Lake is consistently rated one of the top crappie and largemouth bass fishing lakes in the country. Offering year-round bass boat and pontoon boat fishing, Smokies Angling features day and night trips, depending on the season; be sure to acquire a fishing license before getting on the boat. Rates start at $225 for four people for half-day trips.

RAFTING **Big Creek Expeditions** (877-642-7238; bigcreekexpeditions .com), 3541 Hartford Road. Trips offered Mar.–Oct., with multiple trips offered during peak times. When one looks at the Pigeon Rivers—whether the Big or Little version of it—both seem to be sedately flowing waterways. But there's plenty of white-water fun on both, with the Big Pigeon being the more exciting ride, boasting Class III and IV whitewater. $26.95 and up, depending on the season and the choice of river.

SPECTATOR SPORTS ✔ **Tennessee Smokies Baseball** (865-286-2300; smokiesbaseball.com), 3540 Line Drive, Kodak. A double-A affiliate of the Chicago Cubs, the Smokies play in perhaps the only ballpark fronted by the regional visitors center. The lodgelike park affords an excellent view of the action from any seat. Single game tickets start at $6 for children's bleacher seats and go as high as $9 for adults.

✳ Lodging

BED & BREAKFASTS/INNS

There is an abundance of bed & breakfasts in the Smoky Mountains region; resources such as the Smoky Mountain B&B Association (smokymountainbb.com) offers a listing of the association members.

Braeside Inn (866-429-5859; braesideinnbb.com), 115 Ruth Lane. With a huge balcony over-

PRICE CATEGORIES:

Inexpensive	Less than $100 (for hotels, inns, and B&Bs); less than $50 (for campgrounds, state park facilities)
Moderate	$100–200
Expensive	$201–300
Very expensive	More than $300

looking the Smokies, a penchant for all things Charles Rennie Mackintosh, and a Scottish lass for an owner, the pretty two-story inn offers both a Scottish theme and incredible views of the mountains, especially from the second-story porch. There are just three rooms, and all are beautifully appointed, featuring fireplaces and hydrothermal massage tubs en suite. Moderate.

Mountain Harbor Inn (877-379-1313; mountainharborinn.com), 1199 TN 139, Dandridge. This lakefront inn features 15 rooms, a huge waterfront deck with mountain views, and traditional decor. Two room suites and condo-style rooms available; all come with a sunset cruise, dessert, and breakfast. Moderate–expensive, depending on the accommodation and the season.

Persephone's Farm Retreat (865-428-3904; bedandbreakfast .cc), 2279 Hodges Ferry Road. The lush farm setting along the French Broad River really is a retreat, with an in-the-country feel that belies the press of people just a few minutes' drive away. The 1887 farmhouse offers rooms with simple furnishings when compared to other B&Bs, but the friendly atmosphere and the riverfront setting make up for any lack of glitz. Children are welcome in the cabins. Moderate.

CAMPING/RV PARKS Two Rivers Landing RV Resort (866-727-5781; tworiversrvresort .com), 2328 Business Center Circle. Open year-round. An upscale RV park with 55 sites, some of which are riverfront, plus a clubhouse with a fully equipped fitness center, outdoor pool, and playground. Inexpensive.

RESORTS Resort at Governor's Crossing (800-497-5749; gover norscrossing.net), 225 Collier Drive. Governor's resort features a small water park and the added bonus of being close to Parkway attractions and the national park. Full kitchens and fireplaces available. Moderate.

Wilderness at the Smokies (877-325-9453; wildernessatthe smokies.com), 1424 Old Knoxville Highway. A ginormous hotel/water park/condo complex, Wilderness has all the bells and whistles for a family vacation. Its location—a good drive from the national park and other area attractions—is either a blessing or a curse, depending on your patience level. Lodge-y decor runs to wood and plaid and cabinlike furnishings; larger multiroom suites are excellent for those needing a bit more room or traveling in groups, and some units include kitchens. Dining options, minigolf, and real golf available on-site, as well as access to the Sevierville Events Center. Moderate–expensive, depending on the season.

VACATION RENTALS Hidden Mountain Resorts (865-453-9850; hiddenmountain.com), 475

Apple Valley Road. A choice of cabin, villa, and lodge-style accommodations in two locations; some cabins offer pools, and all guests have access to the fishing pond. Inexpensive–expensive, depending on season and accommodation.

Rocky Top Ridge (866-428-3704; rockytopridge.com), 1330 Creek Side. A 15-acre spread with three cabins of varying sizes, but all feature full kitchens and hot tubs, among other amenities. Moderate.

✳ Where to Eat

Note: Sevier County is not a dry county, but where you can get beer, wine, or a cocktail depends on which town you're standing in, and whether you're eating out or stocking up for your accommodation. Restaurants in Gatlinburg and Sevierville offer beer, wine, and mixed drinks, while those in Pigeon Forge only offer beer and wine. There's only one package store in the county, and that's in Gatlinburg; grocery stores throughout the county sell beer, but no wine or liquor.

DINING OUT Bistro 109 (865-453-8899), 109 Bruce Street. Open Mon.–Sun. 10 10. Featuring casual fine dining among antiqued brick walls, Bistro 109 is off the tourist path but worth finding to get a feel for everyday Sevierville. The menu includes American cuisine with a few twists, like a fried goat cheese and tomato jam appetizer, as well as Southern comfort food and classics. Whatever you

PRICE CATEGORIES:

Inexpensive	Less than $16
Moderate	$16–30
Expensive	$31–50
Very expensive	More than $50

choose, it will be plentiful! Brunch on Sat. and Sun. is anything but basic eggs and potatoes. Moderate–expensive.

EATING OUT Applewood Farmhouse Restaurant (865-429-8644; applewoodfarmhouse restaurant.com.), 240 Apple Valley Road. Open daily 8 AM–9 PM. With basic country cooking that's served up hot and fresh in an apple orchard setting, the restaurant is popular with tours, but don't let the thought of a crowd deter you. From fried chicken to eggs with country ham, every meal starts with the restaurant's signature apple fritters. Inexpensive.

🍽 **The Diner** (865-908-1904; thediner.biz), 550 Winfield Dunn Parkway. Open daily at 8 AM; closes Mon.–Thurs. and Sun at 10 PM, Fri.–Sat. at 11 PM. Closing time extended one hour Memorial Day–Labor Day. The '50s-style diner serves up breakfast all day and diner staples—burgers, fries, shakes, and dinner platters—and there's always a classic car or two in the drive.

✳ Entertainment

SHOWS AND DINNER THEATER *Cirque de Chine* (865-

429-1601; cirquedechine.com), Smoky Mountain Palace, 179 Collier Drive. Shows daily; schedule depends on season. A dazzling show of Chinese acrobatics, flying motorcycles, a dragon dance, and more. The show features elaborate costumes and a fast pace, and is a visual delight for children and adults alike. $29.95.

Soul of Shaolin (865-453-8888; easternshanghaitheater.com), 1304 Parkway. Shows daily; schedule depends on season. The martial arts spectacular tells a story of love and loss; the *Soul of Shaolin* was first performed on Broadway and features most of the original cast from the Tony-nominated production. $26.

✳ Selective Shopping

BOUTIQUE SHOPPING Music Outlet (865-453-1031; music outlet.net), 1050 Winfield Dunn Parkway. Open Mon.–Sat. 9:30–6. For the string musician, the Music Outlet is a delight of hard-to-find instruments, from dulcimers and banjos to acoustic and electric guitars. Pianos, keyboards, and other instruments can be found here as well, although in smaller quantity.

OUTLET SHOPPING Tanger Five Oaks Outlets (865-453-1053; tangeroutlet.com/Sevier ville), 1645 Parkway. Open Mon.–Sat. 9–9, Sun. 10–7. More than one hundred outlet stores, including Ralph Lauren, Coach, Nike, Timberland, Brooks Brothers, and more.

✳ Special Events

Mid-May: **Bloomin' Barbeque & Bluegrass Festival** (888-738-4378; bloominbbq.com), downtown Sevierville. The two-day, family-friendly celebration of barbecue and bluegrass music takes over the historic downtown area with live music, activities for the kids, and the barbecue cook-off; it's part of the region-wide Smoky Mountain Springfest. Free.

Late September: **Great Smoky Mountain Annual Auto Festival** (865-680-4193; smokymtnautofest .com), Smokies Stadium, 3540 Line Drive, Kodak. A car show and crafts festival all in one, featuring eight hundred cars, craft booths, and food vendors, as well as a swap meet and classic car giveaway.

Early November–February: **Smoky Mountain Winterfest** (888-738-4378; smokymountain winterfest.com), at locations throughout the region. A regional festival joining Sevierville, Pigeon Forge, and Gatlinburg, when the foothills towns are decorated with millions of twinkling lights and displays; special events take place throughout the festival, including parades, visits with Santa, live music, and other winter-themed events and happenings. Most events are free, although some require admission.

The valley in which modern-day Pigeon Forge sits was popular hunting ground for the Cherokee who populated this area before European settlers discovered it on their expeditions in the early 1700s.

Traveling from the North Carolina side of the Smoky Mountains on the Indian Gap Trail, bands of Cherokee would descend into the valley en route to another path near Sevierville; it's believed the first white settlers were traders and followed the same path to the valley. It was in the early 1800s that the iron forge that gave the town its name was built along the Little Pigeon River; a gristmill and sawmill were eventually added to the property. The gristmill still operates today as the Old Mill, and the forge was dismantled and moved in the 1880s.

Pigeon Forge remained a little hamlet, with a dirt road along the river as the main thoroughfare, until the national park was established in 1934. While the area had attracted visitors for its springs, thought to have healing properties, the official designation as a national park meant huge change was on the way.

Gatlinburg seemed to be the prime candidate for the development of the area, but the town was landlocked by the park, and the limited available land and resources were controlled by a few families. Developers turned their focus to Pigeon Forge, just north of Gatlinburg on the new US 441. Amusements began popping up in town, from a Civil War–themed railroad ride to kiddy rides and two rival amusement parks, one of which eventually became Dollywood.

Today, there are thousands of hotel rooms, multiple family amusement centers, loads of chain restaurants, numerous outlet shops to wander through, and dozens of festivals and events to keep folks entertained year-round in Pigeon Forge. The town is busy almost every day of the year, and one has to head up into the hills to get a feel for the quiet beauty of the area.

GUIDANCE Pigeon Forge Department of Tourism (800-251-9100; mypigeonforge.com), 1950 Parkway. There is no shortage of unofficial visitors centers around the area, but some are disguised as time-share companies—be warned. The Pigeon Forge Web site offers easy links to accommodations and attractions, as well as discount coupons for everything from lodging to dining. Those coupons and information are also available at the two official Pigeon Forge visitors centers at 1950 Parkway and 3107 Parkway.

GETTING THERE *By air:* **McGhee-Tyson Airport** (TYS; 865-342-3000; tys.org), 2055 Alcoa Highway, Knoxville.

By car: Pigeon Forge is about an hour east and south of the Knoxville airport (TYS) via I-40.

GETTING AROUND *By car:* Traffic in and around the Sevierville/Pigeon Forge/Gatlinburg area is often congested; Gatlinburg's trolley bus system and Sevierville and Pigeon Forge's trolley are excellent for those who have the time and patience. Otherwise, driving yourself is the way to go.

Each town has its own set of numbered traffic lights along the Parkway, which is commonly referred to simply as "the Parkway" in all three towns but officially is designated as US 441 or US 321, depending on where you are. Attractions generally advertise themselves as being near a certain traffic light on the Parkway—again, numbered for each town.

By trolley: Pigeon Forge and Sevierville share the **Fun Time Trolley** (865-453-6444; pigeonforgetrolley.org), which runs two routes covering one hundred stops year-round on a seasonal schedule. Fares start at 50 cents.

MEDICAL EMERGENCY If dialing 911 while you're on or near the Parkway, note the exact location by noting the stoplight number. Sevierville, Pigeon Forge, and Gatlinburg all have their own set of numbered stoplights, so be sure to note which town, as well.

LeConte Medical Center (865-453-9355; lecontemedicalcenter.com), 742 Middle Creek Road, Sevierville, is the area's major hospital.

AMPM ER Urgent Care Center (865-908-6402), 2538 McGill Street, Pigeon Forge. Available for more routine ailments.

✳ To See

MUSEUMS Titanic Museum (800-381-7670; titanicpigeonforge.com), 2134 Parkway. Opens daily at 9, with closing hours varied by season; generally 8 PM. Visitors are handed a boarding pass for the ill-fated ship, with the name, class, and background of a real Titanic passenger; one must wait until the end of the tour to find out the fate of their long-ago traveling companion. More than four hundred artifacts from the ship and its passengers are displayed, and interactive exhibits aren't computerized; rather, try to stand on the listing deck (samples range from 12 to 45 degrees) and see how long you can keep you hand in a container of frigid water, set at 28 degrees.

✳ To Do

FAMILY FUN ✎ **Dollywood** (800-365-5996; dollywood.com), 1198 McCarter Hollow Road. Operating times and days change frequently and seasonally; check the Web site or call ahead for the most up-to-the-date information. Closed Jan. 2–late Mar. Dolly Parton's country roots and spunky personality are felt and seen throughout the park, from a replica of the cabin in which she grew up to the friendly attendants at rides and

DOLLYWOOD

food booths. An Appalachian crafts area is dedicated to the mountain crafts tradition, with artists creating functional treasures of glass, iron, and wood. Mountain-themed rides range from wooden roller coasters to water rides. Food at the park runs to hearty country buffets, barbecue, and Southern fried chicken, as well as grab-and-go treats like pork rinds, kettle corn, and funnel cakes. Adults $55.90, seniors $52.50, children 4–11 $44.70.

Dollywood Splash Country (800-365-5996; dollywoodsplashcountry .com), 1198 McCarter Hollow Road. Open late May–mid-Sept., with operating times and days changing frequently. Check the Web site or call ahead for the most up-to-date information. The water park offers something for everyone, from the huge lagoon pools with slides and a waterfall to a padded splash and play area just for the little ones. Adults $45.80, seniors $43.60, children 4–11 $40.25.

Firehouse Golf at Walden's Landing (865-428-0184; waldens landing.com/firehouse_golf.html), 2528 Parkway. Perhaps the nicest miniature golf course I've ever seen, Firehouse Golf has two 18-hole courses and a vintage firehouse theme, set amid an outdoor mall. Adults $8, children 3–11 $6.

Flyaway Indoor Skydiving (865-453-7777; flyawayindoorskydiving .com), 3106 Parkway. Open daily 10–7, with some seasonal adjustments. Be sure to check the Web site or call for details. Take 20 minutes of instruction, gear up, and then you are let loose—sort of—in a wind tunnel where fliers take turns taking off for a faux sky-diving experience without the plane or mile-high jump out of one. In all, each flier experiences about three minutes of airtime, but multiple flights can be purchased at discounted prices, with group rates available, too. Be warned—there are size and weight limits, with a max weight of 230 pounds for men and 200 pounds for women. A single flight is $31.95.

⚓ **WonderWorks** (865-868-1800; wonderworkstn.com), 100 Music Road. Open daily 9 AM–midnight. The entrance to WonderWorks is an upside-down house; an ominous creaking is heard as one enters. Inside, things are upside down, too, as the adults may actually have more fun than the kids when they're landing a space shuttle, trying out a bed of nails, or throwing themselves against a wall, leaving their shadow (and perhaps their dignity) behind. An art exhibit takes some familiar masterpieces and turns them on their heads, allowing for plenty of debate about what one sees, given the angle. Adults $25.75, children 4–12 $14.50, children three and under free.

Zorb (865-428-2422; zorb.com/smoky), 203 Sugar Hollow Road. Generally open daily 9–5, with later weekend closing hours during June, July, and Aug., and 10 AM opening time weekdays Nov.–Mar. So is it really a good idea to roll down a hill inside something that resembles—all too perfectly—a giant hamster ball? Perhaps so. But thousands love to climb into the balls and spin head over feet along the pathways—and have lived to tell about it. A water-feature ride is also available, although I prefer the dry method myself. $37 per person to start, depending on the size of group and style of ride chosen.

✳ Lodging

CAMPING/RV PARKS Foothills RV Park ad Cabins (865-428-3818; foothillsrvparkandcabins.com), 4235 Huskey Street. A full-service RV park with campsites and cabins, free Wi-Fi, and laundry and pool facilities. Pets are welcome with their owners in the RVs and at the RV campsites, but not in the cabins. Inexpensive.

Riveredge RV Park (877-881-7222; stayriveredge.com), 4220 Huskey Street. An upscale-feeling RV park, Riveredge features both campsites and cabins, and a full slate of amenities from a swim-

PRICE CATEGORIES:

Inexpensive	Less than $100 (for hotels, inns, and B&Bs); less than $50 (for campgrounds, state park facilities)
Moderate	$100–200
Expensive	$201–300
Very expensive	More than $300

ming pool to arcade and huge playground for the kids. Inexpensive.

HOTELS Pigeon Forge has several thousand hotel rooms, with every moderate chain well represented; many overlook the bustling, six-lane Parkway. The visitors bureau offers excellent information about all the hotel options.

Inn at Christmas Place (865-868-0525; innatchristmasplace .com), 119 Christmas Tree Lane. It's always Christmas at the inn, from the constant chime of the elaborate carillon bells to the tree and swag-bedecked lobby, all the way to the rooms and bathroom, decorated in red, green, gold, and silver tones. All this good cheer extends to the pool, where the lights turn red and green at night and music is still holiday, albeit with a tropical twist. Kids can write letters to Santa and drop them in a special mailbox, and the big man himself visits frequently. Moderate.

VACATION RENTALS Eden Crest Vacation Rentals (866-254-0249; edencrest.net), 652 Wears Valley Road. Large cabins—with five or more bedrooms—are easy to find through Eden Crest, as are pet-friendly cabins; many are tucked into the hills around Pigeon Forge or scattered throughout the Wears Valley, well away from the traffic of the Parkway. Moderate–expensive, depending on size of rental unit.

Smoky Mountain Dreams (865-365-0240; smokymtndreams.com), 3049 Veterans Boulevard. The company offers cabins and condos of all sizes scattered throughout Pigeon Forge, including some with easy Parkway access. Moderate–expensive, depending on size of rental unit.

✳ Where to Eat

Note: Sevier County is not a dry county, but where you can get beer, wine, or a cocktail depends on which town you're standing in, and whether you're eating out or stocking up for your accommodation. Restaurants in Gatlinburg and Sevierville offer beer, wine, and mixed drinks, while those in Pigeon Forge only offer beer and wine. There's only one package store in the county, and that's in Gatlinburg; grocery stores throughout the county sell beer, but no wine or liquor.

DINING OUT Bullfish Grill (865-868-1000; bullfishgrill.com), 2441 Parkway. Open Sun.–Thurs. 11–10, Fri.–Sat. 11–11. A rarity along the Parkway for its white tablecloths and hip, stylish bar, Bullfish offers fresh seafood flown in daily, prime steaks, and a bit of

PRICE CATEGORIES:	
Inexpensive	Less than $16
Moderate	$16–30
Expensive	$31–50
Very expensive	More than $50

AT THE CHRISTMAS-THEMED INN AT CHRISTMAS PLACE, IT'S CHRISTMAS EVERY DAY.

the country cooking one comes to expect in Pigeon Forge, presented in a more urban style. Moderate.

EATING OUT Mama's Farmhouse (865-908-4646; mamasfarmhouse.com), 208 Pickel Street. Open daily at 8 AM for breakfast, lunch, and dinner; closing times vary by day and season. A one-price, all-you-can-eat extravaganza of country cooking, served up family style—from eggs, bacon, country ham, and biscuits in the morning to fried chicken, sweet potato casseroles, and plenty of Southern side dishes for dinner. Inexpensive for breakfast, moderate pricing for lunch and dinner, and kids under five eat free.

Old Mill Restaurant (865-429-3463; oldmillsquare.com /restaurant.htm), 175 Old Mill Avenue. Open daily 7:30 AM–9 PM.

Huge country breakfasts (and lunches and dinners) are served up in a huge space in a historic gristmill that uses the Little Pigeon River as its power. The mill is still operational and is on the National Register of Historic Places; all the flour used for the fresh pancakes, muffins, baked goods, and even the breading on the fried chicken comes straight from the mill itself. Most breakfast platters come with pancakes (if you prefer, you can order off the lighter menu, which is still a hearty meal), and all breakfasts begin with a fresh glass of orange juice and mini muffins. Inexpensive.

Pottery House Café & Grill (865-453-6002; oldmillsquare.com /cafe.htm), 175 Old Mill Avenue. Open daily 10:30–9 for lunch and dinner. The café at Old Mill provides a true respite from the hustling Parkway; the tranquil setting, Southern comfort food, and small (by Pigeon Forge standards) dining room add up to an excellent meal in a relaxed atmosphere. Many, if not most, of the breads and some of the dishes are created with flour ground right at the mill. Reservations recommended for dinner. Inexpensive–moderate.

✳ Entertainment

SHOWS AND DINNER THEATER
Country Tonight (865-453-2003; countrytonitepf.com), 129 Showplace Boulevard. Show schedule varies by season and day of the week; check the Web site or call ahead for the most up-to-date schedule. A wholesome country music show featuring singers and dancers of all ages, with an emphasis on country but a bit of gospel and patriotic music thrown in the mix. Adults $39, children 12 and under free with a paying adult.

✎ *Dixie Stampede* (800-356-1676; dixiestampede.com), 3849 Parkway. There are generally two shows a night; check the Web site for the most up-to-date schedule. Dolly Parton says the *Stampede*— a combination family-style dinner and horse show—is reminiscent of her childhood, when the family would gather for a big meal and a bit of friendly competition on horseback. The show itself is an extravaganza of horsemanship, Civil War tales, and patriotic songs. The eat-with-your-hands dinner—literally—includes roast chicken, corn on the cob, soup in a sipping bowl, and dessert, delivered at an amazingly coordinated and fast pace. Adults $41.99 and up, children 4–11 $30.99 and up, children under four are welcome to sit on an adult lap and eat from their plate for free (otherwise, a ticket is required).

✳ Selective Shopping

BOUTIQUE SHOPPING
Incredible Christmas Place (800-445-3396; christmas place.com), 2470 Parkway. Open daily 9 AM–10 PM. It's all Christmas, all the time, at this 46,000-square-foot, Bavarian-themed store; individual galleries are arranged by decor and theme. From prelit trees to personalized ornaments, from stockings to tree

THE STORE AT THE OLD MILL

skirts, and from tree lights to giant inflatables for the outdoors, Christmas Place is nirvana for those who can't wait to decorate for the holidays. Our advice is to bring a list of whatever it is you need—decor, gifts, ornaments— and then stick to it. Otherwise, Christmas Place can be overwhelming. But I adore it, anyway.

Old Mill Square (888-453-6455; old-mill.com), 175 Old Mill Avenue. Closing hours at the stores vary slightly, but all are open daily 9–8. The historic mill on the Pigeon River is a favorite stop for photos, but the stores surrounding the mill are a treat not to be missed. The general store is chock-full of fresh-from-the-mill flour, pancake mixes, and more gourmet goodies, including cast-

iron cookware. At Old Pigeon River Pottery, local artists create heirloom quality serve- and dinnerware, as well as charming take-homes, including black bears of all sizes.

✳ Special Events

Mid-January: **Wilderness Wildlife Week** (800-251-9500; mypigeonforge.com/saddleup). Events take place at locations throughout the entire Smokies region, including the national park. An energizing time in the area that celebrates the natural beauty of the Smokies, with experts teaching classes in everything from nature photography to the geology of the region; hikes and field trips throughout the park are led by naturalists and local guides. All the events are free, but some events and hikes/field trips require advance registration.

Late February: **Saddle Up!** (800-251-9500; mypigeonforge.com/saddleup). Events take place at locations throughout Pigeon Forge. Cowboy poets, swing dances, and a chuckwagon cook-off are the highlights of the four-day, cowboy-themed festival. Free.

Mid-March: **A Mountain Quilt-fest** (800-251-9500; mountainquiltfest.com). Events take place at locations throughout Pigeon Forge. One of the top quilting festivals in the country, with more than 80 classes and a quilt show. Free.

Early November–February: **Smoky Mountain Winterfest** (888-738-4378; smokymountainwinterfest.com). Events held at locations throughout the region. A regional festival joining Sevierville, Pigeon Forge, and Gatlinburg, when the foothills towns are decorated with millions of twinkling lights and displays. Special events take place throughout the festival, including parades, visits with Santa, live music, and other winter-themed events and happenings. Most events are free, although some require admission.

GATLINBURG

The Indian Gap Trail served the Cherokee for centuries as an easy connector to the verdant forests and coves filled with wild game that is today's Great Smoky Mountains National Park with the lush valley that encompasses Pigeon Forge and Sevierville. That trail first routed the Indians through modern-day Gatlinburg, which abuts the great mountain.

A white South Carolinian, William Ogle, was the first to permanently settle in these flats, although many hunters and trappers were known to make camp here. But Ogle went one better, cutting his own timber for the cabin he planned to build. But Ogle's dream to build his cabin where the Little Pigeon and Baskins Creek met was not witnessed by him; when he returned to his native South Carolina to gather his family and crops for the move to the mountains, he fell ill and died.

Mrs. Ogle, however, was determined to see her husband's dream become a reality, and she and her brother eventually made the trip over Indian Gap, finding William's logs waiting. They built the cabin, which stands today.

The area became popular with other settlers, many of whom fought in the Revolutionary War or the War of 1812 and were deeded 50 acres of land for their service. (Many descendants of those original settlers still live in Gatlinburg today.) When a post office was established inside Radford Gatlin's general store in the 1850s, the town became known as Gatlinburg. Townspeople tried to remain neutral during the Civil War, although Confederate soldiers moved in to protect the valuable saltpeter mines in Alum Cave, up in the mountains. They were pushed back, and minor skirmishes continued in the area until the end of the war.

As logging grew with the invention of the band saw and the expansion of the railroad, forests were bought up all around Gatlinburg. In addition to hosting loggers, the town soon became a lure for naturalists who had read about the splendor of the mountains and wildlife thanks to regional authors.

Soon, a woman's organization founded a school in the area, noting the lack of educational resources; the school eventually became Arrowmont, dedicated to Appalachian arts and crafts.

With the advent of the automobile, the interest of one determined lady (Ann Davis, who with her husband, Willis, would talk to anyone who would listen about the idea of creating a national park from the Smoky Mountains), and the call of regional businesspeople to protect the Smoky Mountains from further logging, more than 70,000 acres were bought from lumber companies to create the Great Smoky Mountains National

PEDESTRIAN BRIDGE OVER THE LITTLE RIVER

Park. Visitors soon flocked to the park, which is now the most-visited in the national park system, with more than 9 million visitors annually.

The charm of Gatlinburg can sometimes be overshadowed by the crush of visitors, but this little mountain burg is a favorite for a number of reasons: proximity to the park, breadth of attractions, and Alps-like atmosphere. When coming down from a mountain cabin or resort, be sure to simply park and explore on foot.

GUIDANCE Gatlinburg Department of Tourism and Convention Center (800-343-1475; gatlinburg-tennessee.com), 303 Reagan Drive.

GETTING THERE *By air:* **McGhee-Tyson Airport** (TYS; 865-342-3000; tys.org), 2055 Alcoa Highway, Knoxville.

By car: Gatlinburg is about an hour east and south of the Knoxville airport via I-40 to US 441.

GETTING AROUND *By car:* Traffic in and around the Sevierville/Pigeon Forge/Gatlinburg area is often congested; Gatlinburg's trolley bus system and Sevierville and Pigeon Forge's trolley are excellent for those who have the time and patience. Otherwise, driving yourself is the way to go.

Each town has its own set of numbered traffic lights along the Parkway, which is commonly referred to simply as "the Parkway" in all three towns but officially is designated as US 441 or US 321, depending on where you are. Attractions generally advertise themselves as being near a certain traffic light on the Parkway—again, numbered for each town.

By trolley: **Gatlinburg Trolley** (865-436-0535; ci.gatlinburg.tn.us/transit /trolley) operates daily and on a seasonal schedule. Routes include service to the national park and Dollywood. Fares start at 50 cents.

MEDICAL EMERGENCY If you dial 911, be sure to note the exact location by noting the stoplight number. Sevierville, Pigeon Forge, and Gatlinburg all have their own set of numbered stoplights, so be sure to note which town, as well.

LeConte Medical Center (865-453-9355; lecontemedicalcenter.com), 742 Middle Creek Road, Sevierville, is the area's major hospital.

AMPM ER Urgent Care Center (865-908-6402), 2538 McGill Street, Pigeon Forge. Available for more routine ailments.

✳ To See

MUSEUMS Christ in the Smokies Museum and Gardens (865-436-5155; christinthesmokies.com), 510 River Road. Open daily 9–5. Christ in the Smokies is the second coming, so to speak, of Christus Gardens, which for almost 50 years told the story of Christ through dioramas. After the attraction was dismantled in 2008, a few business leaders in Gatlinburg decided to re-create it, using life-sized wax figurines in a variety of biblical scenes, including a depiction of Da Vinci's *Last Supper*, to tell the story of Jesus. Adults $11, children $5.

Ripley's Believe it or Not! (865-436-5096; gatlinburg.ripleys.com), 800 Parkway. Open daily 10 AM–11 PM. Since there are a few Ripley museums around the country, many of the shrunken heads and oddities collected by Robert Ripley throughout his travels and displayed here are replicas, although alongside the displays are the stories that tell the tales of his adventures. Parents of young children, be warned—many of the exhibits deal with death and torture, and may be too graphic for little ones. Adults $14.99, children 3–11 $7.99, children under three free.

✳ To Do

AQUARIUMS AND ZOOS ✎ **Ripley's Aquarium of the Smokies** (865-430-8808; aquariumofthesmokies.com), 88 River Road. Open Sun.–Thurs. 9–9 and Fri.–Sat. 9 AM–11 PM, Labor Day–Memorial Day; daily 9 AM–11 PM Memorial Day–Labor Day. Believe it or not, the Aquarium of the Smokies has the world's longest underwater tunnel, perfect for viewing the sea creatures that call the aquarium's 1.4 million gallons of water home. From a tropical rain forest to a lagoon filled with sharks that's viewed through the acrylic walls of a tunnel, there's an endless array of nose-to-nose wildlife viewing. Adults $21.99, children 6–11 $10.99, children 2–5 $4.99.

FISHING Smoky Mountain Angler (865-436-8746; smokymountain angler.com), 466 Brookside Village Way. Guided fishing available all year; store hours are Mon.–Fri. 8–6, Sat. 8–5, and Sun. 10:30–4:30, with earlier closing times during the winter months. Trout fishing in the Smokies is a delight for experienced anglers and novices new to fly-fishing; Smoky Mountain Angler offers guided fishing throughout the park; locally crafted flies, rods, and reels; and all the necessary gear. Guided trips are personalized to each party's experience and preferences, and loaner gear is provided at no charge. (But licenses and flies are not included in the price of the trip.) Half-day trips are $175 for the first person and $50 for each additional angler; a full-day trip is $250 for the first person and $50 for each additional person. There's a limit on three anglers per guide.

HIKING A Walk in the Woods (865-436-8283; awalkinthewoods.com). Call for seasonal hiking schedules and to make a reservation. Guided hikes through the Smokies, from hikes of just a few hours and half-day and full-day walks and hikes to longer (and more challenging) forays for

RIPLEY'S AQUARIUM OF THE SMOKIES

more experienced or enthusiastic hikers. A hiker shuttle service is offered for those interested in through hikes, as there are few excellent loop hikes in the national park (more experienced hikers will prefer a through hike). $25 and up.

SKIING ✍ **Ober Gatlinburg** (865-436-5423; obergatlinburg.com), 1001 Parkway. Open daily at 9 AM, early Dec.–mid-Mar., with closing hours varying but as late as 10 PM most days. In winter, Ober Gatlinburg offers up eight ski trails served by two quad lifts and one double lift; there are two black diamond runs in addition to the easier blues and greens, as well as a terrain park and tubing area. Another lift is strictly for scenic viewing, offering nonskiers a 15-minute ride each way; a large aerial tram is available to take visitors from downtown Gatlinburg straight up the mountain to the resort. The amusement park side includes huge slides, minigolf, an indoor ice-skating rink, and other games and amusements. The tram ride is $10 for adults, $8.50 for kids six and up; the amusements vary in pricing and require tickets, or an all-access wristband is $30 for adults and $25.50 for kids 7–11. The aerial tram is not included in the

THE TRAM AT OBER GATLINBURG TOTES VISITORS UP THE MOUNTAIN YEAR-ROUND.

wristband admission. Ski lessons are superaffordable, starting at $16, and the runs are open for night skiing. Adults $30, children 7–11 $20, except for holidays, when the rates jump to $47 for adults and $37 for children. Discounts for multiday and night-only skiing are available.

✳ Lodging

BED & BREAKFASTS/INNS

There is an abundance of bed & breakfasts in the Smoky Mountains region; resources such as the Smoky Mountain B&B Association (smokymountainbb.com) offer a listing of the association members.

Buckhorn Inn (865-436-4668; buckhorninn.com), 2140 Tudor Mountain Road. Accommodations at the Buckhorn range from traditional rooms to two-bedroom guesthouses, featuring tasteful decor and antiques, large picture windows or screened porches, and so many on-property amenities that leaving the grounds may not be necessary. A nature trail offers a two-hour, moderately strenuous hike, while a labyrinth gives those seeking peace or solace a chance to mediate. Children 12 and over are welcome at the inn, and holiday weekends require a minimum stay. Moderate–expensive, depending on choice of accommodation.

🍃 Lodge at Buckberry Creek (865-430-8030; buckberrylodge .com), 961 Campbell Lead Road. This mountain lodge is set in the mountains and offers a lush escape from what can often be a hectic pace in the heart of Gatlinburg. Throughout the lodge, Adirondack furnishings provide a rustic yet elegant atmosphere; rooms have chic yet simple decor, from log beds to floral prints. A host of on-site features, from hiking trails to a full-service spa and fine dining, mean one never has to leave the grounds. Every room offers a deck with scenic views and a cozy wood-burning fireplace. Expensive.

HOTELS 🖝 Hilton Garden Inn (865-436-0048; hilton.com), 635 River Road. Tucked on a street behind the busy main drag, the Garden Inn is memorable for a number of reasons, including its silver LEED certification, unexpectedly lush and sleek accommodations, and superconvenient location. Literally, a guest can walk to anywhere in town from this hotel, returning to a hip and upscale atmosphere in the

PRICE CATEGORIES:	
Inexpensive	Less than $100 (for hotels, inns, and B&Bs); less than $50 (for campgrounds, state park facilities)
Moderate	$100–200
Expensive	$201–300
Very expensive	More than $300

evening. The hotel's pool and hot tub feature chemical-free saltwater, and there's in-room recycling for the green-minded. A full bar, restaurant with hot breakfast offerings, and a rustic yet chic lobby create a sophisticated ambience in the heart of Gatlinburg. Moderate.

VACATION RENTALS Jackson Mountain Homes (865-436-8876; jacksonmountainhomes.com), 1662 E. Parkway. This Gatlinburg-based rental company offers fully equipped cabins and chalets for weekly and daily rental, with some properties requiring minimum stays, especially on holidays or peak seasonal weeks. The company Web site gives renters the option to rent by view, community, or number of bedrooms. Moderate.

✳ Where to Eat

Note: Sevier County is not a dry county, but where you can get beer, wine, or a cocktail depends on which town you're standing in, and whether you're eating out or stocking up for your accommodation. Restaurants in Gatlinburg and Sevierville offer beer, wine, and mixed drinks, while those in Pigeon Forge only offer beer and wine. There's only one package store in the county, and that's in Gatlinburg; grocery stores throughout the county sell beer, but no wine or liquor.

DINING OUT Park Grill (865-436-23000; parkgrillgatlinburg

.com), 1110 Parkway. Open daily for dinner. The huge Park Grill is nestled into a space just outside the park, although diners may feel as if they never left it, given the lodgelike decor. Prime steaks grilled over hickory, a huge salad bar, and local favorites including pecan-crusted chicken and slow-roasted pork are served up with sides that run heavy into carbohydrates but are worth the indulgence. Call-ahead seating is available and advisable, especially in the busy summer and fall months. Expensive.

EATING OUT Bennett's BBQ (865-436-2400; bennetts-bbq .com), 714 River Road. Open daily 8 AM–10 PM. Barbecue—it's what's for breakfast, lunch, and dinner at Bennett's, where a huge breakfast bar includes pulled pork and other barbecue treats, as well as the traditional scrambled eggs, bacon, biscuits, and grits. The breakfast bar makes way for a salad bar the rest of the day, and the menu focuses on supremely Southern offerings, including fried green tomatoes and fried okra, slow-cooked ribs and brisket, catfish, and greens. There's also a full bar, which isn't always easy to find in Sevier County. Moderate.

PRICE CATEGORIES:

Inexpensive	Less than $16
Moderate	$16–30
Expensive	$31–50
Very expensive	More than $50

The Donut Friar (865-436-7306; thevillageshops.com/donutfriar .html), 634 Parkway. Open daily 5 AM–10 PM. The heady aroma alone draws the hungry in, and once inside the cute little doughnut shop, the question becomes not which delightful doughnut to indulge in, but how many can one rationalize. Doughnuts are priced individually, not per dozen, so that can help in the process; the warm cinnamon bread is worth the wait. The friars also serve up a fab espresso. Inexpensive.

Flapjacks Pancake Cabin (865-436-2787), 956 Parkway. Open daily for breakfast and lunch. This local chain of pancake houses features huge platters of food at reasonable prices. Breakfast combos are truly gigantic, service is fast and friendly, and special attention is paid to special requests. Inexpensive.

✳ Entertainment

BARS AND NIGHTCLUBS Hard Rock Café (865-430-7625; hard rock.com), 515 Parkway. Open daily 11 AM–midnight. Yes, it's a typical Hard Rock, but it's also one of the only games in town when it comes to live music, and the featured bands are excellent and not a bit country-ish, as you might expect in this part of Tennessee. There's usually no cover charge.

ARROWCRAFT

SHOWS AND DINNER THEATER
Sweet Fanny Adams (865-436-4039; sweetfannyadams.com), 461 Parkway. Nightly shows mid-Apr.–Dec.; shows vary by season and day, with showtime at 8 PM. Vaudeville-style music and comedy are featured at this family-friendly theater; shows include a fairy-tale farce and a special Christmas-themed musical comedy. Adults $24.30, children under 12 $8.90.

✱ Selective Shopping

ARTS AND CRAFTS Arrowmont School of Arts and Crafts (865-436-5860; arrowmont.org), 556 Parkway. Open Mon.–Fri. 8–5, Sat. 8–4:30, and Sun. 1–6. The work or regional artists is featured in Arrowmont's gallery/store space, Arrowcraft, from handcrafted jewelry and furniture to textiles, whimsical stuffed animals, and carefully carved walking sticks. The store also offers books and supplies, and the super knowledgeable staff can answer almost any query—or find an answer if not. They also offer weekend, one-, and two-week-long workshops May–Oct. in everything from ceramics, fibers, and jewelry making to painting, drawing, and glass. Class pricing varies; check the Web site for offerings and fees.

Great Smoky Arts and Crafts Community (gatlinburgcrafts .com). Trail begins 3 miles from downtown on US 321 N.; follow the signs. An 8-mile loop of craft stores and studios showcasing the work of 125 artists. From pottery to woodcarving, basket making and weaving to quilting, the traditional Appalachian crafts are celebrated in this community, believed to be the largest group of independent artisans in North America.

BOUTIQUE SHOPPING The Village (865-436-3995; thevillage shops.com), 634 Parkway. Open at 10 daily; closing times vary by season and go as late as 10 PM in the summer months. Check the Web site for most up-to-date times. The setting is English village at this collection of boutique-type stores, offering up a Thomas Kinkade gallery, an Irish clothing and bookstore, fudge and candy, a hiker's outfitter, and a Christian music shop, to name a few.

✱ Special Events

Mid-May: **Fine Arts Festival** (gfaf.net), downtown Gatlinburg at Ripley's Aquarium and River Road. An arts-themed street fair sponsored by the Southern Highland Craft Guild, the juried festival focuses on regional artists and also offers live music, children's activities, and food vendors. Free admission.

July: **Midnight Independence Day Parade** (800-343-1475; events gatlinburg.com), downtown Gatlinburg. The nation's first parade of July 4th starts in the first seconds of Independence Day, running a mile-long route with lighted floats, marching bands, huge balloons, and more. The party starts earlier, of course, on the evening of the

VILLAGE STORES

third, when downtown streets are blocked off and preparade entertainment takes to the street. Free.

Early November–February: **Gatlinburg Winter Magic** (888-738-4378; smokymountainwinter fest.com), at locations throughout the region. This is Gatlinburg's entry into the larger regional festival joining its Smoky Mountain counterparts, when the foothills towns are decorated with millions of twinkling lights and displays. In Gatlinburg's case, that means LED-lighted displays, a New Year's ball drop, craft shows, and other events. Most events are free, although some require admission.

GREAT SMOKY MOUNTAINS NATIONAL PARK

There's little wonder that the Great Smoky Mountains National Park, with 9 million visitors annually, is the most visited in the whole national park system; after all, the park is within a day's drive of more than a third of the country's population.

It's ironic, then, that at the most visited of all national parks, just a fraction leave their cars for a true exploration. Only one of every six visitors—just 1.5 million people annually—actually hike a trail or spend any measurable time exploring the park, according to park officials.

Drive is the critical word, indeed. On holiday weekends and during peak times—the fall foliage season from mid-September through early November and summertime—a continual parade of cars, motorcycles, and recreational vehicles navigate the winding roads through the park, from the must-visit Cades Cove to the perhaps the most visited point accessible by car, Newfound Gap, which straddles the Tennessee–North Carolina state line.

The parking lot at the main visitors center at the Gatlinburg entrance is usually packed, as is the lot at Newfound Gap, where groups of families and friends pose for pictures in front of the massive stone Rockefeller Monument. Just to the right of that monument is the inconspicuous, almost-overlooked trailhead for a section of the historic Appalachian Trail. Venture a few feet up that incline, and the sudden hush is almost deafening. Gone is the roar of the cars, the rumble of motorcycle engines, and the laughter of visitors. All that's still discernable to the ear is the snapping of twigs underfoot, the laboring breath of hikers, the buzzing of insects, and the twittering of birds.

This is the real Great Smoky Mountains National Park—and the irony is that so few of those who go to the Smokies ever experience its beauty from anything other than a car window.

The delight in finding almost-empty trails and easy walks within the park is matched by the stress relief that hits once you're out from behind the wheel of the car; driving the tight, winding roads while trying to take in the natural beauty all around is a white-knuckle experience.

With all its natural enticements, it's no wonder that Great Smoky Mountains National Park is a lure; one of those "must-checks" from your list of travel to-dos. But it only takes a short hike to realize there's so much more to the park than can be seen through a car window or the back of a motorcycle.

GUIDANCE Great Smoky Mountains National Park (865-436-1200; nps.gov/grsm), 107 Park Headquarters Road, Gatlinburg. Open 24 hours a day, year-round. Visitors centers are located in Townsend, Gatlinburg, and Sevierville outside the park and at Sugarlands, Cades Cove, and

Oconaluftee, North Carolina, inside the park. Sugarlands is the main visitors center, located just inside the Gatlinburg entrance to the park; here there are large-scale models of the park, historic exhibits, and a bookstore. All of the visitors centers are open daily, with the exception of Christmas; refer to the Web site for precise operating hours for the centers. There's no entrance fee for the park.

GETTING THERE *By air:* **McGhee-Tyson Airport** (TYS; 865-342-3000; tys.org), 2055 Alcoa Highway, Knoxville. The airport is about 45 miles west of the Gatlinburg entrance to the park.

By car: To get to the park from points west, take I-40 east toward Knoxville, then US 129 south to Maryville. From there take US 321 to Townsend and the Townsend entrance to the park. Note that the Gatlinburg entrance to the park, directly south of Knoxville, is the most congested and yet is a better route if staying in Gatlinburg or Pigeon Forge.

By trolley: There is no public transportation to the national park from major cities in the area; however, Gatlinburg offers trolley service from Gatlinburg to the Sugarlands Visitor Center and Elkmont during summer and fall. Check the trolley Web site (ci.gatlinburg.tn.us/transit/trolley .htm) for schedules and rates.

FROM ANY ANGLE AND IN ANY WEATHER, THERE ARE STUNNING VISTAS IN THE PARK.

GETTING AROUND *By car:* A car is essential to exploring the park, even if time is limited. Tennessee entrances to the park include Gatlinburg (US 441) Townsend (TN 73), Greenbrier (County Route 416), and Chilhowee (Foothills Parkway). There are only a few major roads in the park itself—Laurel Creek, Little River and Newfound Gap, Rich Mountain Road, and the Roaring Fork Motor Nature Trail. Plan extra drive time if visiting during peak periods, including summer, holiday weekends, and the fall foliage season (mid-September–October).

Note that some roads are inaccessible in winter; be sure to check in with the rangers at one of the visitors centers before setting out.

MEDICAL EMERGENCY If you're in an emergency situation while in the park, 911 isn't the call to make. Instead, keep the Sugarlands ranger station number (865-436-9171) or the Gatlinburg Police number (865-436-5181) in your cell phone. Be sure to know which road or trail you are on, and to look for mile markers or signage to direct emergency personnel. Additionally, carrying a complete first-aid kit is essential for anyone hiking in the park.

✳ To See

PARK HIGHLIGHTS Appalachian Trail/Newfound Gap. At 5,048 feet, Newfound Gap is the lowest pass over the mountains. The real highlight of driving up to Newfound Gap isn't necessarily the stunning views, however; it's the chance to stand with one foot in each state on the well-

marked Tennessee–North Carolina border. There's a trailhead for the
Appalachian Trail off to the side of the restroom buildings.

Cades Cove. The historic settlement inside the park seems worlds away
from the mountains, which almost disappear in the flat valley that was
once farmed extensively. The first homesteaders came here as early as
1820, and life was anything but easy, as they had to clear areas for homes
and fields, and work together with neighbors—about seven hundred folks
at the height of the population—to build a gristmill, church, and other
community buildings in the remote village. In the 1930s, the federal government offered the homesteaders a buyout, and most took the deal; others signed a smaller buyout that allowed them to stay in their homes
inside the new park until they died. A variety of historic buildings still
exist here: three churches, a cantilever barn, and the Cable Mill gristmill.
While driving the 11-mile loop can be a very long and slow process, a
hayride is a treat for those who want to enjoy the ride in an even more
leisurely fashion.

Clingman's Dome. The highest peak in the park, Clingman's Dome
(6,643 feet) features an observation tower at its apex, enticing hikers with
just a few more steps for a stunning, above-the-canopy view. Oftentimes,
that view is muted by haze or clouds, but on clear days, it seems as if one
can see forever, as even Knoxville is visible from the top. Hikers making
their way for Clingman's will want to check the weather before setting
out; it is often cooler and even more wet than the base, and on rainy days,
the view is of rainclouds, not a lush mountain landscape.

Elkmont. Once a logging town, Elkmont is home to the park's largest
campground and one incredible phenomenon: synchronous fireflies,
which gather here every June and put on an amazing, two-week engagement of perfectly synchronized flashing. Although it is an annual light
show, it is also an extremely rare one, taking place at only a few select
spots around the world. The Elkmont Road is closed off during the firefly
show to limit the amount of light pollution, as well as protect the fireflies.
The park service offers shuttles from select visitors centers to ferry folks
to the light show.

Metcalf Bottoms. A scenic picnic and swimming area, Metcalf also
offers an easy, mile-long round-trip hike to the Little Greenbrier School,
a 1800s log schoolhouse with its original furniture still preserved.

✳ To Do

HIKING Hiking in the Smokies doesn't have to be intimidating, as hikes
can be an hour long, a full day, or an overnight adventure. But even for
short hikes, a trail map, available at any of the visitors centers, is a must.
There are 850 miles of trails in the park, so choosing the right hike can be

a challenge. A quick chat with a ranger can help, as will knowing your limits.

For those of almost any ability or age, there's a hike or short walk to match interest or enthusiasm; the stunning views, hidden streams and waterfalls, historic structures, and pervasive quiet are just lagniappe for those who want to go home and be able to proclaim they really did hike the Smokies.

Quiet Walkways and Easy Hikes

The easiest and least-challenging way to experience the park is on one of the "quiet walkways," marked only with a sign and small parking lot, and not on any trail map.

Scattered throughout the park, the walkways are gentle pathways into the forest, often ending at a stream. Most of the walks are about a mile round-trip, and none require great physical strength or endurance. Some of these trails are even paved, providing sure footing for families with children in strollers or for those in wheelchairs or with walkers.

A number of the quiet walks are located just off the Little River Road, Laurel Creek Road, and the lower portion of the Newfound Gap Road.

The **Laurel Falls** trail is one of the park's most popular. The park is also full of easy hikes that end at a piece of history instead of a spectacular view; **Metcalf Bottoms, Little Greenbrier,** and **Old Sugarlands** all offer a chance to walk through a historical area or to a historic building.

Longer Hikes

There's plenty of great scenery at the end of moderate and easy longer hikes. Perhaps the most photographed waterfall is **Abrams Falls,** accessible from the Cades Cove area and a moderate 5-mile round-trip journey. Other hikes from Cades Cove range from easy to strenuous. Two 8-mile loops lure the serious hikers, while the more moderate **Anthony Creek** trail—home to the famed Rocky Top and one of the best vistas—follows the creek to its headwaters.

Challenging Hikes

Popular hikes for those wanting a real challenge include **Chimney Tops,** where the prize at the end of a strenuous 2-mile (one-way) hike is the two towering rock spires and the 360-degree view. An 8-mile round-trip, starting at the Greenbrier area, takes adventurous hikers (read: dedicated and in shape) to the **Ramsey Cascades,** a stunning, 100-foot-high waterfall.

And then there's the mother of all hikes: **Alum Cave Bluff and Mount LeConte.** The 10-mile round-trip hike to Mount LeConte—and the LeConte Lodge—is strenuous and best for the most seasoned of hikers. While the distance from the trailhead to Alum Bluffs (2.3 miles) and from Alum Cave to the top of LeConte (2.7 miles) seem like no distance at all, both sections of the trail are truly a challenge.

VIEW OF THE GREEN RIVER

WATERFALL ON THE ROUTE TO NEWFOUND GAP

SPECIAL PROGRAMS Throughout the year and dependent on the season, the park's rangers lead talks, hikes, and even hayrides to bring visitors closer to nature. On any given day one might partake in a discussion about the 30 species of salamanders that call the park home, or explore Cades Cove during a moonlight hike. Check with the visitors center upon arrival at the park, or on the Web site prior to arrival, to see what ranger-led programs are being offered.

The Great Smoky Mountains Institute at Tremont (865-448-6709; gsmit.org), 9275 Tremont Road, Townsend (inside the park). Tremont offers a variety of programs and classes throughout the year, from summer camps to guided hikes, workshops, and camping trips led by naturalists. Day hikes start at $20 per person, with full-blown backpacking trips going up to a few hundred dollars per person.

The Smoky Mountain Field School (865-974-0150; ce.utk.edu/Smoky /welcome.html). An outreach of the University of Tennessee–Knoxville, the field school offers hikes and adventures for all ages, most with particular themes. In the spring, there are wildflower and waterfall hikes; fall might bring a hike exploring the park's poisonous fungi and spooky historic buildings. Other programs teach compass skills and nature photography. Program rates vary, starting at $49 per person.

✳ Lodging

INSIDE THE PARK

Camping

There are 10 campgrounds in the park, with five on the Tennessee side, for tent, pop-up trailer, and RV camping; some campgrounds are first come, first serve year-round, while others—Elkmont, Smokemont, Cades Cove, and Cosby—must be reserved in advance May 15–October 31.

Each campsite has a fire grate and picnic table, while each campground includes restrooms with cold running water and flush toilets, but there are no showers or electrical or water hookups in the park. Shower facilities are available outside the park; check with the ranger upon campsite check-in to find the nearest location.

The campgrounds range from 12 sites to more than 200, with Big Creek being the smallest (12) and Elkmont the largest (220).

For rates and reservations, call 877-444-6777 or log onto recreation.gov. Campsite reservations can be made through the National Park System for those campgrounds that require them. Rates range from $14/night for most campgrounds and up to $23/night for sites at Elkmont.

Backcountry campers are required to register with the park service and pick up a free backcountry camping permit at one of the park's visitors centers. There are

PRICE CATEGORIES:

Inexpensive	Less than $100 (for hotels, inns, and B&Bs); less than $50 (for campgrounds, state park facilities)
Moderate	$100–200
Expensive	$201–300
Very expensive	More than $300

A NATIONAL PARK MUST-DO: STRADDLING THE STATE LINE ON TOP OF OLD SMOKY

strict rules for the use of back-country sites, and it is recommended that you plan your route in advance, taking into consideration your abilities and pack weight.

There are 17 backcountry camp-sites, plus additional shelters along the Appalachian Trail; all require advance reservations through the backcountry camping office (865-436-1231), which is open daily 8–6.

Lodges

Le Conte Lodge (865-429-5704; leconte-lodge.com), Mount LeConte. You'll note there is no address for LeConte Lodge; that's because the only way to get there is by foot, via one of several hikes up Mount LeConte. Despite its remote location, reservations must be made in advance at the lodge, which features a variety of accommodations in one-bedroom,

rough-hewn cabins or a few multibedroom lodges. Yes, there are linens on the beds and much-needed wool blankets; other amenities include a wash basin and bucket for sponge baths (bring your own towels), kerosene lanterns for light, and covered porches with rocking chairs. And there are bathrooms, but not in each lodging. There are no televisions, telephones, or wireless Internet—and if you can't live without those, then LeConte isn't for you. Provisions arrive via llama; breakfast and dinner are included in the rate, plus lunch if you're staying more than one night. The food is basic—grits, eggs, and Canadian bacon for breakfast; some kind of beef, vegetables, and mashed potatoes for dinner. If you'd like wine with your dinner, there's a $9 additional charge. Moderate.

OUTSIDE THE PARK See "Gatlinburg," "Pigeon Forge," and "Sevierville" for additional lodging options north of the park, including hotels and cabin rentals.

Cabins

🖉 **Dancing Bear Lodge** (800-369-0111; dancingbearlodge.com), 137 Apple Valley Way, Townsend. Just outside the Townsend entrance to the park, Dancing Bear is a chic yet rustic retreat that's ideal for families and couples who want to be in nature but not camp in nature. Log cabins are outfitted with every possible amenity, and there are hike and bike trails, fly-fishing on the Little River, and nature walks right on property. A full-service restaurant

HISTORIC GRISTMILL IN CADES COVE

GREAT SMOKY MOUNTAINS NATIONAL PARK THREE-DAY ITINERARY

Day 1

Get a move on early, especially on weekends and holidays. Stop by one of the park's visitors centers to get a lay of the land, chat with rangers about special events or appropriate hikes, and pick up a trail map. If the traffic is light, head over to the Cades Cove area and choose a hike based on your interests and abilities, then head out of the park toward Townsend for lunch at one of the charming cafés. Pick up a fishing pole and head back into the park to try your luck angling, or simply grab a book and some folding chairs, find a pullout with a nice view, head down to the river, and enjoy the afternoon.

Day 2

Again, start early—but this time, bring your lunch for a full day in the park. Take your time driving up the Newfound Gap Road to Newfound Gap, and take the obligatory photo of your party straddling the state line. There are plenty of photo opportunities at Newfound Gap. Then, head out on a moderate hike on the Appalachian Trail. Be warned, however, that there are few mileage markers, so decide on a length of time as opposed to a set mileage for the hike. Following the hike, head back down the mountain, taking a left on Little River Road. Stop for a late lunch at Metcalf Bottoms, and be sure to wander out of the picnic area to see the historic buildings.

JUST OFF THE NEWFOUND GAP PARKING LOT, THE APPALACHIAN TRAIL LURES HIKERS.

CASTING A LINE IN THE GREEN RIVER

Jim Dyer

Day 3

Start the morning by perusing the gift shop at the Great Smoky Mountains
Institute at Tremont, located along the middle prong of the Little River,
between Cades Cove and the Townsend entrance. Hike one of the trails
from the institute. If you bring a lunch, find a good picnic spot along the
Little River Road, then take off on one of the quiet walkways nearby.
Finally, be an auto tourist and drive the Roaring Fork Motor Nature Trail,
located a few miles past the Sugarlands entrance to the park.

and bar is also on the property, and many of the cabins also include a full kitchen. Moderate–expensive.

Hotels

Blackberry Farm (800-648 4252; blackberryfarm.com), 1471 W. Millers Cove Road, Walland. The lush farm retreat is hidden away a few miles from the Townsend entrance and offers a top-notch, service-oriented escape that few want to leave in order to rough it in the park. There are just 62 rooms, suites, and cottages, all kitted out with the finest furnishings, linens, and antiques. Children are welcome at the farm only during certain times of the year, including the Fourth of July and Thanksgiving; other times, it's adults only. A full-service spa, fishing guides, cooking classes, and arts experiences all await guests at the farm, as does the chance to try sporting clays and trail riding, or to simply enjoy the childlike pleasure of lawn games. Very expensive.

Middle Tennessee: The Heart of Tennessee

2

NASHVILLE AND
SURROUNDING AREA

UPPER CUMBERLAND

NASHVILLE AND
SURROUNDING AREA

NASHVILLE

Yes, it is Music City—but Nashville is so much more than country croon-
ers and record companies. It's a cosmopolitan, progressive destination
that honors both its Southern heritage and its country roots while
embracing the finest in the performing and visual arts, dining, and
lifestyle.

Nashville's history is a rich one, from the time it was inhabited by Mississippian tribes more than a thousand years ago through the later Native
Americans—the Cherokee, the Shawnee, and Chickasaw. Fort Nashbor-
ough was the first permanent European settlement in the region, built on
the Cumberland River in 1779; a replica of the frontier outpost was built
in its place in Riverfront Park, where Broadway meets the river.

In 1796, Tennessee became the 16th state in the Union, with Nashville
chosen as its capital in 1843. While the city was first held by the Confederates during the Civil War, Federal troops occupied the city in 1862 and
held it through the end of the war. Many believe the Federal occupation
is what helped preserve so many of the city's historic plantations and
buildings, including the state capitol, which served as a hospital during
the war. Reconstruction brought with it a renaissance for Nashville, as a
number of colleges and universities were built in quick succession,
including Vanderbilt University and Fisk University, the historically
African American school that's home to the famous Jubilee Singers. The
breadth of academia—more than a dozen institutions of higher education
—coupled with a multitude of cultural offerings helped Nashville become
the Athens of the South; note that the moniker is a self-proclaimed one,
but it stuck nonetheless. Country music first gained wide recognition in
Nashville when a radio station owned by the National Life and Accident
Insurance Company (call letters WSM—for We Shield Millions) began
broadcasting the *WSM Barn Dance* in 1925. The program took off and is

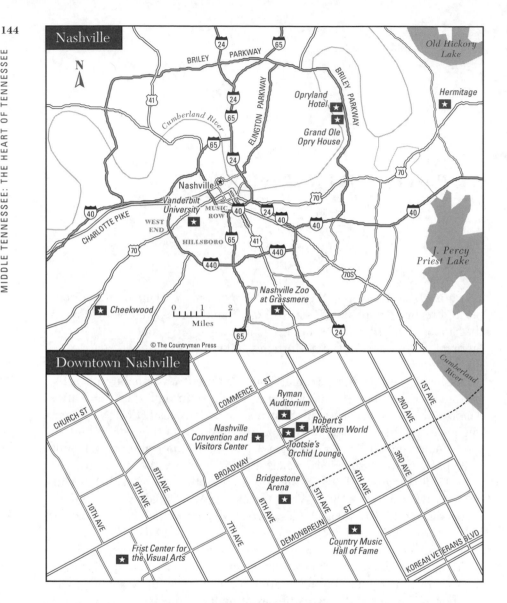

now the longest running country radio program in the country, better known as the *Grand Ole Opry.*

The Nashville lunch counter sit-ins of the early 1960s were among the first of the wave of nonviolent protests for civil rights; the city soon became a magnet for the health care, communications, and insurance industries, as well as manufacturing. In the mid-1990s, Nashville scored two professional sports franchises, the Tennessee Titans of the National Football League and the Nashville Predators of the National Hockey League. The turn of the 21st century brought with it a range of cultural offerings, including the

Country Music Hall of Fame and Museum, the Frist Center for the Visual Arts, and the European-style Schermerhorn Symphony Center concert hall.

Nashville is a neighborhood-centric city; there are many distinctive communities, each with its own flavor and vibe:

The District. Lower Broadway dead-ends at the Cumberland River, forming a T of downtown Nashville's historical district. The old brick warehouses along Second Avenue that once stored cotton and grain for riverboat trading have been converted into restaurants, sports bars, nightclubs, and performance halls, and the honky-tonks of Lower Broadway are doing a booming business, especially after a hockey game or concert. This area was particularly hard hit during the devastating flooding of the Cumberland River in May 2010, but the businesses here quickly restored and repaired themselves. During the summer months you sometimes find

THE LANDMARK BATMAN BUILDING

a concert happening by the river, and the big Fan Fair country music festival happens there in early June.

Hillsboro Village. The totally charming and walkable neighborhood close to Vanderbilt University, Music Row, and Belmont University, Hillsboro Village is more of a collection of cool stores and restaurants than a neighborhood. It's home to the Belcourt, the city's last independent movie theater; Fido coffee shop, a brewpub; several specialty shops; and some of the city's longtime eateries, including Pancake Pantry and the Sunset Grill, as well as newer yet instant favorites like Cabana. Hillsboro Village is a two-block stretch of 21st Avenue, south of Blakemore Avenue.

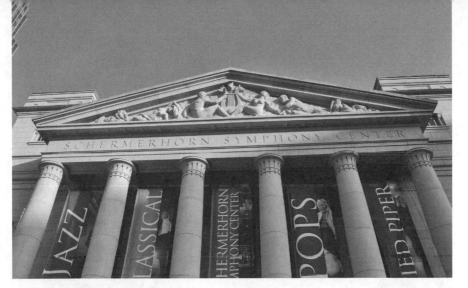

SCHERMERHORN SYMPHONY HALL

The Gulch. Just south of Broadway and near downtown, the Gulch was once a wasteland of old warehouses and empty lots but has become home to the city's most innovative restaurants, its most happening nightspots, and one of the best music performance halls, the Station Inn.

12South. The mishmash of businesses that is 12South, an area of 12th Avenue, south just past Music Row and Belmont University, somehow just works—its funkiness is indeed its success. Within just a few short blocks, one can indulge in a creamy homemade Popsicle, discover vintage country-music-star threads, go on a flight—the wine kind—and find that perfect piece of contemporary decor.

East Nashville. This historic residential area is really a number of individual neighborhoods, including Edgefield and Lockland Springs, joined together by the bustling district known as Five Points, a hot spot for restaurants, bars, and galleries that's adding new tenants seemingly daily. The Tolar House Bakery, Edgefield Sports Bar, Rosepepper Cantina, and the Radio Café are just a few of the diverse offerings; pair these eateries with an old-timey hardware store, a gallery called Garage Mahal, and dozens of other small businesses, and you've got a real feel for the funkier side of Nashville.

From the Mother Church of country music—the Ryman Auditorium—to Andrew Jackson's ancestral home, the Hermitage, to the European-style Schermerhorn symphony hall adjacent to the Country Music Hall of Fame, Nashville is a genuine world-class city packed with cultural offerings, beautifully wrapped in the comforting arms of authentic Southern charm and friendliness.

GUIDANCE Nashville Convention and Visitors Bureau (800-657-6910; visitmusiccity.com), Fifth Avenue S. and Broadway, inside the Bridgestone Arena. Open Mon.–Sat. 8–5:30 and Sun. 10–5. The Nashville

GRAVES OF ANDREW AND RACHEL JACKSON, THE HERMITAGE

Convention and Visitors Bureau is truly one of the best-run tourism operations anywhere in the country, with top-notch navigability on its Web site, friendly and very well-informed folks who can help in trip planning, and excellent services at its downtown visitors center, where live music is often on the menu.

GETTING THERE *By air:* **Nashville International Airport** (BNA; 615-275-1675; flynashville.com), 1 Terminal Drive, Nashville. All major airlines fly into the Nashville airport, just off I-40, about a 30-minute drive from downtown and 15 minutes to the Music Valley/Opryland area. BNA is going through a multiyear, multiproject renovation.

By bus: **Greyhound** (615-255-3556; greyhound.com). Greyhound provides service to Nashville from select cities; a temporary bus terminal is now being used, so be sure to call or visit the Web site for the most up-to-date information.

By car: Nashville is centrally located in the heart of Middle Tennessee, with access from the north and south via I-65 and access from the east and west via I-40. There are two loops around the city center (I-265 and I-440), with the Briley Parkway and Old Hickory Boulevard casting wider loops farther outside the city. There are many parking lots and garages in the downtown area, and, frankly, for the downtown attractions you should just park for the day in a central location and walk. There are a number of good lots near the Schermerhorn Symphony Center and the Country Music Hall of Fame and Museum, both surface lots and parking garages.

GETTING AROUND *By car:* Nashville is a very easy town to navigate by car, and parking is readily available—but in areas like the West End, Vanderbilt, and on Music Row, be sure to double-check parking signs if you park in the street.

A car-sharing service, **WeCar** (615-743-3090; parkitdowntown.com/getting _around/WeCar), is available for on-the-spot rentals, with pickup and drop-off sites throughout downtown Nashville.

By taxi: Taxis are available at the airport and throughout downtown Nashville. A trip downtown, to the West End, or to Opryland costs about $30 from the airport.

MEDICAL EMERGENCY Vanderbilt University Medical Center (615-322-5000; vanderbiltemergency.com), 1211 Medical Center Drive. The teaching hospital of Vanderbilt University is one of the state's premier hospitals, with both a pediatric emergency center at the nearby Children's Hospital (615-936-1000; 2200 Children's Way) and a level-one trauma center for adults at the main hospital.

✳ To See

HISTORIC SITES Belle Meade Plantation (615-356-0501; bellemeade plantation.com), 5025 Harding Road. Open Mon.–Sat. 9–5, Sun. 11–5. The Queen of Tennessee Plantations has a history as rich as any royalty; the plantation was spared from the wrath of the Union army in the Civil War and once reigned over more than 5,000 acres that were devoted to farming and breeding thoroughbreds, most notably Iroquois, the first American thoroughbred to win the Epsom Derby. Now just 30 acres, the mansion and many of the original buildings are well preserved and give a true glimpse into plantation life. The plantation boasts a store well stocked with gifts and decor, with a heavy emphasis on equestrian-themed items, and the excellent Martha's serves up hearty Southern fare. Adults $16, children 13–18 $10, children 6–12 $8, children five and under free.

The Hermitage (615-889-2941; thehermitage.com), 4580 Rachel's Lane. Open daily 8:30–5, Apr. 1–Oct. 15; daily 9–4:30, Oct. 16–Mar. 31. Closed Thanksgiving, Christmas, and the third week in Jan. The ancestral home of President Andrew Jackson is a treat for a variety of reasons; the plantation contains many of its original features and furnishings, including intricately detailed wallpaper, and the love story that took place here—that of the general and his wife, Rachel—brings a dose of romance to this well-preserved home. The Greek Revival house and its formal gardens are the highlights, and there's a museum with many excellent exhibits about Jackson, his slaves, and his presidency, but it's the stories of those relationships—master and slave, husband and wife, president and citizens—that are the secret treasure of the Hermitage.

MUSEUMS ✍ **Adventure Science Center** (615-862-5160; adventuresci .com), 800 Fort Negley Boulevard. Open Mon.–Sat. 10–5, Sun. 12:30–5:30. Children adore this hands-on museum, especially the seven-level Adventure Tower and the Sudekum Planetarium and Space Chase Gallery, where kids can walk on a moonlike surface, feel what it's like to be weightless, and see in-depth, digital astronomy shows. Adults $14, kids 2–12 $9, children under two free. Additional fees for admission to planetarium, laser show, and BlueMax cinema.

Carl Van Vechten Gallery at Fisk University (615-329-8720; fisk .edu), Jackson Street at D. B. Todd Boulevard (18th Avenue N.). Open Tues.–Sat. 10–5; closed on university holidays. Perhaps the state's best art collection as well as the state's best kept cultural secret, the gallery's main floor features more than one hundred pieces from the collection of Alfred Stieglitz, the man who brought the modern art movement to America. Donated by his wife, Georgia O'Keeffe, to the university, the collection includes works by Picasso, Renoir, Toulouse-Lautrec, and Cezanne. The university's **Aaron Douglas Gallery** in the university library is devoted to African American artists, and it's one of the best in the country. Also of note is **Jubilee Hall,** built in 1875. It was the first permanent building erected for African American higher education in the United States. Free, but donations are appreciated.

Cheekwood Botanic Garden & Museum of Art (615-356-8000; cheekwood.org), 1200 Forrest Park Drive. Open Tues.–Sat. 9:30–4:30, Sun. 11–4:30. Closed Mon., with exception of Memorial Day and Labor Day. Nashville's Cheek family made their money in coffee that's good to the last drop and spent much of it on the grounds and mansion that comprise Cheekwood. The 55-acre grounds include several distinct gardens and a sculpture trail, while the mansion boasts an impressive collection of American furnishings and artwork. The picturesque Pineapple Room restaurant is a favorite for ladies who lunch and also offers box lunches to go for alfresco dining among the gardens—don't forget a blanket. Adults $10, students with ID and seniors $5, children under five free.

Country Music Hall of Fame & Museum (800-852-6437; country musichalloffame.com), 222 Fifth Avenue S. Open daily 9–5; closed Tues. in Jan. and Feb. Even those who aren't fans of country music will be dazzled by the impressive hall of fame and museum; the exhibits in the piano-shaped building trace country music from its roots in Europe to its defining in the rural South and finally to the megadollar, megahit music industry it has become. Stage costumes, personal memorabilia, and instruments from the genre's top stars are featured, with special exhibit space for hall of fame members. The extensive archives and library are able to be viewed through giant glass walls. Prices start at $19.99 for adults and $11.95 for children; choose a package with audio tour and

FISK UNIVERSITY'S JUBILEE HALL

BLUE ROOM

GOLD RECORDS AT THE COUNTRY MUSIC HALL OF FAME

Studio B admission for $29.95 for adults and $21.95 for children. Kids under five free.

Frist Center for the Visual Arts (615-244-3340; fristcenter.org), 919 Broadway. The gorgeous art deco post office is the stunning backdrop for the Frist, which has no collection of its own; rather, the city's main art museum exhibits masterpieces loaned from the world's major museums. If at all possible, sign up in advance for a tour from one of the museum's docents; they're a lively and entertaining bunch with the ability to generate contagious enthusiasm for whatever exhibition they're showcasing. Adults $15, children 18 and under free; there's free admission for college students with IDs on Thurs. and Fri.

The Parthenon (615-862-8431; parthenon.org), West End and 25th avenues, in Centennial Park. Open Tues.–Sat. 9–4:30, and Sun. 12:30–4:30 in June, July, and Aug. The world's only full-scale replica of the Greek temple, Nashville's version was originally constructed as a temporary plaster exhibit for Tennessee's Centennial Exposition in 1897 and then was rebuilt with more permanent materials in 1931. A 42-foot, gold-leaf statue of Athena matches the original in Athens; the interior also houses exhibits about the history of the structure, as well as a gallery with rotating shows and permanent artwork by such American masters as Winslow Homer. Adults $6, children and seniors $4, children under four free.

✱ To Do

AQUARIUMS AND ZOOS 🐾 **Nashville Zoo at Grassmere** (615-833-1534; nashvillezoo.org), 3777 Nolensville Pike. Open daily 9–6, Mar. 15–Oct. 14; daily 9–4, Oct. 15–Mar. 14. The zoo, just a few decades old, has come a long way in its short life, transforming from petting zoo to full-blown fabulous and offering a meandering exploration of the unusual and the exotic. An excellent interactive area called Critter Encounters lets kids (and yes, moms and dads) get up close with kangaroos and other animals, while the Gibbon Islands will amaze with its open-air views. There's also a historical farm area, daily keeper talks and animal encounters, and special seasonal events. Adults $14, children 2–12 $12, children under two free.

COUNTRY MUSIC HALL OF FAME

BIKING Hamilton Creek Mountain Bike Trails (615-862-8424; nashville.gov/parks/trails/trails-bike.asp). Call or visit the Web site for location and directions. Open daily dawn–dusk. This hilly park near the airport contains plenty of fun for mountain bikers of all levels, from flat cedar glades to trails cut through limestone. Free.

Shelby Street Pedestrian Bridge (615-862-8400; nashville.gov/green ways/projects), Shelby Street near the Schermerhorn Symphony Center. Open 24 hours. The historic bridge was built in the early 1900s for motor vehicle traffic but is now used as pedestrian bridge connecting downtown to East Nashville's neighborhoods. It was the first bridge in North America to have concrete arched trusses and now features a wide, elevated sidewalk; center bicycle lane; and scenic overlooks of the city and river, with sculptures along the way depicting river life. Free.

BOATING Cumberland River Cruises (615-451-4001; cumberlandriver cruises.com), 450 Cherokee Boat Dock Road, Lebanon. Cruise schedule varies by season; call for the most updated information. Departing from

THE PARTHENON REPLICA AT CENTENNIAL PARK

Old Hickory Lake, these Cumberland River cruises are appealing due to
the small number of folks on the cozy pontoon boats captained by friendly people; it's like having your neighbors invite you to their lake house for
a cruise. Tours include fall foliage and holiday fireworks cruises, as well as
a tour of the waterfront homes of stars. $25 per person.

Four Corners Marina (675-641-9523; fourcornersmarina.com), 4027
Lavergne Couchville Pike, Antioch. Hours vary seasonally; check the Web
site or call for most updated information. Situated on Percy Priest Lake
about 10 miles east of downtown, this longtime marina rents pontoon and
fishing boats, sells bait and fishing supplies, and operates a casual restaurant.

HIKING Radnor Lake State Natural Area (615-373-3467; tennessee
.gov/environment/parks/RadnorLake), 160 Otter Creek Road. Open daily
6 AM–dark. Radnor Lake is a 1,100-acre nature area with extensive hiking
trails located just 6 miles from downtown. It's a favorite for hiking, bird-
watching, or just enjoying the seasonal beauty of Middle Tennessee. Free.

Warner Parks (615-352-6299; nashville.gov/parks/wpnc), 7311 TN 100
(nature center). Parks open daily sunrise–11 PM. Together, the Percy
Warner and Edwin Warner Parks encompass 2,700 acres just 9 miles from
downtown. Although the parks can be accessed at several points, for hikers the best starting point is the Warner Park Nature Center. Not only is
it the trailhead for many trails, but you can also get maps and other information there. Free.

SPECTATOR SPORTS Nashville Predators (615-770-2355; predators
.nhl.com), 501 Broadway. The NHL's Predators were welcomed with the
slogan "hockey-tonk" and have moved from NHL newcomer to Stanley
Cup playoff regulars. The Preds take to the ice at the Bridgestone Arena
Oct.–mid-Apr.

Tennessee Titans (615-565-4200; titansonline.com), 116 First Avenue S.
The National Football League's Titans regularly play at LP Field, just
across the Cumberland River from downtown. Home games often sell
out. If possible, it's best to leave the car and use the Shelby Street pedestrian bridge to cross the river from downtown to the stadium on the east
bank.

✳ Green Space

PARKS ✎ 🐾 Centennial Park (615-862-8400; nashville.gov/parks
/locations/centennial), 2500 West End Avenue. Open daily dawn–dusk. A
fantastic green space in the middle of Nashville and adjacent to Vanderbilt University, Centennial Park includes the Parthenon, several duck
ponds, a train engine, playgrounds, and pretty gardens, plus plenty of

lawn space for spreading a blanket and enjoying a picnic. Spring and fall bring free outdoor craft festivals, and in the summer you can attend free performances by the Nashville Shakespeare Festival and the Nashville Symphony Orchestra, as well as free screenings of family-oriented films. There's also a mile-long walking trail and a dog park. Free.

Shelby Bottoms Greenway and Nature Park (nashville.gov/parks /nature/Shelby.asp), 1900 Davidson Street. Open Tues., Thurs., and Sat. 9–4; Wed. noon–4; Fri. noon–6; and Sun. 12:30–4:30. Just 3 miles from downtown along the Cumberland River in East Nashville, the 800-plus-acre Shelby Bottoms is a beautiful combination of bottomland hardwood forests, open fields, wetlands, and streams; note that if the river is high, then portions of the 12 miles of trails and areas of the park may be closed due to flooding. Naturalists offer nature walks and other programs. Free.

✳ Lodging

HOTELS Courtyard Nashville Downtown (615-256-0900; marriott.com/hotels/travel/bnadt -courtyard-nashville-downtown), 170 Fourth Avenue N. Deals can be had at this hotel, renovated in 2009, a hidden gem that's just a few blocks off Broadway and Second Avenue. Unlike other hotels from the same chain, this Nashville rendition offers much more in the way of style and ambience; a small breakfast room features cooked-to-order meals, and there's a small lounge as well. Free Internet access in guest rooms. Moderate–expensive.

🐾 **The Hermitage Hotel** (615-345-7116; thehermitagehotel .com), 231 Sixth Avenue N. The historic Hermitage, now one hundred years old, is the grande dame of Nashville—and Tennessee— hotels. The luxury is over the top; even the standard guest rooms offer the highest level of comfort and sophistication, offering rich, traditional furnishings paired with

PRICE CATEGORIES:	
Inexpensive	Less than $100 (for hotels, inns, and B&Bs); less than $50 (for camp-grounds, state park facilities)
Moderate	$100–200
Expensive	$201–300
Very expensive	More than $300

all the modern conveniences: marble baths with soaking tubs, glass-walled showers, and modern technology. On-site is one of the city's toniest restaurants, the Capitol Grille, an indulgence that's worth every penny. Pets are very welcome at the Hermitage; in fact, this may be the hotel that started the trend of bringing your pet to a hotel way back in the day, when Roy Rogers brought Trigger here. (And yes, Trigger did indeed stay in a guest room, although the furniture was removed and hay put down to make him more comfort-

TENNESSEE TITANS

Donn Jones

able.) Today, the hotel offers special pet bedding, a dog-walking service, and even an in-room dining option for pets. A $50 nonrefundable pet deposit is charged. Very expensive.

☙ **The Hutton** (615-340-9333; huttonhotel.com), 1808 West End. Taking a basic box of an office building in a fantastic central location and turning it into a hotel isn't exactly a leap, but turning that building into a thoroughly energy efficient, ecofriendly hotel is indeed unusual—and that's the Hutton. The green bells and whistles include EcoDisc elevators (which use hybrid power to transport guests), bamboo furniture and flooring, LED and fluorescent lighting throughout the hotel, dual-flush commodes, and card-key lighting systems in guest rooms that ensure lights are turned off when guests leave. In the Hutton's case, green doesn't mean lean; there's beautifully sleek decor, lushly appointed rooms, and an excellent location—just across from Vanderbilt University, a few blocks from West End shopping and dining, and a bit longer stroll to the sights on Broadway. Expensive.

Maxwell House Hotel (615-259-4343; maxwellhousehotel.com), 2025 Rosa L. Parks Boulevard. Just a few minutes from downtown, the Maxwell House is where President Teddy Roosevelt declared its coffee "good to the last drop," creating a loyal following of not just caffeine addicts but other travelers who want to be a bit off Nashville's beaten path, yet surrounded in luxury. Loads of music memorabilia, lush decor, and beautiful views of the downtown skyline highlight the 287-room hotel, which also offers a fitness center, complimentary parking, and shuttle service to the Broadway music scene. Expensive.

Nashville Marriott at Vanderbilt University (615-321-1300; marriott.com/hotels/travel/bnaav-nashville-marriott-at-vanderbilt-university), 2555 West End Avenue. The location of this Marriott is its main selling point, as it overlooks Centennial Park out the front windows and has an unlikely but fabulous view of the Vander-

bilt football stadium out the back. As one might guess, rooms are hard to come by on Commodore home game weekends, but any other time, this is a perfectly located hotel that offers three hundred well-appointed rooms, wireless Internet connectivity throughout the hotel, a swimming pool and fitness center, a lobby Starbucks, and easy (and inexpensive) in-and-out parking. Moderate–expensive.

Opryland Resort & Conference Center (615-889-1000; gaylordhotels.com/gaylordopryland), 2800 Opryland Drive. Under the glass domes of this city-sized hotel, you'll find almost three thousand hotel rooms and three immense, perfectly manicured garden areas. The Conservatory houses tropical plants, the Cascades boasts multiple waterfalls, and the Delta features an indoor river with guests touring via boats. At Christmas, the hotel has a stunning indoor light display with more than a million twinkling lights, whimsical decor, and an almost over-the-top holiday atmosphere that alone is worth a trip. An excellent, full-service spa; indoor and outdoor pools; and a fitness center are also on-site, although after walking to said fitness center from your room, you may not need to work out after all. Expensive.

Wyndham Union Station (615-726-1001; wyndhamunionstation.com), 1001 Broadway. There's just something utterly charming about the historic train-station-turned-hotel, from the gorgeously restored lobby and the ticket counter that's now the front desk to the sometimes small bathrooms that one doesn't mind so much because they ooze vintage chic. Yes, the corridors are narrow and the elevators painstakingly slow, but the elegant ambience overrides any small inconveniences. The hotel boasts some of downtown Nashville's most reasonable rates, even in the busiest weeks, and I can only account for that by the fact some folks haven't figured out the castlelike former station is actually a hotel. Adjacent to the Frist, the Wyndham offers a cozy bar, a fine restaurant, and a walking-distance location to all the downtown and District clubs and sights. Be sure to ask for one of the rooms overlooking the cavernous lobby with the beautiful wood-framed, arched windows— they're a treat. Moderate– expensive.

✳ Where to Eat

DINING OUT Capitol Grille (615-345-7116; thehermitagehotel .com), 231 Sixth Avenue N. Open daily for breakfast, lunch, and dinner; lunch and dinner reservations recommended. One of those rare eateries that earns top marks in every category, from its seen-and-be-seen clientele to the lush furnishings to the exquisite fare, Capitol Grille (no relation to the

OPRYLAND

DOCENT MANCIL EZELL LEADS A TOUR AT THE FRIST.

chain of steakhouses by the same name) is on the lower level of the century-old Hermitage Hotel. The biggest surprises here come in the form of its side dishes and starters, whether it's the sweet onion bisque or the to-die-for macaroni and cheese. Be sure to take a peek into the men's room adjacent to the restaurant; it's green and black tiled magnificence has been used for music videos, photo shoots, and more. (Ladies, be sure to knock first.) Very expensive.

The Standard at the Smith House (615-254-1277; thestandard nashville.com), 167 Eighth Avenue N. (Rosa Parks Boulevard). Open for dinner Tues.–Sat. Housed in the last remaining 1840s town house in downtown Nashville, the Standard offers an elegant ambience as rich as its signature Tennessee crab bisque. Southern cooking is the highlight here, but don't let that fool you into thinking that means hearty yet plain food. Entrées like seared duck breast with creamy grits, cured pork tenderloin wrapped in bacon (what's not to love about that kind of redundancy?), and lush desserts elevate Southern fare to a must-eat indulgence. A completely different menu for the club-ish lounge offers small plates of com-

PRICE CATEGORIES:	
Inexpensive	Less than $16
Moderate	$16–30
Expensive	$31–50
Very expensive	More than $50

fort food like meatball sliders and sweet potato fries. Reservations required for the dining room, but not the lounge. Very expensive.

Watermark (615-254-2000; water mark-restaurant.com), 507 12th Avenue S. Open Mon.–Sat. for dinner. An eatery with a dash of Southern influence, Watermark prides itself on being skillful and simple in its preparation, with a focus on fresh local and regional ingredients—including the occasional wild boar served with grits, or a Tennessee beef strip with black truffle potatoes. (Foraged mushrooms are a specialty at Watermark.) There's nothing fussy or highbrow about the restaurant; the atmosphere is urban chic yet overwhelmingly elegant at the same time. Weather permitting, rooftop dining is the way to go, with the Nashville skyline the perfect accompaniment in the evenings. Reservations definitely recommended; parking can be tricky in the neighborhood, so be sure to take advantage of the complimentary valet parking. Very expensive.

EATING OUT Cabana (615-577-2262; cabananashville.com), 1910 Belcourt Avenue. Open Mon.–Sat. 4 PM–3 AM, Sun. 4 PM–midnight. Cabana has a bit of a split personality, but in this case, that's a good thing. Canoodling couples can cozy up in the cabana-like booth while social types can indulge in people-watching in the louder, more cavernous space at the back of the restaurant. Huge garage-door-style windows are often opened up, shifting the atmosphere even more. The food is a bit multiple personality as well, best described as Southern comfort food mixed with a dash of everything else, from grilled seafood to wild game. Must-eats include the buttermilk fried chicken—Grandma's got nothing on the folks in the kitchen at Cabana—and the late-night menu, when noshing and being noticed are the rule and smaller plates and more snacky type food are offered. Moderate.

Couva Calypso Café (615-256-3663; calypsocafe.com). With five locations in Nashville, this casual, Caribbean-themed restaurant specializes in rotisserie chicken, black beans, rice, and delicious mustard greens (Martinique Callaloo). A favorite is the Black Bean/Chicken Salad with their signature warm dressing that is a combination of BBQ sauce and salsa; a twist on the traditional Southern meat and-three plate is a bean-and-three—a choice of three sides with Cuban beans. Service is fast, prices are reasonable, and the servings are generous. Inexpensive.

❧ **Flyte** (615-255-6200; flyte nashville.com), 718 Division Street. Open for dinner Tues.–Sat. What's not to love about a place that thinks—nay, knows—that a glass of wine doesn't have to cost more than $10 to be yummy? That's Flyte—sharing the love on reasonably priced wines (the wine menu rotates constantly), a great selection of beers, and food that emphasizes local and/or organic farms. There are some real eye-openers on the menu, including halibut cheeks with house-made bacon (who knew halibut had cheeks? Not us!) and "flytes" of fancy—like a trio of pork portions, chocolate desserts, or salads. Moderate.

Frist Center Café (615-244-3974; fristcenter.org), 919 Broadway. Open Mon.–Wed. and Sat. 10–5:30, Thurs.–Fri. 10–9, and Sun. noon–5:30. I never *need* an excuse to visit the fabulous Frist Center for the Visual Arts, but if I did, the café serves nicely. Tucked into the back of the post-office-turned-museum, the Frist Center Café cooks up some of the city's best lunches, with grilled paninis (the steak/rosemary/horseradish combination is my fave), inventive salads, corn dogs and other kid-friendly foods, and perhaps best of all, a decadent dessert case. The café offers a daily dessert happy hour from 2 to 5 and serves a variety of beer and wine. Moderate.

Las Paletas (615-386-2101; wheresthesign.com), 2907 12th Avenue S. Open Tues.–Sat. noon–7. While it's not a restaurant, Las Paletas is worthy of a visit, especially in Nashville's warm-weather seasons. The Mexican-style fruit Popsicles are a creamy, delightful treat any time of year; for about $2.50 a pop, try flavors like watermelon, honeydew, cucumber, tamarind, or hibiscus. Flavors change daily, so you never know what's being served. The store itself is tiny, so grab your treat and wander through the shopping district or chill out at the nearby Sevier Park. Cash is king at Las Paletas—credit and debit cards are frozen out. Inexpensive.

Lucy Yogurt (615-712-6858; lucyyogurt.com), 4121 Hillsboro Cir. Open Mon.–Thu. noon–9, Fri.–Sat. noon–10, Sun. noon–8. Located a few blocks from Green Hills Mall, Lucy Yogurt serves yummy yogurt with a great selection of toppings. Both are self-serve and sold by weight; this is the part that gets folks in trouble, as they pile on the toppings. Lucy herself usually greets visitors; this little shop is kid-friendly and has easy parking right in front. Beyond fro yo, Lucy offers up sushi to go, a throwback to her former days at the popular Hillsboro neighborhood eatery Taste of Tokyo. Inexpensive.

Loveless Café (615-646-9700; lovelesscafe.com), 8400 Highway 100. Open daily 7 AM–9 PM. The rooms of the former motel on the outskirts of the city now offer art, gifts, and more, while the main café serves up family-style meals—plates filled to overflowing with biscuits, bacon, eggs, grits, pork chops, fried chicken—whatever you ordered, it just keeps coming. There's always a line, no matter the time, day, or weather, and the little stores help diners pass that time. A large barn in back plays home to concerts and the weekly Wednesday WSM

Radio show Music City Roots—a fun evening featuring up-and-coming performers. Moderate.

Pancake Pantry (615-383-9333; thepancakepantry.com), 1796 21st Avenue S. Open daily for breakfast and lunch. The debate (tourist trap or a must-eat?) continues over this Nashville institution, known for its huge stacks of golden pancakes and killer egg combo plates. Country-music-star sightings are common because folks like Keith Urban can come here and not be bothered—Nashvillians are only too happy to give their celebs space. There's almost always a line out the door, but if the line is just out the door, you should be seated within 15 minutes; if it's wrapped around the front, plan on a 45-minute wait.

There's usually hot coffee and cups on a cart outside to keep you warm while you wait. Inexpensive.

San Antonio Taco Company (615-327-4322; thesatco.com), 416 21st Avenue S. Open daily for lunch and dinner. Is it the best Mexican you'll ever eat? No. But it's definitely the best combination in town for casual, cheap dining; a great patio; and a laid-back atmosphere. Grab an order sheet, circle your ingredients (don't forget to write your name), and hand it to the cashier. The guys behind the counter will prepare your order as fast as you can pour a drink. This place is known for its bucket of beers and homemade queso, the latter of which is a must-order. Inexpensive.

THE INFAMOUS, ALWAYS-PRESENT LINE AT THE PANCAKE PANTRY

Sunset Grill (615-244-3121; sun setgrill.com), 2001 Belcourt Avenue. Open for lunch Tues.–Fri. and dinner nightly. There's a reason Sunset is one of Nashville's best-known and oldest restaurants—consistency, from the excellent food to the extensive wine list (filled with a selection of popular labels and a variety of small-production vintages) to the hands-on service of the servers. The range is American with a bit of everything, from seafood and pastas to vegetarian plates and oddities like feta-stuffed lamb meatballs. During the warmer months, the windows are thrown open in the main dining area, creating a festive bistro atmosphere. A hangout for music-industry types, to boot. Moderate.

✳ Entertainment

BARS AND NIGHTCLUBS Fuse (615-458-3873; fusenashville .com), 2800 Opryland Drive. Open nightly 8 PM–until. Surprisingly, the hippest, hottest dance club in Nashville isn't in the Gulch but out at Opryland Resort & Conference Center. The seductive decor and dim lighting of Fuse is sexy and fun, and regularly brings in the city's players—not just of the professional sports variety, although they're often here, too. The music varies from country to hip-hop to rock, and the food runs to funky tapas like salmon lollipops and Kobe beef sliders. A special vodka locker—said to be the first of its kind—ices down the liquor to the perfect temperature. Specialty drinks are mostly candy themed, with rock candy sticks and lollipops often used for stirrers.

Oak Bar (615-345-7116; the hermitagehotel.com), 231 Sixth Avenue N. Opens at 11:30 AM Mon.–Sat. and noon on Sun. Down under the marble floors and brilliance of the Hermitage Hotel lobby, the Oak Bar occupies a small space off the Capitol Grille, recalling the clubby, oak-paneled feeling of a posh men's club. Exceptional service, a star-studded clientele, and quiet conversation are the order of the night, with a limited but excellent menu that's nothing like pub grub. The bar offers an excellent list of wines by the glass, as well as small plates including duck meatballs, fried quail, and a fried green tomato and pimento cheese sandwich.

Wildhorse Saloon (615-902-8211; wildhorsesaloon.com), 120 Second Avenue N. Open Mon.–Thurs. 4:30–10 PM, Fri.–Sat. 11 AM–2 AM, and Sun. 11 AM–10 PM. This well-known country-music club with its 3,300-square-foot dance floor is *the* place in Nashville to scoot your boots. Free daily dance lessons. Cover varies depending on event, with tickets required for some shows. Check the Web site for the most updated information and pricing.

LIVE-MUSIC VENUES Nashville is Music City, and there are more than two hundred live music venues throughout town, so finding a good spot to listen to live music—country and otherwise—is always easy.

Bluebird Café (615-383-1461; bluebirdcafe.com), 4104 Hillsboro Road. Two shows nightly; check the Web site for the weekly schedule. Many a country music star—whether songwriter or singer—launched their careers at the Bluebird. Perhaps the best part of this casual, not-on-Broadway café is the fact that the jam sessions at the Bluebird are always a surprise, both in terms of the talent appearing and certainly in terms of the songwriters and their hits. Songwriters generally appear with others they've collaborated with, making the night feel like an impromptu concert in someone's living room. Don't even think about talking when a show is going on—you'll get shushed, and you'll likely get heckled if you leave early. Be sure to call ahead for reservations. If you don't get a spot, don't give up; stand to the right of the door about an hour before the doors open, and you may luck out with a seat after all. Cover charge is generally $7–20 for shows, but there's no cover on Sun. or for the open mic session on Mon.

Mercy Lounge (615-251-3020; mercylounge.com), 1 Cannery Row, off Eighth Avenue S. Open daily with live music from 9 PM. Country isn't the only music scene in Nashville, which has an abundance of rock clubs. The Mercy Lounge consistently offers the best setting and the best lineups, from local favorites to national midlevel touring acts. There's usually a good chance you'll catch somebody worth seeing. Between sets, grab a spot at one of the three pool tables or vintage pinball machines. Cover varies.

Robert's Western World (615-244-9552; robertswesternworld .com), 416 Broadway. Live music daily from 10 AM. Three doors down from Tootsie's, Robert's (often referred to simply as Three Doors Down among up-and-coming country artists) considers itself the home of traditional country music, and its house band, Brazi-

GUITAR PICK-SHAPED SIGNS HELP LOCATE LIVE MUSIC IN MUSIC CITY

billy, keeps that strain of vintage country alive almost daily. A wall full of cowboy boots serves both fashion and function—if you fancy a pair, they'll make you a deal. Free, unless there's a special event.

The Station Inn (615-255-3307; stationinn.com), 402 12th Avenue S. Open nightly from 7 PM, with music from 9. This has been the best place to hear traditional bluegrass music in Nashville for as long as anyone can remember. Arrive early to get a seat. Cover varies, but there's no cover on Sun. for open bluegrass jam sessions.

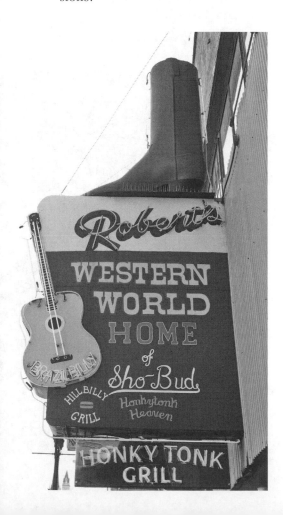

3rd and Lindsley (615-259-9891; 3rdandlindsley.com), 818 Third Avenue S. Open Mon.–Fri. from 11 AM for lunch, nightly for dinner. Shows start at 7 nightly. Perhaps the Music City's most progressive live music venue, 3rd and Lindsley offers multiple floors for dining and taking in up-and-coming artists, and is one of the host clubs for the annual Tin Pan South festival (see *Special Events*). Grill-type menu; admission is 18 and over, and the cover charge varies.

Tin Roof (615-313-7103; tinroof bars.com/Home/Nashville), 1516 Demonbreun Street. Open daily for lunch and dinner. Live music six nights a week, a prolonged happy hour, and a 20-something crowd are the hallmarks of the Tin Roof; grab a booth near the stage for the best view of the stage and the scene. Music ranges from country to rock to everything in between, and the casual atmosphere—from the plastic beer glasses to the simple bar food— adds up to an easy and comfortable way to indulge in Nashville's live music scene. Tickets for special events, otherwise no cover charge.

Tootsie's Orchid Lounge (615-726-0463; tootsies.net), 422 Broadway. Open daily from 10 AM. A lot of country-music history has taken place at Tootsie's, the quintessential honky-tonk if ever there was one. Thanks to its across-the-alley location from the Ryman Auditorium, Tootsie's was the go-

ROBERT'S WESTERN WORLD

to for country stars in need of a quick thirst quencher between their sets at the Grand Ole Opry. Music starts every morning at 10 inside the purple palace, with two separate stages in action in the evening. Knee-deep in grungy charm and full of friendly folks, it's a Nashville must-see. Free.

PERFORMING ARTS *Grand Ole Opry* (615-889-3060; opry.com), 2804 Opryland Drive. Shows Tues., Fri., and Sat. at 7:30 PM, with additional shows on select Sat. at 9:30 PM. The world's longest-running live radio show is a must-do, even if you're not a fan of country music. Sure, there's a bit of down-home kitsch, but the *Opry* is true Americana at its best. The cast is generally made up of names most folks aren't familiar with, like Little Jimmy Dickens, but plenty of Nashville's brightest stars—and certainly those on the

rise—have stood and continue to stand in the famed circle on the *Opry* stage, including Larry Gatlin, Brad Paisley, Loretta Lynn, Carrie Underwood, Garth Brooks, and Alison Krauss, many of whom perform often. In the wake of the devastating May 2010 flooding, the Opry House—located at the Opryland Complex about 10 miles from downtown Nashville—had been relocated to the city's Municipal Auditorium or the Ryman Auditorium. In October 2010 the Opry House reopened, with performances celebrating the restoration of the famed venue, as well as serving as the kickoff for the *Opry*'s 85th season. Tickets start at $42 for adults and $32 for children.

✳ Selective Shopping

ART GALLERIES The Arts Company (615-254-2040; thearts company.com), 215 Fifth Avenue.

Open Tues.–Sat. 10–5. Dedicated to a fresh and diverse collection of art from local and regional artists, the gallery is a destination for bargain hunters, as its art is always reasonably priced. Open late the first Sat. of each month for informal gallery chats with artists and the chance to crack open some vintage art books.

Local Color Gallery (615-321-3141; localcolornashville.com),

AN ASPIRING PERFORMER OUTSIDE THE RYMAN AUDITORUM

1912 Broadway. Open Tues.–Sat. 10–5. While the layout is a bit haphazard and the placement of the artwork rather random, somehow this gallery just works—perhaps it's the eye of the owner, who focuses on a few dozen regional artists, mostly painters and photographers. A great place to wander through.

Tennessee Art League (615-736-5000; tennesseeartleague .org), 808 Broadway. Open Tues.–Sat. 10–4. The nonprofit gallery, housed in a historic building on Broadway, offers an excellent, ever-changing collection of art from local and regional artists. Members of the TAL do more than use this space to exhibit their work; artists can often be found teaching classes in the community, whether at a senior center or in a school.

BOUTIQUE SHOPPING H. Audrey (615-760-5701; haudrey .com), 4027 Hillsboro Pike. Open Mon.–Sat. 10–7, Sun. 12–6. Upscale, trendy fashions for the hip and beautiful from designers including Alexander McQueen and Helmut Lang are offered at H. Audrey, which is owned by Holly Williams, the daughter of country music's Hank Williams Jr. But lineage isn't the only reason to shop at this Hill Center boutique; rather, Williams manages to peg the Music City fashionista with an excellent selection of designer togs with just that dash of Nashville funk.

Katy K's Ranch Dressing (615-297-4242; katyk.com), 2407 12th Avenue S. Open Mon.–Fri. 11–6, Sat. noon–6. The owner of this one-of-a-kind Western shop hails from New York City, where she made a name for herself dressing drag queens and pop divas. Soon she was overrun by country-music stars, so she packed her bags and headed south to Nashville. The shop is a fanciful mix of everything from punk duds to cowboy boots, not to mention a good selection of fancy and everyday Western wear for cowboys and cowgirls. Katy K also stocks gifts, plus a few vintage items such as Manuel suits or gowns from Nudie's of Hollywood.

SHOPPING DISTRICTS AND MALLS Hill Center (hillcenter greenhills.com), 4039 Hillsboro Pike at Warfield Drive. Stores generally open Mon.–Sat. 10–6, Sun. noon–5. The outdoor, pedestrian-friendly Hill Center offers a combination of upscale local boutiques (including Hemline and H. Audrey, owned by Holly Williams—yes, of *that* Williams family) with a smattering of national retailers (including Whole Foods and Anthropologie). While it lacks the charm of 12South or Hillsboro Village, the Hill Center is a worthwhile stop for a discriminating shopper.

Hillsboro Village (hillsboro village.com), Hillsboro Avenue at 21st Avenue. Hours vary by store but are generally Mon.–Sat. 10–5;

select stores open on Sun. A charming collection of boutique-y, locally owned shops, tucked between Vanderbilt University and Belmont College, Hillsboro's stores offer stationery and funky office products to fresh flowers, global oddities, vintage and rare books, and unique gifts. There's also a smattering of excellent restaurants, including Cabana, Sunset Grill, and the funky Fido—a former pet store turned coffee shop/eatery.

The Mall at Green Hills (615-298-5478; themallatgreenhills .com), 2126 Abbott Martin Road. Generally open Mon.–Sat. 10–8, Sun. noon–6, with extended hours over the holidays. With a collection of upscale shops, including Brooks Brothers, Sephora, Restoration Hardware, Tiffany, and Williams-Sonoma, Green Hills is your typical mall, but with a high-end twist—but there's no sprawling food court or movie theater. Be sure to check out the adjacent Bandywood Drive shops and restaurants.

12South, 12th Avenue S., between Sevier Park and Montrose. Most stores are open Mon.–Sat. 10–5, with restaurants serving lunch and dinner daily. 12South is known for its funky mix of stores and small eateries. From vintage Western wear and a chic wine bar to small home decor stores and an Italian pub, this is Nashville's mixed local flavor at its best.

UNIQUELY NASHVILLE
Grimey's (615-254-4801; grimeys .com), 1604 Eighth Avenue S. Open Mon.–Sat. 11–8, Sun. 1–6. The best independent record store in town, Grimey's is cramped but has a good selection of vinyl and "preloved" music. Hosts free in-store performances by both local and nationally known bands, usually in the afternoon or early evening.

Hartmann Luggage (615-449-8000; hartmann.com/shop/outlet .asp), 1303 W. Baddour Parkway, Lebanon. Open Mon.–Sat. 9–6, Sun. noon–6. If you fancy the fanciest luggage, you should make the trip to the Hartmann Factory Luggage Outlet in Lebanon, just a 25-minute drive from downtown Nashville. Located at the Hartmann headquarters, the outlet has deals (relatively speaking—one third to one half off retail price) on this luxury luggage. Expect better prices than at other luggage outlets. If you live in the general region, however, be sure to get on the mailing list for Hartmann's annual tent sale at the factory; the bargains are so good, you'll scream.

Hatch Show Print (615-256-2805; hatchshowprint.com), 316 Broadway. Open Mon.–Fri. 9–5, Sat. 10–5. Hatch is one of my favorite spots in town and a must-visit. Hatch has been around since the late 1800s and is famous for its letterpress printing; it's still operating today if you fancy yourself a custom poster for a special event or a wedding or party invitation. Alternatively, you can pick up a reprint of an original concert poster from stars such as Johnny Cash, Hank Williams, Ernest Tubb, and Elvis, or a more recent addition, say a Harry Connick Jr. tour poster—my most recent purchase.

✳ Special Events

Early January: **Sound & Speed** (soundandspeed.org), various locations. The double-whammy charity event brings together stars of NASCAR and country music to sign autographs and meet fans as a fund-raiser for Victory Junction Gang Camp and the Country Music Hall of Fame and Museum charities.

Late March–early April: **Tin Pan South Songwriters Festival** (800-321-6008; tinpansouth.com), various locations. Highlighting the craft of songwriting, the weeklong

NASHVILLE FARMERS MARKET

HATCH SHOW PRINT

celebration includes club show performances, with more than 80 of the city's live music venues hosting in-the-round-style shows.

April: **Awesome April** (800-657-6920; visitmusiccity.com/visitors/AwesomeApril) is a monthlong celebration of music that includes live public performances, the CMT Music Awards, the Nashville Marathon, and more.

Early May: **Iroquois Steeplechase** (800-619-4802; iroquois steeplechase.org), Percy Warner

Park. The nation's oldest, continuously run, weight-for-age steeplechase is a stylish event benefitting Vanderbilt Children's Hospital. General admission tickets start at $15.

Early–mid-June: **CMA Music Festival** (cmafest.com), various locations. Thousands of country music fans come to Nashville each June for a week full of live music performances, autograph sessions, and even fishing and archery tournaments.

Late September: **Tennessee Arts and Crafts Festival** (615-385-1904; tennesseecrafts.org), Centennial Park. Annual three-day crafts fair in Centennial Park features a juried arts and crafts show and artist demonstrations from more than two hundred exhibitors.

Mid-November–Christmas: **A Country Christmas** (888-999-6779; gaylordopryland.com), Opryland Resort and Conference Center. This is perhaps the mother of all annual events in Nashville, when Opryland is transformed into a winter wonderland thanks to hundreds of thousands of twinkling lights, miles of garland wrapped in glittering ribbon, and lavishly decorated Christmas trees scattered throughout the resort.

CLARKSVILLE

Before Tennessee was recognized as a state, it had been home to tribes of Native Americans—the Cherokee, the Choctaw, the Muscogee, the Yucci, and others. As colonists began to spread westward, the tribes were displaced and eventually marched from "emigration depots" to lands in the Oklahoma Territory. Known as the Trail of Tears, it was an arduous trek, with more than four thousand Cherokee dying en route.

At the successful conclusion of the Revolutionary War, the new government lacked the funds to pay the soldiers of the Continental Army for their services. In 1790, select lands west of North Carolina—which included all of present-day Tennessee—were designated as part of a land grant to pay the soldiers and their families, in lieu of cash.

Clarksville, having already been surveyed, was part of this land grant. The town was named for Revolutionary War general George Rogers Clark, a brother of William Clark of the Lewis and Clark Expedition. Nestled along the Cumberland River, near the confluence of the Red River, Clarksville offered the potential for a prosperous living to those who settled here, with rich soil for crops and trading and shipping possibilities thanks to the river. Tobacco was the king of crops in Clarksville, especially dark-fired tobacco, and in the 19th century Clarksville was the largest market in the world for this type of tobacco, known for its smoky curing and high concentration of nicotine.

Clarksville's strategic location on the Cumberland River—near the Red River as well as close to Fort Donelson and Fort Henry—meant the town was ripe for attack during the Civil War. It was home to three Confederate camps—Fort Defiance, Camp Boone, and Camp Burnet—and thus Confederate forces expected a land assault from the Union, but that attack ended up coming from the water: Clarksville was captured by Union forces in February 1862 as gunboats and troops arrived via the river. Clarksville remained in Union hands for the duration of the war. The slaves who worked in the cotton and tobacco fields in the area, suddenly free men, came into town to live and work, and many joined the Union army.

The military has always been a large part of the history of Clarksville, starting with the land grant to Revolutionary soldiers, then the heavy casualties suffered by its native sons in the Civil War, especially during the battles of nearby Fort Donelson and Fort Henry. That military tradition continued when the U.S. Army opened Camp Campbell in 1942; the camp eventually became home to the 101st Airborne Division and a number of special operations and support divisions. While the present-day Fort Campbell address is in Kentucky, the majority of the 100,000-plus-acre installation is in Clarksville.

Clarksville has the distinction of being home to the oldest bank in Tennessee: the Northern Bank was established in 1854 and is now part of Regions Bank. It is also home to the state's oldest newspaper, *The Leaf-Chronicle*, which first went to press in Clarksville in 1808. Lastly, Clarksville is also home to Austin Peay University, which is located on a campus that has been the site of institutions of higher learning since the early 1800s.

Downtown Clarksville is a charming blend of historic and modern buildings along the Cumberland River—a downtown made even more charming by the fact it has been devastated by two natural disasters within a decade and therefore rebuilt. In January 1999, a rare and powerful F3 tornado ripped through downtown, severely damaging many buildings, including the historic courthouse. And in May 2010, the downtown area was again at the mercy of Mother Nature when the Cumberland River overflowed its banks, cresting at approximately 50 feet following two days of torrential rain in the region.

This pretty river town has taken its share of knocks—from man and nature—over the years, but its rich history and natural beauty still shine through.

GUIDANCE Clarksville Convention & Visitors Bureau (931-553-8467; clarksvillecvb.com), 180 Holiday Drive. The CVB offers a variety of maps for walking and driving through town, as well as comprehensive information on area attractions.

Tennessee Department of Tourism

DOWNTOWN CLARKSVILLE

GETTING THERE *By air:* **Nashville International Airport** (BNA; 615-275-1675; flynashville.com), 1 Terminal Drive, Nashville. Nashville is the closest major airport to Clarksville, about 45 miles away via I-65 N. BNA is going through a multiyear, multiproject renovation.

By bus: **Greyhound** (931-647-3336), 11 Jefferson Street. Provides service to major cities to and from Clarksville.

By car: Clarksville is located off I-24.

GETTING AROUND *By bus:* **Clarksville Transit System** (931-553-2430; cityofclarksville.com/transit), 200 Legion Street. Public bus service around Clarksville, including service to Fort Campbell, is offered daily. Fees range from 60 cents and up, and correct change is required.

By car: Crossland Avenue, Wilma Rudolph Boulevard, and Riverside Drive are the main avenues into Clarksville's downtown district.

By taxi: Taxi service is available in Clarksville, though taxis are not usually found outside hotels as they are in major cities. The local taxi services include **ABC Cab Company** (931-431-3535; abccabinc.com) and **Crown Cab Company** (931-206-5556).

MEDICAL EMERGENCY **Gateway Medical Center** (931-502-1000; todaysgateway.com), 651 Dunlop Lane. Offers a full-service emergency department 24 hours daily.

Doctors Care Urgent Care Center (931-645-1564; drscare.com), 2320 Wilma Rudolph. Features an urgent care clinic open Mon.–Sat. 8–8 and Sun. noon–6.

✳ To See

HISTORIC SITES Fort Donelson National Battlefield Park (615-232-5706; nps.gov/fodo), Highway 79, Dover. Open daily 7:30–6; visitors center is open daily 8–4:30, except for Christmas Day. The Dover Hotel/Surrender House is open noon–4 June–Sept.(closed Oct.–May). In 1862, the capture of Fort Donelson by Gen. Ulysses S. Grant dealt the Confederacy a defeat and changed the course of the Civil War in Tennessee. Approximately 13,000 Confederate soldiers were captured, and the surrender at the Dover Hotel led to the invasion of the Deep South by the Union. The Dover, built as a hotel for riverboat travelers, served as Confederate headquarters during the battle, and it was here that the terms of the surrender were negotiated, leading to the nickname Surrender House. The national cemetery at Fort Donelson was established in 1867; of the almost seven hundred soldiers buried here, the identities of more than five hundred are unknown. The park includes an interactive visitors center with artifacts and a film detailing the fort's history and importance, the Dover House, the battleground, and the cemetery. Admission is free, but donations are accepted.

✎ **Historic Collinsville** (931-648-9141; historiccollinsville.com), 4711 Weakly Road, Southside. Open Thurs.–Sun. 1–5, May 15–Oct. 15. More than a dozen restored log buildings from the 1800s create a historic tableau of frontier life. Most tours are self-guided, but on occasion costumed interpreters offer tales of the frontier and demonstrate candle making and other period tasks. A wildlife center features a variety of Native American artifacts as well as a collection of taxidermic animals that once roamed the Cumberland River Valley, many of which are on the endangered species list. Adults $4, children under five free.

L& N Train Station (931-553-2486; mchsociety.org), 189 19th Street. Tours are offered Tues., Thurs., and Sat. 9–1; call for reservations. The last passenger train ticket was sold at the historic train depot, part of the Louisville and Nashville rail line, in 1968; the station was restored in 1996 and is now home to the Montgomery County Historical Society and the local farmer's market during the summer months. But this station may best be known for being the destination in the Monkees' first hit recording, "Last Train to Clarksville," recorded in 1966. The song went to number one on the charts. Adults $1, children under 18, 25 cents.

Wilma Rudolph Statue (931-645-7476; clarksville.tn.us/info-html/what _to_see.html), Cumberland Riverwalk, College Street and Riverside

Drive. One of the finest athletes to come out of Tennessee, sprinter Wilma Rudolph was an Olympic champion and a native of Clarksville. A bronze statue of a sprinting Rudolph was crafted to honor the hometown heroine. Free.

MUSEUMS Customs House Museum & Cultural Center (931-648-5780; customshousemuseum.org), 200 S. Second Street. Open Tues.–Sat. 10–5, Sun. 1–5. Built as a post office for the tobacco trade, the gorgeous city-block-sized building is now a museum filled with exhibits featuring the art, science, and history of the region. The building itself is worth a visit; built in 1898, the hipped slate roof has flared eaves, and there are 20 dormers, each corner decorated with a copper eagle. Permanent exhibits include the Challenges and Champions Gallery, filled with sports memorabilia from notable Clarksvillians, including Olympic track champion Wilma Rudolph's relay baton; the work of regional artists is showcased in the Peg Harvill Gallery. Adults $5, children 6–18 $1, children under six free.

Don F. Pratt Museum (270-798-3215), 5702 Tennessee Avenue, Fort Campbell. Open Mon.–Sat. 9:30–4:30. Honoring the service of hundreds of thousands of American men and women, the museum at Fort Campbell especially chronicles the history of the 101st Airborne Division—the Screamin' Eagles—and other units that have served at the fort. Memorabilia features items from the Second World War, including a CG-4A glider that carried soldiers into combat in early fighting on the European continent, personal possessions of some of the generals of that era, and personal items of Adolph Hitler and high-ranking Nazi officials. A park across the street from the museum displays military equipment and aircraft, highlighting the C-47 aircraft—the Brass Hat—that carried Gen. Maxwell D. Taylor into Normandy during the invasion of France. Free.

✳ To Do

HIKING ✍ **Cumberland River Walk** (931-645-7476), 640 N. Riverside Drive. Open 7 AM–midnight daily. The riverside park features a 1-mile trail for hiking and biking, as well as a playground, performance stages, and public art. The RiverCenter pavilion features a permanent display of panels detailing the history of Clarksville and the role the river played in that history. During the holidays, the park comes alive with a dazzling light display. Free.

ROCK CLIMBING King's Bluff (seclimbers.org). There's no physical address for the bluff, but merely directions to it: Take I-24 W. to exit 11. Turn left on TN 76 for about 6 miles and make a left onto Max Court. Climbing is permitted during daylight hours only. A limestone cliff along

178

MIDDLE TENNESSEE: THE HEART OF TENNESSEE

THE LEGEND OF THE BELL WITCH

One of the most famous—perhaps infamous—hauntings in American history happened on a farm in Adams, just east of Clarksville.

North Carolinian John Bell moved his wife and children to settle in Robertson County in 1804. It was easy to see why Bell chose this particular site for his farm; the pastoral setting of more than 300 acres was bordered by the Red River, and the soil was rich for growing crops.

Legend has it that the Bell family lived quite happily and grew in prosperity for the first dozen or so years on their pretty farmland. But in the late summer of 1817, strange things began to occur around the farm—unusual animals were spotted. Inside their cabin, strange noises were heard—knocking sounds, heavy thuds on the floorboards, animals gnawing on wood.

The Bells, quite terrified, still waited to ask for help or confirmation of their experiences. Finally, more than a year had passed, and friends from around the community would visit and reported similar experiences. The noises turned from unidentifiable and identifiable sounds to an actual voice; the voice reportedly gave various identities when asked who—or what—it was. Once, it answered that it was the witch of a neighbor, Kate Batts. From that point on, the force was known as the Bell Witch.

The witch terrorized the Bells, apparently intent on killing John because of an old dispute over land. And it seemed the witch also wanted to stop Bell's youngest daughter, Betsy, from marrying. For three years, the family was subjected to physical abuse—hair pulling and pinching, even punches. John Bell seemed to suffer the worst, experiencing bizarre pains, twitching of the facial muscles, and

the Cumberland River offers a variety of climbs from 30 to 80 feet in height and of varying difficulty. The bluff is owned by Southeastern Climbers Coalition, and the entry gate into King's Bluff is locked, so follow the links on the coalition's Web site to access the gate combination. There's no fee for climbing, but donations are welcome.

SPECTATOR SPORTS Clarksville Speedway (931-645-2523; clarksvillespeedway.com), 1600 Needmore Road. Races are held on Fri. and swelling of his throat. Those who visited the farm would report speaking to Kate, who told them their futures.

In December 1820, John Bell died at home, and many believe he was poisoned by Kate—who allegedly told those gathered that she did indeed kill him. In March of the following year, Betsy broke off her engagement, and Kate told the Bells and their neighbors she would leave them for seven years.

Andrew Jackson was said to have heard of the tale and decided to visit the Bell farm for himself. The witch reportedly revealed herself to Jackson and his party, and he's quoted as saying, "I would rather fight the entire British army than deal with the Bell Witch."

John Bell Jr. reported that Kate did return in 1828, visiting him in his home and making predictions for his future—but committed no awful acts against the younger Bell. She again promised to return, this time in 107 years, in 1935. Whether Kate ever left was—and still is—the subject of debate; folks around Adams blame the Bell Witch for strange occurrences, and the tale has been the subject of a number of books and movies, including *An American Haunting* (2006) and *The Bell Witch Haunting* (2004).

The cave on the Bell farm, and a replica of the family's cabin, are both open to the public and available for tours; the cave is small and very narrow, and is closed during and after periods of heavy rains. The cabin features some relics of the Bell family and period furnishings. During October, a special celebration featuring haunted hayrides, psychic readings, and night tours are offered on select Saturdays.

The John Bell Farm/Bell Witch Cave (615-696-3055; bellwitchcave .com) is at 430 Keysburg Road in Adams. It's open weekends in May and Labor Day–October, and daily with the exception of Tuesday June–Labor Day. Cave tours are $11 per person; cabin tours are $7 per person.

Sat. nights at 7:30, Mar.–mid-Nov. For more than 30 years, local and regional drivers have tested their mettle in street-style drag racing on the ⅛-mile strip, or the more challenging oval dirt track, where street cars, drag cars, and motorcycles race. While pros mostly take to the tracks in the UMP-sanctioned races, young adults are offered the chance to race their rides for a $10 entry fee in the track's "midnight madness" competition following the pro racing each Sat. Admission is $12, with pit passes available for $25.

LAND BETWEEN THE LAKES

Since the 1830s, the narrow piece of land between the Tennessee and the Cumberland rivers had been known as the Land Between the Rivers. When the U.S. government, under President Franklin Delano Roosevelt, began what was to become known as the Tennessee Valley Administration, many homeowners lost their land, and when the dam was developed, part of the area was flooded and two lakes were formed—Lake Barkley, on the Cumberland, and Kentucky Lake, on the Tennessee—and the name changed to Land Between the Lakes. Since Tennessee and Kentucky share the area, the land was transferred to the U.S. Forest Service as a national recreation area under President John F. Kennedy.

There's both history and recreation at Land Between the Lakes. The Homeplace, a Revolutionary War land grant, is a living-history farm today. Farmers in period dress work the farm with agricultural techniques from the 1850s, growing tobacco and corn as well as raising sheep and hogs.

The Nature Station offers the chance to view regional wildlife in its habitat or canoe through a lake filled with migrating waterfowl. Bison and elk once roamed this area freely, and a 700-acre range brings both back into their natural habitat. Guided horseback riding, fishing, and hunting are offered here, and there are more than 200 miles of hiking trails through the woods and fields. A planetarium and observatory at the Golden Pond Visitor Center offers daily and seasonal programs for stargazing.

Land Between the Lakes National Recreation Area (270-924-2000; lbl.org), 100 Van Morgan Drive, Golden Pond, KY, is approximately 50 miles from downtown Clarksville. Golden Pond Visitor Center open daily 9–5, year-round, with the south welcome entrance open daily 9–5, March–November. There's no charge for entering Land Between the Lakes, but fees are required for a number of activities, including the bison and elk range, the planetarium, and the farm, with prices starting at $4 per activity for adults and $2 for children.

WINERIES Beachaven Winery (931-645-8867; beachavenwinery.com), 1100 Dunlop Lane. Open Mon.–Sat. 9–6, Sun. noon–5. Ed Cooke began producing his Beachaven wines in 1986, and the Clarksville winery has been winning national and international awards ever since. The winery regularly honors the divisions at Fort Campbell with specially labeled

bottles and currently produces more than 13,000 cases of 22 wines annually. From mid-May to mid-Oct., the winery's free Jazz on the Lawn series
gives folks a chance to bring their own food, lay out a blanket, and enjoy
the scenic, rolling vineyard while sampling Beachaven's best. Free.

✳ Green Space

PARKS Dunbar Cave State Park (931-648-5526; state.tn.us
/environment/parks/DunbarCave), 401 Old Dunbar Cave Road. The park
is open daily 8–sunset. The roomy Dunbar Cave was once home to square
dances and big-band-era concerts; the cave and its surrounds—including
a number of smaller caves—are now a state park located within the
Clarksville city limits. Three hiking trails, including a partially paved trail,
make hiking or strolling available to all. Regular arts and crafts activities
and children's programs are offered at the cave, including children's theater performances. Fishing is allowed on the pretty but tiny Swan Lake,
which is fed from the stream that runs out of Dunbar Cave, although
boating and swimming are not allowed on the lake, given its small size.
Free.

Port Royal State Park (931-358-9696; state.tn.us/environment/parks
/PortRoyal), 3300 Old Clarksville Highway, Adams. Open daily 8–sunset. A
trading post and community along the Red River, Port Royal was settled in
the 1780s and served as a stagecoach stop on the Great Western Road, as
well as a rest stop for the displaced Cherokees as they made their way
along the Trail of Tears. The foundations of the village's businesses can
still be seen, as can the roadbeds for a few trails and roadways, including
the Trail of Tears. A short hiking trail along the Bluff Trail begins at the
covered bridge, and fishing and canoeing are allowed at the park; canoes
must be carried in by hand, and a state fishing license is required for
anglers. Each Oct., nighttime lantern tours of the park are offered, complete with tales of the area's ghosts, campfires, and spiced cider. Free.

✳ Lodging

BED & BREAKFASTS/INNS

✎ ✿ **Lylewood Inn Bed &
Breakfast** (931-232-4203; lyle-
woodinn.com), 110 Camp Lylewood Road, Indian Mound. Built
in 1892, the inn was once the farmhouse of a large operation with
1,400 acres, 24 tenant houses, and
one of the largest smokehouses in
the area. The inn offers three peri-
od-style rooms with fireplaces and

PRICE CATEGORIES:

Inexpensive	Less than $100 (for hotels, inns, and B&Bs); less than $50 (for camp-grounds, state park facilities)
Moderate	$100–200
Expensive	$201–300
Very expensive	More than $300

private baths with claw-foot tubs. During Dec., the innkeepers dress up as the Lewis family—the original owners of the home—and create candlelight, Victorian Christmas experience that includes an optional dinner. Children and well-mannered pets are welcome at the inn. Southern-style breakfasts are included in the room rate and feature farm-produced jams and jellies. Inexpensive.

Magnolia House B&B (931-801-6992; magnoliabb.com), 1231 Madison Street. A more modern B&B—built in the 1940s—Magnolia House offers two lushly appointed guest rooms, each with a private bath, about a mile from downtown Clarksville. A large living room and family room each offer quiet spaces for reading or relaxing, while a gazebo with hammocks beckons with the lure of afternoon naps. Moderate.

HOTELS Riverview Inn (931-552-3331; theriverviewinn.com), 50 College Street. A full-service hotel with river views, a fitness center, Internet access, and on-site restaurant. Breakfast is included in the room rate. Inexpensive–moderate.

✱ Where to Eat

EATING OUT Blackhorse Pub and Brewery (931-552-3726; the blackhorsepub.net), 132 Franklin Street. Open Sun.–Thurs. 11–10, Fri.–Sat. 11–11. With a long wooden bar, plaid carpet, pool tables, and exposed brick walls,

PRICE CATEGORIES:	
Inexpensive	Less than $16
Moderate	$16–30
Expensive	$31–50
Very expensive	More than $50

the Blackhorse has the feel of an authentic British pub. It's the only local brewhouse and crafts a variety of ales; Wed. evenings, a specialty cask is tapped and tasted. One would expect the menu at Blackhorse to be pub grub, but that's not the case, although a nice selection of sandwiches is offered. But amped-up pizzas, flatbreads, and steaks are offered, along with a nice selection of salads. For those who aren't crafted-beer aficionados, a limited but decent wine list is available. Moderate.

Choppin' Block (931-920-2112; thechoppinblock.com), 2212 Madison Street. Open Mon.–Fri. 6–6, Sat. 7–5. A full-service butcher shop/restaurant/cheese store, the Block, as locals call it, serves beefed-up meals like fried pork chops and overstuffed omelets for breakfast, and daily blue plate specials, giant twice-baked potatoes, gyros, and steak sandwiches for lunch. Inexpensive.

Edelweiss Café (931-503-8200; edelweisscafeusa.com), 1984 Fort Campbell Boulevard. Open Mon.–Thurs. 10–8, Fri.–Sat.10–9, and Sun. noon–4. Traditional German and Polish fare served up in a casual setting, with daily specials featuring sauerbraten, potato dumplings, and goulash; a variety of schnitzel dishes, German-inspired side dishes, and a few sandwich options are always on the menu, as is a large selection of German beers. Moderate.

⌂ Front Page Deli (931-503-0325; frontpagedeli.com), 105 Franklin Street. Open Mon.–Thurs. 11 AM–1 AM, Fri.–Sat. 11 AM–2:30 AM. The original downtown deli was destroyed by the F3 tornado that ripped through Clarksville in early 1999; the rebuilt version came back with a vengeance, offering a huge selection of entrées and appetizers—not just deli sandwiches, as one might expect. Fried pickle spears, pot stickers, nachos, and crab-cakes are offered up as appetizers, while entrées include steak and salmon (as the main event or sliced up on salads), a nice selection of pasta dishes, and, of course, a deep offering of deli and po'boy sandwiches. There's an entire beer menu, too, featuring more than 60 beers—both on tap and bottled—and homemade desserts include a yummy selection of cheesecakes. Moderate.

Looking Glass Restaurant (931-552-6344; lookingglassrestaurant .com), 329 Warfield Boulevard. Open Mon.–Thurs. 7 AM–9 PM, Fri.–Sat. 7 AM–10 PM. It started as an art gallery serving coffee and pastries, and turned into a local dining favorite—so it's best to expect the unexpected when dining at the Looking Glass. The menu changes monthly, the table

decor shifts into holiday mode anytime there's a holiday, and the food is made from scratch. Moderate.

Lovin' Spoonful Café (931-553-4080; lovinspoonfulcafe.com), 128 University Avenue. Open Mon.–Fri. 10–4, Sun. 10–2. The groovy Lovin' Spoonful is a retro wonder, kitted out with vintage kitsch from the '60s and '70s, including a variety of paintings depicting Jesus—why, I'm not exactly sure, but I suspect the peace-and-love theme is part of the reason. Regardless, food is simply prepared, with plenty of vegetarian options, homey offerings like Frito pie and cowboy caviar, and a rotating soup selection. Inexpensive.

✳ Entertainment

PERFORMING ARTS
The Roxy Regional Theatre (931-645-7699; roxyregionaltheatre.org), 100 Franklin Street. Productions run year-round; call the theater or visit the Web site for dates and times. The Roxy offers excellent productions of classic plays as well as new works, casting its productions in New York each spring for the upcoming season. The result is top-notch theater in the heart of Middle Tennessee. Tickets start at $15 for adults and $10 for children.

✳ Selective Shopping

ART AND ANTIQUES ART*ifacts* (931-249-0454; artifactsemporium .com), 125 Legion Street. Open

Tues.–Sat. 10–6. A combination art and antiques gallery with more than a dozen artisans and antiques dealers offering everything from handcrafted leather goods and pottery to antique jewelry, vintage tea sets, and architectural oddities.

BOUTIQUE SHOPPING Posh Boutique Outlet (931-905-1500; poshonline.com), 131 Franklin Street. Open Mon.–Sat. 10–6. The outlet for Nashville's upscale designer store, Posh offers designer closeouts at serious discounts. Featured brands include William Rast, MM Couture, Hype, and BCBGeneration; jewelry, shoes, high-end denim, and accessories are refreshed frequently.

✳ **Special Events**

April: **Rivers and Spires Festival** (931-245-4344; riversandspires .com), 50 Franklin Street. Started in 2003 to honor soldiers of the 101st Airborne Division, the festival continues to recognize those returning from active duty. The two-day event features major headline musical acts each evening, with daytime musical performances, parades, a quilt show, a songwriters showcase, and car exhibitions. Free.

Early September: **Riverfest** (clarksvilleriverfest.com), McGregor Park, downtown. The two-day festival celebrates Clarksville's river heritage, featuring live music, children's activities, a lighted boat parade on the Cumberland, and a multigenerational art fair. Free.

COOKEVILLE

Located in the heart of the Tennessee Highlands, Cookeville is a vibrant community that combines all the charm of a small town with many of the amenities of a larger city—offering a nice mix of cultural, retail, and historic offerings in a pastoral setting.

Cookeville was settled in the mid-1850s and is in the first tier of the Cumberland Plateau. Named for local landowner and state senator Richard Fielding Cooke, the town's first building was a log grocery store. The town of Cookeville enjoyed a prime central location in Putnam County; being the halfway point between Knoxville and Nashville on the Walton Road, the village was a natural place for a rest stop. By 1860, more than eight thousand residents had settled in Cookeville, many creating subsistence farms for themselves as the soil in the area wasn't conducive to larger agricultural production.

While this area wasn't prime Civil War battleground, the war still had an impact on those who settled here. Bands of guerillas—both Union and Confederate—attacked and destroyed homes and farms in Cookeville during the war.

Following the war, the expansion of the railway system helped Cookeville become a hub for the newly created Nashville and Knoxville

Railroad. The town quickly grew from the prosperity that the rail line brought with it. Cookeville's location and growth served to create a destination for travelers—as well as a route for business expansion—as state and national highways were built to accommodate the popularity of the automobile. By the 1960s, Cookeville began attracting a variety of industries, and today its major employers include Cummins Filtration, Oreck Vacuums, and Tennessee Tech University.

The city is considered a micropolitan area—a smaller town that operates as a regional economic hub—and the town's population doubles on weekdays, as about 25,000 people from the surrounding area travel to Cookeville for work each day. That extra jolt of population gives Cookeville a bit of a bigger-city buzz, creating a vibrant business and cultural community.

Downtown Cookeville is almost split into two, with one section being the main business district, and the other—the West Side—the main shopping and dining district, centered around the historic railroad depot. Cookeville offers a vibrant performing arts scene, with multiple venues for plays and concerts, a Shakespeare festival, and a free public concert series.

GUIDANCE **Cookeville–Putnam County Convention & Visitors Bureau** (931-526-2211; mustseecookeville.com), 470 Neal Street. The Highlands Visitors Center is open daily 9–5 and features a collection of historic photographs and memorabilia to pique interest in Cookeville's attractions.

GETTING THERE *By air:* Cookeville is approximately 100 miles from the Nashville airport (**Nashville International Airport,** 615-275-1675, fly nashville.com, 1 Terminal Drive) and about 80 miles from both the Knoxville airport (**McGhee-Tyson Airport,** 865-342-3000, tys.org, 2055 Alcoa Highway) and the Chattanooga airport (**Chattanooga Metropolitan Airport,** 423-855-2200, chattairport.com, 1001 Airport Road, #14); all three airports are served by major national and regional carriers.

By car: Cookeville is located between Nashville and Knoxville at the intersection of I-40 and TN 111.

GETTING AROUND *By bus:* The **Cookeville Area Transit System** (931-372-8000; uchra.com/cats) provides bus service throughout the city and to Tennessee Tech; fares start at $1 per trip or $3 for a day pass.

By car: Major routes in town include Washington, Willow, and Spring Street/US 70. The town is easy to navigate, and maps are available at the CVB Web site or welcome center. Once you hit the historic West Side, it's best to park it and walk.

By taxi: Taxi service is available but limited in Cookeville. **Selby's Cab Co.** (931-372-7588), 164 W. First Street, is about the only game in town.

MEDICAL EMERGENCY Cookeville Regional Medical Center (931-646-2628; crmchealth.org), 1 Medical Center Boulevard. Emergency services are offered 24 hours daily.

Physicians Urgent Care Center (931-525-5454; cookevilleurgentcare .com), 225 N. Willow Avenue. Handles minor emergencies.

✳ To See

MUSEUMS ✍ **Cookeville Children's Museum** (931-979-7529; cooke villechildrensmuseum.org), 36 W. Second Street. Open Mon.–Wed. and Fri.–Sat. 10–4, Thurs. 12:30–5:30. Like the children it entertains, the Cookeville Children's Museum is always changing, and it's planning for future growth from its present storefront location on the West Side. The indoor-outdoor, hands-on museum caters to the 2–12 set, with the chance to play dress-up and make-believe in doctor, veterinarian, and farm areas; view changing exhibits in a science area; and and blow off some steam outside on the playground, which features a kid-friendly climbing area, colorful murals, and plenty of swings. Adults $4, children $3, children under two free.

Cookeville Depot Museum (931-528-8570; cookevilledepot.com), 116 W. Broad Street. Open Tues.–Sat. 10–4. The historic depot, the backdrop for a nostalgic visit to the grand era of passenger train travel, features railroad and train artifacts, rolling stock, and a scale model of the city circa 1955. The Tennessee Central Railroad ended operations in 1968; the depot, built in 1909, is one of only three brick depots built by the TCR and is unique for its pagoda-shaped roof. The five pieces of rolling stock that are part of the permanent collection include an original Tennessee Central caboose, as well as a steam engine and track cars. Special train excursions, including fall foliage trips, are offered seasonally. Free.

✳ To Do

ART WORKSHOPS Appalachian Center for Craft (931-372-3051; tntech.edu/craftcenter), 1500 Craft Center Drive, Smithville. A short— and very scenic—drive from Cookeville, this arts-focused satellite of Tennessee Tech University offers intensive weekend workshops for visitors in May and Sept. See "McMinnville, Smithville, and Sparta."

✳ Green Space

PARKS 🐾 **Burgess Falls State Park** (931-432-5312; state.tn.us /environment/parks/BurgessFall), 4000 Burgess Falls Drive, Sparta.

About 8 miles from Cookeville. Open daily 8 AM–30 minutes before sun-down. See "McMinnville, Smithville, and Sparta."

☙ **Cane Creek Park** (931-526-6668; cookeville-tn.org/ls/cane-creek -park), 201 Cane Creek Camp Road. Open daily 7 AM–9 PM, with closing time at 5 PM Nov.–Apr. Bordering the Old City Cave, the park offers something for everyone. A 56-acre lake includes piers for fishing; paddle-boat rentals ($3 and up) are available, and there's a boat ramp for those with nonmotorized and electric-powered boats. Along with snacks and drinks, the concession stand offers sports equipment for rent for those who want to play a game of basketball or volleyball; fishing poles are also available to rent. An 18-hole disc golf course and nature trails wind throughout the park. Dogs are welcome, but in accordance with city law they must be on a leash at all times. Pet disposal stations are available throughout the park. Free.

HISTORIC DEPOT, COOKEVILLE

✳ Lodging

BED & BREAKFASTS/INNS

The Garden Inn Bed & Breakfast at Bee Rock (931-839-1400; thegardeninnBB.com), 1400 Bee Rock Road, Monterey. About halfway between Cookeville and Crossville, the inn offers 11 rooms with private baths, garden or mountain views, and whirlpool tubs or fireplaces. The setting is spectacular, as the house backs right up to the Cumberland Plateau, with a steep, rocky drop right outside the back door. A huge deck allows a safe view of the plateau, as well as the surrounding countryside. A gourmet breakfast, afternoon snacks, and evening sweets are included in the room rate. The Garden Inn is also the site of Bee Rock, an outcropping where Native Americans reportedly used to gather honey from the bee hives once prevalent here. Today, climbers have 30 climbing routes to choose from; the site is open to the public, but

PRICE CATEGORIES:	
Inexpensive	Less than $100 (for hotels, inns, and B&Bs); less than $50 (for campgrounds, state park facilities)
Moderate	$100–200
Expensive	$201–300
Very expensive	More than $300

climbers are asked to leave the grounds at 5 PM if they're not guests of the inn. Moderate.

HOTELS Alpine Lodging and Suites (931-526-3333; alpinelodge .org), 2021 E. Spring Street. A motel with a bit of resort thrown in, Alpine offers standard, hotel-style rooms as well as rooms with fully equipped kitchens and additional space. On the grounds, barbecue grills and a covered picnic area, pool, nature trail, and shuf-

APPALACHIAN CENTER FOR CRAFT

fleboard are offered. Room rates include continental breakfast. Free wireless access is available throughout the hotel. Inexpensive.

Holiday Inn Express (931-881-2000; hiexpress.com), 1228 Bunker Hill Road. Perfectly situated off the interstate for those looking to explore all over the area, the Holiday Inn Express is consistent in its cleanliness and friendliness of the staff. Suites offer a divided space with a pull-out sofa to accommodate families or larger groups; free wireless Internet is available throughout the hotel, from the lobby to the rooms themselves. The hotel offers an indoor pool and small but adequate fitness center, complimentary hot breakfast bar, and morning newspapers. Moderate.

✳ Where to Eat

DINING OUT Maddux Station Restaurant & Wine Bar (931-854-0883; madduxstation.com), 319 E. Spring Street. Open Tues.–Sat. 11–3 and 5–10, Sun. 11–3. A casual yet refined eatery with an emphasis on French techniques, locally raised products, and seasonal offerings, Maddux Station is one of the only upscale restaurants in Cookeville. The owner-chef spends plenty of time visiting with diners and accommodating special requests. Fried green tomato sandwiches are a constant favorite but are usually only available seasonally, as are many of the dishes, which means eating here is never the same

experience twice. Vegetarian and vegan choices are available, too. An excellent wine list complements the entrée selections, and those who enjoy fruity martinis should indulge in the bar's blackberry version. Moderate.

EATING OUT CHAR (931-520-2427; charcookeville.com), 14 S. Washington. Open for lunch Mon.–Fri. 11–4, dinner Mon.–Thurs. 4–9 and Fri.–Sat. 4–10. Take a traditional steakhouse, add a lively bar, and create a live music venue, and that's Char—the see-and-be-seen spot in Clarksville almost any night of the week. Prime steaks, chops, and seafood are accompanied by a down-home menu of sides, from sweet potatoes and mac and cheese to green beans and mashed potatoes and gravy. Moderate.

Crawdaddy's West Side Grill (931-526-4660; crawdaddysgrill.com), 53 W. Broad Street. Open daily 11–11. Authentic Cajun and Creole food in a casual and lively atmosphere. Alfresco dining is available most of the year, with live jazz on Tues. evenings and during Sun. brunch, and more live music throughout the week. Moderate.

PRICE CATEGORIES:

Inexpensive	Less than $16
Moderate	$16–30
Expensive	$31–50
Very expensive	More than $50

Dolce Café (931-528-3200; dolce cafes.com), 323 E. Spring Street. Open Mon.–Sat. 7 AM–10 PM. A chic coffee shop/bakery featuring a heavy emphasis on bold roasts, sweet homemade treats, and eclectic events—from book signings to live music. Inexpensive.

Sweet Sallie's (931-526-6556; sweetsallies.com), 11 N. Oak Avenue. Open Mon.–Fri. 7–7, Sat. 8–3. Decadent daily specials on cupcakes are just the icing on the, well, cupcake at this hip bakeshop/café. While those cupcakes ($2 each or a dozen for $20) do tend to grab all the attention, a variety of espressos, coffees, and other hot beverages dominate the liquid offerings, and there's a daily quiche and salad duo as well as a few other items at lunchtime. Inexpensive.

✳ Entertainment

PERFORMING ARTS Backdoor Playhouse (931-372-6595; tntech .edu/bdph), 805 Quadrangle (the Jere Whitson building on the campus of Tennessee Tech University). For more than half a century, the playhouse has offered productions throughout the year, ranging from classic and modern adaptations of Shakespeare to contemporary plays, original works, and works written and directed by students. Check the Web site for performance times. General admission $12, students $5.

Cookeville Performing Arts Center (931-528-1313; cooke ville-tn.org/cpac), 10 E. Broadway.

The CPAC is more than just one venue—it is a collection of venues, including the main performing arts center, the Backstage Theatre; Dogwood Park; and the Dogwood Performance Pavilion. In these three locations, performances range from weekday lunchtime concerts and under-the-stars productions of Shakespeare to whimsical children's productions staged by the Cookeville Children's Theatre. In the Backstage Theatre, playgoers actually sit on the stage, creating a totally immersive theater experience. Check the Web site for offerings and ticket prices; many of the events are free to the public.

✳ Selective Shopping

ANTIQUES Cherry Creek Antiques (931-526-7834; hand craftedcherry.com), 5589 Cherry Creek Road. Open Mon.–Sat. 9–5. Locally handcrafted and designed cherry and walnut furniture of every description, with a wide array of styles from elegant to casual, European to country.

ARTS AND CRAFTS Muddy Pond Mennonite Community (931-445-7829; bigsouthforkpark .com/muddypond.htm), Hanging Limb Community, Monterey. Stores are generally open 10–5, closed Sun. and holidays. The working Mennonite community, about 20 miles from Cookeville, includes a blacksmith shop, bakery, leather shop, and a general store open to visitors; pottery, home-canned and fresh foods, quilts, handcrafted furniture, and leather goods are offered. The blacksmith shop focuses on creating replacement parts for wagons and historical restorations. On Tues., Thurs., and Sat. in Sept. and Oct., visitors can watch as sorghum molasses is made. Free.

BOUTIQUE SHOPPING Spicer & Company (931-525-3935), 123 W. Broad Street. Open Tues.–Fri. 10–6, Sat. 1–6. Custom jewelry designs, plus an array of fine vintage and antique pieces.

✷ Special Events

Late July–early August: **Putnam County Fair** (931- 528-9316; putnamcountyfair.org), 200 E. Veterans Drive. Agricultural competitions, a huge midway, and fair food—all the makings of the perfect county fair.

Mid-September: **Fall Funfest** (931-525-1109; fallfunfest.com), downtown Cookeville. A two-day festival with live music, a juried arts and crafts show, 5K and 10K runs, and events and competitions throughout the weekend.

FRANKLIN

Franklin, just 20 minutes south of downtown Nashville, was settled in 1799 and grew from a small, quiet farming community into the center of the plantation economy in the region. The Williamson County seat, Franklin was also one of the wealthiest counties in Tennessee in the years leading up to the Civil War.

That all changed on the evening of November 30, 1864, when Franklin became the site of one of the fiercest battles of the Civil War. That deadly evening, referred to as "the Gettysburg of the West," devastated the local economy and way of life for all its citizens. Though it has taken well over one hundred years, I think it's safe to say now that Franklin is back.

Surrounded by the press of suburbanization—strip malls and a megamall, big-box retailers and cookie-cutter subdivisions—Franklin's essence is its downtown area, steeped in historical significance and full of important Civil War era homes and sites. Throw in an incredibly charming public square with its Five Points intersection, and you've got a blend of history and hipness.

Downtown Franklin is alive with strolling shoppers, gallery hoppers, diners, and sightseers. Music of all kinds, especially country and bluegrass, can be heard any day of the week, outdoors and in. I think that Benjamin Franklin (for whom the town was named by his good friend, native son Dr. Hugh Williamson) would heartily approve of the high quality of life led by residents, and the degree of deference paid to the history of the area by its enthusiastic visitors.

Stephanie Jones

FIVE POINTS

GUIDANCE Williamson County Convention and Visitors Bureau (615-791-7554; visitwilliamson.com), 209 E. Main Street. Open Mon.–Thurs. 9–4, Fri.–Sat. 9–5, and Sun. 1–4. Located near the square in the historic McPhail building. For a wealth of current information online, check franklinis.com.

275-1675; flynashville.com), 1 Terminal Drive, Nashville. BNA, just off I-40, about a 25-minute drive from Franklin, is going through a multiyear, multiproject renovation.

By bus: **Greyhound** (615-255-3556; greyhound.com). Greyhound pro-

NEIGHBORS HELPING NEIGHBORS

When the Battle of Franklin erupted on November 30, 1864, some of the fiercest fighting took place between the homes of the Lotz and Carter families. A master carpenter and piano maker by trade, German immigrant Johann Lotz had built his home almost single-handedly, intending it to be a showcase of his abilities to entice those seeking to build plantation homes in the area. A few of the elaborate touches Lotz used to show off his skills included three elaborate fireplace mantles, a gorgeous solid black walnut handrail that stretches two stories, and a whimsical bit of carpentry—using a piano leg, turned upside down, as a balustrade. As beautiful as the home was, it was no match for the threat of flying bullets and cannonballs sure to be let loose by Union and Confederate forces; Union soldiers had dug in just 100 yards from the home following a retreat from Spring Hill. Neighborly Mr. Carter offered the Lotz family refuge in his solid brick home, which also had a brick basement. Both families hunkered down while the 17-hour battle raged, and the next morning, when they emerged unscathed from the basement, the bodies of dead soldiers were reportedly so thick on the ground, one could barely walk without stepping on one. The Lotz home suffered its share of battle scars, from bullet holes to the burn track of a hot cannonball, which crashed through the roof and the floor of an upstairs bedroom before rolling to rest on the first floor.

The home served as a hospital for soldiers from both sides through the summer of 1865, and although Lotz repaired all the damage from the battle, his dream to be a builder of fine homes had evaporated. He eventually moved the family to California, where his daughter, Matilda—six at the time of the battle—made a name for herself internationally as a portrait and landscape painter. Her portrait of California governor Leland Stanford still hangs at Stanford University today.

The Lotz House (615-790-7190; lotzhouse.com), 1111 Columbia Avenue, is open Monday–Saturday 9–5 and Sunday 1–4. Adults $10, seniors $9, children 7–13 $5, and children six and under free.

vides service to Nashville from select cities; a temporary bus terminal is now being used, so be sure to call or visit the Web site for the most up-to-date information.

By car: From I-65, take the Murfreesboro Road exit (TN 96) and go west straight into town.

GETTING AROUND *By car:* Downtown there is some coveted, metered street parking in the square and Five Points area, with small lots tucked behind some restaurants and businesses. Away from the square, you'll need a car to get around.

By trolley: The **Franklin Transit Authority** (615-790-0604; tmagroup .org/trolley) runs a trolley service around town along four routes. Adults $1, children 50 cents (exact change is a must). Ten-ride ticket books and all-day passes are also available.

FRANKLIN'S CHARMING MAIN STREET

Stephanie Jones

williamsonmedicalcenter.org), 4321 Carothers Parkway.

✳ To See

HISTORIC SITES Carnton Plantation and Battlefield (615-794-0903; carnton.org), 1345 Carnton Lane. Open Mon.–Sat. 9–5, Sun. 1–5. Carnton, in one short evening in 1864, went from being one of the most prestigious farms in the region to serving as the largest field hospital in the area, as it was just a short distance from the gruesome Battle of Franklin. The McGavock family witnessed their way of life change forever and later donated part of the farm as a cemetery for the fallen. Call or check the Web site for details on the many special programs offered, including reenactments, events for children, and a truly scary ghost tour. The house and grounds have been meticulously restored. Adults $12, seniors $10, children $6. Grounds-only tour $5.

The Carter House (615-791-1861; carter-house.org), 1140 Columbia Avenue. Open Mon.–Sat. 9–5, Sun. noon–5. The Carter House, a National Historic Landmark, is dedicated to the memory of all who lost their lives in the Battle of Franklin. The 288-acre farm was the scene of the clash on that terrible night, and within hours, the house had become a field hospital. The home and outbuildings withstood the "blackest page . . . in the War of the Lost Cause" (as soldier Sam Watkins wrote of the battle in his memoir, *Company Aytch: Or, a Side Show of the Big Show*) and have been preserved as an incredibly moving historical experience. Adults $12, seniors $10, children $6. Grounds-only tour $5.

Fort Granger (615-794-2103; franklin-gov.com), 405 Murfreesboro Road. Open daily dawn–dusk. The fort was built by Union forces in 1862, and during the Battle of Franklin it served as a command post for Maj. Gen. John Schofield. The Union earthworks remain. A boardwalk meanders through the site, with interpretive signs along the way detailing portions of the battle as well as offering splendid views of Franklin. Free.

Franklin on Foot (615-400-3808; franklinonfoot.com), locations throughout Franklin. Franklin's history is filled with tales of the Civil War, ghosts, scoundrels, and scandals—all of which are told in charming fashion by local guides/history buffs who really know their stuff. Tours range from a 90-minute overview of the historic district and a kid-focused game of I-spy throughout the town to haunted evening tours for the family. $10 and up.

MUSEUMS McLemore House Museum (615-794-2270), 446 11th Avenue N. Open Thurs.–Sat. 10–2. In 1880, ex-slave Harvey McLemore bought a lot in an area called Hard Bargain and built this home, one of the first in what would become a middle-class African American community. The house remained in the McLemore family for more than a century and is in the process of being preserved. $5.

✳ To Do

DISC GOLF Liberty Park Disc Golf Course (615-794-2103), 2080 Turning Wheel Lane. Within the city's Liberty Park, the 10-hole disc golf course covers hilly terrain and winds through scenic woods—a nice challenge for experienced players, but not too difficult for those new to the game. Basket placements switch every few months, keeping the course fresh. Free.

WINERIES Arrington Vineyards (615-395-0102; arringtonvineyards .com), 6211 Patton Road, Arrington. Open Mon.–Thurs. 11–8, Sun. noon–6. A short drive from Franklin, the young Arrington has star power in the form of owner–country crooner Kix Brooks and winemaker Kip Summers, formerly of the award-winning Beachaven (see "Clarksville"). The winery currently offers about a dozen wines and music-filled events throughout the year, some of which feature Brooks and a parade of country-music favorites. During select times of the year, hot-air balloon rides are also offered. Wine tastings are free.

✳ Lodging

BED & BREAKFASTS/INNS
Magnolia House (615-794-8178), 1317 Columbia Avenue. Magnolia House is perfectly situated near the historic Carter House and Carnton Plantation, and within walking distance of downtown Franklin. The Craftsman-style home—with a magnolia-shaded front porch—was built in 1905 on land that was part of the site of the Battle of Franklin and has been tastefully updated. All four guest rooms offer lovely, comfy details, and a full-on Southern-style sit-down-and-have-a-biscuit breakfast awaits guests at 8:30 every morning. Moderate.

Old Marshall House (615-791-1455; oldmarshallhouse.com), 1030 John Williams Road. This

PRICE CATEGORIES:

Inexpensive	Less than $100 (for hotels, inns, and B&Bs); less than $50 (for campgrounds, state park facilities)
Moderate	$100–200
Expensive	$201–300
Very expensive	More than $300

lovely circa-1867 two-story farmhouse is on several acres a short distance from downtown Franklin. Offering three different welcoming rooms and a cozy, private log cabin, the Old Marshall House has a cult following. Could it be the beautiful gardens to gaze upon? The peaceful porches on which to perch? I think their amazing breakfasts might have something to do with it. Moderate.

HOTELS On the outskirts of Franklin, on the I-65 corridor, there are plenty of chain hotel options. I recommend the following if looking for a convenient hotel experience with easy highway access.

Aloft—Cool Springs (615-435-8700; alofthotels.com), 7109 S. Springs Drive. Sleek, slick, and hip, the Aloft is a chain hotel that totally feels like a stylish boutique hotel, with an open lobby with a tiny front desk and a long bar (look for live music or a DJ on the weekends), utilitarian rooms with contemporary furnishings, huge televisions, and a recharge station for electronics. Complimentary wireless and wired Internet access are available throughout the hotel; dining is a selection of snacks, breads, fruits, and beverages from the convenience-style store on the first floor or in the bar. Moderate.

✳ Where to Eat

EATING OUT 55 South (615-538-6001; eat55.com), 403 Main Street. Open Mon.–Thurs. 11–9, Fri.–Sat. 11–10, and Sun. 10–3. Locals flock to all of Chef Jason McConnell's restaurants, but his newest concept, 55 South, is the biggest hit yet. The name is a reference to the highway that runs from Memphis to New Orleans, and the menu features all manner of Southern comfort food and Big

Easy cuisine in a "Southern-rustic" atmosphere. Moderate.

Franklin Mercantile Deli (615-790-9730; franklinmercantile.com), 100 Fourth Avenue N. Open Mon.–Wed. 7–3, Thurs.–Sat. 7 AM–9 PM. "The Merc," as it is fondly known, is a Franklin institution, serving fresh, yummy food in a relaxed, vintage-furnished old building. From plate breakfasts and French toast in the morning to tapas and wine on open evenings, there is truly something delicious on the menu here for everyone. Live music is offered some nights. Moderate.

H.R.H. Dumplin's (615-791-4651), 428 Main Street. Open daily 11–2. Freshly baked bread, still warm. Honey butter. Chicken salad. Fruit tea. Sinful desserts. Enough said. Moderate.

Naticakes (615-807-1133; naticakes.com), 328 Main Street. Open Tues.–Sat. 10–6, Sun. 1–5. The delectable cupcakes and "nati-bites" that make a Naticakes treat the perfect pick-me-up for Main St. sightseers and shoppers also make life sweeter for children in need, as each purchase benefits the Natalie Wynn Carter foundation. Inexpensive.

Red Pony (615-595-7669; redponyrestaurant.com), 408 Main

PRICE CATEGORIES:	
Inexpensive	Less than $16
Moderate	$16–30
Expensive	$31–50
Very expensive	More than $50

Street. Open Mon.–Thurs. 5–10, Fri.–Sat. 5–11. Bar opens at 4. Everything from the freshly made guacamole and the shrimp and grits right through to the Chocolate Demise gets folks swooning over Red Pony. Good thing there is an excellent cocktail and wine list for reviving those in a faint. Reservations suggested. Moderate.

Saffire (615-599-4995; saffire restaurant.com), 230 Franklin Road. Open for lunch Tues.–Sun. 11–3, happy hour Tues.–Sun. 3–6:30, and dinner Tues.–Thurs. and Sun. 5–9, Fri.–Sat. 5–10. Located within the Factory (see *Selective Shopping*), Saffire gets rave reviews for anything prepared on its Tennessee hickory coal-burning grill. (And everything else on the menu.) Lunch is casual, dinner more elaborate, the wine list more than adequate. Moderate.

✳ Entertainment

Franklin's proximity to Music City assures that opportunities for wonderful live entertainment abound. Free outdoor concerts are offered in two beautiful city parks during the summer months, as well. A couple of options are listed below, but check franklinis.com for more current information—click on "entertain" and then "music."

LIVE-MUSIC VENUES Kimbro's Pickin' Parlor (615-599-2946; kimbroscafe.com), 214 S. Margin Street. Open for dinner Wed.–Sat.

5–9:30, with the bar open 5–closing. Check the Web site or give them a call for the entertainment schedule. Everyone describes Kimbro's as "like hanging out at a friend's house," and it is. From the patio to the living room of this old-home-turned-music venue, everything is relaxed and low-key. There is bluegrass almost every Thurs. night. Cover charges: rarely but sometimes.

Puckett's Grocery (615-794-5527; puckettsgrocery.com /franklin), 120 Fourth Avenue S. Showtimes vary, but music happens almost every night, Tues.–Sat., beginning at either 7:30 or 8:30. An offshoot of the famous Puckett's in nearby Leipers Fork, this new location offers the same vibe, down-home food, and great live music as the original. There is a $10 cover charge on weekend nights, and occasionally a $5 cover during the week. Reservations are a good idea. Their Web site has up-to-the-minute performance details.

✳ Selective Shopping

ANTIQUES AND HOME FURNISHINGS The Iron Gate (615-791-7511; theirongateon line.net), 338 W. Main Street. Open Mon.–Sat. 10–5. An interior design team led by Rozanne Jackson is based from this elegant, eclectic shop, full of wonderful, unique home furnishings and gifts. Every piece here has a story. Pretty linens, pajamas, pillows, and candles round out the selection.

Rare Prints Gallery (615-472-1980; rareprintsgallery.com), 420 Main Street. Open Mon.–Sat. 10–5. Their extensive collection of beautiful antique prints is nothing short of dizzying. Find works by Audubon, Piranesi, Gould, and other masters in categories ranging from architecture to quadrupeds.

Scarlett Scales Antiques (615-791-4097; scarlettscales.com), 212 S. Margin Street. Open Mon.–Sat. 10–5, Sun. 1–5. Scarlett's shop, in an old shotgun-style cottage, brings together a crazy mix of antique, vintage, and new, but it works! A great place to find great old painted furniture and garden statuary.

BOUTIQUE SHOPPING

The Factory (615-791-1777; factoryatfranklin.com), 230 Franklin Road. Open Mon.–Thurs. 10–5, Fri.–Sat. 10–6. Some shops are open on Sun. 1–5. Less than a mile from Franklin's downtown square, the Factory at Franklin is a historic 12-building complex that used to house the Dortch Stove Works. It's now home to a thriving mix of creative businesses, shops, and eateries.

Philanthropy (615-794-0074; philanthropyfashion.com), 434 Main Street. Open Mon.–Thurs. 10–5, Fri.–Sat. 10–6. This boutique touts "fashion + compassion" and delivers on both. Sales of each piece of their upmarket clothing,

UPSCALE SHOPPING IN FRANKLIN INCLUDES THE IRON GATE.

Stephanie Jones

including exclusive T-shirt designs, benefit causes both local and global. Look good, do good!

Walton's (615-790-0244; waltons jewelry.com), 410 Main Street. Open Tues.–Sat. 10–4:30. Walton's has a loyal following all over Middle Tennessee. Fans know that they will find a top-notch selection of estate and antique jewelry here, plus wonderful service, repairs, and advice.

SHOPPING MALLS Cool Springs Galleria (615-771-2128; coolspringsgalleria.com), 1800 Galleria Boulevard. Open Mon.–Sat. 10–9, Sun. noon–6. The Galleria is more than just the big mall—it also includes all the retail and restaurant space *around* the mall. The usual suspects—Macy's

and Dillard's, Pottery Barn and Williams-Sonoma, are all represented, plus a few unusual additions, including Plato's Closet (a consignment store) and Texas jeweler James Avery.

✳ Special Events

July 4th: **Franklin on the Fourth** is a celebration worthy of Mr. Benjamin Franklin himself. Held all day and evening in the blocks surrounding the square, the festivities include activities for children (petting zoo, inflatables, rock-wall climbing, pony rides, and more) crafts, live music, a fantastic parade, and, of course, the kind of fireworks display that brings you to your proud American feet, cheering.

COLUMBIA

Columbia is the charming county seat of Maury (pronounced locally as "murray") County. Snuggled in beside the Duck River in hilly Middle Tennessee, it's surrounded by rich farmland and horse country. The downtown district centers around the beautiful old courthouse, built in the early 1900s, and—like many downtowns its size—is currently undergoing revitalization efforts. Famous sons of Columbia include notables such as James Knox Polk, 11th U.S. president; Lyman T. Johnson, a prominent figure in the civil rights movement; and Sterling Marlin, a NASCAR driver.

Tucked in among the rolling farms that surround the town are many well-preserved antebellum houses and churches, most of which are private homes and active places of worship; others are open for tours. Columbia celebrates its self-proclaimed status as Mule Capital of the World with the Mule Day festival each year in early spring. The picturesque courthouse square has been seen on the silver screen as the backdrop in several movies, most recently *Hannah Montana: The Movie* and *Bailey*. Columbia is an excellent jumping-off point for enjoying the area's natural recreation opportunities: cycling, hiking, canoeing, and fishing.

MAURY COUNTY COURTHOUSE

GUIDANCE Maury County Convention & Visitors Bureau (888-852-1860; antebellum.com), 8 Public Square. Open Mon.–Fri. 8–4; closed during lunch. Additional location across from the Polk Home at 302 W. Seventh Street (open Mon.–Sat. 9–4). Both visitors centers have all the same helpful advice and brochures, but parking is easier at the W. Seventh Street spot.

GETTING THERE *By air:* **Nashville International Airport** (BNA; 615-275-1675; flynashville.com), 1 Terminal Drive, Nashville. BNA, just off I-40, about a 30-minute drive from Columbia, is going through a multiyear, multiproject renovation.

By bus: **Greyhound** (615-255-3556; greyhound.com). Greyhound provides service to Nashville from select cities. A temporary bus terminal is now being used, so be sure to call or visit the Web site for the most up-to-date information.

By car: From Nashville, exit I-65 at Saturn Parkway and follow US 31, Nashville Highway, south into town. From Huntsville, Alabama, and other points south, use the TN 50 exit, heading north, and turn right onto US 31.

GETTING AROUND *By car:* There is plenty of street parking in town, with small lots in front of or behind most businesses and attractions. Downtown Columbia is definitely strollable, but a car is a must to explore more of the area.

MEDICAL EMERGENCY **Maury Regional Hospital** (931-381-1111; mauryregional.com), 1224 Trotwood Avenue. Comprehensive 24-hour emergency services are offered through the hospital's emergency center, which includes a fast-track program for those patients whose injuries and illnesses are not life-threatening but still urgent.

✳ To See

HISTORIC SITES **James Knox Polk Home** (931-388-2354; jameskpolk .com), 301 W. Seventh Street. Open Mon.–Sat. 9–5, Sun. 1–5. During the winter months, closing time is 4. This Federal-style brick home is the only surviving residence of our 11th president, except the White House. Polk lived here following his graduation from the University of North Carolina, practicing law and strategizing for his political future. Built by President Polk's father, it now houses more than a thousand items, including paintings, furniture, and the Polks' White House china. Traveling exhibits are on display next door at the Polk Presidential Hall. Allow a little extra time to browse the nice bookshop. Adults $7, seniors $6, youth $4, family $20.

Rippavilla Plantation (931-486-9037; rippavilla.org), 5700 Main Street, Spring Hill. Open Mon.–Sat. 9:30–4:30, Sun. 1–4:30. A visit to gorgeous Rippavilla gives a glimpse of Tennessee's history in a nutshell: frontier farm life, plantation culture, the Civil War, Reconstruction . . . it's all here, with a little romance and family drama thrown in for good measure. The home and gardens have been painstakingly preserved and restored,

Stephanie Jones

ST. JOHN'S EPISCOPAL CHURCH

and many pieces original to the Cheairs family are on display. Adults $10, seniors $8, children $5.

St. John's Episcopal Church, County Route 243 at Polk Lane, Mount Pleasant. The gates aren't often open at this beautiful antebellum "plantation" church, and there is only one service held here each year, on Whitsunday. But if you're riding by, it's worth a stop. Leonidas Polk, who went on to become the Bishop of Louisiana and a Confederate general, built it in the 1840s. If you're able to see the cemetery behind the church, notice that many members of the Polk family are buried here, as well as all but one of the deceased Bishops of Tennessee.

✳ To Do

BICYCLING The Wheel (931-381-3225), 11 Public Square. To take advantage of some of the most scenic riding in the Southeast, check in at the Wheel for trail maps and advice on the best local rides. The friendly folks here will also be glad to supply you with any cycling equipment you may have forgotten. Rentals start at $15.

CANOEING AND KAYAKING Flatwoods Canoe Base (931-589-5661; flatwoodscanoe.com), 11711 TN 13 S., Flatwoods. Open Sun.–Fri. 8–7 (last pickup), Sat. 7–7 (last pickup), May–Oct. The calm waters of the Buffalo River are perfect for paddlers of all ability levels—whether canoers or kayakers—who float through gorgeous scenery, seemingly for miles. Single-day floats (4–14 miles, lasting anywhere from four to eight hours) and overnight trips (14–22 miles, lasting 6–10 hours) are offered, with the morning hours—through lunchtime—being the busiest during summers and weekends. Whether you're bringing your own canoe or kayak, or renting from Flatwoods, shuttle service is available. Single kayak rentals start at $22, while double kayaks or canoes start at $28.

The River Rat's Canoe Rental (931-381-2278; riverratcanoe.com), 4361 US 431. Seasonal operation, Mar.–Oct. Locals recommend this 30-plus-year-old family-owned business for canoe and kayak rentals. River Rat's can also hook you up with a guide for a "catch, photograph, and release" fishing expedition. Trips range from just a couple of hours (and miles) to full-out overnighter expeditions with almost 30 miles of paddling. Trips start at $20 per person.

FISHING Duck River. The beautiful Duck has angling opportunities galore. You must have a fishing license, which can be purchased at Ted's Sporting Goods (see *Selective Shopping*) or at Walmart (931-381-6892), 2101 Brookmeade Drive. Be sure to ask for the scoop on where the honey holes are and what's biting. Toll-free license information is available from the Tennessee Wildlife Resources Agency (800-648-8798).

Williamsport Lakes Management Area (931-583-2477), TN 50, approximately 10 miles northwest of Columbia. Nestled among 1,800 acres, this prime outdoor sporting area offers four different lakes, including one reserved especially for youth under age 16. Call the office for specifics, regulations, and the inside track on what's biting. Boat rental, bait, and tackle are available at the concession.

Stephanie Jones

JACKSON FALLS, NATCHEZ TRACE

✴ Green Space

SCENIC RIVERS AND HIGHWAYS Duck River. Thirty-seven miles of
the Duck River in Maury County have been designated a State Scenic
River. The Scenic section begins on the east side of Columbia at Iron
Bridge Road and flows north to the county line. Information on canoe
launching and routes is available by calling the Maury County Visitors
Bureau at 931-381-7176. Download a guide to the Duck River Blueway at

antebellum.com. (Please see *To Do* for more information on canoeing and kayaking.)

The **Natchez Trace Parkway** (nps.gov/akr/natr; scenictrace.com) is a scenic highway operated by the National Park Service and winds through Maury County a few miles east of town. It offers hiking and horseback riding trails, camping and picnic areas, as well as spots for historical and cultural exploration. The Trace is an extremely popular and well-maintained designated bike route. There are several trailheads and beautiful picnic areas not far from Columbia. Jackson Falls, at mile marker 404.7, is especially beautiful and worth the short but steep hike. Obey the posted speed limit, 50 mph, on the Trace.

✳ Lodging

See "Franklin" or "Nashville."

✳ Where to Eat

EATING OUT Killion's Coffee & Creamery (931-223-5902; killions .net), 40 Public Square. Open Mon.–Fri. 7:30–4. A great spot for coffee drinks, fruit smoothies, and pastries in the morning or a pimento cheese sandwich at lunchtime (go with the spicy version!), Killion's also serves an amazing frozen mocha—just the thing after a day of taking in Maury County's sites. Inexpensive.

Mt. Pleasant Grille (931-379-7228; mtpleasantgrille.com), 100 S. Main Street, Mount Pleasant. Open Tues. 10:30–2, Wed.–Thurs. 10:30–8, Fri.–Sat. 10:30–9, and Sun. 10:30–2. The Grille, located in the former Lumpy's drugstore, anchors one end of Mount Pleasant's tiny town square. Offering old-school ambience, friendly service, and fantastic food, it's well

PRICE CATEGORIES:	
Inexpensive	Less than $16
Moderate	$16–30
Expensive	$31–50
Very expensive	More than $50

worth making the short, scenic drive from Columbia. Menu favorites include fried green tomatoes with roasted red pepper sauce, the Tennessee Trail Salad, and a Mt. Pleasant Po'Boy (made with fried grouper). Dinner is a little dressier, with a full range of steak, pork, and chicken dishes; excellent pastas like the Louisiana Confetti; a nice wine list; and homemade desserts. Moderate.

Nolen's Barbecue (931-490-0007), 100 W. Fifth Street. Open Mon.–Fri. 11–6. Craving a little 'cue? Nolen's serves the best in the area. Very casual, eat in or carry out. My favorite is the pulled pork sandwich with slaw and a little extra sauce, but the ribs are great, too. There are two other locations in town, at 115 E. James Campbell Boulevard (931-381-4322) and 5021C Trotwood Avenue (931-388-1844), that are open on Sat. as well and stay open until 7 each night. Moderate.

Square Market & Café (931-840-3636; squaremarketcafe.com), 36 Public Square. Open Mon.– Thurs. 9–5, Fri. 9–9, and Sat. 10:30–9. Lovely locals Liz Lovell and Debra Mann have been serving up hospitality and great food in their little corner of the square for years. The crowd is a mix of Columbia's ladies who lunch and lawyers and staff from the courthouse across the street. Breakfast burritos and pastries, salads, pani-

MT. PLEASANT GRILLE

Stephanie Jones

Stephanie Jones

BRECKENRIDGE HOUSE

nis, soups, pastas . . . all are home-made, and all are delicious. Live music during dinner most Fri. and Sat. nights. Songwriters night once a month is always special and requires reservations. Moderate.

✳ Selective Shopping

ANTIQUES Breckenridge House (931-379-3399), 205 N. Main Street, Mount Pleasant. Open Tues.–Sat. 11–4 or by appointment. From a lovely circa-1815 Federal cottage (the former Breckenridge Hatter's Shop, the oldest standing home in town), Jerry Tipper and Tim Porter carry a beautiful, carefully edited selection of 18th- and 19th-century American and European art, furniture, silver, and jewelry.

Loblolly Interiors Market Antiques (931-388-4676), 810 Walker Street. Open Mon.–Sat. 10–3. Owner and artist Ellen Calvin finds antique furniture, rugs, and vintage treasures, and tosses them together with her own paintings in flea-market-found frames to great effect. Work by several local artists is also represented. If you're lucky, there will be a cold drink and a piece of chocolate in her fridge to enjoy while you're browsing.

SPORTING GOODS Ted's Sporting Goods (931-388-6387; teds sportinggoods.com), 806 S. Main Street. Open Mon.–Fri. 8–5:30, Sat. 8–4. Heading south from the courthouse square, don't be alarmed by that old-fashioned storefront with the upside-down sign. It's always been that way at Ted's, just as it's been the place since 1955 for locals to find their favorite work and play clothes, boots, and camping/fishing/hunting gear. A visit during the holidays shows that the proprietors' sense of humor extends beyond

LEIPERS FORK

Blink, and you might miss tiny Leipers Fork—so you'll definitely want to keep your eyes wide open. A charming little village located just off the Natchez Trace Parkway about 20 minutes from Franklin, Leipers Fork is home to horse lovers and country music luminaries of varying degree. Founded by land-grant-holding pioneers from Virginia and North Carolina, the village was named for the Leiper family, who had settled along the creek running through town. The town itself is listed on the National Register of Historic Places as it contains so many beautiful examples of 19th-century architecture. (*Note:* The locally accepted spelling of *Leipers* does not use an apostrophe before the *s*, and there is no sense arguing about it. Just relax and enjoy the non-grammar-related delights that the Fork has to offer.)

Along its main street, Old Hillsboro Road, there are low-key but swank shops and galleries, including **Serenite Maison** (615-599-2071), which features a stunning selection of vintage and antique furnishings, jewelry, and gifts; **Leipers Creek Gallery** (615-599-5102; leiperscreekgallery.com), which represents the very finest local and regional artists; and **Yeoman's in the Fork** (615-983-6460; yeomansinthefork.com), offering a wealth of rare and unusual books, ranging in categories from travel and exploration to military and war. These mesh seamlessly with the more divelike joints like **Puckett's Grocery** (615-794-1308; puckettsgrocery.com), a destination for its homey charm, great food, and incredible live music; **Country Boy** (615-591-4245; thecountryboyrestaurant.com), just the spot for ham biscuits and gravy or a plate lunch ("meat and two"); and **Joe Natural's Farm Store** (615-595-2233), where everything is natural, organic, and locally farmed, harvested, or otherwise produced.

PUCKETT'S GROCERY
Stephanie Jones

Just as in its early days as a pleasant stop along the Natchez Trace, Leipers Fork is still a perfect place to pause for a great meal, a little strolling and browsing, and to catch some live music.

the upside-down sign—you'll find the hunting trophies hanging throughout the store wearing festive bows.

✳ Special Events

Late March–early April: **Mule Day** (931-381-9557; muleday.net), downtown Columbia. Since the 1840s, Columbia has set aside four days in early spring to honor the animal that helped shape and build their local economy. Attended by more than 200,000 visitors, the Mule Day celebrations include a parade, traditional Appalachian crafts, music, and dancing—in addition, of course, to the beasts of burden themselves. Most events are free.

BOUTIQUE SHOPPING
Lily Jane (931-381-6554), 1173A Trotwood Avenue. Open Mon.–Fri. 10–5, Sat. 10–3. Savvy young shopkeeper Lucy Fleming chooses the most on-trend clothing, bags, stationery, and gifts for her boutique, Lily Jane (named to honor her grandmothers). This favorite haunt of Columbia's young and stylish conveniently connects to the **Buckhead Coffeehouse** (931-388-0804; buckheadcoffeehouse.com).

LOBLOLLY

Stephanie Jones

TED'S SPORTING GOODS

LYNCHBURG, MANCHESTER, AND SHELBYVILLE

Heading southeast out of Nashville on I-24, through what seems like an endless string of strip malls and fast food franchises all the way past Murfreesboro, one suddenly breaks into the country—wide open spaces with rolling hills, lush green fields, and a hint of the more rocky landscape to come. Dotting this area of Tennessee are tiny towns, huge farms, and some of the state's most notable claims to fame.

Agriculture has always been the mainstay of the counties in this area, including those featured in this chapter—Bedford, Coffee, and Moore. While the land that makes up these counties was once occupied by the ancient Woodland people and later Native American tribes, white settlers began appearing in the very late 1700s as frontier outposts were established, including Fort Nash.

A STATUE OF JACK DANIEL, THE MAN WHO STARTED IT ALL.

When the railroad between Nashville and Chattanooga was established in the early 1800s, the Coffee County town of Tullahoma became an important connector to other lines that led to areas rich in coal, timber, and other natural resources. While the railroad brought prosperity, it also brought both the Union and Confederate armies during the Civil War, resulting in the almost total destruction of the original town.

These three counties share an agricultural heritage as well as each being home to one of Tennessee's most famous offerings. In Bedford County, Shelbyville is most recognized as ground zero for the Tennessee walking horse; it is here in the bucolic rural setting that many horse farms dedicated to the graceful, slow-gaited, and surefooted creature breed champions. In the days leading up to Labor Day, Shelbyville turns from rural escape to horse heaven, as tens of thousands of competitors and fans gather here for "the Celebration," as the annual 10-day Tennessee Walking Horse National Celebration is more commonly known.

Tiny Manchester, with a population of fewer than 10,000, is the seat of Coffee County. In 2001, an enterprising group of friends commandeered a field to host a music festival—not unlike Woodstock—and Bonnaroo, or Roo, was born, turning this tiny hamlet into a rocking musical destination within a very short time. Fans come from across the globe and crowd into the field for the three-day event, bringing RVs and tents, or sometimes just sleeping bags and no change of clothes, to hear a continual lineup of familiar rock stars and up-and-coming acts.

Tennessee's smallest county—Moore—is home to the world's biggest name in whiskey, Jack Daniel's. History tells us young Jack bought his first whiskey still at the tender age of 13 in 1863; he used the pure water found in a local cave, a handcrafted oak barrel, and a bit of mellow charcoal to create his Tennessee sippin' whiskey, as the label heralds his concoction. Tiny Lynchburg does huge business these days thanks to gentleman Jack. The town has a pretty town square, stores proffering whiskey-inspired gifts and a few other specialty stores, and a few nice restaurants. The scenic drive from Nashville through the rolling hills of Middle Tennessee is certainly worth the trip.

GUIDANCE Lynchburg/Moore County Chamber of Commerce (931-759-4111; lynchburgtn.com), 10 Mechanic Street, Lynchburg. The visitors center is located in the town's old gas station just off the town square.

Manchester Area Chamber of Commerce (931-728-7635; macoc.org), 110 E. Main Street, Manchester.

Shelbyville–Bedford County Chamber of Commerce (931-684-3482; shelbyvilletn.com), 100 N. Cannon Boulevard, Shelbyville.

GETTING THERE *By air:* **Nashville International Airport** (BNA; 615-275-1675; flynashville.com), 1 Terminal Drive, Nashville. BNA is the closest major airport to Lynchburg, Shelbyville, and Manchester; all major airlines fly into BNA, which is located off I-40, about a 45-minute drive from Lynchburg. BNA and the Chattanooga airport (**Chattanooga Metropolitan Airport,** 423-855-2200, chattairport.com, 1001 Airport Road, #14) are about equidistant from the Manchester and Shelbyville areas.

By bus: While there is no **Greyhound** (800-231-2222; greyhound.com)
service to these counties, Chattanooga and Nashville both have Greyhound terminals. From Apr. through Oct., **Gray Line** (615-883-5555;
graylinenashville.com) offers Tues., Thurs., and Sat. round-trip shuttles to
Lynchburg from select Nashville hotels. The cost is $45 for adults, $22.50
for children 6–11.

By car: To get to Manchester, take I-24 northwest from Chattanooga or
southeast from Nashville to TN 55; continue west on TN 55 about 30
miles to reach Lynchburg. The town is very small, and one can walk from
Jack Daniel's right to the town square, about a quarter mile. To reach
Shelbyville, take I-24 to TN 64 E.

GETTING AROUND *By car:* There is no local public transportation system in these counties, so a car is essential for exploring the area. As the
area is more rural, street signage is hit and miss, so be sure to keep
detailed map in the car.

MEDICAL EMERGENCY Heritage Medical Center (931-685-5433),
2835 US 231 N., Shelbyville, is a level-two trauma center, meaning there
are emergency services available 24 hours daily, but some diagnostic services may not be available.

United Regional Medical Center (931-728-3586; urmchealthcare
.com), 1001 McArthur Street, Manchester. Offers urgent care.

✳ To See

HISTORIC SITES Falls Mill & Country Store (931-469-7161; falls
mill.com), 134 Falls Mill Road, Belvedere. Open Mon.–Tues. and Thurs–
Sat. 9–4, Sun. 12:30–4. Closed Wed. Set in a cove along Factory Creek,
the pastoral Falls Mill has been many things over the years—cotton mill,
woodworking shop, and now, a working gristmill, with the waterwheel
powering the huge millstones to grind flour, grits, and cornmeal. Admission includes a brief history of the mill, built in 1873, and then visitors
take a self-guided tour throughout the exhibits and grounds. Antique
hand looms and spinning wheels, wool carding machines, and other tools
and equipment from the mill's colorful history are on display; a country
store on the second floor offers freshly ground flour, grits, and cornmeal
to take home, as well as handmade crafts and gifts. A two-story, 1895 log
cabin on the grounds is available for overnight guests. Adults $4, seniors
$3, children under 14 $2.

Old Stone Fort State Archaeological Park (931-723-5073; state.tn.us
/environment/parks/OldStoneFort), 732 Stone Fort Drive, Manchester.
Park open daily 8–sunset, year-round; museum open daily 8–4:30. A
2,000-year-old archaeological site, Old Stone Fort combines walls,

TENNESSEE WALKING HORSE MUSEUM

mounds, and cliffs to create an enclosure, with a hilltop mound believed to be a ceremonial site used by Native Americans. Researchers from the University of Tennessee determined the approximate age of the site, dating back to the Woodland era, and know the site wasn't built quickly, but rather over hundreds of years, with the work completed by at least two different tribes. There's great debate over the fort's purpose, whether for defense or as sacred ground, but researchers found little evidence of continual occupation, and the prevailing theory is the site was sacred. An excellent museum details the excavation of the site and the research into it. Beyond the archaeological ruins, the state park offers visitors a range of athletic options, including a nine-hole golf course, a few short hiking trails of easy and moderate difficulty, river fishing, and canoeing. Fifty heavily wooded campsites—for both tent and RV camping—give a more remote feel than most state park campsites. The sites are first come, first serve and include water and electrical hookups. There's no admission fee for the park.

MUSEUMS Arrowheads to Aerospace Museum (931-723-1323), 24 Campground Road, Manchester. Open daily 10–2. A funky little museum with a hodgepodge collection, including scale replicas of pioneer and colonial-era buildings, Civil War artifacts and documents, and Indian artifacts found in local fields. Of special interest is an exhibit detailing the modern military history of Coffee County; during World War II, open farmland between Manchester and Tullahoma was used as Camp Forrest, an army training camp under the command of Gen. George S. Patton. More than 250,000 troops trained here for the European theater, and the land was eventually turned into the Arnold Engineering Development Center (AEDC), which tests and evaluates space, aircraft, and missile systems. Adults $5, students 7–17 and seniors 65-plus $4, children 2–6 $3. The museum accepts cash or personal checks only.

Tennessee Walking Horse Museum (931-759-5747; twhbea.com/TWH Museum.htm), Public Square, Lynchburg. Open Tues.–Sat. 10–4, but closed noon–1 for lunch. The beautiful Tennessee walking horse hails from this part of the state, and the museum celebrates all things related to this equine perfection. Historic photographs, tack and saddles from championship horses, and a thorough explanation of the breed and its popularity are all explored in this small museum. Rotating exhibits highlight individual trainers, owners, and champion horses. Free.

JACK DANIEL'S DISTILLERY

WINERIES/DISTILLERIES Beans Creek Winery (931-723-2294; beanscreekwinery.com), 426 Ragsdale Road, Manchester. Open Mon.–Thurs. 10–6, Fri.–Sat. 10–7, and Sun. 1–5. Using grapes grown in Middle and Eastern Tennessee, Bean Creek offers an award-winning collection including dry whites and reds, semidry whites, and sweet wines including fruit wines, as well as a few sparkling options. In the fall and spring, sometimes there is live music on Sat. evenings, and folks are invited to bring their picnic dinners to enjoy the festivities. Free.

George Dickel Distillery (800-462-3366; dickel.com), 1950 Cascade Hollow Road, Tullahoma. Open Tues.–Sat. 9–4; last tour starts at 3:30. The Jack Daniel's Distillery is the country's oldest, but it is hardly the only one. About 20 miles from Lynchburg, George Dickel set up shop in Cascade Hollow. Believing that whiskey made in the wintertime was more mellow, George chilled his blend before it went into the vats to age. He believed his whiskey to be so smooth that he spelled it with no *e*, to mimic the fine Scotch whiskies produced in Scotland. The distillery features the only working post office housed at a distillery in the United States. Free.

Jack Daniel's Distillery (931-759-4221; jackdaniels.com), 289 Lynchburg Highway, Lynchburg. Tours of the distillery happen daily every 15 minutes 9–4:30 except holidays. It's ironic that the tiny town of Lynchburg—home to Jack Daniel's Distillery—is in a dry county; you won't get a taste of the famous Tennessee sippin' whiskey anywhere in town, including the distillery. Instead, you'll be offered a refreshing glass of lemonade at the end of the distillery tour. (You can, however, purchase some of the booze to take home with you, as long as it's not Sun. and you're not a resident of Moore County.) The Jack Daniel's story is fascinating, as this legendary Tennessean began making whiskey at the tender age of 13, when he bought a still from a neighbor. The tour highlights the whiskey-making process, and guides regale visitors with tales of Mr. Jack and the characters who worked for him. From the rickyard—where the charcoal that makes the whiskey so mellow is burned—to the huge barrel room, the tour covers 18 stops throughout the sprawling complex in the hollow. No visit would be complete without a visit to Miss Mary Bobo's (see *Where to Eat*), which serves Southern-style comfort food. Tours are free.

✳ Green Space

PARKS ✍ **H.V. Griffin Park** (931-684-9780; shelbyvilletn.org/parksdept), 220 Tulip Tree Drive, Shelbyville. Open daily sunrise–sunset. The 84-acre park offers a huge playground for children featuring forts, slides, and climbing equipment, and other recreation options including horseshoe pits, shuffleboard courts, and a disc golf course. Free.

✳ Lodging

BED & BREAKFASTS/INNS

Cinnamon Ridge Bed & Breakfast (931-685-9200; bbonline.com /tn/cinnamon), 799 Whitthome Street, Shelbyville. The stately, white-columned home with five bedrooms, a large front porch filled with rocking chairs, and antique furnishings is reminiscent of a plantation home, although each bedroom is fully kitted out with all the modern amenities, including a television and private bath. Inexpensive.

🖋 🐾 **Clearview Horse Farm** (931-684-8822; clearviewhorse farm.com), 2291 US 231 S., Shelbyville. Equine enthusiasts will delight in the chance to stay at this working horse farm, home to a number of championship horses of a variety of breeds, as well as a huge riding arena and training operation. The bedrooms are horse themed and offer queen accommodations, with some day beds or connecting rooms available, and there's a pool for guests to enjoy. Breakfast is as one might expect at a working horse farm— continental, meant to be eaten on the run. Or gallop, if you prefer. Trail rides and lessons are available to guests, and the farm is pet friendly. Inexpensive.

Falls Mill Bed & Breakfast (931-469-7161; fallsmill.com), 134 Falls Mill Road, Belvedere. On the grounds of the Falls Mill complex, an 1895 log cabin beckons guests who want an authentic country cabin experience. The

PRICE CATEGORIES:	
Inexpensive	Less than $100 (for hotels, inns, and B&Bs); less than $50 (for campgrounds, state park facilities)
Moderate	$100–200
Expensive	$201–300
Very expensive	More than $300

simply furnished yet completely outfitted cabin offers a huge stone fireplace for cozy nights, a kitchen stocked with homemade breads and all the fixings for a full country breakfast (including samples of the mill's grits and pancake mix to try out), and modern conveniences including satellite television and a DVD player. Downstairs, a queen sleeper sofa is available, while the sleeping loft offers a queen bed and the cabin's only bathroom. Moderate.

Leming House Bed & Breakfast (931-728-5005), 414 E. Main Street, Manchester. A painted lady, the Leming is a pink Victorian home once owned by Manchester's original pharmacist. Featuring Victorian antiques and style, the B&B has three bedrooms, only one of which with a private bath (the other two rooms share). Rates include a full breakfast and midnight access to the kitchen for late-night snacks. There's no minimum stay. Inexpensive.

BELL BUCKLE

Almost sitting on the line between Rutherford and Bedford counties, Bell Buckle is a charming railroad town surrounded by rolling hills, filled with restored Victorian and Arts and Crafts homes, and a smattering of antiques and gifts stores, culminating in a utterly enchanting little spot in which to stop.

The town's first businessman, A. D. Fugitt, gave over some land for the rail depot and rail line, creating an important stockyard between Nashville and Chattanooga. The town blossomed as the rail-boosted economy set in, with major banking and business concerns setting up shop to cater to the growing population, which numbered more than one thousand by the Civil War. A prestigious boarding and day school—the Webb School—was established in the late 1880s and today is one of the state's top college preparatory schools.

The decline of Bell Buckle began with the Depression as the rail trade tapered off, and local businesses began to falter. The charming downtown area was almost a ghost town. Slowly, the plywood started coming off shop windows and homes, as interest in preserving the town's beauty and historic ambience grew, and today Bell Buckle's small strip of downtown stores are selling antiques, gifts, and arts and crafts. The Bell Buckle Café severs up barbecue and lemonade, plus live music on the weekend.

For more information about the Bell Buckle Antiques & Craft District, call 931-389-9663 or log onto bellbucklechamber.com.

Maplewood at Lynchburg (931-636-9254; maplewoodatlynchburg.com), 686 Motlow Barns Road, Lynchburg. This 1858 antebellum residence is the childhood home of Mary Evans Bobo, of Miss Mary Bobo's Boarding House fame. Within walking distance of downtown and of the Jack Daniel's Distillery, the lodging's guest rooms have their own private baths and balconies. Croquet and horseshoes are available on the side lawn. No pets, children, or smoking. Inexpensive.

Mulberry Cottage and Mulberry Manor (931-438-8464; mulberrycottagetn.com), off the downtown square, Lynchburg. Built in the late 1800s, one house is stone and the other wooden, both retaining their charming architectural elements throughout their restorations. Mulberry Cottage was the first jail in town, built in 1865. Breakfast is continental, and the town square is just a short walk from each home. Inexpensive.

The Tolley House (931-759-7263; tolleyhouse.com), 1253 Main Street, Lynchburg. This beautiful white wood house with imposing columns is what a bed & breakfast should look like. The two rooms are adjacent to each other on the first floor, with Miss Ethel's room done in pink, white, and light green, while Mr. Lem's room is more masculine. A full country breakfast is served, and in the evening, sweets are brought out to tempt, including homemade fruit pies. Moderate.

✳ Where to Eat

EATING OUT Cattywampus (931-759-5366; cattywampus restaurant.com), 783 Fayetteville Highway, Lynchburg. Open Mon.–Wed. 11–2, Thurs. 11–2 and 5–9, and Fri.–Sat. 11–9. It's white-tablecloth dining with a twist— and that means corn bread is served up on said white tablecloth right in the iron skillet it was made in. While some might be put off by the overly countrified phrasing on the menu, the food is worthy of a visit, as there are a lot of fresh items on the menu with a nice touch, including some basics like hand-battered cheese sticks,

BONNAROO MUSIC FESTIVAL

Tennessee Department of Tourism

iron skillet fried chicken, and pan-seared catfish. Traditional plate lunches are also served up, with a daily soup special. Moderate.

Gasthaus Bistro and Pub (931-723-1500; gasthaus.baronphork .com), 1401 Hillsboro, Manchester. Open Tues. 5–9, Wed.–Sat. 11–"whenever." But officially, 9. With an authentic German menu with a bit of a Southern twang, Gasthaus offers everything from a wurst salad and bratwurst, sauerbraten, schnitzels, and potato pancakes to chef salads and fried mac and cheese. On the second Tues. of each month, the buffet is kicked up a notch with a beer tasting. The service is super friendly, the prices are insane considering the homemade quality of the food, and the atmosphere is Oma's house meets Granny's cabin. Inexpensive.

Miss Mary Bobo's Boarding House (931-759-7394; jackdaniels .com), 295 Main Street, Lynchburg. Seatings at 1 PM daily, with additional seasonal seatings offered; call the restaurant for the most updated schedule. After your tour at the Jack Daniel's Distillery, visit Miss Mary Bobo's, where the buttery squash casserole, crispy fried chicken, and hot homemade

rolls and corn bread are served family style in a historic home that was once a boardinghouse. Reservations are required. Moderate.

✳ Selective Shopping

ARTS AND CRAFTS Foothills Craft Guild (931-728-9326), 418 Woodbury Highway, Manchester. Open Mon.–Sat. 9–5, Sun. 1–5. The guild is the oldest local guild in Tennessee and features more than two hundred juried artists from the region who work in metal, class, clay, and fiber. Fall and holiday shows make for excellent gift shopping.

Lynchburg Pottery (931-759-5205), 26 Short Street, Lynchburg. Functional and decorative art and pottery, prints, wood carvings, and jewelry.

✳ Special Events

Mid-June: **Bonnaroo** (bonnaroo .com), 1560 New Bushy Branch Road, Manchester. Out on what's now called Great Stage Park, a four-day rock concert has turned from a simple, rural festival of rock to a must-do for American music fans. About 70,000 people descend on Manchester for the event; children are welcome, but this is not a suitable event for kids. RV and tent camping are available on the farm, while motels are available in the surrounding area for those who prefer not to rough it. Tickets are $250 for the four-day event, and a ticket is required for anyone older than six.

Tennessee Department of Tourism

TENNESSEE WALKING HORSE NATIONAL CELEBRATION

June–October: **Noon Time on BBQ Hill** (931-759-6993; jackdaniels.com), Jack Daniel's Distillery, Lynchburg. Fri. and Sat. lunches (11–1) June–Oct. feature live music and games, a huge serving of barbecued chicken and pork and all the sides, plus buckets of tea and lemonade. Reservations are recommended. Adults $25, children $10. Children under three are free.

Late August–early September: **Tennessee Walking Horse National Celebration** (931-684-5915; twhnc.com), Celebration Grounds/Calsonic Arena, Shelbyville. Almost two full weeks of competition and showmanship draw tens of thousands of equine enthusiasts to Shelbyville. Tickets run from $7 and up.

UPPER CUMBERLAND

BYRDSTOWN AND PALL MALL

Byrdstown, the county seat of Pickett County, was named for Civil War Union veteran Col. Richard Byrd, who struggled to keep the state in the Union; when it seceded, he joined Union forces.

The Borderlands, as this area was known, became a political hot potato during the Civil War, as it served as a border between the Union and Confederacy. Here, loyalties were torn between sides, oftentimes within the same family. And many soldiers would begin fighting for one side, then have a change of heart and jump ship for the other. Bands of guerillas roamed the area, terrorizing residents.

At one time, the small county was rich with agricultural resources despite its hilly nature. Corn, wheat, grass, and livestock were all farmed here, but when the Corps of Engineers dammed the Obey River and created the Dale Hollow Reservoir, the best agricultural land was swallowed up—and folks left the area in droves.

Pall Mall has its own military hero—Sgt. Alvin C. York, the small-town sharpshooter who became one of the most decorated veterans of World War I. York and his small patrol were sent out to confront a machine gun unit that was impeding the advance of his regiment; York became separated from his men and single-handedly took on the unit with only a single rifle and a pistol. The fight ended with 20 dead, and York and his team of six accepting the surrender of the rest of the Germans—more than 130 men. York's story is told at his family home and museum in Pall Mall.

The drive to Pall Mall and Byrdstown is a winding one, once you leave I-40—and on a beautiful day, it is definitely worth the time. Open farmland gives way to shaded forests, and the scenery is particularly fetching in the fall, with brilliant colors creating a postcard-perfect setting. Be warned, however, that once out of Crossville, services are few and far between—so be sure to fill up the tank before setting out.

Tennessee Department of Tourism

GUIDANCE Byrdstown-Pickett Chamber of Commerce (931-864-7195), 109 W. Main Street, Byrdstown.

GETTING THERE *By air:* **Nashville International Airport** (BNA; 615-275-1675; flynashville.com), 1 Terminal Drive, Nashville. BNA is the closest major airport to the area, with service from all major and regional carriers.

By car: From I-40 at Cookeville, take TN 111 north to Byrdstown. From Byrdstown, Pall Mall is east via TN 325 and US 127. Alternatively, take US 127 north from Crossville.

GETTING AROUND *By car:* TN 111/Livingston Highway and TN 325/ Main Street are the major thoroughfares in Byrdstown. TN 28/US 127/ York Highway is the major route into Pall Mall, where major streets are the Wolf River Loop and Rotten Fork Road.

MEDICAL EMERGENCY Livingston Regional Hospital (931-823-5611; livingstonregionalhospital.com), 315 Oak Street, Livingston. Offers emergency services to the Upper Cumberland region, including Byrdstown and Pall Mall.

✳ To See

HISTORIC SITES ✅ **Cordell Hull Birthplace & Museum State Park** (931-864-3247; friendsofcordellhull.org), 1300 Cordell Hull Drive, Byrdstown. Open daily 9–5, Apr.–Oct.; daily 10–4, Nov.–Mar. Secretary of state during Franklin D. Roosevelt's administration, Cordell Hull was born in a small cabin that's been reconstructed at the park, the site of which was once part of his father's farm. Hull was considered the father of the United Nations and was awarded a Nobel Peace Prize for his work to create the international organization; a replica of the medal and other memorabilia are on display at the museum. A 2.5-mile (round-trip) nature trail at the park leads to Bunkum Cave, where Hull's father purportedly made moonshine; the cave's entrance is huge—100 feet wide and 50 feet high—and while visitors are welcome to explore the cave, those going farther than the opening are required to obtain a permit from park officials. Free.

Sgt. Alvin C. York State Historic Park (931-347-2664; state.tn.us /environment/parks/SgtYork), US 127, Pall Mall. Open daily 9–5, Apr.–Oct.; daily 9–4, Nov.–Mar. Along the banks of the Wolf River, the York family farm, home, and gristmill tell the story of one of America's most decorated war heroes. The museum is complete with photos, mementos, and personal items; York's son Andrew Jackson York serves as a park ranger. Free.

✳ To Do

OUTDOOR RECREATION ✅ **Dale Hollow Lake** (931-243-3136; lrn.us ace.army.mil/op/DAL/rec/), 540 Dale Hollow Dam Road, Celina. Primitive camping, fishing, hunting, and boating are offered all around the lake, which stretches into Kentucky to the north and as far west as Celina, where the lake headquarters is located. There are hiking and horseback trails, and the lake's crystal-clear waters provide excellent scuba diving. No fee for entrance to the park, although there are fees for camping and other activities.

✳ Green Space

PARKS Big South Fork National River and Recreation Area (423-569-9778; nps.gov/biso), 4564 Leatherwood Road, Oneida. From Byrdstown or Pall Mall, follow US 127 south to County Route 154, and follow 154 east to County Route 297, to the Bandy Creek Visitor Center. Open daily sunrise–sunset; visitors centers open daily 8–6 May–Sept. and daily 8–4 Oct.–Apr. The Big South Fork of the Cumberland River runs through gorges and valleys for 90 miles of this 125,000-acre park, allowing whitewater paddlers a variety of long, challenging runs through incredible scenery; more sedate canoeing is available for those not ready to take on the rapids. There are more than 150 miles of trails in Big South Fork, from 1-mile loops to two-day backcountry treks; camping options include primitive, backcountry, and traditional campsites. Trail rides, mountain bike trails, and stargazing are also available, and there are several archaeological sites housed in the park, including Blue Heron, an abandoned coal mining town. There's no entrance fee to the park; campsites start at $5/night (permits are required), and other activities, including use of the swimming pool or trail rides, are fee based. Fishing licenses are required, and Kentucky and Tennessee have a reciprocal license, good in both states, that's best to use while in the park.

✳ Lodging

HOTELS Holiday Inn Express Crossville (931-707-1035; hiexpress.com), 560 Peavine Road, Crossville. The Holiday Inn Express in Crossville has easy access to I-40, as well as US 127 heading north toward Byrdstown and Pall Mall. Moderate. See "Crossville."

VACATION RENTALS Big South Fork Black Bear Vacation Cabin Rental (734-752-8735; blackbearmountainrentals.com), 3045 Coon Hunter Lodge Road, Jamestown. This 1,600-square-foot rental cabin is decorated with

PRICE CATEGORIES:	
Inexpensive	Less than $100 (for hotels, inns, and B&Bs); less than $50 (for campgrounds, state park facilities)
Moderate	$100–200
Expensive	$201–300
Very expensive	More than $300

antiques and hand-painted artwork; two bedrooms feature queen beds and large baths. Outdoor amenities include a gas barbecue and a fire pit. Two-night

SGT. ALVIN C. YORK HOME

Tennessee Department of Tourism

minimum, with a three-night minimum on holiday weekends.
Moderate.

Buck's Gardens & Grotto (931-
879-5572; buckslodging.com), 99
Buck Lane, Pall Mall. Nestled in
more than 300 acres of rolling
farmland, two historic homes offer
comfortable, rustic accommodations in a pastoral setting. Both
offer full kitchens and are outfitted with antiques, quilts, and
porches with rocking chairs. Be
sure to bring your own food, and
note that there are no laundry
facilities in either accommodation—but one hardly seems to
care, thanks to the relaxing rural
setting of the farm. Moderate.

Dale Hollow Lake Cabins (931-
864-7577; dalehollowcabins.com),
109 W. Main Street, Byrdstown.
Fully equipped lakeside rentals
offer privacy, scenic views, decks,
and in some cases, billiards tables.
Moderate–expensive, depending
on season and choice of cabin.

Dale Hollow Marina (931-243-
2211; dalehollowmarina.com), 440
Arlen Webb Drive, Celina. Two-
to four-bedroom cottages at the
marina are open year-round and
include a discounted slip rate;
daily and weekly rentals are available. The marina also rents a variety of houseboats.
Inexpensive–moderate.

DALE HOLLOW LAKE

Tennessee Department of Tourism

✳ Where to Eat

EATING OUT Bob Cat Den
(931-864-3125), 8550 TN 111,
Byrdstown. Open Mon.–Sat.
11–10. Traditional Southern comfort food at rock-bottom pricing—
including meat-and-three plates
for less than $6. It's a cozy spot
filled with antiques and kitchen
oddities for sale, including an
amazing selection of cookie jars.
Inexpensive.

Dixie Café (931-864-6535), 31
Courthouse Square, Byrdstown.
Open Mon.–Fri. 11–9. Typical
American food served up by a
genuinely friendly staff; huge
breakfast platters include eggs,

PRICE CATEGORIES:	
Inexpensive	Less than $16
Moderate	$16–30
Expensive	$31–50
Very expensive	More than $50

potatoes, breads, and meat, and are worth the visit. Inexpensive.

Wolf River Grill (931-864-4499), 3009 Red Hill Road, Byrdstown. Open Mon.–Thurs. and Sun. 5–9, Fri.–Sat. 5–10. Steaks are a specialty of this restaurant, as well as live music and a children's menu. Karaoke and billiards are nightly attractions. Moderate.

✳ Selective Shopping

ARTS AND CRAFTS Muddy Pond Mennonite Community (931-445-7829; bigsouthforkpark .com/muddypond.htm), Hanging Limb Community, Monterey. Stores are generally open 10–5, closed Sun. and holidays. The working Mennonite community, about 20 miles from Cookeville, includes a blacksmith shop,

bakery, leather shop, and a general store. Free. See "Cookeville."

✳ Special Events

Late March: **Sgt. Alvin C. York Black Powder Shoot** (931-347-2664; sgtyork.org), Valley of the Three Forks of the River, Pall Mall. A shooting competition using only traditional black powder, muzzle-loading weapons. $35 to participate, free to watch.

Early August: **127 Corridor Outdoor Sale** (127sale.com), US 127, Jamestown. The Fentress County portion of the sale, which runs from Michigan to Alabama, is known as the World's Longest Yard Sale and is headquartered in Jamestown. You never know what you'll find along the route.

CARTHAGE AND GRANVILLE

This duo of small towns north of the interstate about halfway between Nashville and Cookeville share Civil War history and civic pride, and offer an authentic slice of small-town Tennessee life.

Located at the confluence of the New Caney and Cumberland rivers, Carthage was quickly becoming a prominent shipping port when the Civil War erupted. When Confederate general Braxton Bragg led his Army of Mississippi into Kentucky, Carthage was on his route, and the town was also the center of Brig. Gen. George Crook's efforts against Confederate guerrilla activity in the area.

Carthage gave rise to two important political figures on both the state and national stages. The first, Senator Albert Gore Sr., who served in both houses of Congress and was known for his sponsorship of the bill that created the interstate highways system, was one of three senators from former Confederate states who did not sign the Southern Manifesto opposing integration. I-65 in Tennessee is named for Gore, who returned to Middle Tennessee in the early 1970s following his senatorial career. His son, Albert Gore Jr., however, is the Gore most people associate with politics; the younger Gore eventually won his father's senate seat, albeit long after his father vacated it, and went on to become vice president under Bill Clinton, as well as win an Nobel Prize for his work to bring attention to global warming.

Upriver, Granville's river town history is told at the Granville Museum and well preserved in its collection of historic buildings.

GUIDANCE Smith County Chamber of Commerce (615-735-2093; smithcountychamber.org), 939 Upper Ferry Road, Carthage.

GETTING THERE *By air:* **Nashville International Airport** (BNA; 615-275-1675; flynashville.com), 1 Terminal Drive, Nashville. BNA is the closest major airport to Carthage, with service from all major and regional carriers.

By car: US 70 N. and TN 25/Dixon Springs Highway are the major routes to Carthage. From Nashville, take I-40 west to exit 258, then go north on TN 53 about 6 miles.

GETTING AROUND *By car:* Main Street and Riverside Drive are the main streets through downtown Carthage.

MEDICAL EMERGENCY Sumner Regional Medical Center (615-328-8888; sumner.org), 555 Hartsville Pike, Gallatin, is the closest medical center to the area offering emergency services.

✳ To See

HISTORIC SITES Sutton's General Store (931-653-4151; granvillemuseum.com), 169 Clover Street, Granville. Open Wed.–Fri. 10–3, Sat. 10–8. The Sutton General Store dates back to 1870, and for the last decade it has become a central meeting spot for Granville residents, as it was back in its heyday as the town's main purveyor of groceries and merchandise. Family-style meals are served, with an emphasis on meat and threes; Sat. evening brings a live bluegrass

GREG HALLUMS, FIDDLE PLAYER FOR THE
SUTTON OLE TIME MUSIC HOUR

Courtesy Granville Museum

radio show, the *Sutton Ole Time Music Hour.* There's no charge to tour the store or listen to the radio show.

MUSEUMS Granville Museum (931-653-4151; granvillemuseum .com), Clover Street, Granville. Open Wed.–Sat. noon–3. Filled with artifacts and historical documents of the tiny river town's history, the museum boasts an excellent photographic history of Granville. Truly, one would have to be a huge history buff to spend any length of time here, but the place is just so charming that its worth a stop if you've got the time. Free.

✳ To Do

ART WORKSHOPS Blue Heron Art Retreat (931-678-4555; theblue heronstudio.com), 576 Carl Dixon Lane, Gainesboro. Along the banks of the Cumberland River and Cordell Hull Lake, the Blue Heron offers workshops in textiles, ceramics, and china painting; on-site lodging is available. Pricing for workshops varies.

OUTDOOR RECREATION Cordell Hull Lake (615-735-1034; lrn.usace .army.mil/op/cor/rec), 71 Corps Lane, Carthage. The lake is a full-out natural experience for hikers, anglers, mountain bikers, and horseback riders; boat and cabin rentals are available, as are a number of designated tent camping sites. The visitors center burned down in 2008 but is slated to reopen in late 2011. Day-use permit is $4/vehicle.

✳ Green Space

PARKS Defeated Creek Park (615-774-3141), 140 Marina Lane, Carthage. Open daily sunrise–sunset, Mar. 15–first weekend in Nov. Located on a small peninsula on Cordell Hull Lake, the park offers a 6-mile hiking trail, bike trails, camping, and swimming. Free.

✳ Lodging

BED & BREAKFASTS/INNS Beech Hill Blue Bed and Breakfast (931-653-4574; beech-hillbluebedandbreakfast.com), 118 Cherry Street, Granville. The 1913 Victorian house has been updated yet still retains its period elegance and is within walking distance of Cordell Hull Lake and Sutton's General Store. Inexpensive.

PRICE CATEGORIES:

Inexpensive	Less than $100 (for hotels, inns, B&Bs); less than $50 (for campgrounds, state park facilities)
Moderate	$100–200
Expensive	$201–300
Very expensive	More than $300

Granville Bed, Breakfast & Antiques (931-653-4511; granville bandb.com), 146 Clover Street, Granville. Two homes offer two bedrooms each, all with private baths, and some rooms feature fireplaces or Jacuzzi tubs. Inexpensive.

HOTELS Armour's Red Boiling Springs Hotel (615-699-2180; armourshotel.com), 321 E. Main Street, Red Boiling Springs. The historic hotel offers a variety of rooms and suites, all with private baths, and the best amenity of all is the mineral bath/steam room/massage treatment ($99 for 60-minute treatment). Inexpensive–moderate, depending on accommodation.

✳ Where to Eat

Carthage and Granville have fast-food options yet few local eateries; see "Crossville" for more distinctive restaurant selections.

RED BOILING SPRINGS

In the 1840s Samuel Hare recognized the commercial potential and medicinal value of this area's unusual boiling springs. He fenced the springs, built cabins, and developed the area as a "watering place." Though Red Boiling Springs (about 25 miles north of Carthage via TN 25, TN 80, and TN 53) was a thriving community in the 1850s, the Civil War and land disputes halted development and resulted in the demolition of most of the community's original buildings.

In the 1880s New York businessman James F. O. Shaughnesy purchased 200 acres, including the boiling springs, and began to develop the area as a summer resort. At its peak in the 1920s and 1930s, the resort boasted nine hotels and more than a dozen boardinghouses. In addition to the mineral treatments, the resort featured horseback riding, tennis, a dammed lake that served as a swimming pool, bowling alleys, and a dance hall.

Three of the historic hotels remain and are listed on the National Register of Historic Places. Springhouses still feature five kinds of mineral water: white, red, and black; double and twist; and freestone. Each has a distinctly different mineral composition related to rock formations in the Highland Rim area, and each is considered a cure for different ailments.

For more information, call 615-666-5885 or log onto redboiling springstn.com.

Special Events

Early October: **Granville Quilt Festival & Fall Celebration** (granvillemuseum.com), downtown Granville. The annual quilt festival is wrapped around a jazz festival and general fall celebration, featuring the quilt show, live music, storytelling, food booths, and children's activities throughout the day. Free.

CROSSVILLE

The seat of Cumberland County, Crossville was truly where two major pioneer-era roads crossed. The Great Stage Road, which connected Knoxville and Nashville, and the Kentucky Stock Road, which connected cattle drives from Chattanooga through Middle Tennessee to Kentucky, intersected in this section of the Cumberland, and when Cumberland County was formed in 1856, Crossville was the natural pick for the county seat.

During the Civil War, both the Union and Confederacy used the Stage and Stock roads to conduct raids, as did more vigilante-type soldiers from both sides. Residents of Cumberland County were equally divided in loyalty between North and South, with men fighting on both sides.

Today, Cumberland County is known as the golf capital of the state, boasting 12 courses, and Crossville's US 127—part of which includes the Kentucky Stock Road—is home to the world's largest yard sale, the Highway 127 Corridor Sale, held every August (see *Special Events*).

GUIDANCE Crossville–Cumberland County Chamber of Commerce (877-465-3861; golfcapitaltenn.com), 34 S. Main Street.

GETTING THERE *By air:* The airports in Knoxville (**McGhee-Tyson Airport,** 865-342-3000, tys.org, 2055 Alcoa Highway) and Chattanooga (**Chattanooga Metropolitan Airport,** 423-855-2200, chattairport.com, 1001 Airport Road, #14) are closest to Crossville, each approximately 70 miles away.

By car: Crossville, just south of I-40 near the intersection of US 70, is approximately 70 miles west of Knoxville, 70 miles north of Chattanooga, and about 30 miles from Cookeville.

GETTING AROUND *By car:* Major roads into town include S. Main Street and Knoxville Highway; main streets in downtown include S. Main Street and West Avenue.

MEDICAL EMERGENCY Cumberland Medical Center (931-484-2311; cmchealthcare.org), 421 S. Main Street. Offers comprehensive emergency services 24 hours a day.

✳ To See

HISTORIC SITES Cumberland Homestead Tower (615-456-9663; cumberlandhomesteads.org), US 127. Open Mon.–Sat. 10–5 and Sun. 1–5, Apr.–Dec. The Homesteads, as the area is better known, was born during the New Deal when the land was opened to put people to work in the stone quarries and building roads and homes for the 250-plus families who would eventually live there. The predominant building material is the locally mined, softly colored Crab Orchard sandstone; there is a striking, consistent appearance of the buildings, evident in the school and the nearby Cumberland Mountain State Park. In the base of the Homestead Tower is a small museum with historical items from the Homestead community, including different types of furniture and appliances a Homestead house in the 1930s would have contained, as well as photographs and memorabilia. Adults $4, children $2.

HOMESTEAD TOWER

Tennessee Department of Tourism

MUSEUMS Military Memorial Museum (931-456-5520; museum .homestead.com/Military.html), 20 S. Main Street. Open Mon.–Fri. 9–4. During World War II, Crossville was home to a prisoner of war camp, Camp Crossville, one of 11 in the state. All of the foreign soldiers held at Camp Crossville were Italian or German, veterans of Erwin Rommel's Afrika Corps. The story of Camp Crossville is told at the museum, which displays artifacts from every American conflict from the Civil War to Operation Iraqi Freedom. Admission is free, but donations are accepted.

✳ To Do

GOLF Bear Trace at Cumberland Mountain (931-707-1640; tn golftrail.net/beartrace/cumberland mtn), 407 Wild Plum Lane. Open daily, with the exception of Christmas. Named by *Golf Digest* as one of the top 10 courses in Tennessee in 2001, the 6,900-yard, par 72 Jack Nicklaus–designed course offers plenty of challenges for the most experienced of golfers. Greens fees vary by season, starting at $24 for walkers and $35 with carts, climbing as high as $60 per round on weekends during peak times.

WINERIES Chestnut Hill Winery (931-707-7878; chestnuthillwinery .com), 78 Chestnut Hill Road Open Mon.–Sat. 9–6, Sun. noon–5. One of the larger wineries in Tennessee, Chestnut Hill's focus is sweet wines, offering red and white muscadine, plus fruit-inspired wines. The winery also produces two more traditional whites. Tastings are free.

Stonehaus Winery (931-484-9463; stonehauswinery.com), 2444 Genesis Road. Open Mon.–Sat. 9–7, Sun. noon–5. This family-owned winery—the first licensed winery in the state—offers a wide range of varietals, including a collection of sparkling wines. Stonehaus also offers homemade fudge, gourmet foods, and ice cream in its gift shop. Tastings are free.

✳ Green Space

PARKS Cumberland Mountain State Park (931-484-6138; state.tn.us /environment/parks/CumberlandMtn), 24 Office Drive. Home to numerous campsites, hiking trails, and fishing holes, Cumberland Mountain also plays host to those who yearn to chase a dimpled white ball across well-kept greens—golfers. The park's Bear Trace Course, designed by Jack Nicklaus, features beautiful sandstone approaches, and greens and fairways designed to take in the natural course of streams, stands of trees, and other elements. (See *To Do.*) Cabins generally sell out up to two years in advance; there are 145 tent and RV campsites as well. The park rents rowboats, fishing boats with electric trolling motors, paddleboats, and canoes; no private boats are allowed. Park entrance is free.

✳ Lodging

BED & BREAKFASTS/INNS
Cumberland Mountain Lodge (931-456-6194; cumberland mountainlodge.com), 1130 Clint Lowe Road. Tucked into a working cattle farm, the lodge is a perfect retreat for larger parties, accommodating up to six guests. The farm's amenities are wide open to guests, from hiking trails to stocked fishing ponds; telescopes await those who want to stargaze. The lodge offers

PRICE CATEGORIES:	
Inexpensive	Less than $100 (for hotels, inns, and B&Bs); less than $50 (for campgrounds, state park facilities)
Moderate	$100–200
Expensive	$201–300
Very expensive	More than $300

hunting and horseback riding packages, as well as golf and wildlife-viewing retreats. Two-night minimum. Moderate.

McCoy Place Bed and Breakfast (931-484-1243; mccoyplace.com), 525 Roy McCoy Road. This three-guestroom bed & breakfast in a family-owned 1920s farmhouse is situated in a state wildlife refuge. All rooms include private baths and antique furnishings. Breakfast includes fruit grown in the McCoy Place orchards and homemade breads. There are old roadways to walk on the 60-acre site and plenty of wildlife for viewing. Inexpensive.

HOTELS Holiday Inn Express Crossville (931-707-1035; hiexpress.com), 560 Peavine Road. With easy access to I-40 as well as a number of state highways, the Holiday Inn Express is perfectly situated for those wanting to make day trips from Crossville to area attractions including the Sgt. Alvin C. York birthplace and Big South Fork National Recreation Area. Suites offer a divided space with a pull-out sofa to accommodate families or larger groups, and free wireless Internet is available throughout the hotel, from the lobby to the rooms themselves. The hotel offers an indoor pool and a small but adequate fitness center, complimentary hot breakfast bar, and morning newspapers. Moderate.

PRICE CATEGORIES:

Inexpensive	Less than $16
Moderate	$16–30
Expensive	$31–50
Very expensive	More than $50

✳ Where to Eat

EATING OUT Bean Pot Restaurant (931-4844633), 590 Peavine Road. Open 24 hours daily, the Bean Pot offers simple food with a Southern flair. Breakfast platters are huge and accompanied by biscuits and gravy, and the vegetable plate includes, unsurprisingly, fried veggies. Homemade cobblers, fudge, and pies top the dessert menu, and there's also an ice cream parlor for a quick hit of sugar. Inexpensive.

Forte's Restaurant on the Square (931-788-6717), 27 E. Fourth Street. Open Tues.–Fri. 11–2, Fri.–Sat. 4–9. The warmth of Forte's—from the friendly greeting at the door to the comfort-food-ish, classic Italian dishes—makes lunch or dinner a relaxing and truly small-town experience. Moderate.

✳ Special Events

Early August: **127 Corridor Sale** (www.127sale.com), US 127, Jamestown. The Fentress County portion of the sale, which runs from Michigan to Alabama, is known as the World's Longest Yard Sale and is headquartered in Jamestown. You never know what you'll find along the route.

The triangle that connects McMinnville, Smithville, and Sparta is an imaginary one, as each of the towns is in a different county and each has its own history. But in this portion of the lower Upper Cumberland, these communities stand out for their small-town charm and their big-time natural resources.

From its earliest days, McMinnville, and its county, Warren, was an agricultural community, and that hasn't changed in the more than two hundred years since Europeans—primarily Scots-Irish and English from nearby North Carolina and Virginia—first settled here. The verdant forests and open spaces, known as the barrens, although not suitable for traditional crop farming, were well suited for raising livestock and plant-

WARREN COUNTY COURTHOUSE AND SQUARE

ing orchards, and the farms of this area provided many of the horses and cattle for the great plantations nearby.

With the advent of the Manchester and McMinnville Railroad came easier access to education and goods, but it also brought the attention of both the Union and Confederacy during the Civil War, as the rail line was an important link to northern Tennessee. The county was under constant battle as both sides fought to control it; the citizens of Warren County sided with the Confederates, and more than two thousand local men fought in the war.

During Reconstruction, attention turned to mining the natural resources of the area, with lumber companies staking a claim on the rich forests. Those companies brought great prosperity to McMinnville, and eventually great economic stress as fortunes were lost during the Depression. It was another kind of tree—those bearing fruit—that became the great provider for the area. The nursery industry continued to bloom, rising out of the apple orchard (and apple-brandy-making) businesses, and today McMinnville calls itself the Nursery Capital of the World, with more than four hundred nurseries shipping plants and trees across the globe.

Named after the Greek city-state, Sparta is the county seat of White County and was a strategic home to Lester Flatt, half of the legendary bluegrass duo Flatt and Scruggs, who performed with Bill Monroe's Bluegrass Boys. Sparta is nicknamed Bluegrass, USA. Nearby Smithville is also known for music—in this case, serious fiddle playing. Smithville is the county seat of DeKalb County and home of the world-famous annual Fiddlers' Jamboree & Craft Festival, held on the first weekend in July (see *Special Events*).

GUIDANCE McMinnville Chamber of Commerce (931-473-6611; warrentn.com), 110 S. Court Square, McMinnville. Or visit the Web site of the Upper Cumberland Tourism Association (931-537-6437; upper cumberland.org), which offers tourism information for all the counties in the Upper Cumberland Plateau.

Smithville–DeKalb County Chamber of Commerce (615-597-4163; dekalbtn.com), 301 Public Square, Smithville.

Sparta–White County Chamber of Commerce (931-836-3552), 16 W. Bockman Street, Sparta.

GETTING THERE *By air:* **Nashville International Airport** (BNA; 615-275-1675; flynashville.com), 1 Terminal Drive, Nashville. BNA is the closest major airport to McMinnville, with service from all major and regional carriers.

By car: Sparta and Smithville are located east of Crossville on US 70 south of I-40; both are about 20 miles from McMinnville, Sparta directly north and Smithville northeast. McMinnville is about equidistant from Nashville and Chattanooga, and can be reached via I-24 and I-40.

GETTING AROUND *By car:* There is no public bus service in McMinnville, so you'll need a car to get around.

By taxi: **AA Cab** (931-473-2451), 201 Black Street, McMinnville.

MEDICAL EMERGENCY River Park Hospital (931-845-1000; riverpark hospital.com), 1559 Sparta Street, McMinnville. Offers comprehensive emergency services 24 hours a day, including an accredited chest pain center.

✳ To See

HISTORIC SITES Rock House Shrine (931-836-3552), 16 W. Bookman Way, Sparta. Open Wed.–Sat. 10–3, or by appointment. The preserved stagecoach stopover for settlers leaving the West settlements to return to the more "civilized" East Coast was built in 1835; two Tennessee sons

FALCON REST

VIRGIN FALLS

Tennessee Department of Tourism

who became president—Andrew Jackson and James K. Polk—stopped here on their way to Washington, D.C. Free, but donations are accepted.

MUSEUMS Falcon Rest Mansion & Gardens (931-668-4444; falcon rest.com), 2645 Faulkner Springs Road, McMinnville. Open daily 9–5. Talk about making a deal: McMinnville businessman Clay Faulkner enticed his wife, Mary, to move closer to his woolen mills—a few miles outside of town—by promising to build her the grandest mansion in Tennessee. Mrs. Faulkner agreed and in return was mistress of a 10,000-square-foot home called Falcon Rest. It was the envy of all for its indoor plumbing, electric lights, and central heat; the mansion was located across the street from Faulkner's Mineral Springs Hotel and was eventually used as a nursing home. The grand mansion—once dubbed the Tennessee Biltmore by PBS—has been refurbished and filled with Victorian antiques; guided tours are offered daily, and the occasional special event includes murder-mystery dinners. There are four suites on the grounds for overnight guests. Adults $10, children $6.

✳ To Do

ART WORKSHOPS Appalachian Center for Craft (931-372-3051; tntech.edu/craftcenter), 1500 Craft Center Drive, Smithville. A satellite campus of the Tennessee Tech University, the Appalachian Center is set on a woodsy campus up in the hills over Center Lake. The center offers intensive workshops for visitors in addition to its full course offerings for full-time students. The focus of all workshops is American crafts, from glass and woodworking to metalwork, pottery, and fiber. Galleries filled with exhibitions by regional artists and a gift shop filled with the works of students and alumni are housed in angular buildings that blend into the surrounding landscape. Check the Web site for workshops and exhibition schedules. An on-site café offers light breakfast and lunch choices Mon.–Fri. 8:30–1 (closed seasonally; call to confirm). Free.

CAVERN TOURS ✍ **Cumberland Caverns** (931-668-4396; cumberland caverns.com), 1437 Cumberland Caverns Road, McMinnville. Open daily 9–5, except for major holidays. The huge cave—so far 32 miles have been explored—was first explored more than two hundred years ago and features large underground rooms, waterfalls, cave pools, and rock formations, some of which are illuminated by a huge crystal chandelier. Soldiers used the mineral-rich caverns to make gunpowder during both the War of 1812 and the Civil War. Overnight spelunking adventures are offered, along with walking tours. Adults $18, children $10, family passes $50. Gem mining is an additional fee.

✳ Green Space

PARKS Bridgestone/Firestone Centennial Wilderness (931-836-3552; firestone100.com/road/wild_bottom_fr.html), Eastland Road, Sparta. Open daily during sunlight hours. This 10,000-acre gift from Bridgestone/Firestone was called the Grand Canyon of the Cumberlands by 19th-century travelers. The area is great for hiking, with more than 26 miles of trails; camping; bird-watching; fishing; kayaking; and cave exploration. There are nine waterfalls within day-hike distance and lush hardwood and pine forests filled with nesting areas for songbirds and other wildlife. Virgin Falls Cave is the source of the Virgin Falls waterfall, which falls about 3,000 feet before disappearing underground. Directions to the entrance: Take US 70 east of Sparta for 11 miles, turn right (south) on Eastland Road, and continue 8 miles to the entrance. Free.

🐾 **Burgess Falls State Park** (931-432-5312; state.tn.us/environment /parks/BurgessFall), 4000 Burgess Falls Drive, Sparta. Open daily 8 AM–30 minutes before sundown. Cherokee, Creek, and Chickasaw used the area for hunting years before the first settlers arrived. Numerous waterfalls and pools from the Falling Water River are formed as the river drops some 250 feet over its course. Naturalist-led programs examine the rich wildlife in the park, including birds of prey, reptiles, and butterflies. Fishing areas for largemouth bass, brim, and carp are generally below the dam and the main falls, and boating is restricted to certain areas, with only trolling motors allowed. There are just a few hiking trails here, including a well-worth-the-workout, moderately strenuous 1.5-mile trail that brings hikers to stunning views of the main canyon and four water-falls. Picnicking below the dam is permitted, with many grills and tables ready for use. Pets should be kept on leash during their time in the park, and pet parents are expected to pick up waste as a courtesy to other park-goers. Free.

Fall Creek Falls State Resort Park (423-881-5298; state.tn.us /environment/parks/FallCreekFalls), 2009 Village Camp Road, Pikeville. Open year-round. The 20,000-plus-acre park is a wonderland of natural

BURGESS FALLS

Tennessee Department of Tourism

beauty, ranging from acres of dense forests to stunning gorges and cliffs, and the 256-foot-tall Fall Creek Falls, the highest waterfall in the eastern United States.

Hikers of all levels can find trails to wander or more challenging paths; the park's 34 miles of trails include two long-distance overnight trails as well as the accessible Fall Creek Falls overlook. Anglers can cast a line in the lake or any of the streams, although no gasoline-powered boats are allowed; canoes and aluminum fishing boats (bring your own trolling motor and battery) are available to rent. Guided trail rides are offered Apr.–Oct. at the park's stables, while the nature center offers hands-on and interpretive displays chronicling the park's geology, natural resources, and wildlife. During the summer, naturalists provide daily programs for all ages.

More than 200 campsites, 30 cabins, and a full-service resort are located within the park, offering accommodations for any taste and budget; an 18-hole golf course and pool at the inn provide a true resort feeling in the park setting.

The park is home to special events throughout the year, including live mountain music performances on Sat. evenings May–Sept., rock climbing workshops in the summer, and a Mountaineer Folk Festival in early Sept. There's no admission fee to enter the park.

❦ **Rock Island State Park** (931-686-2471; tennessee.gov/environment /parks/RockIsland), 82 Beach Road, Rock Island. Open daily 7:30 AM–10 PM. The Caney Fork Gorge and the Great Falls Dam—made by the Tennessee Valley Authority—are the central focus of Rock Island, providing some of the best white-water kayaking in the state, as well as deep pools for fishing and beautiful overlooks for sight-seeing. Cabins and campsites are available, as is a public boat launch on Great Falls Lake. Seasonal ranger-led programs include canoe tours, interpretive hikes, and wildlife viewing. There is no entrance fee for the park.

✷ Lodging

BED & BREAKFASTS/INNS
Bonnie Blue Inn Bed & Breakfast (931-815-3838; bonnieblueinn .com), 2317 Old Smithville Highway, McMinnville. The early-1900s farmhouse, located on a working 52-acre farm, offers two suites with private baths named for Civil War figures—Confederate spy Rose O'Neal Greenhow of Washington and Mary Anna Jackson, the sec-

PRICE CATEGORIES:

Inexpensive	Less than $100 (for hotels, inns, and B&Bs); less than $50 (for campgrounds, state park facilities)
Moderate	$100–200
Expensive	$201–300
Very expensive	More than $300

ond wife of Gen. Stonewall Jackson, whom he nicknamed "esposita." The full breakfasts include jams, jellies, and butters made on-site, and many of the antiques throughout the B&B are for sale. Inexpensive.

Falcon Manor Bed & Breakfast (931-668-4444; falconrest.com/stay), 2645 Faulkner Springs Road,

RUGBY

Rugby, southeast of Jamestown on TN 52, was established as a utopian community, founded by British author and social reformer Thomas Hughes. Hughes saw this area as a cooperative, Christian community, without the class distinctions of England.

With a railroad nearby, the town flourished in the late 1800s as many settlers arrived to be part of an agricultural revolution in the region. More than 300 people became residents and 70 Victorian buildings were built, creating a charming community that enjoyed cultural pursuits, forming dramatic and literary societies in addition to engaging in the outdoor recreation the area offered.

In 1881, a typhoid epidemic took the lives of seven residents, and problems with land titles and financial woes brought on the eventual decline of the community. But today, thanks to the efforts of local preservationists, 20 of the original 70 buildings are still intact, including founder Thomas Hughes's home, the schoolhouse and church, and the town library, with Hughes's 7,000-plus collection of books, virtually unchanged since it opened in 1882. A short but excellent film explores the story and history of Rugby, and guided tours give more information. Holiday-themed events include a ghostly lantern tour of the buildings, a cultural festival celebrating Appalachian and British culture, and the annual pilgrimage, when some of the private homes are open for touring and there are period craft, music, and game demonstrations. There is an admission fee of $14 for adults and $7 for children. For more information, call 423-628-2441 or log onto historicrugby.org.

While Rugby buzzes on weekends and during the summer season, visitors to the village may find themselves a bit spooked during off times if spending the night in one of the historic homes. There's little in the way of streetlights or any light at all, and the quiet is so pervasive that it can be a bit, well, creepy. Suffice it to say, this is not the place to spend the night as a party of one. If you're feeling brave, try the **Grey Gables**

McMinnville. There are four guest suites on the grounds of the Victorian Falcon Rest, including a large two-bedroom cottage with a great room for couples or families. Gourmet breakfast is included, and dinner is offered on Fri. and Sat. nights for an additional charge. Mansion tours are not included in the room rate. Moderate.

Bed & Breakfast Inn (423-628-5252; rugbytn.com; TN 52), or get in touch with **Historic Rugby Lodging** (423-628-2441; historicrugby.org) for information on the various historic accommodations in town.

RUGBY CHURCH

The Inn at Evins Mill (800-383-2349; evinsmill.com), 1535 Evins Mill Road, Smithville. A historic gristmill provides a pastoral setting for a weekend getaway, with creekside and bluff-view lodging in rustic yet well-appointed cabins and rooms. The restored gristmill offers a cozy parlor for game play-ing and gathering, and spa services can be arranged in advance. The inn offers home cooking with a bit of gourmet flair—call it deluxe comfort food. Moderate.

* Where to Eat

EATING OUT Depot Bottom Country Store (931-507-3366), 215 Bridge Street, McMinnville. Open Mon.–Fri. 5:30–3. A downtown deli, coffee shop, and country store featuring big breakfasts, fresh sandwiches and salads, and daily specials for lunch. Cash only. Inexpensive.

PRICE CATEGORIES:

Inexpensive	Less than $16
Moderate	$16–30
Expensive	$31–50
Very expensive	More than $50

FIDDLERS' JAMBOREE, SMITHVILLE

✱ Selective Shopping

ART GALLERIES Stella Luna Art Gallery (615-597-4004), 412 S. College Street, Smithville. Open Wed.–Sun. 10:30–5:30; closed Sun.–Tues. in Jan. and Feb. Beautiful clay pieces and ceramic art objects are made on-site, both straw fired and pit fired. Clay art workshops are held in the studio.

✱ Special Events

Early July: **Fiddlers' Jamboree & Craft Festival** (615-597-8500; smithvillejamboree.com), Court Square, Smithville. Nearly 80,000 music and craft lovers jam tiny Smithville for two days of festivities.

Western Tennessee: Music and the Mighty Mississippi

3

MEMPHIS AND SURROUNDING AREA

NORTHWEST

SOUTHWEST

MEMPHIS AND
SURROUNDING AREA

MEMPHIS

In every language, the word *Memphis* translates as "Elvis," but defining
this river city in Tennessee's southwestern corner isn't nearly so easy. Yes,
Memphis *is* American music—the birthplace of the blues and rock 'n' roll
and soul—and while music definitely unites people in this city, racial
unity, even in the 21st century, can be a little harder to find.

It's surprising to many that Spanish explorer Hernando de Soto actually stood on what was once known as the fourth Chickasaw bluff—present-
day Memphis—and gazed over the mighty river that would be called the
Mississippi. The French had an influence here, too, building a fort on the
bluff, which changed hands frequently as European and Indian groups
battled over the rich soil and strategically elevated position with all-
important river access.

Memphis was founded in 1819 and incorporated seven years later, and
almost immediately the city experienced a land boom that brought quick
progress and prosperity. With the establishment of a naval yard, a rail link
to Memphis, and the explosion in the growth and use of cotton in the
Delta, Memphis became an important shipping port connecting the
South and the Midwest.

By the Civil War, Memphis had become one of the country's top trading posts and river ports; Union forces captured the city in 1862, and
though the South lost the war, the city continued to prosper. The yellow
fever epidemic of the 1870s brought Memphis to its knees, however, as
the city was almost completely devastated by the disease. More than
25,000 Memphians fled the city as the disease spread, leaving those
behind to care for the sick and dying; the death toll in the city alone was
5,000, with more than 20,000 in the Mississippi Valley succumbing. The
city itself had to declare bankruptcy following the outbreak and struggled
to come back from the devastation.

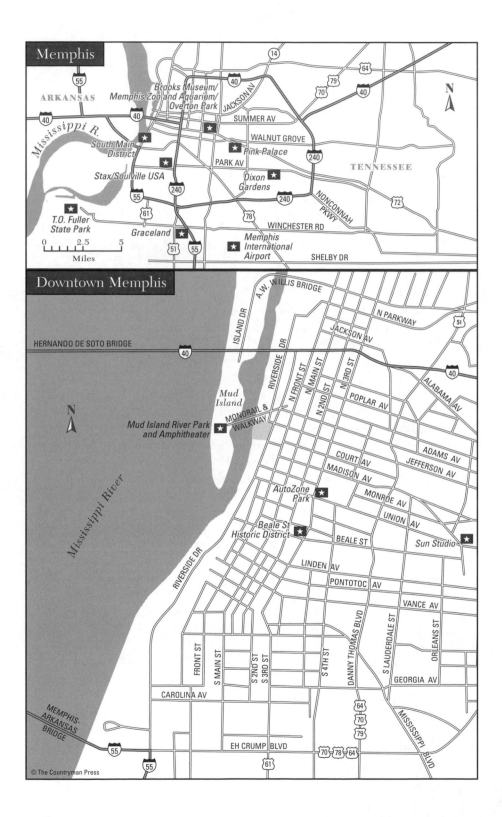

About the time the first bridge across the Mississippi south of St. Louis was constructed in Memphis, a new beat was emerging just off the river, on Beale Street. African Americans who came to Memphis from the Delta brought their music with them; the combination of spirituals sung in the cotton fields with songs filled with lament-filled lyrics that told the story of their woes became known as the blues. Over the next few decades, the music of Beale would continue to gain national attention, as the first black-programmed radio station—WDIA-AM—took blues to the airwaves. Soon, Memphis musicians influenced by the blues were recording more soulful songs, and one day in 1954, a young man named Elvis Presley walked into Sun Studio/Memphis Recording Service and recorded what would become an instant hit and the real start of the rock 'n' roll sound.

Elvis made it no secret that he was heavily influenced by Memphis, the blues, and the African Americans he met; it seemed that having a superstar pay such homage was a sure way to create racial unity in Memphis. But that promising start came to a fast end when Dr. Martin Luther King Jr., who came to town in April 1968 to speak to striking sanitation workers, was shot as he stood on the balcony of the Lorraine Hotel. King's death cast a pall on the city that somehow still remains today, as many leaders and residents will attest.

At the time of King's murder, the city was already experiencing a "white flight," with residents moving out of the downtown area. The pace of the exodus quickened, all but killing downtown businesses, many of which were simply boarded up and left as is.

Little by little, the city has rebounded, renovating and reenergizing the clubs of Beale Street, creating a museum at the Lorraine dedicated to civil rights and King's memory, and pursuing professional

Stephanie Jones

and semiprofessional sports. Native sons like AutoZone founder Pitt Hyde and FedEx founder Fred Smith—told by his Harvard professor that his idea of a worldwide express courier service was a pipe dream—chose hometown headquarters for their companies, boosting the city's business image.

Soon, filmmakers discovered Memphis, using the city and its authentic backgrounds as the setting for dozens of films, including John Grisham's *The Firm* and *The Client,* and native Craig Brewer's *Hustle & Flow* and *Black Snake Moan.*

The metropolitan area of Memphis reaches from the city limits and includes all of Shelby County, plus a number of additional counties in Tennessee, and reaches into Arkansas and Mississippi. Basically, drive an hour in any direction, and you're considered to be within the metro area.

In the city proper, Memphis is defined by its neighborhoods. **Downtown** includes the main business district; the county, state, and federal government offices and courts; and Beale Street, the FedEx Forum, and numerous attractions. There's not much in the way of retail, save for the stores inside the Peabody Hotel and a few remaining holdouts in Peabody

Stephanie Jones

Place, the ambitious mixed-use development that enjoyed a short but spectacular life as a downtown draw. Today, much of that complex is deserted, although plans are under way to convert it to hotel and entertainment space.

The **South Main District,** located downtown, is a historic district known mostly for its well-preserved buildings and the Lorraine Hotel, site of the King assassination and now home to the National Civil Rights Museum. In the wake of the King assassination, South Main was a virtual ghost town, with once-thriving retail businesses closing up shop and moving east. Over the last few decades, a movement has been under way to bring life back to this area, filled with interesting early-20th-century architecture. A collection of art galleries and stores, a few restaurants, and an eclectic mix of businesses, including the local National Academy of Recording Arts & Sciences (Grammy) chapter, now call South Main home, and there's a palpable energy to the area. On the last Friday of the month, galleries and shops open late, and the area takes on a festival feel, with wine flowing at the various stops and a mixed, truly Memphis crowd—all ages, all races, and all income levels—browsing and mingling.

Moving east, **Midtown** encompasses a variety of neighborhoods. There's a bumper sticker that proclaims MIDTOWN IS MEMPHIS, and this is certainly true—meaning there's no one way to categorize this section of town. Huge old homes with lovely yards in **Overton Park** (home to the Memphis Zoo, the College of Art, Brooks Museum, and the Levitt Shell) rub elbows with multifamily apartments and small cottages; some blocks are filled with young families and stately homes, while the next block over might be full of homes needing some serious tender loving care. But the whole area—basically stretching from Danny Thomas Boulevard from the west to Highland Avenue to the east—is full of character. The **Cooper-Young** area of Midtown is making a comeback as a lively dining and nightlife destination for the city, offering a variety of antiques shops and galleries along Central Avenue.

East Memphis—basically considered everything east of Highland to the city limits east—is mostly residential and business, with some of the city's most upscale neighborhoods and shopping. The **Whitehaven** area is home to Graceland and is primarily working-class.

Today, Memphis is still a study in contrasts, but it's a city that's working to bridge every gap, and the result is a promising one, with an atmosphere that's constantly changing—just like the river upon which the city sits.

GUIDANCE The Memphis Convention and Visitors Bureau (901-543-5300; memphistravel.com), 47 Union Avenue. The CVB's Web site offers themed itinerary ideas, as well as lodging specials. Look for their Blue Suede Service folks throughout the downtown area; they'll be wearing uniforms with light blue pith-style helmets and can assist with directions, recommendations, and more.

GETTING THERE *By air:* **Memphis International Airport** (MEM; 901-922-8000; mscaa.com), 3318 Winchester Road, Memphis. MEM is a hub for Delta Airlines; major airlines serving Memphis include Continental, US Airways, AirTran, American, and Air Canada. Most major airlines offer connecting flights to Memphis. Passengers can't help but notice the huge fleet of FedEx planes at MEM, which serves as the global shipping company's home airfield, giving Memphis the distinction of the world's largest cargo airport.

By bus: **Greyhound** (901-523-1184; greyhound.com), 203 Union Avenue. Greyhound offers bus service to Memphis from other metropolitan areas across the United States and select cities in Tennessee. The ticket office is open 24 hours.

By car: Memphis is located in the southwest corner of Tennessee, with I-55 (north/south) and I-40 (east/west) passing directly through the city.

By train: **AMTRAK** (800-872-7245; amtrak.com), 545 S. Main Street.

GRACELAND

Stephanie Jones

The ticket office is open daily 5:45 AM–11 PM. Train travelers can get to Memphis via the City of New Orleans, which offers service from Chicago to New Orleans and back again.

GETTING AROUND *By bus:* The **Metropolitan Area Transit Authority** (901-722-7171; matatransit.com) offers bus service throughout the city, as well as a trolley service throughout downtown and the medical center. Check the Web site for routes and schedules. Base fares are $1.50, with the trolley service free on the last Fri. evening of the month.

By car: Rental cars are available at the airport and at select locations throughout town. The Memphis metropolitan area is easy to navigate, with the downtown area laid out in a grid. The major east–west thoroughfares are Poplar Avenue and Walnut Grove, with Front Street, Parkway, and Highland Avenue as some of the most traveled north–south streets.

By taxi: Taxi service is available throughout Memphis, though outside of the downtown area, cabs are not prevalent and need to be ordered well in advance. **Yellow Cab/Checker Cab of Memphis** (901-577-7777; premierofmemphis.com) operates 24 hours throughout the city. A taxi ride from the airport to downtown hotels will cost about $30.

MEDICAL EMERGENCY Regional Medical Center (901-545-7100; the-med.org), 877 Jefferson Avenue. A top-notch level-one trauma center with comprehensive emergency medical and diagnostic services, located just on the border of downtown Memphis.

Le Bonheur Children's Hospital (901-287-5437; lebonheur.org), 50 N. Dunlap Street. Offers pediatric trauma care and comprehensive medical services.

✳ To See

HISTORIC SITES Graceland (901 332-3322; elvis.com), 3765 Elvis Presley Boulevard. Open daily 10–4, Nov.; Mon. and Wed.–Sun. 10–4, Dec.–Feb.; Mon.–Sat. 9–5 and Sun. 10–4, Mar.–May and Sept.–Oct.; Mon.–Sat. 9–5 and Sun. 9–4, June–Aug. There are special hours during Christmas and other holidays; check the Web site for the most up-to-date times. *Graceland.* The very name is synonymous with Memphis, with rock 'n' roll music, with celebrity mansions. But for the shy young man who bought this house to give himself and his parents a bit more privacy in the wake of his meteoric rise to stardom, Graceland was only one thing: home.

Elvis Presley would go off on concert tours, head to Hollywood and Hawaii to film movies, and he spent two years in the Army. But walk through his home, listen to the recordings and the tour guides, and read the signs, and it's obvious that Graceland equaled home, family, and love for Elvis.

GRACELAND HIGHLIGHTS
Graceland VIP Tour

VIPs get their own shuttles to and from the mansion, plus head-of-the-line access for the entry into the mansion, and never have to wait in a line for return bus—they board at their own spot around back. The VIP ticket buys access to all the exhibits, including a drive-by view of the back side of the property, which includes the escape route the King would take when he wanted to leave Graceland under cover. That extra driveway stretches from the back of the property and comes out right onto Elvis Presley Boulevard, and Elvis was known to put on a hat and sunglasses to avoid recognition.

Stephanie Jones

VIP guests can come and go through the exhibits as much as they want throughout the day. This exhibit area changes yearly, so you never know what special artifacts might be on display.

The Jungle Room

What started as a simple addition to Graceland—a den—ended up as one of the most famous rooms in American pop culture. Exotic-looking carved furniture, bought in Memphis during Elvis's 1974 whirlwind of redecorating, is paired with green shag carpet, faux-fur upholstery, and wood paneling to create the feel of the tropics. A waterfall that Elvis previously added in 1965 completed the room, which was decorated to remind Elvis of Hawaii, a favorite vacation spot and site of his famous worldwide televised concert.

Who would have guessed the thick green shag carpeting—and complementary carpet on the ceiling—would create the basis for a recording studio. But the Elvis did indeed record an entire album in this room in 1976—*From Elvis Presley Boulevard, Memphis Tennessee,* released in May of 1977. Four of the songs recorded in the Jungle Room sessions were used on the *Moody Blue* album, also released in 1977.

According to a Graceland guide, Elvis never called this room any-

Stephanie Jones

thing but the den; it was when Graceland opened in 1982 that the touring public along with the news media gave the room its nickname—and an American pop culture icon was born.

The Meditation Garden

When Vernon Presley, Elvis's father, decided to move the graves of Elvis and his mother, Gladys, to Graceland in the fall of 1977, he did so because fans and the media were overwhelming Forrest Hill Cemetery. Presley understood the power of his son's appeal, and rather than shut out fans who had made a pilgrimage to Memphis to pay their respects, he allowed them access to the new site of the graves, the Meditation Garden, daily for no charge. When Graceland opened to the public in 1982, Elvis Presley Enterprises kept the tradition alive, allowing fans to pay their respects at no charge 7:30–8:30 AM every day. During Elvis week in August and Elvis Birthday Week in January, hours are offered in the evenings as well.

Graceland Gates

It wasn't long after Elvis and his parents moved into Graceland that the young musician contracted with a local company to build gates for Graceland. In April 1957, the gates—featuring a silhouette of Elvis with a guitar and musical notes—were installed. Elvis would occasionally walk down the drive at Graceland, open the gates himself, and greet a few waiting fans, with security officers flanking the gates.

Stephanie Jones

More than 600,000 people visit Graceland every year, and it is the second most famous home in America after the White House. For many fans, a visit to Graceland is like a pilgrimage of sorts. Elvis fans are among the most dedicated in the world, and that quickly becomes apparent to those who might not be as fluent in the King.

Elvis paid a little over $100,000 for the mansion when he bought it in spring of 1957; he was only 22 years old. The understated elegance of the home often surprises first-time visitors, who remark that it seems much smaller than they thought. But the mansion is actually more than 17,000 square feet, including the basement, the den—or Jungle Room as it's more familiarly known—and other additions. For an overview of what you'll see at the mansion, see the *Graceland Highlights* sidebar. Tickets are $30 and up; VIP Tour $69.

Stax—Soulsville USA (901-946-2535; soulsvilleusa.com), 926 E. McLemore Avenue. Open Mon.–Sat. 10–5, Sun. 1–5; closed Mon. Nov.–Mar. The tiny Stax Records had a huge impact on music made in Memphis and around the globe. From Isaac Hayes's theme song "Shaft" to Otis Redding's "(Sittin' on) the Dock of the Bay" to the musical magic of Booker T. and the M.G.s to William Bell, the discography at Stax is as impressive as any label. It was Redding's 1965 track "Respect" that garnered the attention of Aretha Franklin's producer, and she covered the song for a more crossover audience, creating an instant hit. Elvis recorded at Stax, with sessions in July and December 1973; three albums—*Good Times, Raised on Rock,* and *Promised Land*— were produced, and a number of singles resulted from the sessions as well. Today, the Stax history— and that of the surrounding neighborhood known as Soulsville—is told through music and exhibits at the original location of the recording studio. The tour starts with a quick video overview and proceeds through the roots of soul (a church exhibit), then moves through the recording studios through the hall of records (literally, hundreds of records displayed behind glass). It's here you'll find Isaac Hayes's

STAX

Stephanie Jones

tricked-out ride (lean over the rail and he'll admonish—"I told you, don't touch my ride!"). Adults $12, children $9.

MUSEUMS **Brooks Museum of Art** (901-544-6200; brooksmuseum .org), 1934 Poplar Avenue. Open Wed. and Fri. 10–4, Thurs. 10–8, Sat. 10–5, and Sun. 11–5. Closed Mon. and Tues. A small museum that's easy to navigate and comprehensive in scope, the Brooks's excellent permanent collection is highlighted by a collection of Italian renaissance and baroque paintings, along with British, French impressionist, and 20th-century painters including Renoir and Degas, Winslow Homer, and Nancy Graves. Traveling exhibitions range from modern photography to impressionism, and the excellent Brushmark restaurant is worth a stop, even if a day of art is not on the agenda. Adults $7, seniors 65+ $6, students $3, children under six free. Some exhibits require additional tickets. On Wed., there's no admission charged.

Center for Southern Folklore (901-525-3655; southernfolklore.org), 119 S. Main Street. Open Mon.–Fri. 10–5. The South encompasses a distinctive culture, and its stories are told at the Center for Southern Folklore through music, art, and storytelling. The excellent gift shop is chock-full of regional works, and on any given day one can catch a live performance, experience a dramatic presentation, or simply see the South through the eyes of its artists. The center's small café offers up Southern specialties, and the menu changes daily. Depending on what's going on any given day, admission runs anywhere from free to $10.

Elvis Presley Automobile Museum (800-238-2000; elvis.com), 3765 Elvis Presley Boulevard. For hours, see the Graceland listing in *Historic Sites*. There's little argument that Elvis liked more than a bit of flash— and that extended to motor vehicles, not just his clothes. He was a great collector of cars, from fancy imports to luxurious limos and a huge variety of motorcycles, plus a smattering of motorized toys. A huge selection of his cars are showcased in the automobile museum, including the 1955 pink Cadillac Fleetwood he used for road trips with the band as they traveled from gig to gig in the early days. The car was purchased for Elvis's mother, Gladys, whom he liked to spoil with gifts and surprises, although she never drove "her" car as she didn't drive. The museum is part of the Graceland tour package, with the platinum level or above. Prices start at $30 for adults, $30.60 for children 13–17, and $16 for children 7–12. Children six and under free.

Memphis Cotton Museum (901-531-7826; memphiscottonmuscum .org), 65 Union Avenue. Open Mon.–Sat. 10–5, Sun. noon–5. Cotton is still king in Memphis—the largest spot-cotton market in the world. The Cotton Exchange building is where the cotton trading used to take place; the surrounding alleys and buildings were devoted to cotton transportation, classification, and storage before the crops were sent out to the rest of the country and the world. The Cotton Museum recounts the boll's fascinating history in Memphis, including a tour of the old trading floor, films and exhibits exploring the rise of the crop in the Delta, and a self-guided audio tour of Cotton Row, the historic block surrounding the exchange. While the cotton market is still a major force in Memphis and the mid-South, there are no longer truckloads of the crop showing up on Front Street (as some may remember from the chase scene in the Tom Cruise film *The Firm*). Adults $10, children 6–12 $8, children under six free.

Memphis Rock & Soul Museum (901-205-2533; memphisrocknsoul .org), 191 Beale Street. Open daily 10–7. The complete story of Memphis music, from the blues and soul to rock 'n' roll, is told at Rock & Soul; Memphis's rich musical heritage crosses a variety of genres, and all get equal billing here. From the Hayes & Porter Stax recordings to the Sun label, from Beale Street to Graceland, the exhibits pay homage and explain how the city's musical greats were able to cross racial and socioeconomic lines through the power of and the message in their music. While the museum gives an excellent overview of the music that defined (and continues to define) Memphis, the museum is small and can't do justice to the depths of the histories of the individual genres; that's better handled at Stax, Sun, and Graceland. Adults $10, children $7.

✒ **Mud Island River Park/Mississippi River Museum** (901-576-7241; mudisland.com), 125 N. Front Street. Open Tues.–Sat. 10–5, mid-Apr.–

NATIONAL ORNAMENTAL METAL MUSEUM

Tennessee Department of Tourism

late May; Tues.–Sat. 10–6, Memorial Day–Labor Day; and Tues.–Sat. 10–5 following Labor Day–Oct. Closed Nov.–early Apr. Mud Island is part museum and part boat launch, boasts a concert amphitheater, and provides, through an excellent model, the opportunity to walk along the Mississippi from its start in Minnesota to its end at the Gulf of Mexico, seeing how the mighty river widens, narrows, and even floods. Water flow in the model Mississippi mimics that of the real river, and along the meandering river path, historic events and towns are noted. Where the river reaches the Gulf, a spray fountain delights kids, who splash no matter the weather. The island is best reached by the monorail made famous in the movie *The Firm*, but taking the pedestrian walkway is a pleasant option, allowing for a leisurely, scenic stroll. The park is free, as is the pedestrian bridge; a round-trip monorail ride is $4 per person. Museum tickets, which include a monorail ride, are $10 for adults, $9 for seniors 60 and up, and $7 for children 5–12; children four and under are free.

National Civil Rights Museum (901-521-9699; civilrightsmuseum.org), 450 Mulberry Street. Open Mon. and Wed.–Sat. 9–5, Sun. 1–5. Closed Tues. Closing time is 6 June–Aug. The Lorraine Hotel, site of the assassination of Dr. Martin Luther King Jr. in 1968 during the Memphis sanitation workers strike, is eerily preserved and serves as both a reminder of that day and the focal point of the museum. Devoted to the struggle for equal rights, the museum captures the hardship of African Americans in the South but also showcases how the civil rights movement here influenced the world. A lunch counter display is the anchor for an exhibit demonstrating how the quiet lunch-counter sit-ins across the South turned ugly; overhead, video screens continuously play a loop of footage that captured how the silent protestors were cursed and abused, with drinks poured over their heads or food thrown on them. A burned-out bus brings to life the threats hurled at those who participated in the Freedom Rides, and the most chilling exhibit of all leads up to the second floor of the Lorraine Motel, where the room in which Martin Luther King stayed during the Memphis sanitation strike has been reconstructed. Outside, on the balcony where King was shot, a white wreath marks the tragedy. Moving across the street to the boardinghouse where James Earl Ray fired the fatal shot, exhibits examine whether there was a conspiracy or Ray acted alone, and finally, a wall showcasing the museum's Freedom Award winners—including Bill Clinton, the Dali Lama, Bono, and Oprah Winfrey—shows that the work toward civil rights around the world continues. Adults $13, seniors and students $11, children 4–17 $9.50, children three and under free.

National Ornamental Metal Museum (901-774-6380; metalmuseum .org), 374 Metal Museum Drive. Open Tues.–Sat. 10–5, Sun. noon–5; closed Mon. Ironwork is iconic in the South, with gates, railings, and porches intricately fashioned from hot metal. So it is fitting that the only museum in the Americas dedicated to the art of metalwork is in the South, with a permanent collection of more than three thousand pieces dating back more than five hundred years. And new masterpieces in metal are created here daily; artisan workshops and work spaces are constantly in use. From graceful flatware to hammered serveware, the museum store is full of handmade treasures, many of which come from regional artists. Adults $6, seniors $5, students 5–18 $4, children under five free.

The Pink Palace Museum (901-320-6320; memphismuseums.org), 3050 Central Avenue. Open Mon.–Sat. 9–5, Sun. noon–5. Clarence Saunders, the man who started the Piggly Wiggly grocery store, was building his pink marble mansion when he was forced to declare bankruptcy—but the city of Memphis ended up with a real treasure when Saunders turned the mansion over for use as a museum. A fanciful miniature circus, shrunken heads, and opulent decorative accessories are part of the truly eclectic permanent collection, which focuses on the natural history of the area and a bit on the general history of Memphis. The museum turns into an enchanting winter wonderland over the Christmas holidays with the festive Enchanted Forest display that's very vintage in feel and a long Memphis tradition. An IMAX theater and a planetarium round out the offerings. Tickets start at $9.75 for adults and $6.25 for children 3–12 for the museum itself; throw in the IMAX and planetarium, and tickets are $19.25 for adults and $13.50 for children 3–12.

Slave Haven Underground Railroad Museum/Burkle Estate (901-527-3427; slavehavenundergroundrailroadmuseum.org), 826 N. Second St. Open Mon.–Sat. 10–5, June–Aug.; Mon.–Sat. 10–4, Sept.–May. German immigrant Jacob Burkle's home near the banks of the Mississippi was unassuming and plain—a perfect combination for the under-the-radar efforts to move slaves northward so they could become free. Trap doors and hidden passages spark the imagination of what the flight to freedom must have been like for those trying to escape. Adults $6, students 4–17 $4.

✷ To Do

AQUARIUMS AND ZOOS ✆ **Memphis Zoo** (901-276-9453; memphis zoo.org), 2000 Prentiss Place. Open daily 9–4, Oct.–Feb.; daily 9–5, Mar.–Sept. Closed major holidays. Situated in an old-growth forest in the heart of the city's Overton Park, the Memphis Zoo surprises first-time guests with the breadth and quality of its exhibits; few zoos offer as a many opportunities to get as close to the animals as this zoo does. In the Northwest Passage, polar bears come nose to nose with children as they

Memphis Zoo

A POLAR BEAR TAKES A REST AT THE NORTHWEST PASSAGE EXHIBIT
AT THE MEMPHIS ZOO.

cool off in icy waters, the two separated only by a thick layer of glass. The zoo's Chinese pandas often frolic in their outdoor play area, while big cats prowl within feet of visitors behind thin wires, giving an excellent and truly close-up view. The diverse Yellowstone ecosystem is alive in the Teton Trek area, which features grizzly bears, wolves, and elk; a Zambezi River Hippo Camp is next up on the expansion list. The exterior of the zoo pays homage to the city's Egyptian connection, with a templelike facade with colorful hieroglyphics. Once inside, the exhibits are laid out in an orderly fashion, with meandering paths and plenty of shady spots for respite on hot summer days. A tram ($2 for an all-day pass) is a worthwhile investment for those opting to leave strollers behind; special children's rides include a fanciful and brilliantly crafted carousel of Chinese animals and train through the farm area ($2 per ride), as well as a collection of small, carnival-type amusement rides ($1 per ride). Adults $15, seniors $14, children 2–11 $10, and children under two free.

BICYCLING/HIKING Shelby Farms/Memphis Greenline (greater memphisgreenline.org or shelbyfarmsgreenline.org), from Tillman and Walnut Grove in Midtown to Shelby Farms in East Memphis. Open daily sunrise–sunset. The first phase of the Greater Memphis Greenline is the Shelby Farms Greenline, a paved, 7-mile path built upon abandoned CSX rail tracks stretching from Midtown Memphis to the Shelby Farms Park. A straight path from Midtown east, the greenline is open for walkers, joggers, and bicyclists, but not motorized vehicles; it does traverse some of the city's busiest roads and intersections, with those roads well marked for both those on the greenline and drivers on the streets. Shelters, benches, and facilities for users are slowly being added, with plans to extend the greenline north and south, combining street trails with more traditional rails-to-trails sections. Free.

GOLF The Links at Galloway (901-685-7805; thelinksatgalloway.com), 3815 Walnut Grove Road. Open daily, year-round. This links-style course is the city's public golf gem. Set in a neighborhood of stately homes, Galloway features gently rolling hills, inexpensive greens fees, and an excellent pro shop. Golfers find Galloway to be fun and a bit of a challenge. Weekday fees are $18 for walkers and $32 for those who want a cart; fees Fri.–Sun. are $41.

SPECTATOR SPORTS Memphis Grizzlies (901-888-4667; nba.com /grizzlies), FedEx Forum, 191 Beale Street. Play mid-Nov.–Apr. (or beyond), depending on their success on the court. The NBA's Grizzlies take to the court in their very own den, aka the FedEx Forum, a lush and excellent place for watching basketball. Memphis-style barbecue is available for seat-side snacking, while a number of loungelike seating areas are the place to be seen between halves. Single game tickets start at $17.

Memphis Redbirds (901-721-6000; memphisredbirds.com), 200 Union Avenue. Play Apr.–Oct. The triple-A team of the St. Louis Cardinals, the Redbirds consistently finish at the top of the standings and were the 2009 Pacific Coast League champs. Their home field, AutoZone Park, is a treat-filled, old-fashioned-feeling park tucked into a busy corner of downtown Memphis, and it serves up excellent views from every seat (as well as tasty barbecue nachos). Kids can play midway-style games or roll down the outfield hill if they get bored. Advance tickets start at $5 for bluff seating and rise to $18 for club level; expect to pay $2–3 more per seat if purchased on game day.

Memphis RiverKings (662-342-1755; riverkings.com), 4650 Venture Drive, Southaven, MS. Season runs Oct.–Mar. Fast-paced farm team hockey is worth the short drive over the state border, as the team is always a conference contender. $11–27 for single game tickets.

✳ Green Space

GARDENS AND NATURE CENTERS ✍ **Lichterman Nature Center** (901-767-7322; memphismuseums.org/lichterman-overview), 5992 Quince Road. Open Tues.–Thurs. 9–4, Fri.–Sat. 9–5. Smack in the midst of East Memphis, the Lichterman is surprising for both its urban location and the breadth of its natural wonders. A fantastic, three-story forest boardwalk is a woodland treat, while a lake-centered environment and a lush seasonal meadow provide additional insight into the regional environment. The walking trails and boardwalks are very accessible for the disabled. Adults $6, children 3–12 $4.50, children under three free. Free admission on Tues. 1 PM–closing.

✍ **Memphis Botanic Garden** (901-576-4100; memphisbotanicgarden .com), 750 Cherry Road. During Central Daylight Time, hours are

Tennessee Department of Tourism

AUTOZONE PARK, HOME OF THE MEMPHIS REDBIRDS

Mon.–Sat. 9–6 and Sun 11–6; during Central Standard Time, hours are Mon.–Sat. 9–4:30 and Sun. 11–4:30. My Big Backyard opens at 11 on Mon. If you see children searching for fairies in the flowers and gathering fallen petals in the rose garden for a sachet, don't be surprised—creating a love of nature is part of the garden's mission. More than 20 specialty gardens are scattered through the 96 acres of the botanic gardens, including a traditional Japanese garden full of delightful surprises, a labyrinth-like rose garden, and a sensory garden for the disabled. The children's garden, My Big Backyard, is a delight for all ages and abilities, with spots to plant seedlings, tunnel like a worm, explore among the treetops, and catch a view of critters at play. Adults $5, seniors 62+ $4, children 3–12 $3.

PARKS ✅ **Shelby Farms** (901-767-7275; shelbyfarmspark.org), 500 Pine Lake Drive. Open daily sunrise–sunset; visitors center open Mon.–Fri. 8–5. Five times larger than New York's Central Park, Shelby Farms is a recreational oasis at the far eastern reaches of the city, adjacent to the suburban communities of Germantown and Cordova. The farms are home to the national headquarters of Ducks Unlimited and offer hike and bike trails, paddleboats and fishing, trail rides and horseback lessons, and a shooting range. Seasonal events at the Agricenter include a farmer's market and corn maze, and the on-site arena hosts dozens of equine events annually. Free.

✳ Lodging

BED & BREAKFASTS/INNS 🐾

The Inn at Hunt-Phelan (901-525-8225; huntphelan.com), 533 Beale Street. The gorgeous Hunt-Phelan house was built in 1832 and played host to both Confederate and Union leaders during the Civil War; General Leonidas headquartered here while he planned the battle at Corinth, Mississippi, and in 1862, Union general Ulysses S. Grant spent three weeks here, sequestered in the library planning the Vicksburg campaign. His forces used tunnels to relay messages. Through the end of the war, the mansion was a home for soldiers and was then returned to the Hunt family by President Johnson in 1865. The Greek Revival mansion, on the National Register of Historic Places, is now an excellent inn, featuring 10 rooms beautifully decorated with antiques and lush linens. The location is just a few blocks from the delights of Beale Street (I'd recommend taking a cab there and back for safety's sake). There's a lovely bar with brick patio downstairs, as well as a fine-dining restaurant in the restored first-floor rooms. Breakfast is included, and pets are welcome with advance notice. Moderate–expensive, depending on room choice.

⇔ **The River Inn** (901-260-3333; riverinnmemphis.com), 50 Harbor Town Square. The small (28-room) River Inn is just a stone's throw from downtown but feels like it's a big-city boutique hotel tucked away in a hip neighborhood. Four-poster beds, cushy linens, and river views create a cocoon of luxury in the guest rooms, many of which sport terraces or windows that open to allow in the river breezes. Each room offers its own unique feel, with paint colors in hues of blues and browns, and river views are standard. Elegant touches, including a glass of wine or champagne, turndown with chocolates and port, free wireless access and parking, as well as a hearty breakfast, are part of every stay. An intimate rooftop bar provides sunset views over the river, and there are two on-site dining options: the casual and lively Tug's is a neighborhood favorite for Harbor Towners, offering a sports-bar-like atmosphere, patio dining for breakfast, and lunch and dinner daily; the upscale Currents projects a bit of old-world, New Orleans feel with rich fabrics and furnishings, a fireplace, candlelight dining, and attentive service.

PRICE CATEGORIES:	
Inexpensive	Less than $100 (for hotels, inns, and B&Bs); less than $50 (for campgrounds, state park facilities)
Moderate	$100–200
Expensive	$201–300
Very expensive	More than $300

Entrées at Currents tend toward a French and American flair. Moderate–expensive.

HOTELS Hilton Memphis (901-684-6664; hilton.com), 939 Ridge Lake Boulevard. An excellent location for those who want off-the-interstate access for ease of exploring Memphis, the round, glass-mirrored Hilton has been renovated to include furniture upgrades in the guest rooms, which all boast floor-to-ceiling curved windows as well as all the modern conveniences expected by savvy travelers: flat-screen televisions, feather pillows, generously sized bathrooms, and peace and quiet. A contemporary lobby bar is lively most nights, with small plates available. The neighborhood is filled with low-rise office buildings, and there are sidewalks for those who prefer out-of-doors exercise. (The front desk can provide suggested routes.) With the expansion of nearby shopping and dining—mostly of the chain variety, and the more localized restaurants and boutique shopping just a bit farther east—the Hilton is a smart stay for those who may be making just a quick overnight in Memphis and prefer a more suburban locale. Free self parking, and the most reasonable valet rates I've ever seen: $8. Moderate.

☙ **Holiday Inn University of Memphis** (901-678-8200; holidayinn.com), 3700 Central Avenue. The all-suite Holiday Inn is centrally located and a perfect fit for families. Despite its location on the edge of the University of Memphis campus, the hotel is rather quiet in the evenings, although it's busy during the day thanks to its popularity as a prime lunch spot for large association and business meetings. Each of the suites includes a sitting room with pull-out sofa and wood-accented mini kitchen featuring a small refrigerator, coffeemaker, and microwave; accommodations offer a choice of a king or two double beds. The hotel generally sells out during home football weekends Sept.–Nov. $50 pet deposit. Moderate.

☙ **Lauderdale Courts** (901-523-8662; lauderdalecourts.com), 252 N. Lauderdale. The room is not available during Elvis Week in Aug. or Elvis Birthday Week in Jan., as it is open for public tours during those times. The humble brick apartment buildings that made up "the Courts" is where the strains of the young Elvis Presley's guitar could be heard, usually coming from the basement laundry room. One can now stay in the suite of rooms where the King and his family once slept, ate, and bathed: the Elvis Suite—#328—the actual apartment where Elvis and his parents lived, has been refurbished with a vintage flair that includes a nod to the modern conveniences, including a flat-screen TV, wireless Internet, and a microwave oven. Expensive.

☙ **The Peabody Hotel** (901-529-4000; peabodymemphis.com), 149

Union Avenue. The granddaddy of all Memphis hotels, the Peabody exudes Southern charm and grace in every corner; the gorgeous building with the huge rooftop neon sign acts like a beacon for those looking for downtown. A grand lobby bar and choice of dining options are enough to keep some folks in the hotel their entire stay, while the 464 rooms and suites range from quaint to grand. There are pet-friendly perches as well. Red-coated doormen greet guests upon arrival (the head doorman not only carries bags, he's the duck master as well), and opulence is everywhere one looks, from the marble columns to the gilded decor of the lobby bar and Chez Philippe, the grand dining room. Elevators are small and slow, but they decamp guests into hushed corridors, and accommodations are elegant yet simple, with dark wood furniture, a muted color scheme, and crisp linens. Bathrooms are generously sized and include the whimsical touch of duck-shaped soaps. The old-style indoor pool, complete with Greek columns and a private club feel, is popular for its vintage charm and sophistication; an on-site spa, designer clothing stores (see Lansky's in *Selective Shopping*), and graceful atmosphere combine for a memorable place to lay your head. Be sure to take the elevator to the penthouse for a rooftop peek at the revamped digs of the famed flock that calls the

THE PEABODY DUCKS

Take a couple of hunters, thirsty after a long day of stalking, toss down a little Tennessee sippin' whiskey, throw in an opulent hotel with a lobby bar with an ornate fountain and a few live duck decoys, and you've got a tradition that's been part of Memphis legend since 1933. The ducks who paddle in the Peabody Hotel fountain each day began as somewhat of a joke between friends who ended their hunt with a stop at the bar, live decoys in tow. Today, the ducks reign supreme over the lobby and the hotel, arriving and leaving with a fanfare of music, waddling over a red carpet rolled out by the hotel's duck master, also known as the head porter. And did I mention the ride to their lush rooftop digs, via the elevator? Kids and adults alike adore this daily tradition; be sure to arrive a bit early to grab a seat or get in place for photos. Children are usually chosen to be the assistant duck master, helping to ferry the feathered flock to and fro, but every now and again don't be surprised to see a celebrity cast in that role. The Peabody (peabodymemphis.com) is at 49 Union Avenue. The duck parade happens twice daily at 11 and 5. Free.

fountain in the lobby bar its work space; the coddled ducks repair to their rooftop splendor each evening, protected by the weather in a cozy, glassed-in enclosure. (See *The Peabody Ducks* sidebar.) Expensive.

Westin—Beale Street (901-334-5900; westinbealestreet.com), 170 Lt. George W. Lee Avenue. Overlooking the FedEx Forum downtown—home of the NBA's Grizzlies—the Westin is a contemporary glass and brick building that continues the big-city vibe that's taken over this part of downtown since the Grizzlies moved into their new den. The hotel is the choice of traveling NBA teams, as a number of rooms are kitted out for supersized kings of the court, including extra-long beds, extra-tall showers and larger furniture. While most of the guest rooms feature extra-large windows, there's no worry about the late-night noise level, although the room-darkening curtains are a must. With a just-off Beale location, it's a bit of luxury and serenity in the midst of the sometimes frenetic atmosphere of the area. Expensive.

✳ Where to Eat

DINING OUT ✿ **Chez Philippe** (901-529-4188; peabodymemphis .com), 149 Union Avenue. Open Wed.–Sat. 6–10 PM, with a late night menu 9 PM–midnight in the lower tier of the restaurant and the hotel's Lobby Bar. The glamour and gilt at the AAA Four Dia-

mond–rated Chez Philippe, in the historic Peabody Hotel, harkens back to an era of vintage grace and style; the marble-columned dining room features opulent decor, and even the entrance is guarded by an elaborate iron-gated entry. Classic and sumptuous also extends to the food, as Peabody executive chef Andreas Kistler and Chez's young new chef Jason Dallas team up to return the focus to French *haute cuisine*. In a nod to more modern restauranting, however, a Petit Phillipe menu of small plates nicely priced between $8 and $12 is offered Friday and Saturday evenings from 9 PM–midnight, both in the Lobby Bar and the dining room's lower tier. Expensive.

Folk's Folly (901-762-8200; folks folly.com), 551 S. Mendenhall. Mon.–Sat. 5:30–10 PM, Sun. 5:30–9 PM. The local alternative to steakhouse chains, Folk's offers cozy dining and excellent service, plus some of the best aged beef anywhere. The clubby interior screams old-style men's club, with its dark wood and dim lighting and a bar featuring live piano seven nights a week, and the food is certainly on the traditional side, with loads of beef and casserole-style sides. A treat in the bar is the

PRICE CATEGORIES:

Inexpensive	Less than $16
Moderate	$16–30
Expensive	$31–50
Very expensive	More than $50

fried dill pickles—they're complimentary, not to mention addictive. Small private dining rooms are available for special occasions, cozy enough for two but big enough for four to six people. Expensive.

Interim (901-818-082; interim restaurant.com), 5040 Sanderlin. Open for lunch Mon.–Fri. 11–2:30; dinner Mon.–Sat. 5:30–10, Sun. 5–9. There are white tablecloths; dark, intimate spaces; and food that borders on the decadent, but don't be fooled; Interim isn't a fancy dining experience but a comfortable, jeans or suits, mac and cheese or filet (or both) kind of spot. One of the favorites on the menu is the scrumptious

bacon cheeseburger with garlic aioli and a side of hand-cut fries; paired with the crusted macaroni and cheese, it's a slam dunk—and big enough to share. A small bar hops until the wee hours most nights, with the bartenders always willing to pour drinks a bit later than advertised; bar dining is available, although reservations are suggested for bar tables as well as the dining room. Moderate.

Paulette's (901-726-5128; paulettes.net), 2110 Madison Avenue. Open Sun.–Thurs. 11–9, Fri.–Sat. 11–10. There's something just fabulously vintage-y about Paulette's; perhaps it's the traditional European decor or the fact this fine restaurant, regularly voted the best place to get engaged in town, offers early-bird dining specials for less than $13. Why I love it is simple: yummy, traditional European dishes; the perfect popovers with strawberry butter; attentive service; and a lovely atmosphere. Oh, and the scrumptious cheddar cheese soup, a must-order. There's live piano on the weekends and a European-inspired weekend brunch with crêpes and quiches, but also seafood and salad choices. Moderate.

Restaurant Iris (901-590-2828; restaurantiris.com), 2146 Monroe. Open Tues.–Sat. 5–10 PM, Sun. 11–3. A fresh, frequently changing menu with a slight Cajun flair pairs with a to-die-for wine list and a cozy, at-home atmosphere for a great dining experience at Iris. It's a completely casual spot, yet it earned a hard-to-get four-star rating from the local newspaper dining critic, who hailed Iris as a don't-miss dining experience. The Midtown home in which the restaurant lives is reminiscent of a New Orleans eatery (Chef Kelly English hails from Louisiana), and inside, diners practically rub elbows with diners at other tables, but no one seems to mind. The wine list is a great surprise, being both reasonably priced and featuring plenty of half-bottle options, which is so unusual. Book ahead, and in the case of Sun. brunch reservations, book way ahead. Moderate–expensive.

Spindini (901-578-2767; spindini mcmphis.com), 383 S. Main. Open for dinner Sun.–Thurs. 5–10, Fri.–Sat. 5–midnight; lunch Fri. 11–2 and brunch Sun. 11–2. The Grisanti family always brings it when it comes to Italian food. In the case of this hip South Main District eatery, Judd Grisanti (the original chef) went for Italian with a mod twist, like wood-fired pizzas topped with lobster, and a yummy, heady appetizer called Tuscan Butter, which blends goat cheese and mascarpone in a rich fondue served with focaccia. There's a long bar with a hopping bar scene, alfresco dining, and plenty of dark nooks and crannies for canoodling couples inside the exposed-brick building. Moderate.

⤳ **Sweet Grass** (901-278-0278; sweetgrassmemphis.com), 937 S. Cooper. Open Tues.–Sat. 5:30–11 PM, Fri.–Sun. 11–2. An awful lot of plate passing goes on at Sweet Grass, where the focus is low-country cooking with an African/Cajun flair paired with a bit of Southern tradition. The passing comes as there's always major negotiating going on at any given table—as in, "you order the osso buco, and I'll get the shrimp and grits, and we'll share." Starters—or small plates—include a fresh gazpacho of cucumbers and tomatoes, while anything ordered under the medium and large plate category can indeed be considered a meal. The shrimp and grits—a low-country staple—gets an upgrade with scallops and andouille sausage, while that Berkshire pork osso buco is paired with collard greens and bacon shiitake grits. The recent addition of lunch was a great move, as the prices drop and the more casual food is as enticing as the dinner entrées, with huge sandwiches including a burger topped with pimento cheese that is burger nirvana. I have to note that as of this writing the wine list is somewhat disappointing for such a flavorful and ambitious menu—but maybe that's the point. The restaurant is Project Green Fork certified and uses ecofriendly practices including kitchen composting, nontoxic cleaners, and sustainable products. Reservations recommended. Moderate–expensive.

EATING OUT ✍ **The Arcade Restaurant** (901-526-5757; arcadememphis.com), 540 S. Main

Street. Open daily 7–3, with extended hours the last Fri. of the month. The Arcade is Memphis's oldest café, so they say. They also say that its most revered patron, Elvis Presley, preferred the booth in the back corner because of its easy and private access via the side door, and the large mirrored wall just opposite. (Apparently Elvis appreciated being able to sit with his back to the other tables but not miss any of the action.) The food is basic, running to breakfast (all day), burgers, sandwiches, and shakes, and the clientele ranges from truckers to punk rockers to the biggest and richest names in town. Inexpensive.

♪ **Brother Juniper's** (901-324-0144; brotherjunipers.com), 3519 S. Walker. Open Tues.–Fri. 6:30–1, Sat. 7–12:30, and Sun. 8–1. Cokes come in a can and plates are heaping at this practically on campus University of Memphis–area favorite; breakfast is when Brother Juniper's is at its best, and there can be a line out the door on weekends. Omelets are huge and come in just about any combination (or request your own), including portobello mushrooms and pesto—although not together. All the breads are made in-house and alone are worth a visit. Visit early on weekend days, or the wait could be extensive. Inexpensive.

Escape Alley Sundry (901-528-3337), 651 Marshall. Open Tues.–Sat. 11–8. The totally random decor and frankly funky combina-

tion of menu offerings somehow blend to make Escape Alley a treat. Or maybe it's the giant paintings of rockers looking down from the walls, or the whimsical decorative accessories: kiddy bikes and tricycles, wagons, and even street signs serving as the table tops. Food ranges from peanut butter or bologna sandwiches to tamale nachos to my personal fave, the cereal of the day—yes, think a large bowl of Capt'n Crunch for $2, and you've got the idea. Local acts perform a few nights a week (schedule varies), and if there's a cover, it's usually under $10. If there's no cover, then tip the band. Only beer is served, but if you BYO, they'll provide setups; $2 corkage fee. Cash only. Inexpensive.

♪ **Gus's World Famous Fried Chicken** (901-527-4877), 310 S. Front Street. Open Sun.–Thurs. 11–9, Fri.–Sat. 11–10. The unpretentious—*really* unpretentious—building on S. Front might scare some folks away at first, but be brave, walk through the door, and load up. Trust us, fried chicken has rarely tasted so amazing—spicy, crunchy, and juicy—just about perfect, and your particular order doesn't hit the oil until you've ordered. Cold beer (served up in 40-ounce cans) is a nice contrast to the hot chicken. Sides and starters include fried pickles and fried green tomatoes, beans and slaw, and, strangely enough, fried rice. Assuming you have any room left, chess pie is the way to go for dessert. Gus's is a franchise of the original in Mason, about an hour from Memphis; that eatery opened in 1953, and the chicken was served up in a paper sack. There's also a location in Collierville, just east of Memphis. Inexpensive.

Hattie's Tamales (901-775-3757; hattiestamale.com), 1289 S. Lauderdale or 3576 Kirby Parkway. Lauderdale location open Mon.–Sat. 10–11 and Sun. noon–5; Kirby location open Mon.–Thurs. 10–8 and Fri.–Sat. 11–9. For more than 50 years, the folks at Hattie's have been serving up Delta-style beef tamales, based on a family recipe first rolled out for sale to the public in the 1920s. First called Josie's, then Hattie's, the tamales are filled with simmered, spicy beef and are wet—but important here to note that they're not *too* wet—and wrapped, Delta style, in a thin layer of cornmeal and then paper, not a corn husk like Hispanic tamales. Hattie's also serves up yally bowls—tamales in a bowl, covered with add-ons like homemade chili, cheddar cheese, peppers, and onions. What the menu lacks in depth it makes up for with homemade desserts—the perfect, sweet ending to the spiciness of the main feature. Load up on the napkins, whether eating in or taking out. Inexpensive.

☞ **Huey's** (901-726-9693; huey burger.com), multiple locations in town, including downtown at 77 S. Second and in Midtown at 1927

Madison Avenue. Open daily from 11 AM; closing times range from 1:30 AM to 3 AM. The name *Huey's* is synonymous with "heavenly hamburger" in this city, and the atmosphere is about as casual as a burger on the grill. It's a buzzing, family-filled environment pretty much any time of the day, although the downtown and Midtown locations are more adult oriented in the evenings. Service is quick and friendly, menus do dou-

THE ARCADE IS ONE OF ELVIS'S FORMER HAUNTS.

Stephanie Jones

ble duty as place mats (and are sometimes sticky), and the decor runs to posters, sports team T-shirts stapled to the wall, and framed articles about the owners, of which there are many. Whether you're with kids or not, be sure to ask the waiter for a glass of tooth-picks and straws—the favorite pas-time for all ages is seeing if they can shoot toothpicks into the ceil-ing tiles. Local bands play at most locations on Sun.; check the Web site for details and other locations around the area. Inexpensive.

Little Tea Shop (901-525-6000), 69 Monroe. Open Mon.–Fri. 11–2. The Little Tea Shop is a family-owned downtown home-cooking restaurant. The Old Cotton Row eatery is like stepping back in time, with its vintage-lunchroom atmosphere and old-fashioned menu. It's very common to see local business bigwigs chatting up the friendly waitresses, many of whom have worked here for decades; these gals know their regulars well and can even name their children. The food is simple Southern fare, chosen via ballot-style menu—simply grab a pencil, pick up a menu, and start marking off your choices. Turnip greens and other lushly prepared veggies are always on the menu, as is chicken salad, and daily specials include catfish or fried chicken. No matter the day of the week, everything is served with corn sticks on the side, and the home-made desserts are worth skipping dinner for, especially the tasty

frozen pecan ball with hot fudge. And I don't even like pecans! Inexpensive.

⌖ **Miss Cordelia's Grocery/ Table** (901-526-4772; miss cordelias.com), 737 Harbor Bend. Open daily 7 AM–10 PM. Harbor Town's grocery store is a hip gath-ering spot for the varied crowd that inhabits this neighborhood—college students, retirees, young families, and singles of all ages. Specializing in locally grown pro-duce and locally farmed meats, Miss Cordelia's also offers hard-to-find foods and a take-out counter with a variety of entrées, salads, and sides—including daily soup specials and quiches—for a quick picnic or meal. On the café side, sandwiches are deli style or pani-nis—my favorite is their interpre-tation of a croque monsieur—and there are just a few green and pasta salads. A nice by-the-glass or bottle wine list and patio seating add to the casual yet upscale neighborhood bistro feel. Moder-ate.

✿ **Muddy's Bake Shop** (901-683-8844; muddysbakeshop.com), 5101 Sanderlin. Open Tues.–Thurs. 11–9, Fri–Sat. 11–11. Made-from-scratch creations change weekly and are never what one would expect, from cupcakes with nicknames like Prozac (all chocolate and fudge) and straw-berry lemonade to vegan almond bars and honey rosemary cookies. Light sandwiches and snacks not bakery related are also on the menu in this East Memphis favorite. Be warned that the after-school and lunch crowds can be huge—but once you've had a cup-cake, you'll get it. Inexpensive.

Otherlands (901-278-4994; other landscoffeebar.com), 641 S. Coop-er. Open Mon.–Sat. 7 AM–8 PM, Sun. 7–6. Live music 8 PM–mid-night on Fri. and Sat. Otherlands is kind of like that box of choco-lates Forrest Gump talks about—you never know what (or who) you will find inside the brilliantly hued building. Coffee and conversation are the reasons most folks pop in and stay a while; the long drink list is much more than just coffee, with espresso, cappuccino, lattes, and smoothies offered, as well as French- and Italian style sodas and a nice variety of hot and iced teas. Breakfast and lunch/dinner are offered all day, and the menu is about as eclectic as the crowd: Eggo waffles doctored up with butter and syrup, cinnamon toast like your grandma used to make, and lunch/dinner offerings ranging from basic PB&J and egg salad to burrito plates. There's a patio for alfresco hanging out, free wireless, and a gift shop that's full of exotic crafts and amusing gifts. Inexpensive.

Soul Fish (901-725-0722; soulfish cafe.com), 862 S. Cooper. Open Mon.–Sat. 11–10, Sun. 11–9. Cat-fish—it's what the young and hip are eating? Okay, I'll bite, since it can be served up with fresh veg-gies *or* delectable hush puppies and fries. Po'boys, salads, and smoked chicken round out the menu at this Cooper-Young eatery that's one big room with booths and tables. A hodgepodge of Memphians gather here, from grungy students to top executives to families, and the atmosphere is super casual and lively. Inexpensive.

Swanky's (901-730-0763; swankystacoshop.com), 4770 Poplar Avenue. Open Mon.–Sat. 11 AM–midnight, Sun. 11–10. Dur-ing lunch, it's a walk-up-and-order spot, while dinner means table service, but there's no difference in the menu at Swanky's, which features build-your-own burritos, tacos, and salads, plus grilled entrées including fish tacos, que-sadillas, and fajitas. An extensive bar offers sipping tequilas, and those best mixed with other liq-uids, as well as sangria; more than a dozen beer choices; and a full selection of liquor. The star of the menu may just be the white queso—it is super creamy and rich, and practically a meal in itself. Inexpensive.

The Women's Exchange Tea Room (901-327-5681; womans -exchange.com), 88 Racine Street. Open for lunch Mon.–Fri. 11:30–1:45. Ladies who lunch (and yes, men eat here, too!) in Memphis often dine at the Women's Exchange; it's a cozy spot where the food is so much more than chicken salad, although that's on the menu, too. Opened in the early '60s in a Midtown house, it hasn't changed a lot over the years, in terms of the food or the clientele. The menu includes everything from beef tenderloin to fried catfish to the aforementioned chicken salad; the cost of the meal includes beverage, dessert, gratuity, and tax and is one of the best lunch deals in town. The other part of the Exchange is a specialty children's shop with hand-smocked clothing and charming handcrafted gifts, including baby blankets and quilted animals. Inexpensive.

✳ Entertainment

BARS AND NIGHTCLUBS

Ernestine & Hazel's (901-523-9754), 531 S. Main Street. Open nightly 5 PM–3 AM. The nondescript building at the corner of S. Main, a brothel-turned-hotel-turned-bar, is no one's idea of a first-date location. But locals love to roll into Ernestine & Hazel's late in the evening, for the people-watching, the alcohol-absorbing Soul burgers (complete with onions and all the fixings, a truly indulgent treat), and the cool factor.

MEMPHIS BARBECUE

Barbecue. Barbeque. BBQ. Spell it however you wish; it matters not. Just know that pork is the king of Memphis barbecue. There are shacks and roadside stands, old favorites and new(ish)comers, and every Memphian has an opinion on which is the best. The annual Memphis in May World Championship Barbeque Cooking Contest is even known as the Super Bowl of Swine. Five local favorites are all worthy of a visit; it's up to you to make the call on which wins over your palate.

Charlie Vergos' Rendezvous (901-523-2746; hogsfly.com), 52 S. Second Street. There are enough barbecue joints in Memphis to scare a pig at the mere mention of the city, and the most beloved of all is the hidden-from-view Rendezvous. One local politico calls it "ambrosia of pork," but locals call it the 'Vous and order the sausage and cheese plates, barbecue nachos, and full slabs from the perpetually grumpy but loveable waiters. The entrance is actually in the alley behind the address, just across Union from the Peabody. Inexpensive.

Corky's (901-685-9744; corkysmemphis.com), multiple locations, including 5259 Poplar Avenue. Open Sun.–Thurs. 10:45–9:30, Fri.–Sat. 10:45–10. While one could argue a barbecue joint that offers a drive-through should be avoided, there's plenty of good 'cue to be had at Corky's, dine in or drive-through. Ribs come wet or dry, hush puppies are made from scratch, and the dessert menu is not to be ignored. Inexpensive.

Hollywood Disco (901-528-9313; hollywooddisco.com), 115 Vance Avenue. Open Fri.–Sat. 10 PM–4 AM. The former Raiford's Hollywood Disco has been a Memphis institution for decades, and now it's simply the Hollywood. Whatever you call it, you can't call it boring. A light-up dance floor, a pimped-out limo, and 40-ounce beers (domestic only, and the only drink offered) add up to what could be one of those nights you simply can't tell anyone about. $10 cover.

Lobby Bar at the Peabody Hotel (901-529-4000; peabody memphis.com), 149 Union Avenue. Open Sun.–Thurs. 10:30 AM–11:30 PM, Fri.–Sat. 10:30 AM–1:30 AM. The ornate lobby bar is all at once a hot tourist destination and a see-and-be-seen place for locals; the ducks that paddle in the fountain are one draw, as are the opulent surroundings and the always-changing crowd.

Cozy Corner (901-527-9158; cozycornerbbq.com), 745 N. Parkway. Open Tues.–Sat. 11–9. No barbecue joint worth its sauce is pretentious, but Cozy Corner is perhaps the most unpretentious of all Memphis barbecue joints, with its small menu and tiny location. But under it all, the sauce is tangy and the choices are delish—who couldn't love a barbecued bologna sandwich for $3.45? The Corner's real specialty, however, is a roasted Cornish game hen with a spicy sweet rub. Inexpensive.

Interstate BBQ (901-775-3149; interstatebarbecue.com), 2265 Third Street. Open Mon.–Thurs. 11–11, Fri.–Sat. 11–midnight, and Sun. 11–4. Jim Neely is the original Neely in Memphis (see below for dish on nephew Pat's place), and his dive on Third Street is an authentic Memphis barbecue experience. The sauce is tangier than most in town. Try the sampler plate for the best all-out barbecue experience. Inexpensive.

Neely's Bar-b-que (901-795-4177; neelysbbq.com), 5700 Mt. Moriah. Open Mon–Thurs. 10:30–10, Fri.–Sat. 10:30 AM–11 PM, and Sun. noon–8. The Neely brothers—Pat, Tony, Mark, and Gaelin—lay claim to some serious Memphis barbecue DNA: that of uncle Jim, founder of Interstate BBQ. Their wins at barbecue contests and their collective personalities soon won them fans, both in Memphis and around the country, as the guys started showing up on Food Network shows. In addition to owning Neely's, Pat and wife Gina are the hosts of the network's *Down Home with the Neelys*. Inexpensive.

Mollie Fontaine Lounge (901-524-1886; molliefontainelounge.com), 679 Adams Avenue. Open Wed.–Sat. at 5 PM. Midcentury furnishings meld with Victorian elegance in this supposedly haunted hangout that attracts an eclectic mix of Memphians. DJs split the stage with jazz singers, and small plates of comfort food and large pours of fine spirits combine for an unexpectedly chic evening out. No cover.

LIVE-MUSIC VENUES B.B. King's Blues Club (901-524-5464; memphis.bbkingclubs.com), 143 Beale Street. Opens daily at 11 AM. There are other B.B. King's Blues Clubs, but the original is smack in the middle of Beale and promises some of the best regional bluesmen on stage, and even B. B. himself performs occasionally. With live music every night and up to three acts performing on weekends, the club hardly has a chance to go dark. There's lots of Southern-style comfort food on the menu, including fried green tomatoes, barbecue, and po'boys. $5 cover.

Hi-Tone Café (901-278-8663; hitonememphis.com), 1913 Poplar Avenue. Open daily 5 PM–3 AM. The Hi-Tone, with its billiards table and lounge, may seem a bit too college bar–ish for a great live music venue, but don't be fooled—emerging acts are always on the bill. Consistently voted by locals as the best place to see live music—and there are more than three hundred shows a year—the Hi-Tone also serves up traditional pub grub. Ticket prices range $7–20.

Young Avenue Deli (901-278-0034; youngavenuedeli.com), 2119 Young Avenue. Yes, it is a deli—and a great one at that—but Young Avenues double as one of the city's best live-music venues. There's an eclectic mix of bands booked here, even though the atmosphere might scream rock. The cavernous interior offers bil-

It may seem as if there's a church on every corner in Memphis, but there's no other church like **New Tabernacle Gospel Church** (901-396-9192; algreenmusic.com; 787 Hale Road), where one might be lucky enough to hear the Reverend Al Green—yes, *the* Reverend Al Green—sing (and preach) in such an intimate setting. The reverend, known for love songs like "Let's Stay Together," leads a mighty inspirational service, if you can catch him. Services are on Sunday at 11:30 and 4. Call ahead or check the Web to see if he's in town on any given Sunday, and eat a huge breakfast before you head out, as services can last three or more hours. Free.

liards and darts, and plenty of room to mingle. Cover charge for special events only.

PERFORMING ARTS Orpheum Theater (901-525-7800; orpheum -memphis.com), 203 S. Main Street. Performances run all year; check the Web site for schedules and shows. The ornate Orpheum, with massive crystal chandeliers, gilded moldings, and opulent draperies, plays host to everything from classic movies to touring Broadway productions and is an intimate venue for live music performances. Its downtown location at the corner of Beale and Main streets means it's easily accessible from Memphis's entertainment district and downtown hotels, as well as in close proximity to excellent dining options. Tickets for individual shows start about $19.

✳ Selective Shopping

ANTIQUES In Midtown, Central Avenue between Cooper and E. Parkway is where Memphians do most of their antiquing in the city; about a half dozen stores plus a few galleries line Central or are tucked into a side street here and there. This is not the most walkable area—the stores are strung out for the most part, and sidewalks are available but not in fantastic shape—so it's best to park your car and relocate as necessary.

Palladio Antiques & Art (901-276-3808; palladioantiques.com), 2169 Central Avenue. Open

Mon.–Sat. 10–5. The Palladio group of stores includes Palladio, **Market Central** (2215 Central Avenue; open Mon.–Sat. 10–5), and other spots along Central, offering a variety of high-end and more reasonably priced antiques as well as original art from local and regional artists. Both Palladio and Market Central feature dozens of individual booths, many of which focus on findings from a particular country (England, France, American primitives). Small gift items are available at many of the booths, and both locations make for excellent browsing. Inside Palladio, a café offers deli-style lunches daily 11–3.

Wellford's (901-324-1661; wellfordsandcrumpets.com), 262 S. Highland. Open Mon.–Sat. 10–5. The antiques and antique-silver shop housed in a Tudor-style cottage is a delight, with a collection of truly affordable estate silver pieces, Oriental rugs, and a small amount of antique American and European furniture. The staff's knowledge of silver is encyclopedic, especially when it comes to flatware. Accessories—including polishes and cleansers especially made for the care of antiques—are also available. The store fronts a charming tearoom and café.

ART GALLERIES Art Village Gallery (901-521-0782; artvillage gallery.com), 410 S. Main. Open Tues.–Sat. 11–5. The internationally flavored Art Village is owned by

BEALE STREET

The home of the blues didn't have anything resembling a musical start; in fact, Beale was a 2-mile-long street that ran from the river on its western end, filled with commercial businesses, and morphed into an affluent neighborhood filled with lovely homes on its eastern end. In the middle of the two areas, Beale was sometimes referred to as the "underworld"; saloons and other places of entertainment called this area home, and during Prohibition, this section of Beale was regularly in the crosshairs of the Memphis Police Department, which worked to put bootleggers and gamblers out of business.

Stephanie Jones
A. SCHWAB FIVE AND DIME, BEALE STREET

But it is the period between the late 1890s through the early 1930s for which Beale is best known. During this time, the many clubs and gambling halls, including Peewee's, Hammitt Ashford's, the Panama Club, and the Monarch, offered places for musicians to gather. According to the history outlined for the city's application to have Beale named a National Historic Landmark:

> Piano players, guitar players, and musicians of all descriptions liked to gather. It was in such an atmosphere that (W.C.) Handy heard many of the things that went into his blues. Theaters held an important place in the life of Beale Street. The largest show house for blacks in the South was the Palace Theater on Beale. It was famous for its traditional Tuesday night amateur shows. The old Pastime, opened in 1909, was the first theater for blacks on Beale Street. The first Beale Street theater established by black capital was the Lincoln, between Hernando and Fourth Streets. In this setting, William Christopher Handy played a key role at the beginning of the era when the blues became a form of music popular and imitated across the country. (Source: Beale Street Historic District application, National Park Service.)

W. C. Handy arrived in Memphis in 1909 following a career as a music teacher and minstrel band leader; in his travels with his band, he spent time in the Mississippi Delta, listening to the lament-filled songs of workers, many of whom would use crude instruments to accompany their sad lyrics. When he arrived in Memphis with his band, the songs of the Delta still resonated, and Handy incorporated the 12-bar blues into his songs, most notably "Mr. Crump"—a campaign song for political boss E. H. Crump. Handy reworked and retitled the song as "Memphis Blues," which became a hit. Handy then went on a composing streak, and his place as the father of the blues was cemented. He lived in a modest home a few miles from Beale Street, and the shotgun-style home, relocated to 352 Beale, is now a small museum dedicated to Handy and his time in Memphis.

Today, the Beale Street National Historic Site (901-526-0110; bealestreet.com) centers on the area between Second and Fourth avenues, which are shut down in the evenings to allow only pedestrian traffic for club-hopping to hear the best blues—from local groups to national acts and legends like B.B. King. The atmosphere is French Quarter–ish, with street musicians and music from the various clubs—many with open windows—competing for attention. Most of the clubs are open daily 11 AM–5 AM, and most clubs don't charge a cover unless there's a special event; tables are always turning over as patrons hop from one club to another. While the blues is indeed played here, there's also a mix of other music. Most of the clubs offer food as well, which ranges from the alcohol-absorbing burgers at Dyer's Café to ribs and catfish at Blues City Café—a can't-miss spot that's a bit grimy but a real slice of the city. A visit to the funkiest five-and-dime ever—A. Schwab's—is a must; be warned that it's not always open at night. While Beale is a fine spot for families to visit during the day, it's an adult destination in the evenings.

BEALE STREET COMES ALIVE AT NIGHT. Stephanie Jones

Nigerian artist Ephraim Urevbu, a delightfully energetic man whose passion for art—and for Memphis—flows from his fingertips. Urevbu bought the gallery when the S. Main revitalization had barely taken hold, repairing the old building with its holey roof and other challenges to create one of the district's first—and most enduring—galleries. His work, as well as that of other artists with international connections, are the focus here and include sculpture, pottery, and paintings.

David Lusk Gallery (901-767-3800; davidluskgallery.com), 4540 Poplar Avenue. Open Tues.–Fri. 10–5:30, Sat. 11–4. David Lusk is one of those galleries that makes one question everything—including why lovers of art must be subjected to snooty art gallery employees. But once one gets over the snobbery, one does enjoy the breadth of artists represented at Lusk, from local sculpting wonder Joyce Gingold to national and international names.

D'Edge Art & Unique Treasures (901-521-0054), 550 S. Main. Open Mon.–Fri. 10–5, Sat. 10–4. D'Edge is loaded with the work of local artists, many of whom focus on the blues, Memphis settings, and regional themes. This is the place to stop if you can only hit one gallery and want an authentic Memphis experience. During the Fri. night trolley tours on S. Main, the gallery hops with collectors and artists, and is a must-stop.

BOOKSTORES Davis-Kidd (683-9801; daviskidd.com), 387 Perkins Extended. Open Mon.–Thurs. 7:30 AM–9 PM, Fri. 7:30 AM–10 PM, Sat. 8 AM–10 PM, and Sun. 9–8. Bookshops like Davis-Kidd are the reason there will always be books and people who can't get enough of 'em. A staff filled with incredible literary knowledge, an easy-to-roam layout, gifts and cards, and an expansive children's section are just the "shop" portion; throw in the popular bistro that serves breakfast, lunch, dinner, and wine, and there's barely a reason to leave.

BOUTIQUE SHOPPING Charlotte Ehinger-Schwarz (901-522-0100; charlotte.de), 526 S. Main. Open Tues.–Sat. 10–6. You can preview this German jewelry online, but seeing it in person, at one of the only U.S. retailers of the line, is a treat. The modern engineering—yes, engineering—of the pieces is astounding, with the ability to swap out pearls and stones, metal and flannel, flowers and animals, to create stunning, unique combinations. And even with German engineering and fine stones, the Lego-like jewelry isn't cost prohibitive.

Joseph (901-767-1609; joseph stores.com), 418 S. Grove Park Road. Open Mon.–Sat. 10–5:30, until 7 Thurs. Featuring a delectable selection of designer clothing, shoes, handbags, and jewelry for women, Joseph isn't a huge store but offers a wide variety of women's fashion, with the best designer shoe department in town. Clothing varies from casual to evening wear, with dresses a particular focus; those who wear anything over a standard size 12 will find little to try on, however. The best part of the store is the service-oriented cosmetics section, which features Laura Mercier, Bobbi Brown, and other top skin-care and makeup lines, including the affordably priced Kiehl's.

Lansky's at the Peabody (901-525-5401; lanskybros.com), 149 Union Avenue, inside the Peabody Hotel. Open Sun.–Wed. 9–6, Thurs.–Sat. 9–9. The modest Lansky Brothers store on Beale Street had always been known in Memphis as fashion forward, but when the world discovered that Elvis bought virtually all his clothing at Lansky's, the store became known as "the store that permanently changed how America dresses." Lansky's has outfitted every major star who came through Memphis or got their start here; B. B. King, Roy Orbison, Johnny Cash, and others were among those dressed by the Lansky brothers. The store moved to the Peabody Hotel in 1981, and among its many designer brands carries a line of exclusive Elvis-inspired fashions, Clothier to the King—the nickname for the store since the brothers became known as Elvis's fashion source.

Oak Hall (901-761-3580; oakhall .com), 6150 Poplar Avenue. Open Mon.–Sat. 10–6, until 7 Thurs. Traditional clothing (read: expensive, preppy, and chic) for men and women, with plenty of American and British designers to choose from. The men's department features particularly helpful service, while the women's side can be a bit intimidating (they are known to ask who your husband is and where he works, as if that matters anymore).

Spruce (901-682-5513; spruce shop.com), 5040 Sanderlin Avenue. Open Mon.–Fri. 10–5, Sat. 10–3. Designer Selena McAdams brings a bit of chic, modern, and got-to-have-it contemporary style to East Memphis in a small space that bursts with ideas, furniture, gifts, and more. The easy-to-take price point is perhaps the best surprise of all, although her knack for finding just the perfect things keeps locals on a short leash.

World's Apart (901-272-0777; worlds-away.com), 2161 Central Avenue. Open Mon.–Sat. 10–5. Furnishings manufacturer Worlds Away—known as the go-to source for Neiman Marcus and Horchow as well as other upscale market retailers—offers its signature designer pieces, including antique mirror containers and furniture, iron tables and accessories, and lighting and case goods, at a deep discount. It's one of those shops you just can't seem to leave without picking something up, and there's plenty to choose from. The best part of all is that this really isn't a scratch-and-dent kind of outlet, so for the most part the goods you're taking home are almost always first quality.

* Special Events

Early January: **Elvis Birthday Week** (901-332-3322; elvis.com), locations throughout Memphis. All hail the King of Rock 'n' Roll, on the anniversary of his birth, January 8. The week is filled with Elvii—my pet name for tribute artists and fans—and there are a hunka-hunka events, even though this is a much quieter week than Elvis Week in August.

May: **Memphis in May** (901-525-4611; memphisinmay.org), Tom Lee Park. The monthlong festival honors one country and includes the three-day Beale Street Music Festival, the World Championship Barbeque Contest, and the Sunset Symphony—all taking place on May weekends in the riverfront Tom Lee Park.

May–September: **Live at the Garden** (901-636-4107; liveatthe garden.com), Memphis Botanic Gardens. The summer concert series boasts the best live music venue in town—the Memphis Botanic Gardens. General admis-sion lawn tickets start at $44; bring a picnic and wine, or order food from the on-site vendors.

Mid-August: **Elvis Week** (901-332-3322; elvisweek.com), locations throughout Memphis. What the locals affectionately refer to as Dead Elvis Week, this is the mother of all weeks in Memphis. Activities range from tribute artist contests (don't you dare call them impersonators), car shows, a 5K run to benefit the King's favorite charity, and a candlelight vigil when tens of thousands converge on Graceland.

Late November–December: ✦ **Starry Nights** (901-767-7275; starrynightsmemphis.com), Shelby Farms. An ecofriendly holiday light display featuring more than 1.5 million LED lights. Mon. during the month are limited to foot and bike traffic.

Year-round: **Friday Night Trolley Tours** (901-578-7262; south mainmemphis.net/trolley-nights), South Main District. The historic area's decidedly urban feel is bolstered on the last Fri. of the month, when shops, galleries, and businesses open 6–9 PM, offering libations, live music, and lively conversation.

ARLINGTON, SOMERVILLE, AND LA GRANGE

At one time a bustling town along the Memphis-Ohio Railroad, Arlington's history is like that of many once-busy farm towns that saw a population drop due to the decline of agriculture as a primary industry. But this historic little town is making a comeback, and how: Arlington's population has exploded since 2000, as people look to leave Memphis proper and make a lifestyle change in a smaller town. Settlers first came to Arlington in the 1830s, when the town was called Hays, named after the original landowner, Samuel Jackson Hays. During the horrific Memphis yellow fever epidemic of 1878, in which thousands died, the town of Arlington, too, was affected, with leaders closing off the town to outsiders, many of whom fled Memphis to escape. Arlington's historic Depot Square is truly the town center, with a charming collection of boutiques and shops that make for pleasant browsing.

Nearby Somerville and La Grange are much smaller communities. Somerville was incorporated in 1836, named after Lt. Robert Somerville, who was killed in 1814 while serving under Gen. Andrew Jackson during the Battle of Horseshoe Bend in Alabama. Tiny La Grange (population 160) was occupied by Union forces from 1869, and the Immanuel Episcopal Church was used as a hospital during that time. With its rich collection of well-preserved antebellum mansions built between the late 1860s and the 1920s, La Grange is on the National Register of Historical Places. It is also home to the remote Ghost River Section of the Wolf River, a beautiful spot for outdoorsmen, hikers, and canoers to explore.

GUIDANCE Visitor Information Center (901-543-5333; memphistravel .com or visit the town of Arlington site attownofarlington.org), 12036 Arlington Trail, Arlington. This branch of the Memphis CVB offers plenty of information for exploring this part of the Greater Memphis area. Pick up walking tour maps for both Arlington and La Grange here, as well as detailed maps.

GETTING THERE *By air:* **Memphis International Airport** (MEM; 901-922-8000; mscaa.com), 3318 Winchester Road, Memphis. MEM, the closest airport, is about 29 miles from Arlington via I-240 E. and TN 205. Major carriers are Delta, American, United, and AirTran. Arlington is located in far eastern Shelby County, while both Somerville and La Grange are in Fayette County.

By bus: There is no bus service to Arlington, Somerville, or La Grange, nor local bus service. Memphis has the closest Greyhound bus terminal.

By car: From Memphis, take I-240 E. toward Nashville to exit 24A for Arlington. Somerville is southeast of Arlington at the intersection of US 64 and County Route 222, with La Grange just south of Somerville at the intersection of CR 222 and TN 57.

GETTING AROUND *By car:* You'll need a car to explore this area. For Arlington, head north off the highway and simply follow the signs to get to the downtown area. Most attractions are within walking distance of one another, as is the case for Somerville and La Grange.

MEDICAL EMERGENCY Saint Francis Hospital (901-820-7000; saint francisbartlett.com), 2986 Kate Bond Road, Bartlett. There is no hospital in Arlington; this is the closest.

Baptist Memorial Hospital (901-861-9000), 1500 W. Poplar Avenue, Collierville. The closest hospital to Somerville and La Grange.

✳ To See

HISTORIC SITES Ames Plantation (901-878-1067; amesplantation .org), 4275 Buford Ellington Road, Grand Junction. The research and educational facility on almost 20,000 acres is also the site of the National Championship for Field Trialing Bird Dogs (see *Special Events*) and home to a local hunting club. But first and foremost, it is a research facility, with thousands of acres of commodity crops being harvested annually; beef cattle are raised here, and the quail bred here are used to restock quail habitats across the country. The grounds and historic buildings are open to the public a few times a year during the Heritage Festival (see *Special Events*) and other special events.

NATIONAL BIRD DOG MUSEUM

Arlington Depot Square (901-867-2638; townofarlington.org), Chester and Walk streets, downtown Arlington. The historic eight-block center of Arlington was a stop along the Memphis Railroad and was the center for this rural community outside of Memphis. With the recent boom in population, Depot Square is once again thriving as the center of town and features small museums, shops, and cafés. It includes the **Blacksmith Shop,** a working shop with a bellows, a brick forge, and many tools and accessories, which holds demonstrations during special historic weekends, and the **Historic Post Office,** a museum of postal memorabilia that honors those who served in the armed forces.

Historic La Grange Driving/Walking Tours, La Grange Town Hall, 20 Main Street. Pick up a brochure at the town hall to walk or drive by the collection of antebellum homes on the tour; all are privately owned, but the brochure details the history of the homes or buildings. Free.

MUSEUMS National Bird Dog Museum (731-764-2058; birddog foundation.com), 505 W. TN 57, Grand Junction. Open Tues.–Fri. 9–2, Sat. 10–4, and Sun. 1–4. The museum honors the top dogs in the world of field, trail, and shooting sports with photographic and historical memorabilia; there's both a Retriever Hall of Fame and Field Trial Hall of Fame. The museum also explores conservation efforts for waterfowl and upland game birds. Free.

✳ To Do

CANOEING The Ghost River Section of the Wolf River (901-878-0855; state.tn.us/environment/na/natareas/ghostriver), La Grange; check Web site for detailed driving instructions. About 2,200 acres of protected bottomland hardwood forests, open marshes, cypress-tupelo swamps, and upland fields create an almost mystical nature experience, and certainly an unspoiled wilderness area to visit and enjoy. Fourteen miles of the Wolf River run through the Ghost section, named for the loss of river current as the water "flows" through open marshes and bald cypress–water tupelo swamps. Canoe routes are marked with blue route signs, which are truly needed in this labyrinth of trees. A short boardwalk/walking trail provides noncanoers with the chance to view the beauty of the ecosystem. Free.

✳ Green Space

PARKS ✐ Hughes–College Hill Park (901-867-2620), 5980 Chester Street, Arlington. This charming park offers exercise stations and walking paths, plus the Playground of Dreams, a community-built, accessible-for-all playground.

✳ Lodging

Since Arlington is a day trip from Memphis, it is easy to fit into a visit to the larger city. But for those looking to stay closer to Arlington (in which there are no hotels), there are a few nearby options from which to choose.

BED & BREAKFASTS/INNS

The Old Church House (901-466-1503), 14655 County Route 194, Oakland. A former Methodist church has been born again as an interesting B&B; each of the three rooms (named Faith, Hope, and Charity) features stained-glass windows original to the church, country furnishings, and soothing colors. Modern amenities offered in each of the rooms belie the country church feel, including comfy gel-top mattresses, Egyptian cotton linens, gourmet chocolates at turndown, and flat-panel televisions. There are private baths in all three rooms, and two feature large soaking tubs. Massage services are available. Children over 12 are welcome. Inexpensive.

HOTELS **Hampton Inn & Suites Wolfchase Galleria** (901-382-2050; hamptoninn.com), 2935 N. Germantown Parkway, Bartlett. Just a few miles toward Memphis from Arlington, the Hampton Inn is an excellent choice for those wishing to stay closer to points east, as hotel options farther east on I-40 are generally along the freeway and hum with traffic all

PRICE CATEGORIES:

Inexpensive	Less than $100 (for hotels, inns, and B&Bs); less than $50 (for campgrounds, state park facilities)
Moderate	$100–200
Expensive	$201–300
Very expensive	More than $300

night long. This Hampton Inn is located just adjacent to the Wolfchase Galleria Mall, with plenty of national stores and national chain dining options in the immediate area. Furnishings at this hotel are not as modern as those at more recently built Hampton Inns, but rooms are very clean and comfortable, and the hotel's signature hot breakfast is part of the deal. Moderate.

✳ Where to Eat

EATING OUT **Vinegar Jims** (901-867-7568; vinegarjims.com), 12062 Forrest Street, Arlington. Open for lunch Tues.–Fri. 11–2; dinner Tues.–Sat. 5–9. This is the oldest restaurant in Arlington and

PRICE CATEGORIES:

Inexpensive	Less than $16
Moderate	$16–30
Expensive	$31–50
Very expensive	More than $50

the home of the fried pie, a Southern delicacy: each individual pie is filled with chocolate, apples, or peaches; fried; then coated in powder sugar. Before dessert, the meal is typical meat and three, with homemade meat loaf the house specialty. Inexpensive.

✳ Selective Shopping

ANTIQUES S.Y. Wilson and Company (901-867-2226), 12020 Walker Street, Arlington. Open Mon.–Sat. 10–5. Once the general store, this is still a family-run business, now filled with antiques and art, as well as hardware, candy, and soft drinks. Wilson's was the center of commercial and social life in Arlington; the store opened in 1893 and stocked the necessities that took customers from cradle to grave. In fact, the mezzanine displays one of the store's original baby carriages, from 1930, and there are still caskets in the attic. The store sports its original tin ceilings and wide-plank wood floors, and you can still play checkers on the porch, like the townsfolk did way back at the turn of the 1900s.

ARTS AND CRAFTS Arlington Quilting Barn/The Stichin' Station (901-867-4824; arlington quiltingbarn.com), 12019 Walker Street, Arlington. Open Tues.–Sat. 10–5. Quilters can get lost for hours in this barnlike space full of quilting fabrics, patterns, and anything quilters might need to create a masterpiece by hand or machine. Classes and workshops are offered, and many quilts on display are for sale.

✳ Special Events

Early February: **National Championship for Field Trialing Bird Dogs** (901-878-1067; amesplantation.org), 4275 Buford Ellington Road, Grand Junction. The two-week championship plays out over the fields at Ames Plantation, home to the competition since 1915. Spectators follow the action on horseback (bring your own horse; no stallions allowed). Free.

June–October: **Fayette County Farmers Market** (901-465-5233), 125 E. High Street, Somerville. Produce available on Tues., Fri., and Sat. 7–1 or until sold out. Product is locally grown, and organic produce is available.

Early October: **Ames Plantation Heritage Festival** (901-878-1067; amesplantation.org), 4275 Buford Ellington Road, Grand Junction. A one-day festival celebrating the history and heritage of Ames Plantation, with tours of the plantation's historic buildings, Civil War artillery demonstrations and encampments, and demonstration by craftspeople. Adults $4, children 5–16 $2, and children under five free.

AMES PLANTATION HERITAGE FESTIVAL

Courtesy University of Tennessee Knoxville

GERMANTOWN AND COLLIERVILLE

Memphis's two largest suburban communities, Germantown and Collierville, are not themselves master planned communities but certainly give off the feel of suburban utopia once one leaves the Memphis city limits.

Germantown's first white settlers came to the area in the 1820s; the Neshoba Plantation was one of the first residences and working plantations, albeit a plantation that supported the idea of free men working the land, not slaves. Known as Pea Ridge in its early days, Germantown was named for the surveyor who laid out the town lots, N. T. German. During World War I, the town name was changed briefly to Neshoba.

The Memphis-Charleston Railroad line came through Germantown and into Collierville in the late 1850s, which opened the door during the Civil War for both communities to feel the sting of the battle. Collierville was a Union garrison, built to protect the railroad and the supplies being transported on it; two battles and two minor skirmishes in town make up what is known as the Battle of Collierville. Despite smaller Union forces on the ground, Confederate soldiers were unable to take the garrison during four skirmishes over about a month's time. One of the skirmishes was led by Gen. William T. Sherman.

Both Collierville and Germantown saw their populations decline during the yellow fever epidemic, and with the destruction wrought by the war and the epidemic, both fought to restore their towns. When Memphis began experiencing the infamous white flight in the middle of the

20th century, East Memphis and Germantown, then eventually Collierville, became the prime relocation communities. Due to this, there's not a lot of diversity or uniqueness in either town, economically, racially, or socially—a real departure from the more urban feel of Memphis.

Today, both towns are home to populations of more than 40,000, and neighborhoods are well designed, filled with large homes, large lawns, sidewalks, and parks. Local parks are excellent, and Germantown's greenway system is a gem for runners, walkers, and bikers. Like many suburban areas, there's not a lot to define each of these towns—they meld together, connected by Poplar Avenue and lined on that main thoroughfare with franchise shopping and dining. But dig a little deeper, and there's more to be found.

Old Germantown, as that town's historic district is called, includes just a few buildings, many of which are residential. A few have been turned into shops and restaurants, and add a touch of charm to the town's south side. Collierville's historic town square area and the surrounding homes have been the focus of much restoration and redevelopment, and today is a vibrant focal point to Collierville's town spirit. Businesses around the square include clothing and antiques stores, offices for lawyers and architects, and even a funky army surplus store; a number of fine and casual eateries dot the area, giving it a vibrancy that many Tennessee town squares are sadly missing these days. Collierville is a particularly pleasant day trip from Memphis.

GUIDANCE **City of Germantown** (901-757-7200; germantown-tn.gov), 1930 Germantown Road S., Germantown.

Main Street Collierville (901-853-1666; mainstreetcollierville.org), 125 N. Rowlett, Collierville.

GETTING THERE *By air:* **Memphis International Airport** (MEM; 901-922-8000; mscaa.com), 3318 Winchester Road, Memphis. MEM is the closest major airport to Germantown and Collierville. The airport is a hub for Delta Airlines; major airlines serving Memphis include Continental, US Airways, AirTran, American, and Air Canada. From the airport, travel via I-240 E. to TN 385/Bill Morris Parkway for the Germantown and Collierville exits.

By bus: **Greyhound** (901-523-1184; greyhound.com), 203 Union Avenue. Greyhound's Memphis terminal is the closest to Germantown and Collierville. The ticket office is open 24 hours.

By car: Germantown and Collierville are located in the southwest corner of Tennessee, in Shelby County. Both are accessible via I-40 east (Germantown Road exit), TN 385/Bill Morris Parkway, and I-240 E. (Poplar Avenue exit).

GETTING AROUND *By bus:* The **Metropolitan Area Transit Authority** (901-722-7171; matatransit.com) offers bus service throughout Memphis, Germantown, and Collierville. Check the Web site for routes and schedules. Base fares are $1.50.

By car: Rental cars are available at the airport. The Germantown and Collierville areas are easy to navigate, with Poplar Avenue being the main thoroughfare in each town, as well as connecting the towns. Exits off TN 385 are at the western edge of each town; Germantown Road is a main north–south thoroughfare in Germantown. Collierville's historic district is just off Poplar Avenue, turning south on Main Street. Note that the Germantown police are notorious speed watchers, especially along Poplar Avenue; speed limits are strictly enforced, and the city employs the use of traffic light cameras to catch those who cruise through stop lights as they change from amber to red.

By taxi: Taxis are available throughout Germantown and Collierville, but they are not prevalent and need to be ordered up well in advance. **Yellow Cab/Checker Cab of Memphis** (901-577-7777; premierofmemphis .com) operates 24 hours throughout the area. A taxi ride from the airport to outlying hotels will cost about $40.

MEDICAL EMERGENCY If you need to dial 911, be sure to note whether you are in Germantown or Collierville, as each town has its own emergency services system.

Baptist Memorial Hospital (901-861-9000), 1500 W. Poplar Avenue, Collierville. Offers comprehensive emergency and medical services.

✳ To See

HISTORIC SITES Historic Collierville Walking Tour (901-853-1666; mainstreetcollierville.org), 125 N. Rowlett, Collierville. Start at the historic depot—that's where you pick up the map—and tour the town's historic buildings, many of which are well preserved or restored. The stories of the various town square buildings are especially interesting, as many have gone through numerous transformations; the square is on the National Register of Historic Places. Maps and detailed descriptions are available online as well. Free.

MUSEUMS Bible Resource Center & Museum (901-854-9578; biblical-museum.org), 140 E. Mulberry, Collierville. Open Tues.–Sat. 10–5. Run by a nondenominational organization dedicated to education about the historic significance of the Bible, the small museum space features a permanent collection of biblical artifacts, including a replica of the Rosetta stone and other reproductions; there's also space for special exhibitions. The gift store offers a variety of religious and bible-themed gifts. Free.

✳ To Do

BICYCLING/HIKING Germantown Greenway (901-757-7375; german town-tn.gov), access points around Germantown. Open daily dawn–dusk. The greenway system will eventually circle the city, and about half of the 22 miles is paved and open for bikers, runners, and walkers. Some areas wind through forests and parks, along creeks or the Wolf River; others are in wide-open spaces or cruise through neighborhoods. While at some points the greenway enjoys excellent lighting (thanks to nearby business-es, not because the path itself is lighted), once the sun goes down it is dif-ficult to see where you're going. Visit the Web site for a trail map. Free.

✳ Green Space

PARKS ✎ ☙ Wolf River Nature Area (901-757-7375; germantown-tn .gov), 7014 Wolf River Boulevard, Germantown. Open daily dawn–dusk. The Wolf River winds through this nature preserve within the German-town Greenway system, offering a variety of tracks and trails for biking and hiking. Interpretive stations along the way explore and explain the flora and fauna of the river habitat; creative use of natural materials—including a hollowed-out tree trunk—entice children, as well as educate them on conservation and ecology. There are rest areas and restrooms in a few key locations. The bike trails in the nature area connect up with the greenway and can get a bit crowded during the spring and fall, when fam-ilies hit the trails. A map of the nature area is available on the town's Web site. Free.

✳ Lodging

There are a handful of chain hotel options in the Germantown and Collierville area, but no inns or B&Bs; the properties listed here are good choices if specifically exploring this area. Other more distinctive options are available in Memphis—see that section, at the beginning of this chapter, for rec-ommendations.

HOTELS Courtyard by Marriott at Carriage Crossing (901-850-9390; marriott.com), 4640 Mer-chants Park Circle, Collierville. Tucked behind the outdoor mall, the Courtyard offers quite an

PRICE CATEGORIES:	
Inexpensive	Less than $100 (for hotels, inns, and B&Bs); less than $50 (for camp-grounds, state park facilities)
Moderate	$100–200
Expensive	$201–300
Very expensive	More than $300

upscale and stylish atmosphere for a typical chain motel, with rooms and suites that offer plenty of space for families. The hotel has an indoor pool and spa, a fitness center, free parking, and, of course, an easy walk to the retail shops and restaurants in Carriage Crossing. About 2 miles from the Collierville historic district. Moderate.

Hilton Memphis (901-684-6664; hilton.com), 939 Ridge Lake Boulevard, Memphis. An excellent location for those who want off-the-interstate access for ease of exploring East Memphis and Germantown. Moderate. See "Memphis."

✳ Where to Eat

DINING OUT Elfo's (901-753-4017; elfosrestaurant.com), 2285 S. Germantown Road, Germantown. Open Mon.–Sat. 4–until. The Grisanti family is food royalty in Memphis, with three generations of Grisantis offering their own individual take on Italian cuisine throughout the area. At Elfo's, the Grisanti in charge is Alex, who along with his wife, Kim, offer up Tuscan-inspired dishes as basic as homemade ravioli and thin, crispy pizzas to more complicated combinations of thinly sliced eggplant layered with tomatoes, zucchini, and cheese served over pasta, or a filet stuffed with Gorgonzola and

PRICE CATEGORIES:	
Inexpensive	Less than $16
Moderate	$16–30
Expensive	$31–50
Very expensive	More than $50

served up on wild mushrooms. Expensive.

Pasta Italia (901-861-0255), 101 N. Center Street, Collierville. Open Tues.–Thurs. 5:30–9:30, Fri.–Sat. 5:30–10:30. The small and charming restaurant on the town square reeks of old-world ambience, even if it is American in style, with exposed brick walls and a tin ceiling. The northern Italian food is hearty and filling, and meals start with a bit of sharp Parmesan cheese to get the palate in gear for what's to follow. Entrées can be ordered in two sizes, which makes sharing a snap, and for a special treat, one can indulge in the "feed me" option—where the chef, at his whim, prepares a six-course meal for two. Every meal ends with a cup of mulled wine—an authentic touch. Moderate.

EATING OUT Café Piazza (901-861-1999; cafepiazzaonline.com), 139 S. Rowlett Street, Collierville. Open Mon.–Sat. 11–9. An early-1900s home just off the historic Collierville square has been turned into a lush but unpretentious spot by the Lucchesi family, yet another Italian-American family keeping locals well fed. In a departure from their casual offering in East Memphis, Café Piazza is closer to a fine-dining experience with no airs; the service is friendly and quick, the food is rich and served up in large portions. Choices range from pizzas and traditional dishes with freshly made pastas to steaks; desserts are all homemade and come in portions large enough to share. Moderate.

The Germantown Commissary (901-754-5540; commissarybbq .com), 2290 Germantown Road, Germantown. Open Mon.–Sat. 9–9, Sun. 11–8. The Commissary was just that—a small store offering just about anything to the folks in Germantown—and operated for more than 90 years as such until the building was bought and turned into one of the best barbecue spots in the Memphis area. The dining room is actually a number of rooms, and this is not the place to come if you mind rubbing elbows—or backs—with folks at neighboring tables. The 'cue here is slow cooked over hickory, and the aroma can be sniffed from blocks away. There are a multitude of combo plates to choose from if you can't make a decision between ribs or pulled chicken or pork; sides are mostly homemade and include a not-too-creamy slaw that offers a tangy alternative to the heat of the sauce. Be warned: the trains come through this part of town frequently, and right outside the front door, so close you could spit on them (but don't)—that's what is causing the sudden noise and shaking inside the restaurant. Moderate.

Ø **Gus's World Famous Fried Chicken** (901-527-4877), 215 S. Center Street, Collierville. Open Sun.–Thurs. 11–9, Fri.–Sat. 11–10. The Collierville version of the downtown Memphis favorite is in a converted old house just off the historic town square, and while it lacks a bit of the grit of the Front Street location, the chicken is still a treat—spicy, crunchy, and juicy—that's just about perfect. Your particular selection doesn't hit the oil until you've ordered. Sides and starters include fried pickles and green tomatoes, beans, and slaw, and strangely enough—fried rice. Assuming you have any room left, chess pie is the way to go for dessert. Gus's is a franchise of the original in Mason, about an hour from Memphis; that eatery opened in 1953, and the chicken was served up in a paper sack. Inexpensive.

Ø **Huey's** (901-726-9693; huey burger.com), multiple locations, including downtown Memphis at 77 S. Second and in Midtown Memphis at 1927 Madison Avenue. Open daily from 11 AM; closing times range from 1:30 AM to 3 AM. Inexpensive. See "Memphis."

Mensi's Dairy Bar (901-853-2161), 162 Washington St., Collierville. Open Mon.–Sat. 11 AM–8 PM. It's basic burgers, dogs, and ice cream treats at the walk-up Mensi's Dairy Bar; burgers come wrapped in paper, and fries are perfectly crispy. There are no tables, but you can wander over to the town square just a block away and find a bench to use as a perch. Inexpensive.

Petra Café (901-754-4440; petra cafe.com), 6641 Poplar Avenue,

Suite 101, Germantown. Open Mon.–Sat. 11–9. Due to decor that's a bit basic—paper-topped tables and posters of the famed Petra on the walls—one might not expect much when it comes to the food, but that's a mistake. At lunch, Petra's salads and sandwiches are anything but meat-and-potatoes, featuring lamb, steak, and muffuletta salad options, and a large variety of gyro-, pita-, and deli-style sandwiches—such a huge selection that it's almost overwhelming. Hummus, tabbouleh, and spanakopita compete for appetizer attention during lunch and dinner, and in the evenings, walk-up ordering is replaced with table service and a sharper focus on traditional Greek entrées including braised lamb shanks, dolmades, and kabobs. Moderate.

Silver Caboose & Sidecar Market (901-853-0010; silver caboose.com), 132 E. Mulberry Street, Collierville. Open Mon.–Sat. 11–2, Fri. 5–8, and Sun. 10:30–2. The Sidecar is open Mon.–Fri. 7–3 and Sat.–Sun 11–2:30. The charming restaurant is a favorite spot for local ladies who lunch, with a menu that's as varied as it is large. Dinner turns up the elegance notch just a bit with steaks and other more substantial entrées. The soda fountain—one of the state's last original fountains—is a favorite spot for kids and serves up traditional sundaes and sweets in an old-timey setting. Next door, the

Sidecar is the bakery arm of the operation, offering fresh homemade pies, cookies, and rolls; casseroles and other main dishes are frozen and ready to take home to bake. Inexpensive–moderate.

Swanky's (901-737-2088; swankys tacoshop.com), 6641 Poplar Avenue, Suite 109, Germantown. Open Mon.–Sat. 11–midnight, Sun. 11–10. There's a second location at 4770 Poplar Avenue in Memphis (901-730-0763). Swanky's features build-your-own burritos, tacos, and salads, plus fish tacos, quesadillas, and fajitas. Inexpensive. See "Memphis."

West St. Diner (901-757-2191; weststreetdiner.com), 2076 West Street, Germantown. Open Mon.–Fri. 6:30 AM–8 PM, Sat.–Sun. 6:30–2. A small, classic diner complete with oilcloth table covers, huge platters of food, and those little lined tickets written out by the waitress—there's usually just one, and she covers all of the eight or so booths at the speed of light. Breakfasts range from grits, biscuits and gravy, and egg platters to waffles and pancakes, while lunch is typical diner fare but better than that sounds: charbroiled chicken in the chicken salad, homemade veggie soup, and grilled turkey and ham sandwiches with crisp bacon and melted cheese. Inexpensive.

✳ Selective Shopping

ANTIQUES The George (901-757-9455), 7609 Poplar Pike, Germantown. Open Tues.–Sat. 10–5.

The small beige house looks like a bit of a hoarder's place, what with all the furniture and "stuff" on the wraparound front porch, and there always seems to be a trailer or container in the back drive that promises treasures from England. Inside, loads of English furniture is crammed into every conceivable space, making for a bit of a claustrophobic experience, but all that's forgiven if you're lucky enough to find that perfect piece—and loaded enough to pay for it. Even if you're not, it's a fun place to meander through.

Past & Presents (901-853-6465; pastandpresentsonline.com), 307 W. Poplar Avenue, Collierville. Open Mon.–Sat. 10–5. The little house offers big fun for antiques shoppers, with rooms filled to overflowing with furniture, rugs, and accessories. In addition to primitives from around the South, there's a great selection of Swedish finds, something one doesn't see much of around these parts. Architectural pieces tend to go fast and are worth seeking out—and make for fun browsing.

Sheffield's Antiques Mall (901-853-7822; sheffield-antiques.com), 684 W. Poplar Avenue, Collierville. Open Mon.–Wed. 10–5, Thurs.–Sat. 10–6, and Sun. noon–6. A former megastore space has been turned into a giant antiques mall mostly populated with great finds at really reasonable prices. Few large pieces of furniture are found here—most booths run more to collectibles,

accessories, and the like—but the browsing is excellent, and the in-store café is surprisingly top-notch as well. Estate jewelry and silver are kept up front, and large garden and architectural pieces are out in what used to be the former store's garden center on the east side of the building.

Town Square Antique Mall (901-854-9839), 118 E. Mulberry Street, Collierville. Open Mon.–Sat. 10–5. Featuring a mix of antiques and reproductions, plus a lot of collectibles, the two-story mall places a heavy emphasis on Christian-inspired art and gifts. A winding staircase in the front and back of the store provides the only access to the second-floor offerings.

BOUTIQUE SHOPPING Bella Vita (901-850-0892; shopbella vita.com), 3670 Houston Levee Road, Collierville. Open Mon.–Sat. 10–6. A home decor store, Bella Vita features a nice mix of well-known brands, with a collection of art and decor by local and regional craftsmen. There's also a small selection of clothing, jewelry, and accessories for women— the store can serve as a one-stop shop for a lot of gift buying.

Hewlett & Dunn Jean & Boot Barn (901-854-3806; hewlettdunn .com), 111 N. Center Street, Collierville. Open Mon.–Sat. 10–6. A no-nonsense purveyor of jeans, boots, and work clothes for the regular guy (or gal), the old Collierville staple also offers more dressy Western wear, boots that

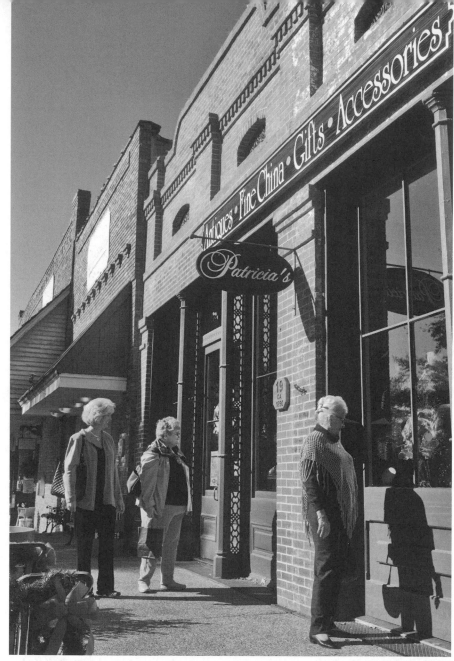

SHOPPING AT COLLIERVILLE'S HISTORIC TOWN SQUARE

Tennessee Department of Tourism

aren't just utilitarian, and belts and buckles worthy of a rodeo, along with barn jackets, work pants, and a selection of Stetson hats.

Indigo (901-755-6909), 7509 Poplar Avenue, Germantown.

Open Mon.–Sat. 10–6. *Chic* and *trendy* are the buzzwords at Indigo, which caters to older teens and their 40-ish moms, who can both find something to wear (although usually not the same thing). Designer brands include local boy Justin Timberlake's William Rast line, and loads of accessories are available. A very unrelenting return policy means you'd better leave the store in love with your purchases; otherwise, you can only return items for store credit.

James Avery—Saddle Creek (901-756-5715; jamesavery.com), 7615 W. Farmington, German-town. Open Mon.–Sat. 10–8, Sun. noon–5. The Texas craftsman opened his first store in the 1950s, and his silver pieces—charms and chains, bracelets and rings—can be both simple and intricate in design, with charms often hanging from basic black silk cords. While the store is best known in Texas, Avery is starting to be seen across Tennessee, and the distinctiveness of his pieces (he's now retired, but many of the most popular designs are still his originals) are worthy of a visit to the store.

Spoiled Sweet Boutique (901-757-9797), 2011 Exeter, German-town. Open Mon.–Fri. 10–6, Sat. 10–5. A children's boutique, Spoiled Sweet features smocked clothing for boys and girls, plenty of coordinating hair bows, and a large selection of baby and chil-dren's gifts, including soft stuffed animals, blankets and nursery accessories, and keepsakes.

SHOPPING AREAS Avenue at Carriage Crossing (901-854-8240; carriagecrossing.shopthe avenue.com), 4674 Merchants Park Circle, Collierville. Open Mon.–Sat. 10–8, Sun. noon–6. Restaurants have later closing hours. Two large department stores anchor the outdoor "lifestyle" shopping center, which includes almost any chain retailer one finds in a snazzy suburban mall. Macy's and Dillard's are the department stores, and names like Sephora, Build-a-Bear, Jos. A. Bank, and Chico's are here, among dozens more. A variety of chain restaurants—Firebirds, Red Robin, and Bonefish—are also on-site.

Collierville Town Square (901-853-1666; mainstreetcollierville .org), 125 N. Rowlett, Collierville. Most stores are open Mon.–Sat. 10–5 and closed on Sun.; the cafés usually have longer hours. Around the town square, a collection of gift, decor, and antiques stores make for a day of pleasant brows-ing and dining. **C. J. Lilly's** and **First Fruit** offer upscale home decor and accessories; **Wish! Memories** sells stationery, custom stamps, and cards; **Village Toy-maker** sells fine toys and play-things for babies and children.

Shops of Saddle Creek (901-753-4264; shopsofsaddlecreek .com), 7509 Poplar Avenue at West Street/Farmington Boule-vard, Germantown. Open Mon.–Sat. 10–8, Sun. noon–5:30. Split over two pieces of property on opposite sides of Poplar Avenue, the outdoor shopping area offers upscale and more bou-tique-type chain retailers, with just a few locally owned stores mixed in. Apple, J.Jill, Anthropologie, and Williams-Sonoma are among the offerings.

✳ Special Events

Early June: **Germantown Charity Horse Show** (901-754-0009; gchs.org), Charity Horse Show Arena, 7745 Poplar Pike, Germantown. The five-day competition brings the best in the hunter, jumper, and show classes to Germantown; proceeds benefit the Exchange Club Family Center. Adults $5, children $3.

June–July: **Concerts on the Square** (901-853-1666; main streetcollierville.org), town square, Collierville. The Thurs.-night concert series brings a variety of music to the town square, with bands setting up in the gaze-bo; restaurants and shops stay open late (if not already open) to welcome concertgoers. Free.

Courtesy Germantown Charity Horse Show

GERMANTOWN CHARITY HORSE SHOW

MILLINGTON, COVINGTON, AND HENNING

Heading north out of downtown Memphis, there's a palpable change in the energy, moving from high wattage to low voltage—and that's not a bad thing.

US 51 heading out of Memphis is indeed a road less traveled, but it opens up a beautiful slice of rural Tennessee that continues to the Kentucky state border, starting with Millington; this section explores northern Shelby County, moving through Tipton County and, finally, Lauderdale County. This region is highly agricultural, thanks to the rich soil of the Mississippi Delta; there are a few larger towns—Millington and Covington—and a smattering of smaller burgs, including Halls, Henning, Mason, Ripley, and Nutbush.

Once part of the Chickasaw Nation, Millington was a rural farming community until the Chesapeake and Ohio rail line came through; local landholder George Millington offered some of his holding for a town and station to be built along the rail line, and Millington was born. The land was part of the Chickasaw Bluffs and was higher ground along the Mississippi River for many of the people who built homes on the donated land. Millington wasn't officially a town until the early 1900s and was the first town in all of Shelby County to provide a school bus—actually a wagon— to transport children to school.

North out of Millington, wide fields stretch as far as the eye can see; cotton was and still is the primary crop grown in this part of West Tennessee. The flat land with its rich, river-fed soil, combined with a long and hot growing season, created the perfect conditions for growing cotton and other crops. Huge plantations once dominated this landscape, and slaves were brought in to pick the crops. West Tennessee, in fact, had the largest population of slaves in the state; outside this area, few farms kept slaves as laborers.

During the Civil War, this area was vital to both armies, as controlling the Mississippi River was critical. Union forces occupied Covington and most of the area around it in Tipton County from an early point in the war, and in Henning, Fort Pillow—a Confederate stronghold along the Mississippi—was occupied by both sides during the war and eventually abandoned by the South.

The small towns of this area have produced some of the best-loved names in entertainment—some household names, others known only to those who are students of the blues. *Roots* author Alex Haley first heard the stories of his African ancestors at his grandparents' home in Henning; Tina Turner hails her tiny hometown in "Nutbush City Limits," although *city* is definitely a misnomer when it comes to Nutbush; and major bluesmen—including John Henry Barbee, Sleepy John Estes, and Peetie Wheatstraw—called this area home. Perhaps the most famous native son of this area—who still visits frequently and remains a force in the local music and philanthropic community—is pop superstar Justin Timberlake.

GUIDANCE City of Millington (901-872-2211; millingtontn.gov), 7930 Nelson, Millington. There's limited information on Millington's attractions at city offices; the Memphis Welcome Centers in Arlington and downtown Memphis are better spots to pick up information on attractions throughout the area.

GETTING THERE *By air:* **Memphis International Airport** (MEM; 901-922-8000; mscaa.com), 3318 Winchester Road, Memphis. MEM is the closest airport, about 30 miles from Millington via I-240 W., I-40 E., and US 51. Major carriers are Delta, American, United, and AirTran. Millington is in Shelby County, Covington is in Tipton County, and Henning is in Lauderdale County.

By bus: There is no Greyhound bus service to Millington, Covington, or Henning, although Greyhound does have a station in Memphis (901-523-1184; greyhound.com) at 203 Union Avenue.

By car: Take I-240 W. toward Little Rock, to exit 2A for Millington; Henning is north on US 51 thorough Millington, another 30 miles. Covington is located a little more than halfway between the two towns, also via US 51. Continue north for Ripley and Halls; follow TN 59 out of Covington to get to Mason, about a 20-minute drive.

GETTING AROUND *By car:* US 51 is the main drag in Millington, with the majority of stores, restaurants, and businesses located between Paul Barrett Parkway and Union Street.

MEDICAL EMERGENCY As you drive north on US 51, you travel through three counties—Shelby, Tipton, and Lauderdale—so be sure to note the town you are closest to when calling 911 and pay special attention to road markers.

Methodist North Hospital (901-516-5200; methodisthealth.org), 3960 New Covington Pike, Memphis. The closest hospital to Millington features a 24-hour emergency room.

✳ To See

HISTORIC SITES ✽ **Fort Pillow State Park** (731-738-5581; state.tn.us /environment/parks/FortPillow), 3122 Park Road, Henning. Open daily 8–sunset, year-round. Both a natural wonderland and an important historic site, Fort Pillow stretches for almost 1,700 acres along what was known as the Chickasaw Bluffs of the Mississippi River. The Confederate Army built extensive fortifications here in 1861, and today the remains of the long-ago abandoned earthworks are in excellent condition, even after 150 years. The battle fought here in April 1864 was bloody; the African American Federal troops that fought the battle surrendered, only to be massacred by the Confederates. There are some restored fortifications in the park, as well as a museum featuring Civil War artifacts and more information about the battle.

Beyond history, Fort Pillow offers fishing (fishing boats and trolling motors only) and canoeing; a valid Tennessee fishing license is required. There are no boat rentals in the park. Almost 40 tent sites are available, but there is no water or electrical hookup. Pets on leash are welcome, and pet owners are expected to pick up waste. There's no entrance fee for the park.

MUSEUMS Alex Haley State House Museum (731-738-2240), 200 S. Church Street, Henning. Open Tues.–Sat. 10–5, Sun. 1–5. Tiny Henning gave birth to a huge player in the American literary scene, *Roots* author Alex Haley. His modest boyhood home is now a museum featuring memorabilia and family heirlooms; Haley lived here with his mother and maternal grandparents, and it was the stories told by his grandparents that gave him fodder for *Roots*. While many call the home Haley's birthplace, the author was born in Ithaca, New York, and moved to Henning to live with his grandparents when he was just six weeks old. The Haley home is the first state-supported historical site devoted to a black Tennessean. Haley is buried here, just a few steps from the porch where he listened to the family stories. Adults $5, children $3.

Veterans Museum (731-836-7400; dyaab.us), 100 Veterans' Drive, Halls. Open Sat.–Tues. 2–5. During World War II, the Dyersburg Army Air Base served as a training facility for B-17 bombers; it was the only such facility east of the Mississippi River, and at the height of its activity the crews flew more than one hundred cycles every 24 hours, with both day and night training flights. Following the war, the base was quickly dismantled, with just a few storage buildings remaining. It was in the mid-1980s, when then-governor Lamar Alexander initiated a statewide homecoming to celebrate the history of Tennessee, that the idea of a museum on the old air base came up. Area residents who worked at the base shared their stories, photos, and mementoes from their time there, and an air show was put on. Fund-raising started in earnest, with the museum completed in 1997. Its collection includes photos and documents about the base from the National Archives, the diaries and personal artifacts of pilots and crew members, and a series of murals from the era. There's also an excellent history of the infamous Memphis Belle, the first heavy bomber of the war to carry out 25 combat missions. An air show and dance take place every Sept. as a fund-raiser for the museum. Tickets are $5 in advance and $10 at the gate.

ALEX HALEY HOME, HENNING

✳ To Do

GOLF ↝ **Mirimichi Golf Course** (901-259-3800; mirimichi.com), 6195 Woodstock Cuba Road, Millington. Yes, pop superstar Justin Timberlake is the owner of Mirimichi, and yes, he plays a round here practically every time he's in town, which is frequently. Beyond the star factor, however (and Timberlake has pumped $15 million in improvements into the course since he purchased it with partners), there's the green factor, as in environmental. Lush greens are accented by natural elements—wood and stone—and the course also practices intense sustainability efforts, including recirculating creeks and runoff landscaping. The course has been named a GEO (Golf Environmental Organization) course, one of just 10 in the world and the only one in North America. And how's the golf? Beyond pretty, the main course is a 7,400-yard par 72 course with rolling hills and mounds to frame fairway shots. Rates are $49 and up for the regular course, with lower rates for the nine-hole Little Mirimichi course.

RIPLEY TOMATOES

The Ripley tomato is the king of fruits and vegetables in West Tennessee. With smooth skin, the large tomatoes are a deep red color and offer an intense flavor; people eat them whole like apples. While they are easy to grow for home gardeners anywhere, it's the mineral-rich soil of the Mississippi River Delta that makes all the difference when it comes to the flavor. Increasingly the Ripley is becoming a must-have for chefs throughout the region, and it is fast becoming popular outside of the South as well.

Drive through Ripley during the growing season, and there's no shortage of roadside stands from the larger farmers offering the tomatoes and other fresh vegetables for sale; some farmers even just leave out a tent at the end of their drive, tables underneath filled with baskets of tomatoes, with a scale and paper sacks. Simply choose your tomatoes, fill a sack, weigh it, and leave your money—all on the honor system.

The Ripley growing season is from June through September, with the annual festival celebrating the famed tomato taking place each July in Ripley's downtown square (see *Special Events*). A list of growers can be found on the Ripley city Web site (ripleytn.com), but it's just as easy to find fresh tomatoes on a drive up US 51 or through town.

FISHING AT MEEMAN–SHELBY FOREST STATE PARK

Tennessee Department of Tourism

WINERIES Old Millington Winery (901-873-4114; oldmillingtonwinery
.com), 6748 Old Millington Road, Millington. Open Wed.–Sat. 10–6, Sun.
1–5. The small winery grows its own Chambourcin grapes for its red
wines and blends its other wines from a variety of grapes grown throughout the region. Sweet wines, with an emphasis on fruit wines, are a specialty. Label collectors will enjoy the whimsical artwork for each bottle.
Tastings are free.

✳ Green Space

PARKS Meeman–Shelby Forest State Park (901-876-5215; tn.gov
/environment/parks/MeemanShelby), 910 Riddick Road, Millington.
Open daily 7 AM–10 PM. At almost 14,000 acres, much of it bordering the
Mississippi River, the park is a delight for bird- and wildlife watchers, as
well as anglers and hikers. Most of the park is made up of bottomland
hardwood forests of huge trees, including cypress, oak, and tupelo. More
than 20 miles of hiking trails meander throughout the forests and along
the river, and wild turkey and deer are abundant. Anglers can rent a john-
boat at the park to explore the two lakes in the park; boats with electric
motors are allowed, but boats with gas motors are not permitted. Canoes
are also available to rent. There's no entrance fee for the park.

✳ Lodging

Hotels in downtown Memphis are also a good option for those who plan a day trip through Millington to Lauderdale County. There are no lodgings between Covington and Halls; if continuing your trip through northwest Tennessee, then options in Union City and Dyersburg are a good choice (see the "Northwest" chapter).

HOTELS Hampton Inn & Suites Millington (901-872-4435; hamptoninn.com), 8838 US 51 N., Millington. With the Hampton's rich color scheme and hip black-and-white photos, it's hard to believe that it isn't a unique boutique hotel. But the Millington version of this popular chain hotel is right on the money—clean rooms, sparkling lobby, easy to find location. There's a free hot breakfast, or grab a to-go bag if you're in a rush. Other amenities include an outdoor pool, fitness room, and business center. Inexpensive–moderate.

Holiday Inn Express Covington (901-476-9700; holidayinn.com), 120 Deena Cove, Covington. The Holiday Inn offers both regular rooms and suites decorated in soothing tones with contemporary furnishings. It's located off the highway, so the hotel is quieter than most in the area. Amenities include a large business center with computers and free wireless, and a surprisingly sleek lobby with a breakfast area and conversational seating. The indoor pool is salt-

PRICE CATEGORIES:	
Inexpensive	Less than $100 (for hotels, inns, and B&Bs); less than $50 (for campgrounds, state park facilities)
Moderate	$100–200
Expensive	$201–300
Very expensive	More than $300

water filtered, and there's a nicely kitted-out fitness room. Inexpensive–moderate.

✳ Where to Eat

DINING OUT Marlo's Down Under (901-475-1124; marlosdu.com), 102 Court Square E., Covington. Open Tues.–Sat. 11–2 and 5–9, with the bar open until 10 each evening. Marlo's is a bit hidden—it is, after all, truly down under in the basement, the former dry goods storage for the long-gone grocery that used to occupy a prime corner of Covington's town square. And it is certainly worth searching out, with some simple yet elegant offerings from seared steaks and crispy onion rings to more exotic fare like creatively crusted seafood options with a variety of creamy risottos. Moderate–expensive.

EATING OUT ✍ Bozo's Hot Pit Bar-B-Q Mason (901-294-3400), 342 US 70 W., Mason. Open Tues.–Sat. 10:30–9. Across the

PRICE CATEGORIES:

Inexpensive	Less than $16
Moderate	$16–30
Expensive	$31–50
Very expensive	More than $50

highway from Gus's, Bozo's draws folks simply with the aroma of slow-cooked barbecue like an irresistible siren song. Bozo's has its own long history, having opened in 1923 by Thomas Jefferson "Bozo" Williams. The eatery was so small there were no tables, only counter seats, and a pork sandwich (back then called a pig sandwich) sold for 15 cents. The location of Bozo's jumped back and forth across the highway, settling in its present location in the 1950s, and it was one of the first air-conditioned buildings in town. Inside the narrow building, plastic red and white checkered tablecloths cover the tables, and the menu hasn't changed much over the years—the most recent addition being onion rings in 1991. There are barbecue sandwiches and plates (all pork or chicken) with mild and hot sauces, slabs of ribs (Fri. and Sat. only), and traditional sides including baked beans and potato salad, plus a really scrumptious choice of either sweet or vinegar coleslaw—either is a tasty option. A variety of sandwiches and hamburgers are also available; salads, catfish, and chicken tenders round out the entrée portion of the menu. The main event for some folks is pie, however; a

variety of freshly made pies are offered daily, ranging from pecan and lemon meringue to apple or a German chocolate pie—the selection is rarely the same on any given day. Inexpensive.

✍ **Gus's World Famous Fried Chicken** (901-294-2028), 520 US 70 W., Mason. Open daily 11–6; the last "eat-in" is 5:15. The original location of the Gus's mini chain is, like the others, a small, unpretentious building filled with friendly folks ready to help you clog your arteries. Inexpensive. See "Memphis."

Just Divine Tea Room (731-836-6113; charlenes.net), 2257 County Route 88, Halls. Open for lunch Tues.–Sat. 11–2; dessert served until 3. The tea shop is part of Charlene's Colony of Shoppes, housed in what was once a

THE HISTORY OF GUS'S WORLD-FAMOUS FRIED CHICKEN

Gus's was opened in 1953 by Napoleon "Na" Vanderbilt and originally named Maggie's Short Orders after Mrs. Vanderbilt. The couple ran the small but popular eatery that brought folks in from as far away as Memphis—an hour's drive—until their deaths in 1983. Their son Gus and his wife reopened the restaurant a year later and have been fixtures on the local food scene ever since.

COVINGTON'S TOWN SQUARE

Mississippi River–side country church. The clapboard building was moved to the Charlene's property in three installments and underwent a renovation, including the addition of a full kitchen. The church's former sanctuary and Sun.

school rooms provide a cozy setting for a meal, with each room having its own color scheme and coordinating decor—and most of what's on the walls and the pieces of furniture are for sale. The food is indeed pretty divine, yet simple—

a favorite comes from Charlene's personalized take on chicken salad, made fresh daily: freshly cooked chicken, almonds, and chopped grapes and peppers with a tangy honey-mayo dressing. Gourmet sandwiches and salads and a variety of twists on Southern staples— including orange-y corn bread— are nice additions. Desserts are homemade, thoroughly decadent, and served up in portions large enough to share. During Nov., the tearoom offers evening meals on Thurs. 5–7:30. Moderate.

Old Timers (901-872-6464; old timersrestaurant.com), 7918 C Street, Millington. Open Mon.– Thurs. 11–2 and 5–8, Fri. 5–9, Sat. 8 AM–9 PM, and Sun. 8–2. The cuisine is pretty basic at Old Timers, but read that to mean standard fare served up fresh, with a bead on Southern favorites: Memphis barbecue, large breakfast platters with grits and biscuits, fried chicken and catfish, and sides of greens, beans, and gravy. The ambience is old-timey, indeed: housed in a brick building that had once been a dry goods and grocer, the restaurant's exposed brick interior walls are covered with historic photos of Millington. Inexpensive–moderate.

✳ Selective Shopping

FOOD PURVEYORS Shelby Forest General Store (901-876-5770; shelbyforestgeneralstore .com), 7729 Benjestown Road, Millington. Open daily 8 AM–9 PM. What started as the general store

for rural residents in 1934 has turned into a must-stop for the million visitors to Meeman–Shelby Forest State Park. The store offers everything from fishing lures and live bait to what some call the best cheeseburger in West Tennessee (it is pretty darn good). And yes, for those tracking local boy Justin Timberlake, he does still pop in here on occasion—he went to school across the street. Don't be surprised if you see him ordering a cheeseburger.

SHOPPING AREAS Charlene's Colony of Shoppes (731-836-5418; charlenes.net), 2257 CR 88, Halls. Open Tues.–Sat. 10–5. Charlene—pronounced like the "char" in *charcoal*—has gathered a variety of old homes on a pretty hill and filled them with everything from antiques to smocked children's clothing to women's trendy clothing. The main attraction is a huge, barnlike space that's decked out for whatever holiday that's upcoming. The Christmas season starts in late Sept., with each room bedecked and beribboned, from fanciful, colorful pink and purple trees and ornaments to more traditional silver and gold. There's a little bit of everything in this main barn, including traditional upholstered furniture, rugs, dining tables, and chairs—and just about any accessory one could need to create a custom-designed look on a reasonable budget.

✳ Special Events

July: **Lauderdale County Tomato Festival** (731-635-9541; lauderdalecountytn.org/living_tomato.html), downtown Ripley. A two-day event paying homage to the Ripley tomato, the festival at the scenic town square includes a tomato-themed art exhibition and tomato cooking contests—one recent entry was a chocolate and tomato cake. Traditional festival-style fun includes a baby crawling contest and talent show, and the occasional attempt to break the world's record for the largest tomato sandwich.

Mid-September: **International Goat Days Festival** (901- 873-5770; internationalgoatdays.com), USA Stadium, 4351 Babe Howard Boulevard, Millington. All things goat are celebrated at the annual Goat Days, where activities include goat chariot races, a best-dressed goat contest, pancake breakfast, a painted goat art exhibit (not live goats, of course), a rodeo, and live music. There's no admission charged, but parking is $5.

NORTHWEST

PARIS AND LAND BETWEEN THE LAKES

The oldest municipality in West Tennessee, Paris is the seat of Henry County, and its courthouse in the still-charming downtown area was built in 1823. It was there on the courthouse lawn that Confederate regiments formed, with hundreds of volunteers signing up for the war; folks called Henry County the "volunteer county of the Volunteer State," as more than 2,500 Henry County men would join Confederate troops.

The town saw much action during the war, as Gen. Ulysses S. Grant attacked an encampment of soldiers here but soon retreated toward Paris Landing after that unsuccessful engagement. About two years later, Gen. Nathan Bedford Forrest began his Johnsonville campaign at Paris Landing, where he made the stunning capture of four Union gunboats, multiple barges and transport, artillery, and more than 150 prisoners.

Paris Landing had been a steamboat landing on the Tennessee River in the mid-1800s, but it wasn't until a century later that government action gave the town a resort feel. The Tennessee Valley Authority cut a channel between the Tennessee and Cumberland rivers in 1963, creating an inland peninsula and a lake out of each river. Lake Barkley and Kentucky Lake both straddle the Tennessee-Kentucky state line and offer a rich camping and outdoors experience, including fishing, hiking, and houseboating. The national recreation area known as Land Between the Lakes (or LBL, as some Tennesseans refer to it) is a must-see destination for history buffs and nature lovers alike, as well as a great family recreation destination. It's part of Fort Henry, a Civil War–era fortification, and the Homeplace, an 1850s living-history museum, both located within the park; the ruins of the Great Western Iron Furnace, a major force in Tennessee's post–Civil War iron industry, are on the park's Trace Road.

The creation of Land Between the Lakes was opposed by many of the families in both Kentucky and Tennessee whose land was acquired for the project; more than 2,700 people were bought out or moved to make way

HENRY COUNTY COURTHOUSE, PARIS

for the recreation area between Kentucky and Barkley Lakes. Those in favor of the move had promised displaced residents that they'd be rewarded with a boom in tourism and recreation that would more than make up for their inconvenience. But the economic boom has yet to happen, as a series of budget cuts chopped the programs and amenities in the recreation area, which was eventually passed to the U.S. Forest Service.

Agriculture still plays a large role in Henry and the other counties around Land Between the Lakes, and recreational tourism is a prime economic factor in the area as well. But the quiet towns and small businesses in the area are testament to underdevelopment—and that's not such a bad thing for those looking to take in wide, quiet natural spaces, peaceful vistas, and a bit of small-town charm.

GUIDANCE Northwest Tennessee Tourism Council (731-364-2233; kentuckylaketourism.com), 231 South Wilson Street, Dresden. The NTTC has the best information about the LBL area and limited information about other attractions in the area. The **Village of Paris** (800-345-1103; visithenryco.com) offers additional attraction and lodging information for the town of Paris and surrounding area.

GETTING THERE *By air:* **Memphis International Airport** (MEM; 901-922-8000; mscaa.com), 3318 Winchester Road, Memphis. MEM is the closest major airport, about 140 miles from Paris via I-40 to US 641. Major carriers are Delta, American, United, and AirTran.

By bus: There is no Greyhound bus service to northwest Tennessee; the closest terminal is Jackson, about 70 miles southeast of Paris.

By car: Paris is located on US 79 at the intersection of US 641, north of I-40.

GETTING AROUND *By car:* There is no public transportation in the region, so a car is essential; the area is well marked in terms of finding the marinas and state park facilities on the Western Tennessee lakeshore.

MEDICAL EMERGENCY Henry County Medical Center (731-642-1220; hcmc-tn.org), 301 Tyson Avenue, Paris.

✳ To See

HISTORIC SITES Eiffel Tower Replica (731-644-2517; visithenryco .com/eiffel.htm), 50 Volunteer Drive. The replica is located in the city's Memorial Park; park hours are generally daily sunrise–sunset. There are a few dozen towns in the United States named Paris, and one is right in Tennessee. But it was farther south, in Memphis, that the idea for a replica of the namesake city's Eiffel Tower was born. Engineering students at Christian Brothers University had constructed a 60-foot replica of the famed Parisian landmark and weren't quite sure what to do with it when their project was finished. One of the university's administrators contacted Paris city officials to see if they would like it—and the answer, unsurprisingly, was a resounding *oui!* Dismantling the tower was as complicated as building it; all five hundred pieces of Douglas fir and thousands of steel rods were taken apart, trucked to Paris, and reassembled in the city's Memorial Park. There's no fee to visit the park.

EIFFEL TOWER REPLICA

Tennessee Department of Tourism

MUSEUMS Paris/Henry County Heritage Center (731-642-1030; phchc.com), 614 N. Poplar Street. Open Tues.–Fri. 10–4, Sat. 10–2. Housed in an Italian Revival mansion, the center features photographs and historical displays from Paris and Henry County, including a collection of Civil War memorabilia from battles fought in the area or from local soldiers. The building itself has been lovingly preserved, and tours are given daily. Walking tour maps of the historic downtown district area available here, and the museum is just a short walk from the court square. Free.

Tennessee River Folklife Museum (731-584-6356; state.tn.us /environment/parks/NBForrest), 1825 Pilot Knob Road, Eva. Open daily 8–4:30, but closed 11–noon for lunch. Atop the highest elevation in West Tennessee, the museum explores the life of river towns and people from the late 1800s through the 20th century. The tools of the museling and commercial fishing trades are exhibited, giving insight into the unique fishing communities that once ruled here, including a preserved john-boat—a flat-bottomed boat used in the stump-filled waterways. There's no admission fee.

✳ To Do

BOATING Birdsong Resort & Marina (birdsong.com), 255 Marina Road, Camden. The marina offers slips and overnight docking for those with boats, as well as everything one might need on a fishing trip or camping trip, from gas for the boat to every kind of tackle and bait imaginable, groceries and hot food, and fishing and hunting guide services. Boat rentals (canoes, pontoons, fishing boats, and water toys) skis, wakeboards, and tubes are also available. There are full-service RV sites, and campsites are located in shady, grassy areas along the lake.

Buchanan Resort & Marina (731-642-2828; buchananresort.com), 785 Buchanan Resort Road, Springville. The full-service marina offers fishing licenses, bait, tackle, groceries, and ice. Boat rentals, including fishing boats, pontoons, and houseboats, are also available, as are slips for those with their own craft. Local fishing guides are easily booked through the marina, and guide service includes free cleaning and freezing for easy transport of the catch.

WINERIES Paris Winery (731-644-9500; pariswinery.com), 2982 Harvey Bowden Road. Open Mon.–Sat. 10–6, Sun. 1–6. Despite its setting in a town called Paris, this working family farm has an Italian flair. The young winery offers 13 varieties, most made directly from the grapes grown in its extensive vineyard. An Italian bistro, summer concert series, and lush setting combine for a nice afternoon of wine tasting. Wines on offer include traditional Italian offerings like pinot grigio and a sparkling spumante, as well as a number of fruit-flavored wines. Wine tastings are free.

✳ Green Space

PARKS Land Between the Lakes National Recreation Area (lbl.org), 100 Van Morgan Drive, Golden Pond, KY. Welcome centers

TENNESSEE FRESHWATER PEARL FARM

The freshwater pearl is the state gem of Tennessee, and in an embayment of Kentucky Lake, the Tennessee Freshwater Pearl Farm—the only freshwater pearl farm in North America—cultures these iridescent beauties. Tours of the farm range from a quickie drop-in look to an intensive three to five hours exploring the world of musseling and cultivating pearls; a jewelry shop offers a wide array of pearls to take home. Walk-ins see a video and can tour the farm and shop for no fee; the longer, guided tours start at $29.50 and require a 15-person minimum. (Rest assured, there are plenty of tour groups that come through, and singles or small groups can be added to them.) Located at 255 Marina Road in Camden, the pearl farm is open Monday–Saturday 8–5 and Sunday 1–4. For more information, call 731-584-7880 or log onto tennesseeriverpearls.com.

open daily 9–5, year-round, with park hours generally sunrise–sunset. The Homeplace, planetarium, and nature center operate varying seasonal schedules but are generally open daily 10–5. Indians and early settlers called this area "between the rivers" as the land was bordered by the Cumberland and Tennessee, but the area didn't get its name until the early days of the Tennessee Valley Authority, when the TVA constructed a canal between the two rivers, creating a large inland peninsula now known as Land Between the Lakes. The result of this action was the creation of Kentucky Lake and Lake Barkley, providing a slew of recreational opportunities, especially placid waters for houseboating and fishing. From Mar. through Nov., the Homeplace, a Revolutionary War land grant that became a farm, provides a living history of the mid-1800s. Fourteen of the 16 log buildings are original, creating an impressive and accurate historical backdrop for the daily farming that takes place during the Homeplace season. A 700-acre elk and bison range and a Nature Station offer the chance to view regional wildlife in their habitat, or you can canoe through a lake filled with migrating waterfowl. Guided horseback riding, fishing, and hunting are offered here, and there are more than 200 miles of hiking trails through the woods and fields. A planetarium and observatory at the Golden Pond Visitor Center offers daily and seasonal programs for stargazing. There's no charge for entering Land Between the Lakes, but fees are required for a number of activities, including the bison and elk range, the planetarium, and the farm, with prices starting at $4 per activity for adults and $2 for children.

Nathan Bedford Forrest State Park (731- 584-6356; state.tn.us /environment/parks/NBForrest), 1825 Pilot Knob Road, Eva. Open daily

7 AM–10 PM. The site of Confederate cavalry commander Gen. Nathan Bedford Forrest's operational area during the 1864 Battle of Johnsonville, the park is also home to Pilot Knob, one of the highest points in West Tennessee, and the Tennessee River Folklife Center. The park, located on Kentucky Lake, contains more than 30 miles of hiking trails that range in difficulty from easy, scenic strolls to rugged and challenging hikes; the trailheads for most trails come off a 20-mile loop and allow for customiz-

ing a hike to fit your experience and durability. Two primitive campgrounds are available, one of which is on Kentucky Lake, and a full-service campground is also on-site. Reservations for the lakeside campground are required; all others are on a first-come, first-served basis. There's no entrance fee for the park.

Paris Landing State Park (731-641-4465; state.tn.us/environment/parks/ParisLanding), 16055 US 79 N., Buchanan. Small as state parks go, Paris Landing is less than 900 acres yet is packed with plenty to do. On Kentucky Lake, the park offers abundant wildlife viewing and water sports; two large fishing piers and shoreline fishing lure anglers year-round, as does the promise of more than one hundred kinds of fish in these waters. The park includes a lakeside golf course, a beach for lake swimming, a pool for those who prefer chlorine with their water, and a full-service marina with slips available, but no rentals. There is no entrance fee for the park.

Tennessee National Wildlife Refuge (731-642-2091; fws.gov/tennessee refuge), 306 Dinkins Lane. Open daily sunrise–sunset. A devastating flood in 1937 in the Tennessee and Ohio river valleys wiped out farms

BISON, LAND BETWEEN THE LAKES

Tennessee Department of Tourism

and families throughout the Tennessee Valley and was the catalyst for building the Kentucky Dam across the Tennessee River. The dam created Kentucky Lake, and more than 50,000 acres of the water, forests, and lands around the lake make up the refuge. The refuge is a prime wintering habitat for migrating waterfowl, which feast on the abundant natural resources in the wetlands and forests. While providing a habitat for migratory waterfowl was the initial intent of refuge, it's also home to year-round species, including almost 90 reptiles and amphibians, dozens of mammals, and more than 140 species of fish. Recreational opportunities within the refuge are almost unlimited, from fishing and hunting to wildlife photography and hiking. There are three hiking trails, a handful of wildlife observation decks, and boat ramps and docks scattered throughout the refuge. There is no entrance fee.

✳ Lodging

BED & BREAKFASTS/INNS

Mammy & Pappy's B&B (731-642-8129; mammy-pappysbb.com), 7615 Elkhorn Road, Springville. A pretty farmhouse with a colorful history is the setting for this B&B, which has been in the same family for more than one hundred years, earning it a Century Farm designation from the state. In operation since before the Civil War, the farm's main crops are wheat, corn, and soybeans, and cattle and mules are raised here as well. The home itself was chosen to showcase new electrical wonders in the early 1950s, and while it has been updated, it still retains the charm of a number of eras. There are four large bedrooms with en suite baths, vintage matelasse coverlets, and pretty antiques; the innkeepers can also arrange guided hunting and fishing. Inexpensive.

PRICE CATEGORIES:

Inexpensive	Less than $100 (for hotels, inns, and B&Bs); less than $50 (for camp-grounds, state park facilities)
Moderate	$100–200
Expensive	$201–300
Very expensive	More than $300

CABINS Buchanan Resort & Marina (731-642-2828; buchananresort.com), 785 Buchanan Resort Road, Springville. A variety of cabins, motel-style rooms, and condo-style suites are available at the resort, many with lakefront views. All have standard furnishings, coffee pots, and microwaves, and some have full kitchens. Many of the cottages and cabins feature porches or decks. Rates are based on two people, and children are an additional (but inexpensive) fee. Inexpensive–moderate, depending on the style of accommodation chosen.

❦ **Cypress Bay Resort** (731-232-8221; cypressbayresort.com), 110 Cypress Resort Loop, Buchanan. Nine cabins offer one to three bedrooms, full kitchens, and a single bath; boat and slip rentals are available for those who bring their own craft or want to rent. The full-service marina also offers licenses, bait, ice, and groceries, but there is no restaurant on-site. Each cabin includes a grill for cooking out. Inexpensive–moderate. There's an additional charge if you want to bring Fido.

❦ **Paris Landing State Park** (731-641-4465; state.tn.us /environment/parks/ParisLanding), 16055 US 79 N., Buchanan. Ten nicely appointed cabins feature three bedrooms and two bathrooms, and each sleeps up to 10; one of the cabins is ADA accessible. All come with linens, fully stocked kitchens, cable television, and air-conditioning/heating units. There's a launderette and full-service restaurant in the park, as well as a small convenience store for supplies and groceries. Inexpensive–moderate, depending on the season. Pets are an additional charge and must be leashed.

CAMPING/RV PARKS ❦ **Birdsong Resort & Marina** (birdsong.com), 255 Marina Road, Camden. A resort, campground, and marina all in one, Birdsong is also home to the Tennessee Freshwater Pearl Farm (see sidebar) and sits on almost 60 acres on the shore of Kentucky Lake. The resort offers 50 full-service RV pads with electrical and water hookups; some of the pads also feature sewer. Campsites are located in shady, grassy areas along the lake. The marina offers slips and overnight docking, as well as boat rentals and water toys. Inexpensive.

❦ **Paris Landing State Park** (731-641-4465; state.tn.us/environment/parks/ParisLanding), 16055 US 79 N., Buchanan. In addition to cabins, Paris Landing offers 45 campsites with water and electric hookups as well as 18 primitive campsites. All the sites are open year-round, and none require a reservation; the sites are first come, first serve. The launderette and public restrooms are open 24 hours daily, year-round, and there is a full-service restaurant in the park, as well as a small convenience store for supplies and groceries. Inexpensive. Pets must be on a leash, but there's no additional charge for bringing Fido along to the campground.

HOTELS Hampton Inn Paris (731-642-2838; hamptoninn.com), 1510 E. Wood Street. Perfectly situated for those who want to explore both Paris and LBL, the AAA Three Diamond–rated Hampton Inn offers a more lush feel than other area chain hotels, the muted color scheme and hip black-and-white photos providing the buzz of a boutique hotel. There's also free hot breakfast, or grab a to-go bag if you're off to explore the LBL area. An outdoor pool, fitness room, business center, and free wireless Internet in guest rooms round out the amenities. Inexpensive.

PRICE CATEGORIES:

Inexpensive	Less than $16
Moderate	$16–30
Expensive	$31–50
Very expensive	More than $50

✷ Where to Eat

EATING OUT Ace's Pizza (731-644-0558), 1031 Mineral Wells Avenue. Open Mon.–Sat. 11–9. The Chicago-themed Ace's dishes up Chicago-style pizza, Vienna beef hot dogs, and plenty of cold beer. Inexpensive.

Tom's Pizza and Steakhouse (731-642-8842), 2501 E. Wood Street. Open Tues.–Sun. 11–9. A very casual atmosphere reigns at Tom's, and plates are heaped with food, whether it's the square-cut pizza or a spicy steak with sides. The restaurant also offers a large salad bar and full-service bar area. Inexpensive–moderate.

✷ Special Events

Late April: **World's Biggest Fish Fry** (731-644-1143; worldsbiggest fishfry.com), Henry County Fairgrounds, Paris. The fish fry offers up more than 12,500 pounds of catfish, and for just $10, it's an all-you-can-eat extravaganza. But the fun doesn't stop there; there's also a carnival midway, beauty contest, rodeo, tractor pulls, and crafts fair. Some events are free; fish tent is $10 per person, and carnival armbands are $20.

April–October: **Raptor Program** (731-641-4465; state.tn.us/environ ment/parks/ParisLanding), Paris Landing State Park Motel. On Fri. evenings, naturalists from the park bring birds of prey into the lobby of the park motel to educate the public about the creatures. Free.

May–July: **Summer in the Park** (731-641-4465; state.tn.us/environ ment/parks/ParisLanding), Paris Landing State Park. A Sat.-night summer concert series featuring regional bluegrass, gospel, and country musicians in a lakefront setting. Free.

REELFOOT LAKE, UNION CITY, AND MARTIN

West Tennessee's great northwest area is a vast playground for hunters, anglers, and nature lovers, with miles of shoreline to explore and migratory birds to watch. But it's also rich with history and culture.

Between the Mississippi and the Tennessee rivers, the deltalike area of northwest Tennessee offers small town upon small town; Martin, Dyersburg, Union City, and Tiptonville are the largest of those, each offering a slice of true small-town Tennessee and none with a population more than 18,000.

Much of the land in northwest Tennessee was Chickasaw land, especially the western portion. Through an 1818 treaty—the Jackson Purchase—the tribe ceded the land to the U.S. government, and settlers moved in to claim land. The region is highly agricultural due to the rich soil and long growing season, and cotton, soybeans, alfalfa, and other staple crops flourish here. In fact, Lake County—home to Reelfoot—produces more cotton than any other county in the nation, according to local tourism officials.

Reelfoot Lake, created during the New Madrid earthquakes, a series of tremblers between December 1811 and February 1812, is part of the Mississippi Flyway and home to thousands of migratory birds during the winter months, including golden and bald eagles. Reelfoot is a year-round fisherman's paradise with bass, catfish, crappie, bream, and more to lure anglers to the lake, even when there's snow on the ground.

Union City is home to a number of industries, including Goodyear Tire and Jiffy Steamer Company, the world's largest manufacturer of garment steamers. It is the site of a new, $100 million educational museum and complex funded by the Kirkland Foundation called Discovery Park America, set to open in late 2012.

GUIDANCE Reelfoot Tourism Council (731-253-2007; reelfoottourism .com), 4575 TN 21 E., Tiptonville. The RTC offers excellent advice for those interested in the Reelfoot area, as well as information for much of northwest Tennessee.

GETTING THERE *By air:* **Memphis International Airport** (MEM; 901-922-8000; mscaa.com), 3318 Winchester Road, Memphis. MEM is the closest airport, about 125 miles from Reelfoot Lake or Union City via I-55 N. to TN 181 east to TN 78. Major carriers are Delta, American, United, and AirTran.

By bus: There is no Greyhound bus service to northwest Tennessee; the closest terminal is Memphis, 125 miles to the south.

By car: From Memphis, there are two ways to get to the Reelfoot Lake area: via the scenic route, US 51 north through Millington to Dyersburg, then cutting west on TN 78 to TN 21, or the faster route, taking I-55 N. through Arkansas, then cutting east on TN 181/the Great River Road to TN 78 to TN 21.

GETTING AROUND *By car:* There is no local bus service, so a car is essential for exploring the area, as is a detailed map. Dyersburg and Union City are accessible via US 51, while Reelfoot Lake and Tiptonville are accessible via TN 21. For Martin and Dresden, take US 51 to US 45 and follow the signs.

REELFOOT LAKE

MEDICAL EMERGENCY Dyersburg Regional Medical Center (731-287-4245; dyersburgregionalmc.com), 400 Tickle Street, Dyersburg. Offers comprehensive emergency services 24 hours daily, including a dedicated pediatric emergency room.

✳ To See

MUSEUMS Davy Crockett Cabin-Museum (731-665-7523), 219 Trenton Street, Rutherford. Open Tues.–Sat. 9–5; Sun. (Memorial Day–Labor Day) 1–4:30. Rutherford was where colonel and congressman Davy Crockett lived from 1822 until the fall of 1835; it was around these parts that Crockett is said to have hunted and killed 105 bears. Crockett also served three terms in Congress representing the people of this area. A replica of his cabin, complete with furniture and accessories dating back to that time, plus copies of Crockett's letters, are on display. His mother's grave is also located here. Each Oct., the town celebrates Crockett Days, with parades, pioneer crafts, a bluegrass concert, and fireworks. Adults $2, children $1, family $5. (The museum is free during Crockett Days in Oct., but donations are welcome.)

Dixie Gun Works, 1412 W. Reelfoot Avenue, Union City. Open Mon.–Fri. 8–5, Sat. 8–noon. A traveling jewelry salesman fascinated by guns started buying and selling antique black powder firearms on the side, and soon he dumped jewelry sales for a full-time job and what would become Dixie Gun Works, a mail-order business that offers more than 10,000 parts and accessories for thousands of antique and reproduction black powder guns. The Old Car Museum offers the chance to see a few dozen antique cars, plus a host of antique and vintage mechanical devices, and also feature an 1850s-period log cabin gun shop. Adults $2, seniors $1, family $5.

Dr. Walter E. David Wildlife Museum (731-286-3200; dscc.edu), 1510 Lake Road, Dyersburg. A random little museum housed on the campus of Dyersburg State Community College bears the collection of wildlife enthusiast Walter David, literally. Bears—both polar and grizzly—a lion, a huge collection of ducks from the Mississippi Flyway, and an assortment of other animals, from bighorn sheep to wildebeest to leopard, are just some of the sport animals David hunted over the years, and as one can imagine, his trophy room at home was getting a bit crowded. So he offered pieces of his collection, a little at a time, to the college and kept on hunting. Free.

Great River Road Interpretive Center/R.C. Donaldson Museum (731-253-9652; state.tn.us/environment/parks/ReelfootLake), 2595 TN 21 E., Tiptonville. The park is open daily sunrise–sunset. The complex's

REELFOOT LAKE

nature center features a variety of animals native to the Reelfoot ecosystem, including raptors unable to be rereleased into the wild and snakes. The small museum offers an excellent glimpse into the rustic life of the area, as well as a history of the legend of Reelfoot, which holds that the lake was created when a Chickasaw Indian chief named Reelfoot stole the daughter of a Choctaw chief. Reelfoot had fallen in love with the daughter and ignored the warning of the Great Spirit, who appeared and told him the earth would move and the mighty river—the Mississippi—would flood the earth if he should steal the girl for his wife. When Reelfoot stole his bride, the Great Spirit was said to have stamped his foot, causing the earthquake and flood from the Mississippi, which created the lake. In reality, it was the New Madrid quake in the early 1800s that caused the ground to collapse and the Mississippi to flow backwards for more than a day, filling in the newly depressed ground, which created Reelfoot. But plenty of folks prefer the legend over reality. Admission is free.

Obion County Museum (731-885-6774; ocmuseum.com), 1004 Edwards Street, Union City. Open Sat.–Sun. 1–4. The small museum started with a collection of toys and tools from one county resident and has grown into a full recounting of the county's history. A variety of exhibitions showcase life in the county, including a kitted-out dentist office with some truly scary-looking equipment, a country store, and post office and printing shop displays; the big draw, however, is the woolly mammoth skeleton unearthed in Siberia and on loan from a local resident. Free.

✳ To Do

BOAT TOURS Reelfoot Lake State Park (731-253-8003; state.tn.us /environment/parks/ReelfootLake), 2595 TN 21 E., Tiptonville. Open daily sunrise–sunset. A variety of boat cruises and scenic tours are offered at Reelfoot, including a deep swamp canoe tour, bald eagle and waterfowl tours, and scenic pontoon boat tours. Each operates on a seasonal schedule, the bald eagle and waterfowl tours during Jan., Feb., and early Mar.; the swamp canoe tours in Mar. and Apr.; and the scenic boat tours May–Sept. All the cruises and tours should be reserved in advance, and prices vary depending on the option selected.

FISHING Reelfoot Lake State Park (731-253-8003; state.tn.us/environ ment/parks/ReelfootLake), 2595 TN 21 E., Tiptonville. Open daily sunrise–sunset. Fishing Reelfoot is an experience unlike most other lake fishing, not only for the year-round ability to drop a line but also for the natural beauty of the lake, which contains thousands of cypress tree stumps to navigate around. Seasonally, crappie are most active Mar.–early May, and again through the winter; largemouth bass enjoy a long run Mar.–Oct.; and catfish are pretty limited to the spring and summer. A valid Tennessee fishing license is required of all anglers older than 13, and those older than 16 also must carry a lake permit. Fishing the bank, piers, and boardwalk is permitted in addition to boat fishing, and there are a few cleaning stations throughout the park. There's no entrance fee for the park; lake use permits are available at the visitors center.

HUNTING There is hunting at **Reelfoot Lake State Park** (see *Green Space*). The following are area hunting guides.

The Cooper Hole Guide Service (731-885-5861; thecooperhole.com), 3414 Walnut Cove, Union City. The Cooper Hole's blind—which can accommodate up to 13 hunters—is just 50 or so yards from the edge of the national wildlife refuge, giving excellent access to the migrating birds. In a nod to comfort, the blind is kitted out with lights and heat. Shooting starts at 3 AM and continues past lunch. Both breakfast and lunch are included in the hunting rates, which start at $100 per person.

Water's Edge Guiding (731-592-2529; watersedgeguiding.com). Two local hunters offer guided goose and duck hunting, either in a cypress hole or a blind; rates include one meal. $125/person.

✳ Green Space

PARKS Reelfoot Lake State Park (731-253-8003; state.tn.us/environ ment/parks/ReelfootLake), 2595 TN 21 E., Tiptonville. Open daily sunrise–sunset. Considered one of the finest hunting and fishing preserves in

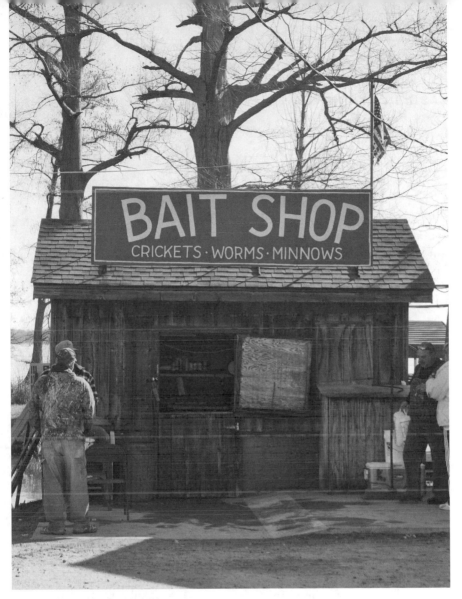

BAIT SHOP AT REELFOOT LAKE

the country, Reelfoot Lake is actually a series of waterways connected to one another via bayous and streams, and covers more than 25,000 acres, of which more than half is water. There's excellent birding during the winter months, as Reelfoot is a migratory destination for a variety of northern waterfowl. During the winter, the park is home to both golden and American bald eagles, and naturalists offer a variety of wildlife viewing programs that allow visitors the chance to see these creatures in their habitat. Campground facilities are available for both tent and RV camping. There are just a few hiking trails, including a 1.5-mile trail along the shoreline, and all are easy hikes. There's no entrance fee for the park.

✳ Lodging

CABINS/CAMPING Cypress Point Resort (731-253-6654; cypresspointresort.com), 3535 TN 21 E., Tiptonville. A lakefront resort with both tent/RV campsites as well as cabin accommodations, Cypress Point also offers a full-service marina for boat rentals; ice, bait, and gas; and guided fishing/accommodation/boat-rental packages. Fishing piers allow those who prefer to remain on land the chance to make a catch, and on Mon. and Thurs. mid-Mar.–mid-May, the resort includes a barbecue dinner for guests. Moderate.

Eagles Nest Resort (731-538-2143; eaglenestresort.com), 256 W. Lakeview Drive, Samburg. A combination of motel-style accommodations and cabins nestled along the shore of Reelfoot Lake include space big enough to house large families and groups; the two cabins include full kitchens. The property offers a fishing pier and boat ramp, fish cleaning stations, and guide/accommodation packages for hunting or fishing. Inexpensive–moderate.

Our Backyard Town (731-587-1918; ourbackyardtown.com), 520 N. College Street, Martin. An old farm property with a variety of vintage buildings—a smokehouse, a church, and a few other log cabins—was renovated and updated to create a small village tableau, including two log cabins for overnight guests. The owner's car collection fills one building, while

PRICE CATEGORIES:

Inexpensive	Less than $100 (for hotels, inns, and B&Bs); less than $50 (for campgrounds, state park facilities)
Moderate	$100–200
Expensive	$201–300
Very expensive	More than $300

a soda fountain, grocery store, and barbershop fill the others, complete with antiques exclusive to the era in each spot. Weddings are held in the small church, and the "town" opens up for a Sat. each Oct. when the owners host folks and tour them around in exchange for a donation to the local food pantry. Breakfast each morning takes place in the owner's home, at the large kitchen table with other guests, and includes typical Southern fare. Moderate.

HOTELS Blue Bank Resort (877-258-3226; bluebankresort.com), 813 Lake Drive, Hornbeak. Blue Bank offers everything from a huge lodge that can sleep 19 to basic motel-style accommodations. The lakefront property includes a marina, and guests can literally dock their boat right outside their lodge or motel room. The motel-style property is just a few minutes away. A concession store, swimming pool and hot tub, game room with bar, and full-service restaurant are all on property, and the resort offers hunting and fishing packages that include boat and motor rental, bait, and ice. Moderate.

✳ Where to Eat

DINING OUT Sassafrazz (731-884-1877; sassafraz.net), 2205 W. Reelfoot Avenue, Union City. Open Mon.–Sat. 11–10. The unassuming brick building, on the main highway into Union City, is a pleasant surprise amid the chain restaurants throughout the area. While there are no huge surprises in terms of the menu—traditional offerings for an upscale American restaurant—the food is some of the freshest I've had, ever. The Caesar salad, for example, is dressed with scrumptious homemade croutons and Parmesan that was obviously shaved just before making its way to the table. Many of the sides—such as garlicky red-skinned mashed potatoes—were also obviously freshly prepared. Desserts feature a touch of Tennessee, including a Jack Daniel's pecan sauce topping a lush bread pudding. Moderate–expensive.

EATING OUT Blue Bank Rod and Reel Grill at Blue Bank Resort (731-253-6878), 3330 TN 21 E., Tiptonville. Open daily 11–9. I'm the first to admit that I was surprised to see homemade rolls served up with strawberry butter at a restaurant where camouflage tablecloths are used, and I was equally impressed with the menu, huge in terms of the meals

offered, and varied enough to suit just about any palate. Appetizers run to Southern fried—fried dill pickle slices, fried green tomatoes, fried mushrooms. A loaded baked potato soup was my favorite dish, and the traditional Southern favorites like catfish or country ham platters come with two sides—the debate being which to order out of a long list including baked apples and homemade potato chips. Moderate.

Boyette's Dining Room (731-253-7307; reelfoot.com/boyettes), 10 Boyette Road, Tiptonville. Open daily 11–9. Country cooking is the theme at Boyette's, which is Reelfoot's oldest restaurant and a longtime favorite of those who regularly fish and hunt here. No matter what is ordered—from catfish to fried chicken to steak, the portions are overly generous, although smaller portions are available. The homemade hush puppies are to die for. Note that on weekends there's often a long line out the door for a table—but no one seems to mind the wait. Moderate.

✳ Selective Shopping

ARTS AND CRAFTS Six Toe Studio (901-573-3743; sixtoe studio.com), 204 Main Street,

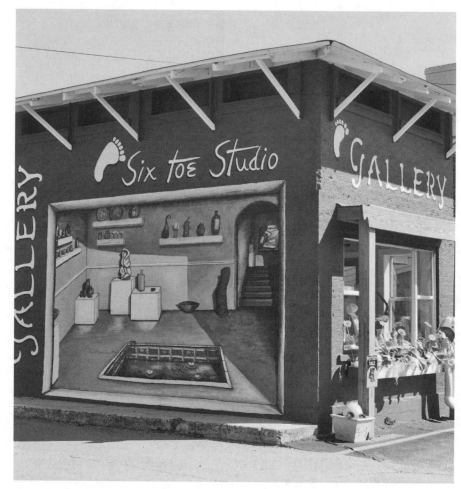

SIX TOE STUDIO

Martin. Open Mon.–Fri. 10–5 and by appointment. Potter Clint Riley throws pieces of art—like functional pottery, including cups, plates, and bowls—in his just-off-the-square studio. The name of the studio comes from his son's unique characteristic—a sixth toe on one foot.

✳ Special Events

Early February: **Reelfoot Lake Eagle Festival** (731-253-9652; reelfoot tourism.com/eagle.html), Reelfoot Lake State Park. The yearly festival pays homage to the eagles that nest here during the winter months and features a variety of contests, including art, photography, and geocaching; nature walks and naturalist-led programs offer the chance to spot eagles in the wild or see them up close. Free.

Late April: **Tennessee Iris Festival** (731-364-5101; tennesseeirisfestival
.com), various locations in Dresden. What started as an Easter parade
turned into a celebration honoring the state flower and brings thousands
of visitors to tiny Dresden each Apr. Including beauty contests, tricycle
races, a midway, craft show, and, of course, a horticultural show featuring
irises, the festival is somewhat like a county fair and is a delightful time
for families. Most events are free.

Early October: **Crockett Days** (731-665-7253; townofrutherford.org/davy
crockettdays.cfm), Davy Crockett Cabin. The weeklong festival honoring
Crockett includes pioneer crafts and demonstrations, activities for children, and free admission to the museum.

SOUTHWEST

JACKSON

Located about halfway between Memphis and Nashville, Jackson is a small city caught in the shadow of those two larger metropolitan areas. But despite its smaller stature and small-town feel, Jackson, too, has big musical names to call its own.

During the great railroad expansions of the mid-19th century, Jackson quickly developed as a hub for a number of railroads; three lines—the Mobile & Ohio, the Tennessee Central, and the Mississippi Central—all ran through Jackson, and each developed a maintenance shop here. Jackson eventually became home to two depots and numerous lines that criss-crossed the country, hauling both freight and passengers; for a few decades, the town offered daily passenger service on at least 15 different train routes.

The growing railroad industry was just taking root in Jackson when the Civil War began; Tennessee's railroads were constantly under fire as both sides attempted to control the flow of supplies. For about three weeks in December 1862 and January 1863, Confederate and Union troops skirmished to gain control of the Mobile & Ohio line, in order to thwart Grant's movement of supplies. The Union forces held off the attacking troops and kept the line open for their use.

Jackson's most famous railroad connection, however, isn't a train line, but an engineer. Casey Jones—made famous when he crashed his speeding train into another (after telling his coalman to jump)—lived in Jackson at the time of his death; the resulting folk hero ballad spawned huge interest in Jones, who posthumously became a national celebrity.

Some of Jackson's native sons and daughters have been an integral part of the state's music scene. Carl Perkins, who some consider the originator of the rockabilly sound, is from Jackson, and the city is home to the Rockabilly Hall of Fame. He lived in Jackson—and owned a restaurant here—until his death in 1998. Bluesman John Lee "Sonny" Williamson (there are two bluesmen known as Sonny Williamson; John Lee is the Jackson Sonny) played the harmonica, or what blues players call the harp. Williamson was best known for his work in the Chicago blues scene. Other notable musicians with a Jackson connection are Bertha Dorsey, who recorded country music as Ruby Falls, and blues shouter Big Maybelle.

Surrounding Jackson are a number of small agricultural towns with a smattering of interesting spots worth seeing; those are also covered in this section.

GUIDANCE Jackson, Tennessee Convention & Visitors Bureau (731-425-8333; jacksontncvb.com), 197 Auditorium Street, Jackson.

GETTING THERE *By air:* **Memphis International Airport** (MEM; 901-922-8000; mscaa.com), 3318 Winchester Road, Memphis. MEM is the closest major airport to Jackson. The airport is a hub for Delta Airlines; major airlines serving Memphis include Continental, US Airways, AirTran, American, and Air Canada. From the airport, travel via I-240 E. to I-40 E. to Jackson.

By bus: **Greyhound** (731-427-1573; greyhound.com), 407 E. Main Street. Greyhound's Jackson terminal is open daily 8–7.

By car: Jackson is located 80 miles east of Memphis via I-40 E. and about 120 miles west of Nashville via I-40 W.

GETTING AROUND *By bus:* The **Jackson Transit Authority** (731-423-0200; ridejta.com) offers bus service throughout Jackson. Buses run Mon.–Sat. 6 AM–10:30 PM; check the Web site for routes and schedules. Base fares are $1, with free transfers.

By car: Most of the attractions in Jackson are located south of I-40 and between US 45 and TN 1/Dr. F.E. Wright Drive, including the downtown area. The city is laid out in a grid downtown, with the grid expanding a bit as one travels outside the main business district.

MEDICAL EMERGENCY Jackson Madison County General Hospital (731-541-5000; wth.org), 620 Skyline Drive. Offers emergency room services 24 hours daily.

✳ To See

HISTORIC SITES Casey Jones Village/Home (731-668-1223; caseyjones.com), 56 Casey Jones Lane. Open daily 9–8, Memorial Day–Labor Day; daily 9–5 the rest of the year. The legendary railroad engineer, who took over for an ailing friend one night on a race to get a train to its destination on time, was killed when his locomotive rounded the final corner and plowed into a stalled train. Jones had just enough time to get his

Tennessee Department of Tourism

CASEY JONES HOME

coalman out of the train. His speedy journey and death were an inspiration to a former roundhouse coworker who sang a ballad to remember him by; the song was passed off to a professional song-writing team and recorded, and it became one of the most popular American songs of the early 20th century, spawning a book, movie, and radio series. The Jones home was moved to its present location and is now a museum, along with a number of preserved rail cars; other attractions at the village include a traditional country store with restaurant and ice cream parlor, and a variety of retail shops featuring local craftsmen. Museum admission: adults $6.50, children 6–12 $4.50. Most of the other attractions and stores are free, as are most special events, although some concerts require a ticket.

Pinson Mounds Archaeological State Park (731-988-5614; state.tn.us /environment/parks/PinsonMounds), 460 Ozier Road, Pinson. Open Mon.–Sat. 8–4:30, Sun. 1–5. The Pinson Mounds are the largest Wood-land-period mound group in the United States, dating back to about AD 1500. It's believed the mounds, discovered in the early 1800s by a land surveying crew led by Joel Pinson, were used primarily for ceremonial purposes, although the smaller mounds were believed to have been used for burial rites. The park features a museum with archaeological library and the original survey map drawn by Mr. Pinson; hiking trails include a boardwalk over the Forked Deer River. Throughout the year, a variety of archaeologically themed programs are offered. There's no entrance fee for the park.

Riverside Cemetery (731-424-1279), corner of River Drive and Sycamore Street. Open daily sunrise–sunset for self-guided tours. One of the oldest cemeteries in Tennessee, Riverside's first interment was in 1824—the eight-year-old daughter of the man considered to be the father of Jackson, Dr. William E. Butler. Riverside is the final resting place for 180 Confederate soldiers, only 40 of whom are identified. Free.

Salem Cemetery Battlefield (731-424-1279; salemcemeterybattlefield .com), 58 Cotton Grove Road. Open daily sunrise–sunset. The Battle at

Salem Cemetery was quick and fierce; as the cavalry of Gen. Nathan Bedford Forrest rode toward Jackson on December 19, 1862, they were ambushed by Union troops. The Union forces had hunkered down in the cemetery, and despite their surprise attack, ended up retreating toward Jackson. Union troops lost just two men, but 65 Confederate soldiers were killed in the four-hour battle. The battlefield and cemetery have remained virtually untouched since the war, with local groups donating their time and energy to maintaining the site. Tours are self-guided, and there are a few monuments honoring the men on both sides who fought here. Free; donations welcome.

MUSEUMS ✐ **Green Frog/Cotton Museum of the South** (800-663-0603; greenfrogtn.com), 71 Green Frog Lane, Alamo. Open Tues.–Sat. 10–5. Green Frog Village is the vision of one man, who built his own log home and soon realized he wanted to build more. John Freeman's vision was to create a historic rural village that harkened back to the turn of the 20th century in West Tennessee. Freeman's interest in history created Green Frog Village—the name is borrowed from a local country store. Green Frog's restored buildings date from the early 20th century and include a chapel, general store, and blacksmith's shop as well as the centerpiece of the village, a 1915 cotton gin moved from Alabama. Now home to the Cotton Museum of the South, the former gin is where the story of cotton is told through photos and farming implements. The one-room schoolhouse in the village is a great place for today's kids to visit, as

PINSON MOUNDS ARCHAELOGICAL STATE PARK

Tennessee Department of Tourism

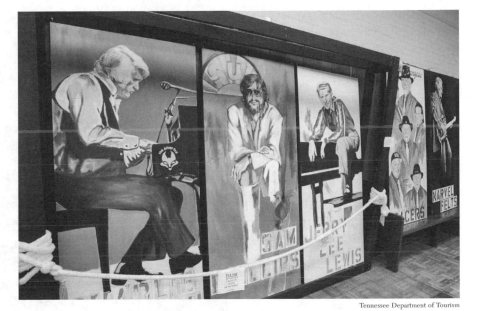

Tennessee Department of Tourism

INTERNATIONAL ROCK-A-BILLY HALL OF FAME

they see what kind of school their great-grandparents very well could have experienced—one big room, hard seating, and even the schoolbooks of the era. The town's working print shop is another spot kids and adults are fascinated by, especially the century-old linotype machine, which at the time was a huge revolution in printing. JaJa's—the country café that's in the village center—offers up homemade ice cream and Southern fried pies as well as simple meals. Free.

International Rock-A-Billy Hall of Fame (731-427-6262; rockabilly hall.org), 105 N. Church Street. Open Mon.–Thurs. 10–5, Fri.–Sat. 10–2. Line dancing lessons are offered Mon. and Tues. evenings at 6 and Fri. evenings at 7, when there's also a live rockabilly band. For hard-core music—and especially rockabilly—fans, this is a must-tour, but for those not passionate about the genre, I'd suggest a pass. The museum highlights the stars of the rockabilly world, most notably Carl Perkins, who was born in Jackson. A room filled with Elvis Presley memorabilia may entice the King's fans as well. Tours are $10.

N.C. & St. L. Depot and Railroad Museum (731-425-8223; jackson recandparks.com), 582 S. Royal Street. Open Mon.–Sat. 10–3. The beautiful brick depot, built in 1907, was part of what helped Jackson become a thriving city—the railroad. Inside the depot, a large model train, historic photographs, and memorabilia explore the importance of the railroad; outside, guests can climb aboard an engine and a dining car. Free.

Trenton Teapot Collection (731-855-2013; teapotcollection.com), 309

College Street, Trenton. Open daily at any time; enter through the Trenton Police Department for a self-guided tour. Tiny Trenton is home to an astonishing collection of porcelain Veilleuse-Théières teapots crafted between 1750 and 1860. The collection of more than five hundred pieces is valued at over $3 million. Guided tours are available by reservation. Free.

West Tennessee Agricultural Museum (731-686-8067; milan .tennessee.edu/museum), 3 Ledbetter Gate, Milan. Open Mon.– Fri. 8–4. Tracing the rich history of West Tennessee's pioneers and agricultural communities, the museum offers the chance to experience daily life in pioneer times, as well as explore a variety of historical artifacts, photographs, and implements. A visit to the museum may include the chance to see a demonstration of traditional skills; almost three thousand farming

Tennessee Department of Tourism

TRENTON TEAPOT COLLECTION

implements and tools make up the collection. Each year in Oct., the Fall Folk Jamboree brings together craftspeople skilled in historic crafts including blacksmithing, weaving, and wood carving with folk musicians and artists. Free.

✱ To Do

AQUARIUMS AND ZOOS ✐ **Alamo—Tennessee Safari Park** (731-696-4423; tennesseesafaripark.com), 637 Colony Road, Alamo. Open Mon.–Sat. 10–4:30 and Sun. 12–4:30, early spring–late fall (generally Mar.–Nov.). Lots of kids want to be a zookeeper when they grow up, but few really become one. Claude Conley, however, knew from an early age that wanted his very own zoo and has spent his life since then acquiring a unique collection of wildlife that calls northwest Tennessee home. From the first herd of buffalo brought back to the state in the 1960s from an Oklahoma buffalo preserve to the more recent additions of a red kangaroo and dromedary camel, Conley's collection has grown to fill the farm that was originally a land grant from President Andrew Jackson to his family. Hillcrest, as the farm is known, dates back to 1867 and has stayed in the Conley family the entire time, which is a rarity for century farms in Tennessee. The Conley family still farms about 200 acres, growing cotton and raising cattle, but most of the crops have been replaced with animals—more than 400 from 80 different species. Visitors can drive on the 2.5-mile loop to view the animals, as well as stop at the petting zoo for more true interaction with some of the animals, including giraffes. Adults $12, children two and older $8.

FAMILY FUN Donnell Century Farm (731-424-4526; donnellcentury farm.com), 3720 US 70 E. Open Sat. 10–5 and Sun. 1–5:30. The working cattle and cotton farm, in the same family for more than 175 years, opens on weekends during select months in the fall for the general public, offering a petting zoo, pumpkin picking, corn mazes, and more fun. Admission $6; children under two free.

FISHING Lake Graham (731-422-0950; tennessee.gov/twra/fish/pond /TWRAfamlake/lakegraham.html), 300 Hurts Chapel Road, Jackson. The family fishing lake is designed for anglers of all ages and includes an accessible fishing pier, boat ramps, boat and motor rentals, and a bait and tackle shop. There are limited concessions and vending machines, picnic facilities, and restrooms. A valid fishing license is required and available at the shop. There's no entrance fee charged for the park.

SPECTATOR SPORTS Jackson Generals (731-988-5299; diamond jaxx.com), Pringles Park, 4 Fun Place. A double-A minor-league club of the Seattle Mariners, the Generals play in the Southern League with home games at Pringles Park, named after the crowd-pleasing potato chip made here in Jackson. Games are generally Mon.–Sat. at 7:05 or Sun. at 2:05. Tickets range from $4 to $8.50.

✱ Green Space

PARKS Cypress Grove Nature Park (731-425-8316; jacksonrecand parks.com), US 70 W./Airways Boulevard near US 45 bypass. Open daily 7 AM–dusk. With a winding wooden boardwalk through a cypress forest, the nature park is a beautiful introduction into the ecosystem. A center for injured raptors is located within the park, and visitors are allowed to see the birds as they are nursed back to health. Gazebos and benches along the boardwalk offer quiet spots along the 2-mile round-trip to rest or simply enjoy the peace. Free.

✳ Lodging

A variety of chain hotels and motels are available in and around Jackson, with most located on the I-40 corridor; bed & breakfasts and inns are more difficult to find.

BED & BREAKFASTS/INNS

Highland Place Bed & Breakfast Inn (731-427-1472; highland place.com), 519 N. Highland Avenue. Just a few minutes out of downtown, the Highland Place offers four rooms in a turn-of-the-20th-century Colonial Revival mansion. Each room has a different theme and is decorated to match; a large library offers a wide choice of entertainment. Guests have the choice of a full or continental breakfast. Moderate.

HOTELS **Jameson Inn** (731-860-6651; jamesoninns.com), 1292 Vann Drive. The Jameson is nothing if not consistent, with an always-friendly staff and consistently clean rooms. The location right off I-40 is convenient to downtown Jackson and the outlying areas featured in this section. Upgraded premium rooms offer a microwave, refrigerator, and coffeemaker; a serve-yourself breakfast area with a waffle maker, cereals, fruits, and breads is included for all guests. Inexpensive.

Signature Boutique Hotel (731-660-0077; signatureboutiquehotel .com), 1935 Emporium Drive. The surprisingly chic hotel amid the usual suspects is a delight, featuring individually decorated

PRICE CATEGORIES:	
Inexpensive	Less than $100 (for hotels, inns, and B&Bs); less than $50 (for campgrounds, state park facilities)
Moderate	$100–200
Expensive	$201–300
Very expensive	More than $300

rooms with colorful walls. Special children's rooms with themed decor and suites are available. Complimentary use of a local gym is included, as is a hot breakfast. Inexpensive.

✳ Where to Eat

EATING OUT **Baker's Rack** (731-424-6163), 203 E. Lafayette. Open Mon.–Thurs. 7–5, Fri. 7–3. While it's true there's breakfast and lunch served at the Baker's Rack, the desserts—including a scrumptious treat nicknamed "BTS" (Better Than Sex)—is enough reason to pop in. Sandwiches, baked potatoes, and salads are standard lunch fare, while breakfast runs to yummy French toast, egg platters, and fresh-from-scratch biscuits. Inexpensive.

Brook Shaw's Old Country Store (731-668-1223; caseyjones .com), 56 Casey Jones Lane. Open daily 6:30 AM–9 PM. When Brooks Shaw liked something, he liked it, and how. The founder of the Country Store at Casey Jones Village liked antiques—not the fancy kind, mind you, but the little pieces of history best found in barns and sheds all over the state. Those odds and ends now cover the walls of the Country Store, where Shaw started by serving plate lunches and moved up to full buffets at breakfast, lunch, and dinner that offer up much better food than one expects from a typical buffet. An ice cream parlor, candy store, and souvenir store are also part of the huge building. Moderate.

Dixie Castle (731-423-3359), 215 E. Baltimore. Open Mon.–Fri. 10:30–2 and 5–9, Sat. 5–9. The iconic Jackson eatery is a favorite with locals, and sometimes there's a wait for the large plates of basic—but excellent—items: hamburgers and plate lunches at lunch, hearty pork chops, steaks, and full chicken dinners in the evening. Inexpensive.

Downtown Tavern (731-424-1995; downtowntavern.com), 208 N. Liberty. Open Mon.–Thurs. 3–midnight, Fri. 3 PM–2 AM, Sat. 6 PM–2 AM, and Sun. 6–10 PM. A huge space, the Downtown Tavern hums with live music most evenings—including an open mic night on Tues. The upstairs lounge offers clubby chairs and couches, and screens for watching sports, as well as a limited menu and totally

smoke-free environment. The main bar area, with exposed brick walls, sports a long bar with a giant chalkboard above it spelling out styles of beer and drink specials. Moderate.

✳ Entertainment

LIVE-MUSIC VENUES Brook Shaw's Old Country Store (731-427-9616; music.caseyjonesbulletin.com), 56 Casey Jones Lane. Throughout the year, the Old Country Store plays host to a variety of live music showcases, including the Song Writer's Depot (check the Web site for schedule; tickets $10), the Jackson Area Plectral Society Club Jams (Thurs. evenings mid-Apr.–Oct.; free), and the Casey Jones Barbershop Chorus (third Tues. of the month at 6:30; free).

Miss Ollie's Piano Bar (731-868-1120; missollies.com), 111 E. Lafayette. Open Tues.–Thurs. 5–10 PM, Fri. 5 PM–2 AM, and Sat. 6 PM–3 AM. A swanky nightclub featuring sleek furnishings and a chic setting, Miss Ollie's—named after one of Jackson's finest madams from the early 20th century—is an elegant oasis in town. There's a piano bar and a dance floor; the two are separated so as not to conflict with one another.

✳ Selective Shopping

ART GALLERIES Art Under a Hot Tin Roof (731-427-2772; artunderahottinroof.com), 114 E. Lafayette Street. Open Tues.–Fri. 10–5:30, Sat. 10–4. There really is

PRICE CATEGORIES:	
Inexpensive	Less than $16
Moderate	$16–30
Expensive	$31–50
Very expensive	More than $50

a tin ceiling in this downtown art gallery, which is a nice contrast to the mostly contemporary art displayed far underneath the loftlike space. Most of the artists shown here are from the region, with works including contemporary jewelry, paintings, and sculpture, as well as more traditional thrown pottery pieces.

✳ Special Events

Early August: **International Rockabilly Music Festival** (731-427-6262; rockabillyhall.org), Rock-A-Billy Hall of Fame. A three-day festival featuring rockabilly's legends, plus up-and-comers. Single-day tickets $25 and up; $75 for three-day ticket.

Early September: **Pinson Mounds Archeofest** (731-988-5614; state.tn.us/environment/parks/PinsonMounds), Pinson Mounds Archaeological State Park. A celebration of Native American culture, the festival includes representatives from a number of tribes and features craft and food demonstrations, traditional singing and dancing, and historical artifacts and story-telling. Free.

Mid-October: **Bagels & Bluegrass Bicycle Century Tour** (731-616-7474; bagelsandbluegrass.tn.org). The 100-mile bike ride through southwest Tennessee starts with bagels at Jackson State Community College and winds through a few state parks before looping back to Jackson and a dinner at the college. $25 registration fee includes bagels and dinner.

SAVANNAH, ADAMSVILLE, AND PICKWICK

In the Western Valley of the Tennessee River, Hardin County is one of Tennessee's most desired recreation spots, thanks to the river and the dam built to control the flow of the river, creating Pickwick Lake.

Evidence of early human occupation of Hardin County can still be seen in the mounds built by prehistoric people of the Woodland and Mississippian eras; the county seat, Savannah, is built within a line of 14 trenches on a mound that runs parallel to the Tennessee River. With its rich natural resources—the river and its creeks, the vast bottomlands—the area that makes up present-day Hardin County was prime hunting ground for many Native American tribes prior to the occupation of European settlers starting in the early 1800s, following the Revolutionary War.

The first settlers to Hardin County came after land claims for veterans were approved by the North Carolina legislature; the county was named for Col. Joseph Hardin, who fought in the war and served in the early territorial legislatures. While Joseph Hardin himself never made it to this part of Tennessee, his two sons, daughter, and their families were among the first settlers here.

Hardin County is home to one of the bloodiest battles in the Civil War, the Battle of Shiloh; that two-day engagement saw more than 20,000 soldiers from both sides killed or wounded. The residents of the primarily agrarian county were split in their allegiances during the war; those to the eastern side of the river tended to side with the North, while those on the western side of the river favored the South. Gen. Ulysses S. Grant headquartered at Cherry Mansion in Savannah in the days leading up to the Battle of Shiloh; he reportedly was eating breakfast when he received news that the fighting had commenced.

Though soldiers from both sides crisscrossed Hardin County during the war, there was little evidence of the war beyond the huge, silent battlefield and cemetery at Shiloh. Industries tied to the Tennessee River— mills for grinding the local grains and processing the abundant lumber in the area, and the mining of rocks and minerals—soon rivaled the work of farmers in the area, and many businesses of those same industries continue today.

Hardin County borders both Mississippi and Alabama, and is home to much of the Tennessee portion of Pickwick, the general name for the huge watery playground that's comprised of Pickwick Lake, the Tennessee River, and the Tombigbee Waterway. The dam was built in 1938 and created a huge recreational playground. Today, Hardin County calls itself the catfish capital of the world thanks to Pickwick and its abundant waters, and is home to the National Catfish Derby.

GUIDANCE Hardin County Convention & Visitors Bureau (731-925-8181; tourhardincounty.org), 320 Main Street, Savannah.

GETTING THERE *By air:* **Memphis International Airport** (MEM; 901-922-8000; mscaa.com), 3318 Winchester Road, Memphis. MEM is the closest airport to Savannah, about 125 miles via I-240/I-40 to US 64 E. Major carriers are Delta, American, United, and AirTran.

By bus: There is no Greyhound bus service to Savannah; the closest terminal is Jackson (731-427-1573; greyhound.com), about 60 miles northwest of Savannah.

By car: Follow US 64 east from Memphis, about 120 miles.

GETTING AROUND *By car:* A car is essential in this part of Tennessee, as there is no public transportation and limited taxi service. Be sure to keep a detailed map handy, as rural areas aren't always well marked, and it is easy to miss signs.

By taxi: **River City Taxi** (731-925-0366), 364 Horse Creek Road, Savannah.

MEDICAL EMERGENCY Hardin Medical Center (731-926-8000; hardinmedicalcenter.org), 935 Wayne Road, Savannah. Offers 24-hour emergency care.

✳ To See

HISTORIC SITES Cherry Mansion (731-607-1208), 265 Main Street, Savannah. Tours by appointment only. Originally built as a wedding gift for W. H. Cherry and his bride about 1825, the riverfront Cherry Mansion was occupied by Union forces—specifically Gen. U. S. Grant—in the days leading up to the Battle of Shiloh. The Cherry family, however, remained in residence, and it is said that Grant, out of deference to the pro-Southern ladies, did not wear his uniform in their presence. Grant had just sat down to his breakfast when the news of the battle came to him; his steamer was tied up at the dock, and Grant ordered the boat to head upriver toward the battle. Only a few of the original furnishings from that period are still in the house. The mansion is privately owned, and as of this writing the owners do offer tours on a limited basis; one must call ahead to schedule a tour. Adults $10, children $5.

Shiloh National Military Park (731-689-5696; nps.gov/shil), 1055 Pittsburg Landing Road, Shiloh. Open daily dawn–dusk; visitors center open daily 8–5. One of the first major battles in the Western Theater of the Civil War, the battle of Shiloh was also one of the most critical, as well as one of the bloodiest. After capturing Fort Donelson and Fort Henry, General Grant led his Federal troops to Pittsburg Landing on the west bank of the Tennessee River, but he didn't believe reports that Confederate troops were in the area. Confederate generals Johnston and Beauregard marched toward Pittsburg Landing and surprised Grant with an attack on April 6, 1862. The Union soldiers were forced to retreat, but Grant was able to stop the Southern advance that day; Confederates attacked again the next morning, but the Union forces held. When the fighting ended, more than 20,000 soldiers had been killed or wounded. The visitors center tells the story of Shiloh through artifacts, dioramas, and interpretive presentations. The **Shiloh National Cemetery** is located in the park; 3,584 soldiers are there, of whom 2,359 are unknown. A well-marked driving tour of the battlefield has plaques describing the position of the regiments and details of the battle. **The Shiloh Indian Mounds** are also in the park; the site is an archaeological treasure, largely undisturbed due to its almost-hidden location. Six mounds of earth—flat topped and rectangular in shape—are believed to have been the platforms for important buildings in what was once an Indian village; a seventh mound, rounded in shape, is likely a burial site for the village's VIPs. Cost for a family visit is $5 for a seven-day pass; NPS Golden Age, National Park, and Golden Access passes are accepted.

MUSEUMS Country Cabin Records & Museum (731-658-0383; doles enterprises.com), 14135 Parker Street, Hornsby. Open Mon., Tues., and Thurs.–Sat. 11–5. Part recording studio, part museum dedicated to the music history of Hardeman County, Country Cabin is a funky little spot that's a must for diehard music fans. Ed Doles and his wife, Loretta, both members of the Rockabilly Hall of Fame, have collected recordings, news clippings, mementoes, and memorabilia from the county's famous musicians, featuring Carl Perkins and Eddie Bond, and pay homage to the musicians in what can only be described as a labor of love. Housed in a log cabin, the museum's walls are covered from floor to ceiling with costumes, instruments, records, and photographs. Free.

Hockaday Broomcorn Farm, Store & Museum (731-645-4823; hh brooms.com), 2074 TN 172, Selmer. Open Wed.–Sat. 10–5. Jack Hockaday's family has farmed this land in Selmer since before the Civil War, but making brooms was more of an afterthought for his ancestors. His great-grandfather made brooms from the broomcorn he planted just for that purpose, and it was just another way to use the land to produce a product to support his family. Jack started making brooms when he was a

SHILOH CANNONS

child, watching his grandfather craft them from the dried stalks of the broomcorn. Each broom is handcrafted on the broom-wrapping table his great-grandfather made. Jack's brooms are available in the store or online and range from small brooms to sweep out a hearth to a heavy-duty house broom. Brooms can even personalized, with names carved into the handles.

The Tennessee River Museum (931-552-8366; tourhardincounty.org), 495 Main Street, Savannah. Open Mon.–Sat. 9–5, Sun. 1–5. This small museum has exhibits chronicling life in the Tennessee River Valley, from prehistoric times to the Civil War and steamboat eras to the modern shipping that takes place today. Artifacts include an effigy pipe from the Shiloh Indian mounds, Civil War uniforms, arrowheads, and more. Adults $3, children under 18 free.

✳ To Do

BOATING Grand Harbor Marina (662-667-5551; gograndharbor.com /boat_rentals.htm), 325 County Route 380, Counce. Pontoon boats powerful enough to pull tubers and skiers are available at the Grand Harbor Marina; rentals include a full tank of gas (renters must refuel before returning the boat), and only full-day rentals are available.

BOAT TOURS *Pickwick Belle* (877-936-2355; pickwickbelle.com), Pickwick Landing State Park. The paddle-wheel riverboat offers cruises year-round, some with holiday and special themes, from a moonlight Christmastime cruise to romantic Valentine's cruises; depending on the type of cruise, meals may be served. Some of the cruises leave out of Florence, Alabama, while others leave out of Pickwick Landing State Park; be sure to note the departure location. Tickets start at $9.99 for sight-seeing cruises and go up to $49 for adult dinner cruises.

✳ Green Space

PARKS Pickwick Landing State Park (731-689-3129; state.tn.us /environment/parks/PickwickLanding), Park Road, Pickwick Dam. Open daily dawn–dusk; park office is open daily 8–4:30. A playground for Memphians and many central Tennesseans, Pickwick is another dam project of the Tennessee Valley Authority, which was looking to boost public construction projects during the Depression. The park itself—Pickwick Landing—was a riverboat landing dating from the 1840s; the lake is a complicated waterway that flows to and from the Tennessee River and the Tombigbee canal. Folks generally just refer to the whole area as Pickwick. Waterskiing, rafting, and tubing are huge sports here, and the state park includes hotel lodging (see *Lodging*), campgrounds, a golf course, a full-service restaurant, and year-round fishing. Anglers, take note that the lake

WALKING TALL

McNairy County hardly seems like the place one would consider a hotbed of crime, but in the 1960s, there was plenty to keep a young sheriff named Buford Pusser busy—and in the headlines. Pusser had no patience for the moonshiners, criminals, and lowlifes terrorizing the county, which sits on the border of Tennessee and Mississippi. Pusser took a hard line against those running illegal gambling and prostitution operations, and during his decade in law enforcement, he became a national hero for his tough-guy, gun-slinging ways.

In a single year, Pusser destroyed almost 90 whiskey stills. He once fought six men by himself, sending three to the hospital and the other three to jail. He was shot eight times, knifed seven times, and even jumped onto the roof of a speeding car, smashing in the windshield to subdue the man who had attempted to run him over.

The sheriff received a call at home late in the evening of August 12, 1967, the caller revealing that a bunch of drunks were getting out of hand and violence was starting to break out. Pauline Pusser told her husband she would ride with him, since she was awake and the kids were at their grandmother's for the night. But the call was a trap—as Pusser drove down New Hope Road, a black Cadillac pulled out behind him, and shots rang out. Pauline was hit, and as Pusser pulled over to check on her, more shots were fired, striking him in the face and hitting Pauline a second time. Pauline was killed that night, and Pusser spent 18 days in the hospital recovering from his injuries.

Pusser's tough-guy persona and colorful career garnered the attention of the media, and his career was retold on the big screen in the *Walking Tall* movies starring Joe Don Baker and in a television series. Pusser served three terms as sheriff of McNairy County and was killed in a fiery one-car traffic accident in 1974.

His home in Adamsville has been turned into a museum, the **Buford Pusser House & Museum** (731-632-4080; bufordpussermuseum .com); it's at 342 Pusser Street.

is in three states—Tennessee, Alabama, and Mississippi—and a valid license is needed in each state. The Pickwick marina offers overnight slips, full-service gas, and fishing boat rentals, and also has a good list of local guide services, most of which are phone-number-only folks. There's no entrance fee for the park.

✳ Lodging

CABINS AND CAMPING Pickwick Landing State Park (731-689-3135; state.tn.us/environment/parks/PickwickLanding), Park Road, Pickwick Dam. Eight contemporary cabins are surprisingly hip for a state park; the sleek design of the outside is juxtaposed on the inside with typical cabin-ish furnishings, but they are clean and nicely appointed. Cabins all sleep up to eight people and include fully stocked kitchens, wood-burning fireplaces, and televisions. Cabins can be booked a year in advance—and people do just that, so plan ahead. One cabin is ADA accessible. The full-service camping area for tent and RV camping is pleasantly wooded, allowing for a bit more privacy and at least the illusion of remoteness. Two of the 48 sites are specifically designed as handicapped sites, and all feature water and electrical hookups. The primitive area includes 43 campsites, with some waterfront; a bathhouse and boat ramp are nearby. The full-service sites are open year-round, while the primitive campground is open only Apr.–Oct. All the campsites are available on a first-come, first-served basis. Inexpensive (for both cabins and camping).

HOTELS 🐾 Pickwick Landing State Park Inn (731-689-3135; state.tn.us/environment/parks/PickwickLanding), Park Road, Pickwick Dam. Every one of the inn's

PRICE CATEGORIES:	
Inexpensive	Less than $100 (for hotels, inns, and B&Bs); less than $50 (for campgrounds, state park facilities)
Moderate	$100–200
Expensive	$201–300
Very expensive	More than $300

119 modest rooms offers a balcony with a lake view—a pretty good deal for the inexpensive price tag. Suites with full kitchens are available, and the inn features a full-service restaurant, laundry facilities, swimming pool, and tennis courts. Some accommodations are pet friendly (must be reserved in advance); dogs must be kept on a leash in public spaces. The inn books up quickly, so advance reservations are necessary, even in the winter months. Inexpensive.

VACATION RENTALS Grand Harbor Condominiums and Marina (662-667-5551; gograndharbor.com), 325 CR 380, Counce. Lush one- to three-bedroom condos in a midrise building offer lake views, balconies, kitchens with granite countertops, and soaking tubs in the master bathrooms. While there are plenty of luxury amenities (including tennis courts, a lakeside pool and fitness center, and a medical spa) on-site, there's no restaurant, although there is a convenience store at the marina with snacks, beverages, and limited groceries. Moderate–expensive, depending on the choice of accommodation and the season.

PRICE CATEGORIES:

Inexpensive	Less than $16
Moderate	$16–30
Expensive	$31–50
Very expensive	More than $50

✳ Where to Eat

EATING OUT Hagy's Catfish Hotel (731-689-3327), 1140 Hagy Lane, Savannah. Open daily 11–9. Whole catfish and fillets—and those are the only choices—are served up at this local favorite, where you can choose the all-you-can-eat option or just a simple plate with a choice of sides. Inexpensive.

Historic Botel (731-925-4787; thehistoricbotel.com), 1010 Botel Lane, Savannah. Open 11–9 Thurs.–Sun. A fully restored houseboat—docked on high ground, mind you—serves as the setting for this casual restaurant that features an all-you-can-eat catfish buffet along with steaks and salads, as well as homemade seasonal cobblers. Beverages are basic—sweet tea, the Coca-Cola line, plus milk and buttermilk. Not something one sees every day.

WorleyBird Café (731-926-4882), 990 Pickwick Street, Savannah. Seasonal hours, but generally open daily 8 AM–9 PM. Country music's Darryl Worley's namesake café serves up a little bit of everything, from steaks to homemade fried green tomatoes and a lunch buffet. The restaurant features loads of

memorabilia from Worley, and there's a patio for alfresco dining, although it's now the favorite spot for smokers, who can no longer light up inside. Moderate.

✳ Selective Shopping

ANTIQUES Shiloh Civil War Relics (731-438-3541; shilohrelics .com), 230 Guinn Street, Savannah. Open Mon.–Fri. 9–5. The owner, featured often as an expert on *Antiques Roadshow,* has a vast collection of Civil War relics, not just from Shiloh but certainly with an emphasis on the local battle. Tiny uniform buttons, bullets, buckles, documents, and newspapers, and even photographs and political mementoes, are available in the store.

✳ Special Events

Early June: **National Catfish Derby** (731-234-3188; kenfreeman outdoorpromotions.com), Pickwick Landing State Park. A simple, no-entry-fee, six-week fishing rodeo ends with a bang when the top-weighing fish (and the lucky angler who caught it) is named the winner.

APPENDIX:
THE CIVIL WAR IN TENNESSEE

With the exception of Virginia, Tennessee saw more battles during the Civil War than any other state. Due to its central location, with Illinois, Kentucky, and Virginia to the north and Mississippi, Georgia, and Alabama to the south, and the geographic boundaries of the Mississippi River to the west and Appalachian and Smoky mountains to the east, Tennessee was vitally important to both the Union and Confederacy. If the North were to win the Civil War, it was important to control Tennessee: the Mississippi and the Tennessee rivers, the railroads, and the well-known roads were vital to transporting war materiel and men.

There were some 35 battles—large and small—fought in Tennessee. Of the five major battles, the Union won three and the Confederacy two, all at a terrible price. At Stones River more than 28,000 died; at Chattanooga and Chickamauga, more than 34,000 were lost. In Nashville, Union colored troops helped defeat the Confederates. If Grant could be defeated at Shiloh, the Confederates would regain control of much of Tennessee. Alas, it was not to be. As in other states, small towns—such as Collierville, Murfreesboro, and Franklin—became household names because of the severe fighting in those areas.

Tennessee was the last state to join the Confederacy due to strong opposition—the western areas were for secession, and the eastern mountainous regions were more pro-Union. Many families were split apart because of differing sentiments. What was initially seen as a glorious cause soon turned to devastation: the loss of young lives, destruction of property, and a major change in a way of life for both sides.

There a number of excellent resources for discovering the stories and locations important to Tennessee during the Civil War. A number of the battles mentioned here are part of **The Civil War Trail** (civilwartraveler.com/WEST/TN); trail maps can be downloaded online or picked up at all the state welcome centers, and often at local attractions. The **Ten-**

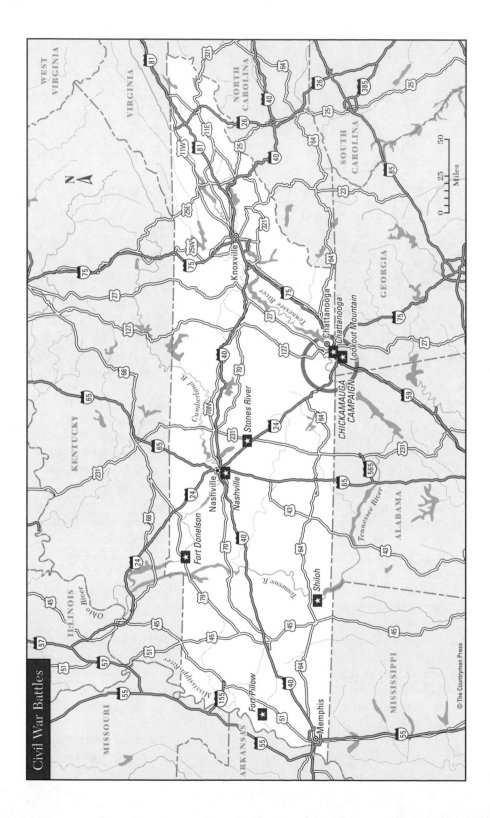

Civil War Battles

WEST VIRGINIA

VIRGINIA

NORTH CAROLINA

SOUTH CAROLINA

GEORGIA

Knoxville

Tennessee River

Chattanooga
Chattanooga
Lookout Mountain

CHICKAMAUGA CAMPAIGN

KENTUCKY

Cumberland R.

Stones River

Nashville
Nashville

Fort Donelson

Tennessee River

ALABAMA

Shiloh

Tennessee R.

Ohio River

ILLINOIS

MISSOURI

Mississippi River

ARKANSAS

Fort Pillow

Memphis

MISSISSIPPI

N

0   25   50
        Miles

© The Countryman Press

nessee **Department of Tourism** also offers excellent and very detailed battlefield and historic site information on its Web site, tnvacation.com /civil-war.

In 2011, Tennessee celebrates the 150th anniversary (the sesquicentennial) of the Civil War with a variety of reenactments, memorials, and other events. Be sure to check the battlefields' Web sites or the state Web site (tnvacation.com/civil-war) for the most up-to-date information on events.

MAJOR BATTLES IN TENNESSEE

Fort Donelson (Middle Tennessee, February 11–16, 1862)
Fort Donelson National Battlefield (931-232-5348; nps.gov/fodo), Dover. The Fort Donelson Visitor Center is open daily 8–4:30 (closed Christmas Day), and the park is open daily 8–4:30, except during daylight savings, when it is open 7–6. Free admission.

Getting there: From Nashville, take I-24 W. to Clarksville (exit 4). Take a left on Wilma Rudolph Boulevard and continue until you reach 101st Airborne Division Parkway/TN 374. Take a right at this intersection. Follow TN 374 until you reach US 79. Turn right on US 79 S. Follow signs to Dover (approximately 30 miles). The Battlefield is located 1 mile west of Dover.

FORT DONESLON NATIONAL BATTLEFIELD, DOVER

Tennessee Department of Tourist Development

MONUMENT TO THE FALLEN SOLDIERS OF TENNESSEE, SHILOH NATIONAL MILITARY
BATTLEFIELD

After Union general Grant captured Fort Henry, he sent his troops
toward Fort Donelson, where Union gunboats were preparing an attack.
The Confederate army had positioned heavy artillery above the water and
decimated the six Union boats. Grant now had to change his battle plan,
and he surrounded the fort. The Rebels broke through the line, intending
to escape, but were called back to their previous positions, and Grant
charged, closing the escape route. Brig. Gen. Simon B. Buckner, commander of Fort Donelson, was not able to hold out against Grant's
25,000-man force and asked for terms of surrender. "No terms except an
unconditional and immediate surrender can be accepted" was Grant's
reply. Buckner acquiesced. The victory opened up Tennessee to Union
supply lines, and Grant, who from then on was known as "Unconditional
Surrender Grant," was promoted to commander of all Union forces.

This was the first victory of the Civil War for the Union. More than 1,800
are buried at the cemetery here, with 504 of the soldiers unidentified.
The visitors center displays Confederate and Union weapons, including
cannon; articles of clothing and gear, such as shoes, uniforms, and blankets; and a short film describing the battle and its significance, which
runs throughout the day. There are maps at the visitors center for self-
guided tours of the fort, and there are more than 6 miles of hiking trails
throughout the battlefield.

Shiloh (West Tennessee, April 6–7, 1862)
Shiloh National Military Park (731-689-5696 or 901-689-5275), 1055
Pittsburg Landing Road, Shiloh. The park is open daily dawn–dusk
(closed Christmas Day). The visitors center and gift store are open daily

8–5. Cost for a family visit is $5 for a seven-day pass; NPS Golden Age, National Park, and Golden Access passes are accepted.

Getting there: Shiloh is 110 miles from the Memphis airport and 150 miles from the Nashville airport. From Memphis, take US 72 to Corinth, Mississippi, and TN 22 N. From Nashville, take I-40 W. to the Parker's Crossroads exit and TN 22 S.

The battle of Shiloh was one of the most critical battles of the Civil War. After capturing Fort Donelson and Fort Henry, General Grant led his Federal troops to Pittsburg Landing, on the west bank of the Tennessee River. Grant, believing that the quick victories over the Southern forces had demoralized them, did not accept the information that Confederate troops were in the area. Confederate generals Johnston and Beauregard had retreated to Corinth, Mississippi, and then marched toward Pittsburg Landing, surprising Grant with an attack on April 6, 1862. The Union soldiers were forced to retreat, but Grant was able to stop the Southern advance. Federal gunboats and Southern cannon poured a seemingly unending barrage at each other. The next morning, the Confederates

GRAVE MARKERS AT SHILOH

Tennessee Department of Tourist Development

FORT PILLOW STATE HISTORIC PARK

attacked again, but the Union forces held. When the fighting ended and the North had won, Beauregard had lost more than 15,000 men, either killed or wounded, and retreated to Shiloh Church and then back to Corinth, Mississippi.

The Shiloh National Cemetery is located in the park; 3,584 soldiers are there, 2,359 of whom are unknown. The rows and rows of monuments are a haunting reminder of the consequences of war. A well-marked driving tour of the battlefield has plaques describing the position of the regiments and details of the battle. The visitors center tells the story of Shiloh through artifacts, dioramas, and interpretive presentations.

Fort Pillow (West Tennessee, May 1862)
Fort Pillow State Historic Park (731-738-5581; state.tn.us/environment /parks/FortPillow), 3122 Park Road, Henning. Open daily 8–sunset, year-round. There is no entrance fee for the park.

Getting there: From Memphis, take I-40 to exit 66 (US 70). Turn right on TN 19 to US 51 S. to Henning, then west to County Route 87 to TN 207.

The Confederate Army built extensive fortifications here in 1861, and today the remains of the long-ago abandoned earthworks are in excellent condition, even after 150 years. A strategic location overlooking the Mississippi River was necessary for the Union to control river traffic, but Gen. Nathan Bedford Forrest successfully attacked and defeated the Union soldiers in the May 1862 battle. The battle fought here in April 1864 was bloody; the African American Federal troops surrendered, only to be massacred by the Confederates.

Stones River
(Middle Tennessee, December 31, 1862–January 2, 1863)

Stones River National Battlefield (615-893-9501; nps.gov/stri), 3501 Old Nashville Highway, Murfreesboro. Battlefield, museum, and bookstore are open daily 8–5 (closed Thanksgiving and Christmas Days). Free.

Getting there: From the Nashville airport, take I-24 E. 30 miles to exit 76 and follow the signs.

Known in the South as the Battle of Murfreesboro, the Stones River battle was short and bloody; the Confederacy lost 10,266 soldiers and the Union 18,249. No battle during the Civil War had a higher percentage of casualties.

The Union Army of the Cumberland, under the command of Gen. William S. Rosecrans, left Nashville to attack Chattanooga. Intent on stopping the Union advance, Confederate general Braxton Bragg picked Murfreesboro as the location for the battle. The winding nature of the Stones River required Bragg to locate troops on both shores, hindering his battle plan. Twice the Confederates attacked, but twice they were repulsed, forcing Bragg to withdraw, giving the Union a much needed political, though not a decisive military, victory. The withdrawal ended the hopes of the Confederacy to hold Middle Tennessee for the South, and Fort Rosecrans was built on the site by the Union.

Park rangers give guided tours, with participants traveling in their own

A REENACTMENT AT STONES RIVER NATIONAL BATTLEFIELD   Tennessee Department of Tourist Development

cars. Also, there are walks, talks, and history programs available. Allow about two hours to view the museum and take a self-guided tour; be sure to allow time to watch the movie in the visitors center detailing the battle. A bookstore offers books and other mementos.

Chattanooga (East Tennessee, August 21, 1863)

Chickamauga & Chattanooga National Military Park (Chickamauga Visitor Center, 706-866-9241; Lookout Mountain Battlefield Visitor Center, 423-821-7786; nps.gov/chch), 1 E. Brow Road, Lookout Mountain. There is no fee to visit Chattanooga National Military Park. Each of the battlefields has its own visitors center; refer to the Web site for detailed directions and a map. Visitors center open daily 8:30–5; park itself open daily dawn–dusk. There's no charge to enter the Chickamauga battlefield, but admission to Point Park, the location of the Lookout Mountain battlefield, is $3.

Getting there: To get to Chickamauga from Chattanooga, take I-75 S. to Georgia exit 350 into Fort Oglethorpe. Follow the signs and turn left off Battlefield Parkway onto Lafayette Road. The visitors center entrance is about a mile ahead. To get to Lookout Mountain from Chattanooga, take I-24 to exit 178 and turn left on US 41. Turn left on TN 148 to the top of Lookout Mountain, and take a right on E. Brow Road.

Chattanooga was an important rail center providing access to the Deep South. After the Battle of Stones River, neither side—the Confederacy under Braxton Bragg and the Union under William Rosecrans—left its encampment until June 1863. President Lincoln pressured Rosecrans to take Chattanooga, but Bragg also was criticized for his lack of activity against the Union.

In June 1863, Rosecrans finally took action by forcing Bragg to retreat to Chattanooga, and then to Chickamauga, where the Union suffered a major defeat. Rosecrans lost more than 16,000 men in the battle, and Bragg's army lost more than 18,000. Rosecrans retreated to Chattanooga, where his supply lines were cut by Bragg. The battle at Chickamauga was the last major Confederate victory of the war. Bragg pursued the Union army and occupied Missionary Ridge and Lookout Mountain.

President Lincoln had had enough and replaced Rosecrans with Gen. Ulysses S. Grant. Grant then sent his troops to Lookout Mountain and Missionary Ridge to continue the campaign.

Lookout Mountain and Missionary Ridge (East Tennessee, November 24, 1863)

Lookout Mountain is not a national battlefield, and there are but a few markers denoting the battle fought here. It is now home to Ruby Falls, the Incline Railway, and Rock City.

The Battle of Lookout Mountain gave the Confederates an opportunity to block supplies from reaching Grant's troops in Chattanooga. Bragg used artillery on the heights to fire on the Union soldiers and to disrupt communication and supply lines. General Grant then ordered generals Thomas and Hooker to attack Lookout Mountain, and in two days, in the Battle above the Clouds, Bragg was forced to abandon the site and move his troops to Missionary Ridge. Thomas and Hooker were joined by General Sherman's forces, and Bragg took his fleeing troops into Georgia. Bragg resigned his command.

Nashville (Middle Tennessee, December 15–16, 1864)
Battle of Nashville Preservation Society (615-862-8400; bonps.org), 419 Battle Park Road, Nashville. The battlefield is not preserved, and much of it is now covered by residential and commercial development. The Battle of Nashville Preservation Society offers a variety of trailheads and informational plaques for portions of the battlefield.

In a desperate attempt to make Union major general William T. Sherman leave Georgia, Gen. John Bell Hood moved his Army of Tennessee troops toward Nashville, where Gen. George H. Thompson began fortifying the area. Hood suffered terrible losses at Franklin as he headed to meet Thomas. Thomas decided to hit both of Hood's flanks and succeeded, even though Hood was still confident of a victory. Fighting was fierce, and the Union finally routed the Confederates. Eight regiments of U.S. colored troops helped defeat Hood, whose soldiers fled from the battle. The Union soldiers followed for 10 days until the beaten Confederates crossed the Tennessee River. Hood, who had taken a superb Army of Tennessee and destroyed it with poor strategies at both Franklin and Nashville, retreated to Tupelo and resigned his command.

REGIONAL BATTLES IN TENNESSEE

Smaller skirmishes and conflicts impacted seemingly every corner of the state, and while these battles did not see the huge casualties—or gain as much glory—as the aforementioned, each was important in its own right. Few of the locations listed here have been preserved, but all are on the Civil War Trail.

West Tennessee
Fort Henry (February 6, 1862). To continue to gain and/or maintain control of the Tennessee River, General Grant attacked Fort Henry, a poorly occupied and equipped fort on the Tennessee/Kentucky border. The Confederate commander, Brig. Gen. Lloyd Tilghman, removed his garrison and proceeded to Fort Donelson, some 10 miles away. Tilghman then returned to Fort Henry and surrendered, opening the Tennessee River to Union gunboats.

Memphis (June 6, 1862). Nine Union and eight Confederate ships fought for control of the Mississippi River, which was vital as it would allow the North to transport troops and supplies. Although commanded by civilians, the North was able to crush the Confederate River Defense Force.

Hatchie Bridge (October 5, 1862). A small but fierce battle near Pocahontas, Tennessee, that allowed the South to escape to defend Vicksburg.

Jackson (December 19, 1862). Confederate general Forrest had a partial success in stopping Grant's supplies as the confederates cut the Mississippi Central Railroad and Mobile and Ohio Railroad shipping activities.

Johnsonville (December 31, 1862). Gen. Nathan Bedford Forrest attempted to destroy the supply storehouses that were supporting the Union drive across Georgia. Situating his forces across the Tennessee River from Johnsonville, Forrest began firing on the supply depot. Union gunboats and artillery countered, but Forrest's position was superior, and he was able to destroy gunboats and other batteries. The Union feared being overrun and burned the gunboats, but the fire spread to the warehouses, and many supplies were lost. Although a victory for the South, it did not stop General Sherman's march across Georgia.

Collierville (November 3, 1863). A Confederate attempt to capture the Memphis & Charleston Railroad to stop Union troop movements resulted in four battles, with no significant winner.

Parker's Crossroads (November 4–5, 1864). The Union troops pursued Forrest and attempted to cut off the Confederates from crossing the Tennessee River. General Forrest, positioned on a knoll, used artillery and made two successful attacks on the Union lines, until a brigade arrived behind the Confederate line. Fighting both ahead of and behind his lines, Forrest was still able to escape and cross the Tennessee River.

Middle Tennessee

Hartsville (December 7, 1862). Hartsville, north of Murfreesboro and on the Columbia River, was defended by Col. Absalom B. Moore's 39th Brigade to prevent raids by Confederate cavalry. In an early-morning invasion, Confederate general John H. Morgan and his troops, said to be dressed in Union uniforms, crossed the river and attacked the camp. After a two-hour battle, the Confederates had surrounded the Union troops, who surrendered.

Thompson's Station (March 5, 1863). Union forces left Franklin to travel to Columbia but met two Confederate regiments near Spring Hill, Tennessee. Three separate attacks resulted in the loss of the Union wagon train. Quickly becoming surrounded and out of ammunition, the Federals surrendered.

Vaught's Hill/Milton (March 20, 1863). After Stones River, Union and Confederate forces replenished their supplies and troops, and limited their activities to reconnaissance. Leaving Murfreesboro, Col. Albert S. Hall encountered a Confederate cavalry under the command of Brig. Gen. John Hunt Morgan. Morgan attacked repeatedly but was unsuccessful and, with reinforcements arriving from Murfreesboro, removed his troops from the site.

Hoover's Gap (June 24–26, 1863). As Confederate losses increased, the Union believed that the Confederate line at Duck River would withdraw to counter the siege of Vicksburg. General Rosecrans attacked Braxton Bragg's defenses and forced the Confederates to retreat, with Union soldiers pursuing. Although not able to capture Bragg, the soldiers did destroy Confederate railroad track near the Elk River, further disrupting the South's ability to compete.

Columbia (November 24–29, 1864). Wanting to disrupt communications between the Federals and Nashville, Confederate generals Hood and Forrest crossed into Tennessee. General Schofield erected earthwork fortifications to withstand the Confederate assaults. Hood moved his troops toward Davis Ford on the Duck River, and Schofield elected to retreat to Columbia, a victory for the South.

Spring Hill (November 29, 1864). The Union army was retreating to Nashville when it encountered the Army of Tennessee and became involved in a number of skirmishes. The day was spent fighting charges until the Union reinforced their positions and beat back an attack, allowing them to leave Spring Hill overnight for Franklin.

Franklin (November 30, 1864). A year earlier, Franklin had been the site of a minor skirmish, but in 1864 the Union had constructed a number of fortifications near Franklin. Leaving Spring Hill, Gen. John Bell Hood's Army of Tennessee, with 20,000 men, was determined to defeat the Union. Numerous assaults were launched, with an enormous loss of Confederate soldiers and officers. Fourteen Confederate generals were killed, captured, or wounded, and 55 regimental commanders were lost. The Confederate Army of Tennessee was permanently decimated.

East Tennessee

Blue Springs (October 10, 1863). The Battle of Blue Springs was the result of the Confederates trying to disrupt communications while the Union was attempting to control the roads and passes to Virginia. The Rebels were headed to Bull's Gap but met a Union force at Blue Springs. Not knowing the size of the Confederate force, the Union retreated, but after a number of skirmishes, the Union advanced to meet the enemy. After fighting through the day and until dark, the Union had broken Confederate lines. After dark, the Confederates withdrew to Virginia.

Wauhatchie/Brown's Ferry (October 28–29, 1863). Chattanooga, though held by the Federal troops, faced starvation due to Confederate placement of forces surrounding the city. To relieve the situation, Grant ordered his commanders to secure the Brown's Ferry bridgehead so that supplies could be ferried to Brown's Ferry and then transported by road to Chattanooga. The Confederates attacked Wauhatchie Station at night to disrupt communications to the south, but Union reinforcements forced a retreat to Lookout Mountain. Weapons, food, and other supplies were able to be received in Chattanooga.

Campbell's Station (November 16, 1863). Union general Burnside was proceeding to Knoxville while Confederate general Longstreet hurried to reach Campbell's Station to stop him. Burnside arrived at Campbell's Station slightly before Longstreet and set up defenses. Longstreet attacked both flanks, but only one was successful. Burnside withdrew and continued his march; however, he may not have reached Knoxville if Longstreet had arrived at Campbell's Station first.

Fort Sanders/Fort Loudon (November 29, 1863). To capture Knoxville, the Rebels picked Fort Sanders as the most vulnerable spot to attack the Union. The fort was on higher ground than the area surrounding it, and a wide, deep trench outside the fort made scaling the sides of the trench almost impossible. The Confederates attacked, and few were able to survive the cannon and rifle fire. The skirmish only lasted about 20 minutes, with another defeat for the Confederacy and much of East Tennessee.

Bean's Station (December 14, 1863). After the defeat at Nashville, Lt. Gen. James Longstreet retreated northeast, with Maj. Gen. John G. Parke pursuing to Bean's Station, where Longstreet decided to fight. The battle lasted all day, with the Union repelling attacks until Southern reinforcements arrived. The Union retreated and dug in at Blain's Crossroads. Longstreet left the area. It was a Confederate victory but not significant enough to prevent Union progress.

Mossy Creek (December 29, 1863). The Federals headquartered in Dandridge, Jefferson County, received word from scouts that Confederate cavalry was in the area. While Union troops were sent to meet the cavalry, the Confederate force attacked the remaining troops in Mossy Creek. Union troops returned to the battle, and the Confederates retreated, returning to their original location.

Dandridge (January 17, 1864). Union general Parke and Confederate general Longstreet met near Dandridge, where Longstreet was advancing toward New Market to attack the Union base. After an initial engagement near Kimbrough's Crossroads, the Union cavalry retreated under enemy artillery. The next day the Confederates attacked, with fighting continuing until dark. The Federals fell back to New Market but were not pursued because the Confederates were short of ammunition, shoes, and cannon.

Fair Garden (January 27, 1864). After the battle at Dandridge, Union cavalry disrupted Southern operations and captured many wagon trains. To reduce or stop these raids, Longstreet sent his cavalry and artillery to meet the North. With the Confederates holding the Fair Garden Road, the Union sent cavalry and routed the Rebels. After another raid against a Confederate cavalry troop, the Union suffered heavy casualties and, running out of ammunition, withdrew.

Bulls Gap (November 11–13, 1864). Another attempt to drive Union forces from East Tennessee had Maj. Gen. John C. Breckinridge attack the Federal force at Bulls Gap. The fighting lasted over a three-day period, when the Union withdrew because of a lack of supplies and ammunition. Although Breckinridge pursed, the Union received reinforcements, and Breckinridge returned to Virginia.

INDEX